NAPOLEONIC PROPAGANDA

"What is truly vicious is not propaganda, but a monopoly of it." —NEW YORK TIMES

September 1, 1937

Napoleonic Propaganda

by

Robert B. Holtman

ASSOCIATE PROFESSOR OF HISTORY
LOUISIANA STATE UNIVERSITY

Louisiana State University Press

Baton Rouge

"*The greatest orator in the world is success.*"
                                    —NAPOLEON

"*To attach no importance to public opinion is a proof you do not merit its suffrage.*"
                                    —NAPOLEON

"*Government is nothing unless supported by opinion.*"   —NAPOLEON

"*The truth is not half so important as what people think to be true.*"   —NAPOLEON

PREFACE

Every schoolboy knows of Napoleon's great military prowess; but even historians tend to limit their view of his attempts to control opinion; they are prone to notice only his censorship activities and his preoccupation on St. Helena with building up a Napoleonic legend. Various studies have considered both these phases.

Fully as important is Napoleon's recognition that every ruler must use propaganda as a necessary tool of politics and statesmanship. For this reason the present book deals only with the period during which Napoleon was actually in power and concentrates its attention on France and the regions occupied by France. Because a study of this phase derives its value from a demonstration of the method by which Napoleon's propaganda was disseminated, approximately one half of this work, Chapters II through VII, is an analysis of how Napoleon employed his governmental machinery to exploit the existing means of communication.

Throughout the study, dates have been cited in terms of whichever calendar was official, the Revolutionary or the Gregorian. The name "Bonaparte" has been used to refer to Napoleon Bonaparte for the period of the Consulate; "Napoleon," for the period of the Empire or for a reference which concerns the whole period from 1799 to 1815. Attention of the reader is especially called to Footnote 10 in Chapter I, without which much of the material in the chapter would be meaningless.

The author does not claim that this is a definitive work—nor can it be so without utilization of sources available only in foreign countries. He has reason to believe, however, that material gleaned from them would substantiate the conclusions of this study, based on the material available in the United States.

Despite the shortcomings of the book, for which he alone is responsible, the author wishes to express his appreciation to those whose aid has speeded the work and improved its quality. His mother and sister have endured the agonies of authorship with him and have given unstintingly of their time in bettering the style and in typing the manuscript. Professor John H. Wildman, of the Department of English, Louisiana State University, has gone over the entire manuscript from the standpoint of style; Professor Cecil G. Taylor, of the Department of Romance Languages at Louisiana State University, has reviewed all the translations from the French and offered suggestions on their rendering. Lastly, the author is grateful to Professors C. P. Higby and C. V. Easum of the University of Wisconsin for their advice and constant encouragement.

ROBERT B. HOLTMAN

Baton Rouge
 May, 1950

CONTENTS

INTRODUCTION: *DE PROPAGANDA*

MOST ACTIVITIES OF ANY RULER, NAPOLEON OR ANOTHER, MIGHT be called propandistic to the extent that through them he hopes to build up a public opinion favorable to himself. On the other hand, Napoleon never spoke of engaging in "propaganda," a term which came into common usage only with the war of 1914.

Failure to give his activities the appellation does not mean that Napoleon did not carry on propaganda or that the term had not been used before his day. History shows that one of the early uses of the word "propaganda" was in the official title of a committee of cardinals in charge of foreign missions in the seventeenth century.

This usage can aid in defining and delimiting the subject of this study. It implies a definite creed about which numerous individuals and groups are to be brought to think in a certain way, a way they would not have adopted by themselves. Although the cardinals could use any means of influence they were able to exert to carry on their proselyting, we shall eliminate from our discussion any deeds which change elements in the environment other than the people themselves. All decrees, legislation, and projects such as public works, even though designed primarily to sustain public opinion, are deemed outside the scope of this book unless they act directly on the public itself. More precisely, for the purposes of this study the definition will be: Propaganda is a conscious effort to affect the attitudes of large numbers of people toward definite doctrines by direct manipulation of social suggestion.

Note that no stigma attaches to such a definition. That is not to say, however, that propaganda thus defined and education are coterminous. Education endeavors to show people why they think and act as they do and to present every side of a question; propaganda presents only one side of an issue and discourages its subjects from seeking the reasons for their attitude and behavior.

How good a propagandist was Napoleon? To ascertain the

answer, it will be necessary to examine his activities in the light of the best present-day thought on the subject.[1] What requirements do experts lay down for the propagandist to meet? What techniques are available to him to solve the problems he faces?

The first step of the propagandist, as of anyone dealing with the public, should be to analyze his audience. He will find that he must appeal to the pre-existing beliefs of these potential subjects if he is to influence them. Should any of these attitudes be at variance with the beliefs he wishes the people to hold, he will have to effect the conversion gradually—perhaps by cleverly intermingling with the old ideas the new ones that will eventually modify them.

Since these pre-existing attitudes depend largely upon custom and upon previous and contemporary events, the propagandist must adapt his message to happenings and movements—indeed, to all the components of history in general. Furthermore, the propagandist must appeal to the various groups in the population before he can achieve his final goal of unified action. In time of peace this means that the government will seek primarily to win and hold the support of the people by emphasizing how beneficial to them its rule has been.

Propaganda especially flourishes during times of tension and struggle. It is important to keep this fact in mind, since Napoleon was at war with at least one power for all but fourteen months of his reign. First and foremost among the subsidiary aims of propaganda during war is that of instilling into the populace a desire to fight the enemy. This can be promoted partly by getting the public to believe that the enemy is responsible for the outbreak of the war and for the failure to negotiate a just and lasting peace and by citing examples of insolence and depravity on his part. In addition, the propagandist must justify his own participation in

---

[1] In addition to the more valuable books on propaganda cited in the section of the bibliography dealing with propaganda in general, the following works have been utilized with profit: Harwood L. Childs, "Propaganda and Society," *Seventh Yearbook* of the National Council for the Social Studies (1937); Martin Conway, *The Crowd in Peace and War* (New York, 1915); Siegfried A. Evjen, "English Propaganda Against Napoleon 1802–1805" (unpublished M.A. thesis; Chicago, 1932); Jay McKee and R. E. Heiges, "Our Magazines, an Unbalanced Ration," *Social Studies*, XXVII (1936); and two books by Lucy M. Salmon, *The Newspaper and Authority* (New York, 1923), and *The Newspaper and the Historian* (New York, 1923).

the war on religious and ethical grounds, including self-defense, and by contrasting the war aims of the two sides.

Once having aroused a will to fight, the propagandist must strive to maintain morale at home (as expressed in enthusiasm or confidence, determination, and absence of complaint) and to break down that of the enemy. Especially is this true in the case of a protracted war. His first step is to emphasize the soundness of friendly alliances—meanwhile expressing esteem for his allies— and the disagreements and weak bonds of enemy leagues. While playing up the unity and confidence of his own side, he endeavors to sap confidence in enemy leaders and to separate enemy populaces from their governments. He works to prevent neutrals from becoming belligerents except on his side. Since people do not like to admit setbacks, the propagandist, to maintain the illusion of constant victory, minimizes any enemy triumph by claiming it was obviously gained through a surprise attack or temporary superiority in numbers. At the same time that he portrays the war as one in behalf of civilization against the forces of reaction, the propagandist tries to show that it will be profitable to those on his side.

What means does he have of driving home his points? He will naturally utilize all the existing organs of public expression; in addition, if at all possible, he ought to devise new methods of reaching the public.

He should also be the first to discuss an item or to use a particular medium of social control. This is important because propaganda deals largely in stereotypes—symbols essentially dogmatic and intolerant, allowing no "if's" or "but's." If the propagandist can implant his stereotype before the opposition functions, his antagonists will have great difficulty in dislodging it.

Although the role of stereotypes means that propaganda is generally statement and conclusion rather than argument, one of the devices the propagandist should exploit to increase his effectiveness is an appeal to reason. He may do this either by using logic or by employing statistics.

Examples of other devices used recently come readily to mind. The tales about "Commando" Kelly, for instance, illustrate the adventure and heroism which help maintain morale by giving an aura of romance to events. Such personalization is necessary because warfare is so vast that without some simplifying it seems remote and incomprehensible to the average person. For instance, it is much easier for him to grasp the shortcomings of the enemy if they are attributed to one individual—say to Hitler, who alone was responsible for the war of 1939. Then, too, this device is effective in stressing the benevolence of the government to the people at home. If the propagandist knows sympathetically the people to whom he is appealing, sarcasm, irony, and ridicule may be very effective. Because of the force of social ridicule the average person likes to feel that he is doing the accepted thing, that all the people who really count think as he does; he must have quality as well as numbers on his side. The testimonial-seeking vendors of patent medicines have long recognized the advisability of being able to cite organizations and people with sufficient prestige to influence favorably the potential subjects. The propagandist must decide whether revelation at any given time of his identity and of the type of action he desires will strengthen or weaken his efforts. The Nazis have shown us *ad nauseam* the value of repetition. This device is especially effective if there is sufficient variation to arouse related attitudes or if the repetition is of an emotionally charged catchword. Such an emotional vocabulary may also be extended to show that God and history are on the side of the propagandist. The Nazis also fully utilized falsification, with Hitler cynically declaring that if a lie were big enough, people would believe it. Our contemporary press is well aware of the several important techniques that can be employed to advantage, such as having material appear as straight news, varying the amount of space devoted to topics, choosing the location for the story, and altering the size or type of print.

It is the propagandist's task to adapt these various devices to the groups he is seeking to influence.

Organizing his agencies of control is another problem of the propagandist. The war of 1914 showed that the best system of organization provided for a central office equal in importance to a policy-making cabinet post, whether or not the director was actually in the cabinet. This office should have its own special agencies and not be forced to operate through other governmental bodies such as the diplomatic corps. These agencies should function both to stimulate propaganda, which is most effective when it is positive and presents an ideal, and to exercise censorship.

There are, with their ramifications, two usable types of censorship. The first is preliminary or preventive and calls for submission of material to the authorities before it appears. They may then approve it, alter it to suit their demands, or prohibit its appearance. The second is punitive and provides that whoever is responsible for the material must pay the penalty if he turns out something the authorities had earlier told him not to distribute. As the number of periodicals rises, there is a tendency to replace the former type of censorship by the latter. There may even be a tendency for influential and popular papers to be immune to either of these types of control.

When the government has control of printed matter, it may select news to suit its aims, often furnishing its own news to replace that provided by the journalists. It may also "doctor" official reports before allowing them to be published.

But no matter what changing means the propagandist uses to his end, the philosophy behind his procedure remains eternally fixed: dexterity and persistence are the keys to his success.

CHAPTER I

THE MESSAGE [1]

When Bonaparte came into power on 18 Brumaire, Year VIII, France was utterly exhausted. For over seven years it had been constantly at war with one or more powers. Its finances were depleted and the government had had to default on its securities. The government itself was split into factions, and a civil war was raging in the Vendée, with the Catholics and royalists aligned against the republicans and those opposing re-establishment of a state church.[2] Above all else, therefore, public opinion was demanding peace, both foreign and domestic.[3] But it also desired a more stable administration, with better functionaries and less fraud; a balanced and public budget and the end of forced loans; a permanent judiciary; the development of domestic and foreign commerce; and encouragement to industry and education.[4] The general dissatisfaction with the *status quo* appreciably lightened

[1] Since many of the points in the official propaganda of the French government were emphasized over a considerable period of time, any specific footnote could be only an indication of *one* time when a certain argument was made. For such protracted arguments, therefore, the author will give footnotes only if the material does not come from newspapers of the period. In principle, newspapers are cited in this chapter with reference to statements of a less general nature. The contemporary papers which the author has examined are complete files of *La Gazette nationale ou le Moniteur universel* (hereafter referred to as the *Moniteur*), the *Journal des Débats et Loix du Pouvoir législatif* (after 1805 entitled the *Journal de l'Empire*), the *Mercure de France*, most of the *Journal de Paris* (hereafter referred to as the *Journal*), and smaller portions of several other papers. These and all other French papers mentioned throughout this book were published at Paris unless the place of publication is otherwise indicated.

[2] For the historical facts cited in this chapter, any survey work such as that of Leo Gershoy, *The French Revolution and Napoleon* (New York, 1933), may be used.

[3] François V. A. Aulard (ed.), *Paris sous le consulat: recueil de documents pour l'histoire de l'esprit public à Paris* (Paris, 1903-1909), I, *passim*.

[4] Citoyen Fonvielle aîné, *Résultats possibles de la journée du 18 brumaire an VIII* (Paris, Year VIII), *in toto*.

Bonaparte's first task, that of persuading the country to support his new government.

On the day of his accession to power, Bonaparte claimed that the actions taken by his group were necessary to retain a republic based on civil liberty and national representation. On the following day the Legislative Body said that the change was necessary in order to escape factions and instability and to guarantee individual rights. To win the many who were still attached to the Constitution of the Year III, Bonaparte emphasized that it was the principles, rather than the act itself, which counted.[5] In addition to public support based on grievances against the Directory, the government could rely on the name "Bonaparte," which to the average Frenchman connoted military invincibility. Bonaparte himself did not fail to point out that upon his departure for Egypt he had left France peaceable and triumphant and upon his return had found it humiliated and divided, its armies destroyed or conquered.[6]

To sustain this initial, favorable attitude, Bonaparte promised to end the war in the Vendée and to re-establish peace on the continent of Europe; but he warned that a moderate government could establish the republic on the bases of "civil liberty, internal happiness, victory, and peace"[7] only with the union and confidence of all patriots.

To hasten the glorious end of the foreign war by inspiring the troops, he lavished praise upon the soldiers for their bravery, devotion, and generous enthusiasm[8] and promised that their needs would be cared for. Further to instill into his men the desire to fight, Bonaparte told them how dastardly was the enemy with whom they had to deal. Inasmuch as Napoleon was at war during all but fourteen months of his rule, this type of material bulked large in his propaganda.

[5] Napoleon, *Correspondance de Napoléon Ier* (Paris, 1858–70), VI, 3.

[6] Auguste de Marmont, *Mémoires du maréchal Marmont, duc de Raguse de 1792 à 1841 imprimés sur le manuscrit original de l'auteur* (2d ed.; Paris, 1857), II, 95.

[7] Theodore Iung, *Lucien Bonaparte et ses mémoires, 1775–1840* (Paris, 1882–83), I, 304.

[8] Bonaparte hoped that constantly repeating to the men that such qualifications characterized them might create the desire to live up to their appelations.

CRITICISM OF ENEMY

Each of France's enemies was the recipient of verbal abuse, but Napoleon always realized that England was his major (as well as his most persistent) opponent and concentrated his attacks upon it.[9] This verbal offensive against France's enemies began immediately upon Bonaparte's assumption of office with the charge that England was paying the brigands in western France,[10] and throughout the period of Napoleon's rule, England and its allies were accused of continuing to incite revolts in France and other countries. Not content with furnishing supplies, England, according to Napoleon, had urged the brigands to exterminate their opponents and to devastate the countryside and had encouraged fanaticism and royalty. Napoleon further charged that in 1802 England had deliberately tried to prolong the civil war in Switzerland; that Austria in 1805 had endeavored to foment a revolution in Bavaria; and that in 1807 Russia had attempted to stir the Serbs to open revolt against the Turks.[11]

Even worse, the British government had participated in plots to assassinate the legitimate head of a sovereign government, having had a hand in the plot of 3 Nivôse against Bonaparte's life. The role played by the British caused Bonaparte to give vent to his feelings. "When a state has no resource except crimes . . . then that nation is badly governed." "One nation is responsible to another for all the acts of its citizens. The English government has nothing to gain, as the French one is more firmly established. If it cannot prevent actions, there is not any government." "It is unworthy of the character of the British nation for the ministry to try to isolate Bonaparte from the government, and the government from the French people." [12] Though he did not directly state

[9] The similarities between the charges made by Napoleon and those made by Hitler are quite interesting.

[10] *Journal*, 23 Brumaire, Year VIII. Any statements in the remainder of the chapter on men and events of the period may be assumed to be propaganda claims rather than historical facts. The two may, of course, coincide.

[11] *Moniteur*, 23 Prairial, Year XI and 19 Brumaire, Year XIV; *Journal*, April 26, 1807. The items cited in the text are merely a few examples, and the list could easily be extended.

[12] *Moniteur*, 16 Ventôse, Year XII. The French government, to show the

that the British had been responsible for the assassination of Paul
I, Napoleon did imply that there was a definite connection between his death and the passage through the Sound a week later of
a British squadron.[13] Even before the plot of Georges Cadoudal
broke, France charged that Baron William Grenville and William
Windham were involved with him. The French exploited very
well the rather convincing evidence that Spencer Smith and a
certain Drake, England's diplomatic representatives at Stuttgart
and Munich, were plotting in 1804 to kill Bonaparte, or at least to
upset the government.[14] Napoleon also accused British assassins in
the pay of Marquess Richard Wellesley and Spencer Perceval of
an attempt on the life of the King of Denmark.[15]

The enemy was furthermore charged with conducting a lying
campaign. Its papers might with impunity print any libels, and in
England the ministerial papers had been the worst offenders. England had spread false rumors designed to attenuate the effects of
French victories, and, in addition, it had falsified even official reports before publishing them. As for Austria and Russia, their
official bulletins told the exact opposite of the truth.

Naturally Napoleon said that whoever he was fighting had provoked the war against the pacific desires of the French government. As early as 1800 the *Journal des Débats* quoted the *Spectateur du Nord* as saying that the desire of England to abase France
was the sole cause for continuation of the war.[16] Had it not been
for England, the peace established by Lunéville could have been
a general one. Bonaparte showed no reluctance to voice what he
thought of British leaders who refused to make peace.

> When there exist in a nation furious men who are the enemies
> of humanity enough to desire perpetual wars of extermination,

---

extent to which England was inculpated, published *Papiers saisis à Bareuth: et à
Mende, département de la Lozère* (Paris, Year XII), warning that all the correspondence could not be included because of police considerations.

[13] Therese Ebbinghaus, *Napoleon, England und die Presse (1800–1803)* (München, 1914), 46.

[14] *Moniteur*, Year XII, *passim;* Gilbert Stenger, "Histoire de la société française
pendant le consulat," *Le carnet historique et littéraire*, 4th year (1902), 195–96.

[15] Léonce de Brotonne (ed.), *Lettres inédites de Napoléon Ier* (Paris, 1898),
351. Perceval was at this time Prime Minister and Wellesley Foreign Minister.

[16] *Journal des Débats* (henceforth referred to as *Débats* or *Empire*), 9 Fructidor, Year VIII. The *Spectateur du Nord* was published at Hamburg.

they ought to be prevented from entering councils and forced to spend entire years far from their families and country on cutters blockading the roads beset by the tempests of winter, or placed in the middle of the Arabian desert or on the field of carnage on the day of a battle; if every sentiment of humanity were not smothered in their hearts, they would doubtless abjure all these atrocious principles. Those who cry "War to the Death" at the top of their lungs in an assembly are cowards who have never left the bosom of indolence, for the brave man makes war for the honor, glory, and well-being of his country and uses his vigils and speeches to bring the nations back to sentiments of fraternity, conciliation, and justice.[17]

It was England which violated the Peace of Amiens and declared war. Bonaparte's outburst upon the resumption of war reminds one of the famous "War is Hell," a remark attributed to General William T. Sherman. "It is too bad Hell is not at England's disposal; she would vomit it over the whole universe." [18] Austria in 1805 and Prussia in 1806 had no motives for desiring war, yet because of England's gold and incitation they declared war on France. "Do not blame the greed of France for the war; it is your own ambition. Since our army was scattered, you thought you could fight with impunity. Divine Providence is on our side." [19]

When Russia refused to ratify the treaty concluded with France in 1806, France claimed that England was responsible for the rejection.[20] England itself had refused to ratify a friendly agreement made with the United States by its own plenipotentiary, Lord David Erskine. Its attack on Holland in 1809 had been designed primarily to prevent peace, because it was headed by men who madly wanted perpetual war. Russia had fought Turkey in 1807 and Austria had begun hostilities in 1809 only because they thought the moments opportune: Russia because France and Prussia were at odds, Austria because France was busy in Spain.[21]

[17] Antonin Périvier, *Napoléon journaliste* (Paris, 1918), 159.

[18] *Moniteur*, 12 Prairial, Year XIII.

[19] Bulletin 13, October 20, 1806, in Napoleon, *Correspondance de Napoléon Ier* (Paris, 1858–70), XIII, 378–79.

[20] *Archives parlementaires 1787–1860: recueil complet des débats des chambres françaises,* Series 2 (Paris, 1862–1913), IX, 459.

[21] It is noteworthy that there was comparatively little vituperative material against Austria in 1809. Perhaps Napoleon was already thinking about using

English intrigues had been responsible for the Spanish troubles of 1808, and Russia had started hostilities in 1812 even at the expense of violating its treaty of alliance with France. There is a grim, unconscious humor in one of Napoleon's accusations: after he had returned from Elba, the allied powers had refused even to accept couriers bearing pacific messages from him!

The allies had begun all their campaigns against France primarily because they were ambitious. England wanted universal dominion over the seas and desired to reduce all other nations to poverty by ruining their industry and agriculture; Russia hoped to be supreme on land. In 1815 the allies had aimed at dismembering France for their own aggrandizement.

Napoleon also charged that his enemies had no respect for international law and recognized only the law of force. As instances of his point, he accused Austria of invading neutral Bavaria to destroy its independence and accused the allies of not respecting the neutrality of such states as Switzerland and Saxony. In direct contravention of international law, Austria had furthermore refused to recognize passports and to permit the passage of provisions for the duchy of Warsaw.[22]

In the matter of maritime law, especially, the English were arrogant, treating all foreigners as inferior. England had flagrantly disregarded the rights of neutrals at sea. It had impressed American sailors even when they had been born in the United States. It had stopped and searched ships on the high seas and had extended its list of contraband. It had refused to recognize that a neutral flag made goods neutral and that the mere existence of a convoy was sufficient guarantee of the legitimate use of a neutral flag. Following the code of pirates, England had seized ships before issuing a declaration of war; and the British blockade of France and her allies was illegal, for it existed only on paper. Such actions had shown the workings of England's maritime law, resulting from the maritime wars of the eighteenth century, all of which England alone had started.[23]

Austria after peace was signed, or even about marrying an Austrian archduchess.
[22] *Archives parlementaires*, X, 280.
[23] Alexandre Hauterive, *De l'état de la France à la fin de l'an VIII* (Paris, Year IX), 183.

Napoleon incessantly harped on the bad faith of all countries hostile to France. England and her allies had entered into negotiations merely in order to give themselves time to perfect their military arrangements. They had not respected surrender terms signed with French or pro-French commanders. After signing a treaty with France, Sweden had allowed British goods into its ports, whence it could flood the Continent with them.[24] Later it had not lived up to the terms of the treaty signed at Jönköping. The actions of Austria had been in direct violation of its treaties. Prussia, after having been saved by Napoleon and having become his ally, had changed sides as soon as the fortunes of war had shifted against France. England had broken the Convention of El Arish, the Treaty of Amiens, and an agreement not to seize or destroy fishing vessels. It had, moreover, violated international custom and good faith by making public its negotiations and treaties with Continental powers and by shipping millions of francs in counterfeit money to the Continent.

Nor did the French government forget to depict the utter inhumanity of its enemies. The Austrians had killed French couriers in Croatia; and Tyrolese rebels, with the permission of the Austrian General Jean Chasteler, had slaughtered 2,600 Bavarians and Frenchmen.[25] One French citizen had been forced to pay the British proconsul in Turkey a ransom to be allowed to escape alive. An English agent had tried to assassinate a French officer. The British had manhandled a ship captain in a vain attempt to wring a false confession from him, and they had set adrift in a small bark two sailors whom they had stripped.[26] Even England's misdeeds of the past received publicity. During the American Revolution the English had thrown wounded men off a cliff, and an English colonel had run the sword of surrender through a defending officer.[27]

In addition to such specific acts of violence, the enemies of France were accused of indulging in cruelties which were more widespread and which lasted for a longer period. The conduct of

[24] *Archives parlementaires*, XI, 604.
[25] Napoleon, *Correspondance*, XIX, 191.
[26] *Moniteur*, Thermidor, Year VIII, *passim;* 13 Nivôse, Year IX; 15 Nivôse and 4 Messidor, Year XIII.
[27] *Journal*, Prairial, Year XI, *passim.*

Naples had been atrocious; the officials had allowed captured officers to be insulted by the masses and chained with their faces to
the wall. In the American war for independence, England had
hired barbarous, butchering Hessians. Both before and after the
United States had declared war in 1812, England had encouraged
the Indians to massacre the whites. England had not treated properly the prisoners it held: many were held in disease-ridden barges,
some had been kept in violation of agreements, and none of them
had been given adequate food or clothing. England had consistently refused a fair exchange of prisoners. Yet the British prisoners
had been the first to revolt.

The French propagandist loved to make the havoc thorough-
going and wanton. British "uprightness," he said, had been demonstrated by the massacres of Copenhagen and by the threat that the
whole city would be burned down if the Danes sank their fleet.
Nelson had burned all the ships in port and had deliberately sunk
all those of less than one hundred tons. The English had also used
infernal machines against the French fleet. Such, and worse atrocities the British papers had directly encouraged; for in the hands
of the English, human blood was nothing but merchandise. Foreigners who had grown old in its service England threw on hostile
coasts, penniless, in rags, and covered with wounds. It was reputed
to have thrown poisoned bales of cotton onto the coast in order
to call epidemic diseases to its assistance.[28] In Spain and in Portugal the British were devastating the entire countryside, and wherever they had effected a temporary landing, they had pillaged
indiscriminately, not even respecting church property.

The Russians were taunted particularly for their infidelity and
their barbarism: they pillaged even the territory of their allies;
and they showed even more clearly their barbarity by firing their
own cities when they could no longer defend them, thus forcing
innocent women, children, and old men to suffer. Count Feodor
Rostopchin, it was said, had even freed five thousand criminals
so they could burn Moscow.[29]

---

[28] Michel Ney, *Memoirs of Marshal Ney*, 2 vols. (London, 1883), II, 204. Were
this instance of chemical warfare true, it would demonstrate the modernity of
warfare in the early nineteenth century. The memoirs are spurious.

[29] *Moniteur*, October 14, 1812.

The real barrage of atrocity stories, however, began with the invasion of French territory by the allies in 1814. The cowardly Cossacks, who had stripped houses of their thatched roofs to feed their horses and had stolen everything they could lay their hands on, had cut off the noses of peasants striving to defend their property. The allies had mistreated women, slaughtered or driven off all the farm animals, pillaged, and burned. They had cut off fingers to get gold rings and torn off ears to get earrings. They had made requisition upon requisition, sparing not even the churches. And their goal was the pillage of Paris, whose fate had been foreshadowed by the Russians' slaughter of 80,000 people in cold blood and by the excesses committed against the Jews in Warsaw.[30]

The French saw in their opponents, once again particularly England, many other traits to expose, although these were of a less bloodcurdling nature. The privateers of England and its ally Sweden were more piratical than the Algerians. The British were selfish and mercenary, acting only when their trade was at stake. Themselves deceitful and corrupt, they sought to corrupt others, and the ministerial London *Times* was so bigoted that it had advocated prohibiting the study of French.

These traits resulted in acts that were unworthy of a nation calling itself civilized. The British, for instance, had restored Egypt to ignorance and barbarism and had promoted slavery of the whites in Santo Domingo. They had seized a storm-beaten Spanish ship, even though Spain had refused to treat so piratically a British vessel in similar plight. Although its Alien Law authorized their deportation, England had continued to harbor royalist *émigrés*.

In fact, England had in many ways adopted the worst features of revolutionary governments. For example, it had never treated the Catholics decently. Forcing 90 per cent of a nation to accept a religion contrary to its belief was the worst possible form of tyranny; yet that was what England had done in Ireland. The English landholders in Ireland paid nothing toward maintenance of the roads.[31] The same people shouting "No Papism" at home

---

[30] *Empire*, March 13, 1814.   [31] *Moniteur*, 15 Prairial, Year XIII.

were the ones supporting a government in Spain which would re-establish the Inquisition.

The baseness of Prussia was especially emphasized. The propaganda charged that it fought merely because it was opposed to France, not for any principles. Though helped by Napoleon, it had shown itself ungrateful.[32] Actions it had allowed, such as the gendarmes' sharpening their swords under the window of the French ministry, were revolting.[33]

Napoleon also used the past actions of all his enemies to predict what they would do if once again victorious. Austria, for example, had not spared anyone in Italy who had served the Cisalpine Republic.[34] Napoleon, therefore, pointed out that his supporters did not dare let their foes win, and in this way sought to build up morale.

Napoleon likewise launched out against the Pope for his refusal to proceed with the investiture of men whom Napoleon had appointed. Violating the Concordat, which provided that no diocese should be without a bishop for more than three months, the Pope had left twenty-five sees vacant.[35]

Russia, like other foreign countries, was criticized harshly. Some critics, in their efforts to please Napoleon, sometimes went beyond what he would have desired. Thus in 1812, the August 6 issue of the *Moniteur*, the official French newspaper published at Paris, criticized the *Tableau historique, géographique, militaire et morale de l'Empire de Russie* by Damaze de Raymond for picturing Peter the Great merely as a barbarous and ferocious ruler. But it was permissible to call the Russians cowards exercising military tyranny and to point out that Russia had abandoned Westphalia instead of aiding it.[36] When Russia criticized the seizure of the Duke of Enghien, it was advised to remember the death of Paul I.[37]

Napoleon considered the Bourbons just as much his enemies as the rulers of any foreign state and criticized them accordingly.

---

[32] *Empire*, September 20, 1806.   [33] Napoleon, *Correspondance*, XIII, 434.
[34] *Ibid.*, VI, 328.   [35] *Ibid.*, XXII, 256–59.
[36] *Empire*, August 6–7, 1812. These answers by a French grenadier and a German to Russian proclamations seem quite obviously to have been officially inspired.
[37] François de Chateaubriand, *Mémoires d'outretombe*, 4 vols. (Paris, 1899), II, 457.

The Bourbons should never rule again, he said, for a country was always more fortunate under the first members of a new dynasty than under the last members of an old one. He contrasted as follows the Bourbon and Bonapartean regimes: "The throne of the Bourbons was illegitimate as it was raised by foreign hands and proscribed by the wish of the nation, and because it offered a guarantee only to the interests of a clique opposed to our rights. The Imperial throne alone was able to guarantee the rights of the people, and especially the first of our interests, our glory." [38] Once off the throne, the Bourbons urged war against France and civil war within it. Their allies claimed that they would respect the independence of France, yet they refused it that first prerogative of an independent government, freedom to select its form of government.[39]

EXPOSURE OF ENEMY CONDITIONS

Napoleon hoped that the propaganda barrage against the enemies of France had raised the temper of the French to a fighting pitch. In order to maintain it at that level, he caused one facet of his propaganda to be a depiction of how little success the enemies of France were having, how many problems they were forced to face.

As Napoleon had blamed British subsidies for being the cause of Continental powers' fighting France, he encouraged the French to believe that England would have to discontinue them because its finances were growing progressively worse. Its increasing budget would soon cause the already heavy taxes to become almost intolerable. The interest on its debt, which was so large that it would never be paid, was already greater than England's real income.[40] It had to rely upon paper money which did not even cir-

---

[38] Speech of Napoleon on the Place du Carrousel, March 21, 1815, as quoted in Napoleon, *Messages et discours politiques*, pub. by Georges Barral (Paris, 1896), 174.

[39] *Archives parlementaires*, XIV, 431.

[40] That is, the income derived from sources other than commerce. The *Moniteur*, 13 Pluviôse, Year VIII, cleverly played up the statement by Sheridan, a Whig leader, that half of England's national debt was due to the attempt to destroy the Bourbon family and the other half to the expense involved in re-establishing it.

culate at par. The finances of countries siding with England were also in very bad shape.

The British government relied largely on commerce for its revenue, but that commerce was steadily deteriorating.[41] French corsairs made British merchants uneasy. Because the Continental System barred British goods from Europe, Britain was overstocked with colonial wares of which it could not dispose, and the number of bankruptcies increased daily. In a few years the continuation of this System would prove fatal to England. Its only hope lay in smuggling, which was discouraged by the burning of all British goods found on the Continent.[42] England's inability to sell goods also damaged industry, and hundreds of thousands were out of work.

The unemployment, coupled with a dearth of specie and with prohibitively high grain prices, had caused widespread crime and riots among the workers. The spirit of revolt was not manifested by the industrial population alone, however. The Irish were a constant source of worry to England. The newly acquired colony of Barbados was revolting,[43] Jamaica was troublesome, Canada was proving difficult, and India was in revolt or on the verge of it. Even in the fleet dissatisfied and impressed sailors caused trouble. One could say that the morale of England was really at the breaking point.

Napoleon pointed out that England would be unable to support a coalition for any length of time and showed that even the ones already existing were therefore none too stable. Since England thought of its allies only at the beginning of a war and forgot them at the end, it was only natural that they had all suffered as a result of their alliances. Their losses were caused by two things: British inability to render sufficient aid, and British activity in favor of only its own interests rather than those of the whole coalition. England did not hesitate even to desert its allies if such a step served its selfish interests, which had nothing in common with those of the Continent; for example, it had been willing to sacrifice its allies to France if that country renounced Belgium.[44]

---

[41] In 1808 the *Moniteur* cited specific figures for the decline in Britain's export trade.   [42] This policy was begun in 1810.
[43] *Empire*, January 31, 1812.   [44] A. Hauterive, *De l'état de la France, passim.*

Ever since the Treaty of Utrecht, England, the modern Carthage demonstrating Punic "good faith," [45] had followed a policy inimical to all other maritime nations. If things did not turn out well, it placed all the responsibility on the other members of a coalition; and it took all the glory for any victories. It so looked down on its allies that it even refused to exchange French prisoners for their nationals held by Napoleon. All Britain could do for its allies was promise them money, which it paid tardily or not at all and for which they shed their blood.

Hence it was no wonder that England's allies distrusted and disliked it. The Spaniards had come to an open break with the British, the British and Portuguese were not amicable, the Swedes did not come to Britain's aid, and the Sicilians hated England. Although papers should not have any weight in affairs of state, those of Britain criticized its allies more harshly than did those of France. A piece, tending to show why England should be isolated, was borrowed from the Paris *Argus* by the *Moniteur* for 6 Messidor, Year XI. It was a supposed "Note handed the King by Hawkesbury"—in retaliation for the insertion in a British paper of a note supposedly by Talleyrand. Among other things this note stated: "The Eternal . . . has seemed to establish us as supreme arbiters, dominators, and natural supervisors of what happens. . . . We are strong only by the divisions of Continental powers, happy only by their disasters, rich only by their poverty. If ever we permit them twenty years of peace, it will be necessary to yield the empire of the seas. . . . Twenty years of peace and we lose all glory, all wealth, and all hope. . . . The British ministry has constantly worked at this great task of weakening Continental powers, especially France. . . . Russia is, with France, the power most formidable to us."

Dissension in the other enemy camps was also depicted. Both Prussia and Austria disliked the arrogance shown them by Russia. The Austrians were very discouraged because the Russians forced them to fight despite the protests of their officers, because they received their pay in depreciated paper, because the French beat them so easily, and because the Germans hated them so.[46] Prussia

[45] Such a charge would meet with a good reception from the populace during a classical age.　　[46] Napoleon, *Correspondance*, XI, 344–51.

and Russia accused each other of nonsupport, and Austria had to bear the brunt of any war waged by Russia and itself against France. The spirit of the Russians themselves, who were already disgruntled by the plans of Prince Mikhail Barclay de Tolly, was grievously affected by the capture of Smolensk. The Spaniards in 1815 did not want to fight the French,[47] the Saxons under General Gebhard von Blücher actually did mutiny, and allied soldiers constantly deserted. To increase this dissension, Napoleon repeatedly pointed out to the various German states that Austria had constantly sacrificed their interests to its own, and he promised the Hungarians liberty, protection, and a constitution, if they revolted from Austria. He also gave important stress to the speech by Count André Palfi-Karoli in the Hungarian Diet in 1805 which pointed out that Hungary would not support Austria in its war.[48] An appeal by the General Confederation of Poland to the Poles in the service of Russia to desert their barbarian leaders and fight with civilized peoples for the independence of their country was widely publicized.[49]

All efforts of the enemies of France were portrayed as being futile. The *levée en masse* attempted in England and regions under its control had been a dismal failure. Each attempt of England to make a landing on the Continent resulted in failure, and not a single one of its expeditions since 1793 had turned out successfully.[50] Though the British attacks on French ports showed that England could not harm France, Britain was vulnerable at home and throughout its empire. History showed that no empire based on commerce could endure. The immoral Orders in Council disturbed Continental and American commerce, but could never destroy it; their important effects were to damage British commerce and to give an impetus to industry in the countries affected by the Orders. As a result of them France would soon be able to compete with British textiles. The blockade hindered commerce

---

[47] *Moniteur*, May 3, 1815.

[48] Count André Palfi-Karoli, "Discours prononcé dans la diète de Hongrie," *The Empire: Contemporary Pamphlets 1805-1815*, in Boulay de la Meurthe collection of pamphlets, Widener Library, Harvard University. The portion of this collection relating to the Napoleonic period had never been previously exploited.

[49] *Empire*, August 1, 1813; Napoleon, *Correspondance*, XXIV, 68–70.

[50] *Moniteur*, December 18, 1811.

somewhat, but it was far from effective. Fleets, either of merchant or naval vessels, were able to leave even closely blockaded ports. Although England's navy was as strong as the combined navies of all other European states, the British captured fewer ships than did the French privateers. Britain's actions against Copenhagen had cost Napoleon a few ships, but he had made the much more valuable gain of a new ally with its many experienced sailors, and England had lost any opportunity of forming a coalition on the Continent.[51] With each campaign, England thus lost allies while France gained them.

Much worse than the inability of the enemy to achieve any benefits by his actions were the defeats suffered by England and its allies. Even if they won ephemeral victories, their losses were much heavier than those suffered by France and its allies. Visible proof of these losses was found in the thousands of prisoners streaming through French towns. The net results of England's acts to 1810 were the ruin of Sweden, the loss of two armies in Spain, a war with Russia, and a probable war with the United States.[52]

This constant losing was one reason that the opponents of France did not have the support of their own populations. In England only the oligarchic *nouveaux riches* supported the war; the masses were opposed to it. The Austrian peasants and workers resented having to leave profitable employment to enroll in the militia. This lack of support appeared in the frequent desertions to the French side and in a revolt in Galicia.[53]

The privations which foreign countries had to undergo because their resources were strictly limited also contributed to the lack of popular support. There was a dearth of food, especially of grain. The army did not have enough supplies and, because of the fatigues which it was forced to endure, suffered greatly from disease.

Still a third reason for the unpopularity of the war was the poor leadership. The Swedish king, for example, let personal hatreds dictate his actions. The Duke of Brunswick's conduct of the war was very stupid, and he was foolish to let himself be in-

[51] *Ibid.*, 8 Floréal, Year IX; *Empire*, August 29, 1810.
[52] *Journal*, January 23, 1810.   [53] *Moniteur*, October 9, 1809.

fluenced by a woman and a poet.[54] The British, assuming that people were ignorant, always used the same plan of campaign. The royal family did not inspire confidence because the King was on the verge of insanity and the conduct of the other members was scandalous. The British ministers had foolishly insisted upon prolonging the Walcheren expedition in the midst of the malaria season, demonstrating once again that British foreign policies were the result of political considerations on the part of the ministers.[55] The political leaders did not exhibit any consistency; for instance, they had warred on Prussia for annexing Hanover and had allied with it when it fought France for retention of Hanover. They were perfidious, avaricious cowards who had never waged war and who now misled a populace which had many good points. Furthermore, they were unknowns with no knowledge of politics, opposing the most important men in the country and unable to co-operate even among themselves.

Failure of the British government to have its acts coincide with its words was a further cause of popular disapproval. The British ministry had stressed that one of the main objectives for which it was fighting was preservation of the British constitution. Yet England had suspended habeas corpus and frequently put an embargo on papers.[56] Although the constitution guaranteed the right of petition, the government refused to honor petitions. The electoral system was bad: the ministers returned to power by buying votes and by relying on rotten boroughs, and riots always characterized the elections. The license allowed the opposition was often harmful.[57] The ministers kept the House of Commons in such ignorance on Anglo-French affairs that it was compelled to rely on French papers for information.[58] The English boasted of liberty and equality, yet it was in Britain that rank and wealth had most sway.[59]

[54] *Journal*, November 11 and 14, 1806. The woman was of course Queen Louise of Prussia, the poet Goethe.

[55] *Empire*, March 31, 1809.   [56] *Débats*, 19 Fructidor, Year XI.

[57] Napoleon was evidently never aware of the inconsistency between this statement and the charge of British tyranny. Propaganda experts would not hold such inconsistency to be harmful, however; all that is necessary is consistency within a time period and topic.

[58] *Mercure de France*, 17 Ventôse, Year XI.

[59] *Journal*, 7 Fructidor, Year XI.

In enemy countries, the leadership of incapable and corrupt men, whose actions flouted the very ideals for which the masses were struggling, prevented even unprecedented sacrifices from winning any important successes. This fact created among the enemies of France an utter lack of self-confidence. Many of them were afraid to face the invincible French armies. The civilian populations were nervous about what their allies might do and about the financial, mercantile, and industrial situations. Aware that a huge majority of the invasions attempted since William the Conqueror had been successful,[60] they realized that an invasion of England could succeed. The preparations in Dutch ports had obviously worried England, whose voting of an inquest on the Walcheren expedition showed its mistrust of the government.

PORTRAYAL OF FRENCH CONDITIONS

Depicting the troubles besetting the enemies of France could not in itself suffice, however, to maintain the morale of Napoleon's supporters. It was a negative step, and something positive was needed. Napoleon could not be content with exposing the failures of Britain and its allies; he had to play up the contrast between them and France, showing that for the latter, things progressed smoothly.

In France, for example, the public was unanimously behind the government, and there was a complete community of interests between it and the army. Offers of aid came from many private organizations as well as from all the government agencies. Confident that the result would justify the means, all France was willing to make temporary sacrifices, such as those entailed by the Continental System and by military service.

The draft was completed easily and quickly, more so each year than at any previous time, and young men were eager to get into the honor guards. The army was thus constantly reinforced by new troops who fought as well as the regular army. There were also many who volunteered—witness the man who had enlisted

---

[60] Ebbinghaus, *Napoleon, England und die Presse*, 80–81. Napoleon spent a good deal of effort, especially from 1803 to 1805, to make these points regarding invasions.

after refusing to be a paid substitute.[61] Yet France, though it possessed the largest army of any nation, had the smallest percentage of its citizens in the army. The morale of the fighting men was splendid, they had all the provisions they needed—many captured from foreign magazines—and very few became ill. Relying on their desire to gain his approval, Napoleon praised those soldiers who had conducted themselves well, and even had the legislature pass laws that certain corps had deserved well of the country. Napoleon also praised auxiliary troops: the Poles for their fine spirit, the Belgians for their defense against the British, the Italians for being worthy of the Grand Army.

Such praise was one means of directly inspiring both the troops and the inhabitants of regions such as the Cisalpine Republic and Poland, which were told to demonstrate that they merited the benefits they hoped for or had already obtained.[62] With the same end—to inspire his allies—in mind, Napoleon also promised to lead the army in person. Later, on the eve of battle, assuming that victory would come as a matter of course and that the people would support him, he exhorted the soldiers to defeat once again the enemy they had so often beaten and to obtain revenge on those who had violated their treaty obligations. He showed the troops that victory was possible, and declared that the enemy forces, despite their claims on paper, were really ridiculous. His own desire for revenge was revealed in his vow to build a large fleet which would allow him to wreak vengeance on England before coming to terms with the latter's warmongering ministry.[63] Knowing the sacrifices which military life entailed, he tried to steel the soldiers by asking them to await patiently the advent of better times and by assuring them of his solicitude, which endeavored to spare them every adversity.

Giving publicized rewards to the army was another way to

[61] *Moniteur*, 18 Floréal, Year VIII.

[62] One of the more surprising features of public opinion is that the Poles supported Napoleon so devoutly despite his failure to promise the restoration of their country. The nearest France came to making such a promise was the following: "Although unable to re-establish Poland, Napoleon has a very friendly feeling for it and the day of its restoration will come." *Journal typographique et bibliographique* (Paris, 1799–1810), X, 33, February 24, 1807.

[63] *Aurons-nous la paix? ne l'aurons-nous pas? est-il possible de la faire avec l'Angleterre?* (Paris, 1800), 40. This was a semiofficial pamphlet.

maintain morale. The old soldiers received pensions, and widows and orphans of military men were provided for. Because of Napoleon's assumption that ambition was the main motive of men,[64] the enlisted men might receive bonuses and the officers titles and income-bearing property while they were still in active service. The men might also win promotions, either to the Guard or to higher ranks. During the Consulate, drumsticks, trumpets, guns, grenades, swords, rings, and boarding pikes of honor were awarded as signs of merit.[65] In 1804 all men who had received such awards automatically became members of the Legion of Honor, which replaced all previous signs of distinction. The government praised this organization because every Frenchman could earn membership in it, because it was a guarantee against the reestablishment of a privileged nobility, and because it was another step toward unifying the country and binding the institutions of other European states closer to those of France.[66] Napoleon also extolled the flags he awarded and exhorted the soldiers to defend them.

The best of all ways to maintain morale, however, was to write about the victories France had won, always without heavy cost to itself. Doing this was facilitated by the fact that until 1809 the French had received virtually no setbacks on the Continent. If at all possible, doubtful actions were described as victories; for example, when the British won a fleet action, the French claimed that they had really been the victors, inasmuch as they had achieved their aim.[67] These victories were reported in the army bulletins, which, until the famous Bulletin 29 of the campaign of 1812, contained no mention of losses except for a few minor setbacks in Spain and always portrayed deeds performed by the army and Napoleon as heroic.[68] Proof of victories was seen in the

---

[64] J.A.C. Chaptal de Chanteloup, *Mes souvenirs sur Napoléon*, ed. by E. A. Chaptal de Chanteloup (Paris, 1893), 324.

[65] Joseph Durieux, "Les écharpes d'honneur sous le consulat," *Revue des études napoléoniennes*, VI (1914), 253.

[66] *Archives parlementaires*, III, 746; *Débats*, 30 Messidor, Year XII.

[67] *Moniteur*, 25 Thermidor, Year XIII.

[68] *Débats*, 2 Germinal, Year VIII, and cf. the bulletins as printed in the *Moniteur*. Bulletin 29, written December 3, 1812, gave the following account of the French disaster in Russia: "Up to November 6 the weather was perfect, and the movement of the army was executed with the greatest success. The cold began

number of prisoners entering France—and those from Spain were listed in detail.[69] Very cleverly did the bulletin of October 13, 1806, point out that the King of Prussia's desire that the territory included in the Confederation of the Rhine be cleared of troops

---

on the seventh; from this moment on, we lost each night several hundred horses who died in bivouac. We had already lost many cavalry and artillery horses by the time we reached Smolensk. . . . More than thirty thousand horses died in a few days. We had to destroy a goodly part of our guns, our munitions, and our food supplies.

"This army, so fine on the sixth, was very different after the fourteenth, almost without cavalry, artillery, or transportation. Without cavalry, we could not reconnoiter even as much as a quarter of a league; yet, without artillery, we could not wait resolutely and risk a battle; we had to march so as not to be forced to a battle which the lack of munitions prevented us from desiring; it was necessary to occupy a certain space so as not to be turned, and that without cavalry to reconnoiter and join the columns together. This difficulty, joined to an excessive cold coming upon us suddenly, made our situation grievous. Some men, by nature not tempered strongly enough to be above all the chances of fate and fortune, appeared shaken, lost their gaiety and their good humor, and dreamed only of misfortunes and catastrophes.

"The enemy, who saw on the roads the traces of this frightful calamity which was striking the French army, sought to take advantage of it. It enveloped all the columns with its Cossacks, who, like the Arabs in the deserts, robbed the trains and the carriages which wandered to one side. This contemptible cavalry, which makes only noise and is not capable of routing a company of riflemen, became redoubtable through the favor of circumstances. Yet the enemy had to repent for all the serious attempts it undertook; having placed itself in front of the viceroy, it was thrown back by him with the loss of many men. . . .

"Yet the enemy occupied all the crossings of the Berezina, . . . a difficult obstacle to overcome. . . .

"Having deceived the enemy by various movements made on the twenty-fifth, the Emperor had two bridges thrown over the river at daybreak on the twenty-sixth. . . . The first brigade of the Partouneaux division . . . got lost, . . . went to the right instead of the left and . . . was probably captured. This cruel misunderstanding cost us two thousand infantrymen, three hundred horses, and three pieces of artillery.

"On the twenty-eighth . . . the combat became brisk. . . . The fourth and fifth regiments of cuirassiers routed the enemy cavalry which was coming to the aid of its infantry: six thousand prisoners, two flags, and six cannons fell into our power. . . .

"In the battle of the Berezina, the army of Volhynia suffered greatly. . . .

"The army, without cavalry, weak in munitions, horribly fatigued by fifty days of marching, dragging in its wake its sick and the wounded of so many fights, needed to reach its magazines. . . .

"To say that the army needs to re-establish its discipline, to remake itself, to remount its cavalry, artillery, and supply wagons is the result of the exposé which has been made. Rest is its first need. Material and horses are arriving. . . . The artillery has already repaired its losses. The generals, officers, and soldiers suffered much from fatigue and hunger. Many lost their baggage as a result of the loss of their horses, some by the ambushes of the Cossacks. The Cossacks have taken many isolated men.

had been carried out; only, the French had crossed the Saale instead of the Rhine, continuing their advance toward Prussia rather than retreating toward France.[70]

Even so, some news showing that things were not going perfectly well for France could not be repressed completely, even though it might be kept out of the *Moniteur;* consequently, some rather disadvantageous items made their appearance. Napoleon, for instance, complained that various supposedly loyal countries were refusing to support France, and might even be working against it. Occasionally he thought it necessary to reprove soldiers who had not performed their duties. One such reprimand was that administered to the Seventeenth Light Corps for abandoning its position: "Are all the braves of Castiglione . . . dead? . . . The Fourth and Twenty-second Light . . . in the midst of the desert without bread or water said victory would yield bread, and you, you desert your flags! . . . I shall check daily on the conduct of all corps. . . . They will remember I had confidence in them!" [71] In making such criticisms, he hoped to shame the men into better deeds through their personal attachment to him.

In order to attenuate the possible effect of adverse news items, they were either reported in a one-sided manner or accompanied by material favorable to France. Thus, any French losses—witness the report of a defeat sustained by Marshal Michel Ney's advance guard—were always caused by inferiority of numbers,[72] though the French were generally able to win even against odds. Victories might be reported simultaneously with losses in order to

---

"In all these movements the Emperor always marched in the midst of his Guard, the cavalry commanded by the marshal Duke of Istria, and the infantry commanded by the Duke of Danzig. His Majesty was satisfied with the good spirit which his Guard showed. . . .

"Our cavalry was so dismounted that it was necessary to group the officers who still had horses to form four companies of one hundred fifty each. Generals performed there the functions of captains, and colonels those of noncommissioned officers. This devoted squadron, commanded by General Grouchy and under the orders of the King of Naples, did not lose sight of the Emperor in all the movements.

"The health of His Majesty has never been better."

[69] This might mean that the Spanish affairs were the ones which caused Napoleon most anxiety with regard to public opinion.

[70] Napoleon, *Correspondance*, XIII, 345.

[71] *Ibid.*, VI, 39.   [72] *Moniteur*, 10 Thermidor, Year VIII.

offset the latter. While admitting that the situation in the Vendée was bad, the government exposed how much worse was the comparable situation in Ireland.[73] When attacks on Napoleon by members of the English Parliament appeared in the French papers, the speakers were frequently ridiculed, and what they said was refuted in footnotes. And as long as possible the government claimed that affairs were progressing well. Napoleon even stated that the French had been victorious at the Battle of Leipzig but had withdrawn because they were running short of cannon balls.[74]

In its account of the parliamentary debates of January 22, 1806, the *Journal de l'Empire* printed the statement that a large part of the French naval forces had been destroyed at Trafalgar and that England's maritime supremacy was thus signally confirmed.[75] The authorized account of Trafalgar merely said that if all the French and Spanish vessels had fought with the courage exhibited by two of the captains, victory would not have been in doubt.[76] The British blockade, it was said, was making navigation of the Sound difficult.[77] In 1813 the papers began admitting retreats in Germany, and by January of the following year they stated that the war had now become one of self-defense.[78] Near the end of the 1813 campaign, the *Journal de l'Empire* stated that the French soldier was struggling against weather and want, and in 1815 it admitted the desertions in Murat's army. The *Gazette de France* stated that Murat was continuing his retreat beyond hostile Tuscany and Rome, and that Sweden was making huge military preparations.

Other troubles were also admitted. Among them were those connected with the draft. Some conscripts had purposely mutilated themselves, and the Grand Judge urged that laws on crimes

[73] *Ibid.*, 17 Ventôse, Year VIII.

[74] Napoleon, *Correspondance*, XXVIII, 374–79.

[75] *Empire*, January 29, 1806. Such a statement speaks very well for the authenticity with which the *Empire* translated English accounts of the debates.

[76] *Journal*, August 29, 1806. The battle took place on October 21, 1805. Even this much did not get into the *Moniteur*.

[77] *Moniteur*, July 20, 1810.

[78] On September 4, 1810, the *Journal de l'Empire* said that Masséna had been forced to retreat in Portugal; on December 12 the *Journal de Paris* admitted the retreat but claimed it was voluntary.

relative to the draft be strictly enforced.[79] The skeleton army decreed by the legislature had not been filled.[80] The French army was not always as well led as it should have been. The *Journal de Paris* printed a report of the London newspaper, *Courrier de Londres,* that French soldiers were dying by hundreds in the hospitals;[81] it also printed an article from the London *Times* claiming that Napoleon had had to put forth more effort for the campaign in 1809 than before.[82] On 15 Ventôse, Year VIII, the *Journal de Paris* carried a rather disparaging article on the public debt.[83] A letter to Foreign Minister Jean Champagny from the American minister John Armstrong, protesting French seizure of American ships, appeared in the *Journal de l'Empire* of August 9, 1810.

British criticisms of France also appeared in French papers.[84] One of these criticisms pointed to the fact that the British were not the first to take steps contrary to international law: they had not started a blockade of the territory under French control until November, 1807, and then in reprisal against the Berlin Decree of November, 1806.[85] France was also the first to violate the Treaty of Amiens by the seizure of new territories immediately after the signing of the treaty. The *Moniteur* itself printed the speech of the King of England,[86] who placed on French ambition the responsibility for renewal of the war and who claimed that France had arranged for election of a docile Grand Master of the Knights of St. John. The *Moniteur* also printed an exposé of how badly the French army in Hanover had conducted itself.[87]

Napoleon, however, tried at all times to justify the actions of the French and his own demands and measures. To make the

---

[79] *Moniteur,* October 5, 1806; Ernest Picard and Louis Tuetey (eds.), *Correspondance inédite de Napoléon Ier conservée aux archives de la guerre* (Paris, 1912–25), I, 358.

[80] A. Hauterive, *De l'état de la France,* 284.

[81] March 8, 1807.   [82] November 10, 1809.

[83] As this was shortly after Bonaparte's assumption of power, he would later have a chance to point out the improvement he had wrought.

[84] The author has omitted enemy criticisms when it was impossible to be certain of their circulation in France.

[85] *Journal,* September 3, 1810.   [86] May 17, 1803.

[87] 28 Messidor, Year XI.

draft law more acceptable to civilians, he told them that the draft
was necessary to obtain freedom of the seas or to keep in Spain
an army large enough to prevent the prolongation of the revolution there which was blocking his aim of peace. Claiming that
among the French, rules of humanity were stronger than those
of war, he called attention to the fact that his brother Jerome had
helped the suburbs of Breslau after the enemy had fired them, and
that the soldiers occupying conquered territories had acted with
such moderation and had kept such discipline that the inhabitants
regretted their departure.[88] The taxes levied on Saxe-Gotha and
Saxe-Meiningen were to be refunded. France had allowed Denmark to remain neutral even though such an act of generosity
allowed England the advantage of carrying on trade in its ports.[89]

To make the war popular, the French government pointed out
—in addition to its indictment of the enemy—that its own war
aims were invariably either self-defense, peace, or championing
the cause of respect for independent governments. France was
the only great power which had been interested in a general
balance of power for the last hundred years.[90] Napoleon was always in favor of making peace, providing it was an honorable and
glorious one. Time and again the moderate peace terms he had
offered immediately after a decisive victory had shown that
France was not self-seeking. Instead, it had been attempting ever
since the Peace of Westphalia to maintain the balance of power
in Europe. A large France was beneficial to the Continent, as it
would frighten England and offset its power. France had therefore
taken action against Portugal and Spain and had annexed several
territories in order to obtain more sailors and, by gaining a longer
coast line, to close the Continent to England. In these ways it was
going to compel Britain to re-establish freedom of the seas.[91] It
had annexed Genoa only in order to protect it from England and
the Barbary pirates.[92] Other countries, such as Russia, were going
to join France in opposition to England, which had to fight

---

[88] Napoleon, *Correspondance*, XIV, 88, 103–104.
[89] *Empire*, October 5, 1807.
[90] A. Hauterive, *De l'état de la France*, 37, 40.
[91] Napoleon, *Correspondance*, XVII, 87.
[92] *Moniteur*, 8 Prairial and 24 Floréal, Year XI; Napoleon, *Correspondance*,
X, 476.

alone.[93] When the tides of war had turned against France, especially in 1814, Napoleon constantly stressed that he was on the verge of making peace with the allies.

Any such action as that of opening and publishing intercepted letters or burning British goods was taken merely in reprisal against similar measures by the British. Similarly, the *Mémoire sur la conduite de la France et de l'Angleterre à l'égard des neutres* showed that everything the French had done against neutrals was merely in reprisal,[94] for one of the principles of French foreign policy was recognition of neutral rights.

France also considered treaties inviolate. The idea that it wanted to split European Turkey was chimerical.[95] France denied England's claim that it had violated the Treaty of Amiens: although England complained of French activities in Piedmont, Etruria, and the Ligurian and Italian Republics, they had taken place before the treaty was signed; and, despite Britain's protests against French commercial activities, nothing in the treaty denied France the right to send commercial agents to England.

But if England was critical of and hostile to French actions, French publicity could at least claim that the other nations were very friendly. This friendship might have resulted in large part from the oft and loudly proclaimed assertion that French acts were justifiable. France also praised the British ministry which had made the peace of Amiens, and expressed confidence in France's friends, saying that they would realize the wisdom of not breaking their engagements.[96] According to French statements, countries always benefited, sometimes even more than they had dared hope, by allying with a France determined to help them. Napoleon also stressed the benefits other regions would experience by having Napoleon or his subordinates as rulers. They assured freedom of worship, abolished feudalism and established equality before the law, removed internal customs barriers, and effected a more equitable distribution of wealth. He emphasized that in Italy he had established a better administrative system, transplanted most of the French civil code, reformed finances, undertaken

[93] *Journal,* 29 Fructidor, Year XI, and 1807, *passim.*
[94] *Moniteur,* December 19, 1810.   [95] *Débats,* 3 Vendémiaire, Year XIII.
[96] *Journal,* 2 Frimaire, Year XI.

public works, given the clergy an adequate endowment, standardized education, equalized departmental expenses, and promised that taxes would not rise.[97]

ATTEMPT TO WIN ALLIES

Part of the purpose in publicizing the benefits accruing to countries on the side of France was to appeal to hostile or neutral states. Obviously, the more countries supporting France and the fewer supporting England, the more easily could Napoleon fulfill his very natural desire that the fighting come to a favorable end as rapidly as possible.

Napoleon therefore tried to wean England's allies from it and to win all neutrals for himself. The French pointed out that all countries but England had the common interest of trying to restore freedom of the seas. Napoleon expressed friendliness toward recent enemies and pointed out that states were no better off as neutrals than they would be as belligerents because England would not allow the enjoyment of their neutral rights.[98] The pamphlet *Du Jacobinisme des Anglais sur les mers et des moyens d'en triompher* urged neutral nations to make common cause against England.[99] To show they would not be alone or unwise if they did so, Napoleon traced step by step the growing hostility of the United States toward England, stressed the victories of American ships in duels with the British, and gave prominence to the acts of any nations with viewpoints similar to those of France. One such act was the declaration of war on Portugal by the King of Spain.[100]

Conquered regions were also to feel a unity of interests with France. Many inspired newspaper articles expressed Napoleon's contentment with them. Napoleon vowed that he would not surrender a single captured village even if enemy headquarters were Paris itself: all inhabitants in regions incorporated into the French Empire were French and would be treated exactly as those in old France.

The most concentrated campaign to win public favor in a

[97] Napoleon, *Correspondance*, X, 484-88.
[98] A. Hauterive, *De l'état de la France*, 175-83.
[99] Ebbinghaus, *Napoleon, England und die Presse*, 132.
[100] *Moniteur*, 3 Ventôse, Year IX.

region ruled by a subordinate of Napoleon was directed at Spain. There Napoleon promised to repay to the Spanish estates the sums they had advanced to the French troops.[101] He urged the French soldiers, who would get back the difference they lost on the money exchange, to treat the Spaniards with consideration.[102] Various means were used to convince the Spaniards, who were exhorted to have confidence in Napoleon, that Charles IV and his son, Ferdinand, had voluntarily and without mental reservation submitted to Napoleon the settlement of the quarrel as to who should rule.[103] Napoleon also assured them that he had the highest esteem for their country, that he was planning only advantageous things for it, and that the two nations could now be consolidated. He promised that he would not infringe upon Spain's territory or integrity,[104] and that it would retain all its privileges.[105] All that he personally wanted was the regeneration of Spain, for which the credit would go to himself.[106] He reminded the Spaniards that he had already given them a liberal constitution and destroyed every obstacle to their prosperity.[107]

On French initiative, articles appeared in the Spanish papers to make the people realize they no longer had a king, to point out the maladministration of the past several years, and to stress the need for Spain to improve its administration and to march along with France. These articles also said Napoleon had given Ferdinand a good reception.[108]

Notifying the grandees that he positively would not recognize Ferdinand, Napoleon urged the support of himself: the fate of Spain, he declared, depended upon their conduct.[109] Charles IV also sent out a proclamation telling the Spaniards not to heed people speaking against France, warning that these were enemies

---

[101] Napoleon, *Correspondance*, XVI, 396.

[102] *Ibid.*, 396–97.

[103] L. Lecestre (comp.), *Lettres inédites de Napoléon Ier (an VIII–1815)* (2d ed.; Paris, 1897), I, 186–87.

[104] Napoleon, *Correspondance*, XVII, 31. A few days later, however, Napoleon threatened to dismember Spain if its tranquillity was troubled and the safety of his troops compromised. Napoleon (Lecestre, comp.), *Lettres*, I, 188.

[105] Napoleon (Lecestre, comp.), *Lettres*, I, 186.

[106] Napoleon, *Correspondance*, XVII, 202.

[107] *Ibid.*, XVIII, 103.   [108] *Ibid.*, XVII, 40.

[109] Napoleon (Lecestre, comp.), *Lettres*, I, 188.

of Spain or agents of England, and repeating that Spain could have prosperity and security only if it was friendly to Napoleon.[110] After assuring the Spaniards that their fate was in their own hands, Napoleon warned that if they did not respond, he would make himself king of Spain and treat it as a conquered region.[111]

To quell any desire on the part of the Spanish possessions not to acknowledge French control in Spain, Murat told the Spaniards that Napoleon was sending ships to the colonies.[112] The Emperor of Morocco, in whose territories Spain had the cities of Ceuta and Melilla plus special treaty privileges, also received warning via the papers that if he listened to the English, he would have to deal with 300,000 united French and Spanish.[113]

In Spain several state bodies asked Napoleon to let them have Joseph as king, so he wrote Joseph and published the answer that his brother would leave Naples immediately.[114] In answer to an address from the Junta, Joseph said that the reason he desired to enter Spain in the near future was to conciliate the various interests and begin his reign by acts of clemency and pardon. At the same time he expressed his sorrow at the thought of having to use force to repress Spain's rebellious elements when reason and conviction would do as well.[115]

FRENCH CONFIDENCE IN THE GOVERNMENT

Napoleon wisely felt that it was not enough merely to show that his foreign affairs were progressing smoothly and favorably and that he could not fail to win the war. He wanted the French to feel that at home he was accomplishing things for them, that their domestic situation was as superior to that of the enemy as was their military situation. Both his foreign and his domestic policies warranted popular confidence in his government, and the results accomplished by them explained that confidence.

---

[110] Napoleon, *Correspondance*, XVII, 59.

[111] *Ibid.*, XVIII, 103.   [112] *Ibid.*, 163.

[113] *Ibid.*, XVII, 202. Napoleon had written a letter in this same vein to the ruler of Morocco.

[114] *Ibid.*, XVII, 260. These requests were of course staged.

[115] *Ibid.*, XVII, 311; Joseph, *Mémoires et correspondance politique et militaire*, ed. by A. Du Casse (Paris, 1853–54), IV, 335.

While the Luddite riots kept England uneasy, France was becoming more confident and serene. The finances of the country became more sound year by year, so that France could continue fighting indefinitely. Napoleon did not even have to ask for new taxes at the opening of the legislative session. If regions under French control thought their financial burdens were heavy, Napoleon showed them how much more France was gladly paying.[116] Yet French taxes were only one half those in England, and France did not have any debt.

French commerce had gradually improved, partly because the United States was doing more trading with France. Agriculture was much advanced and the industrial situation was splendid. The Continental System had opened new markets to the products of French factories.[117] Some of the economic enterprises begun or stressed because of the war were raising silkworms, merinos, and cotton; producing an artificial substitute for indigo; improving pottery, glass, and textiles; and extracting sugar from grapes and beets. As a result, the income of France was larger than ever. All of the successful efforts along these lines were emphasized, and the government offered bonuses and prizes to stimulate the work.[118]

The official news from French colonies was always very favorable. General Charles Leclerc had been making steady progress in Santo Domingo. All the colonies were economically sound and quite able to defend themselves. Yet, when the government had to admit that it had lost colonies, it said their loss was beneficial to France.

The reason for the loss of colonies was the marked superiority of the British navy. Nevertheless, the French were led to believe that the French navy, though still in the early stages of its development, was doing splendidly. Praises of it were sung in Trublet's *Histoire de la campagne de l'Inde par l'escadre française,*

[116] Napoleon, *Correspondance*, XII, 283. At this time (1806) Napoleon had Eugene insert in the Italian papers that France would have to face a salt tax and a higher levy.

[117] In the Year IX, France had admitted that the budget was not balanced and that industry had been hard-hit. But it was declared war industries would replace those which were suffering. A Hauterive, *De l'état de la France,* 251, 284.

[118] *Journal,* March 7, 1808; Aulard (ed.), *Paris sous le consulat,* II, 213.

which was reviewed in the *Moniteur* for 7 Fructidor, Year X. Napoleon also set about convincing the French that the admitted superiority of the British fleet did not foredoom any attempted invasion of England. The *Journal de Paris* quoted an English paper of 1756 to the effect that some British admirals had said a strength even double that of the enemy would not guarantee England against a landing.[119] In 1801 the *Annuaire de la marine de la France et des colonies* appeared for the first time since 1790. Publication of this showed that there was at least a renewed interest in the navy.[120] Although England had seized Denmark's ships, the Danes had only twenty-eight fewer vessels than at the start of the war.[121] France was constantly building new vessels, and the first effect of the Anglo-American war would be to draw English ships to America and thus facilitate Napoleon's developing the navy.

The French had every reason to be confident. A pamphlet, *France en 1709 et en 1809*, showed how much the situation of France had improved.[122] All types of French resources were superior to those of their enemies, and all the benefits of war accrued to France. It was gaining new allies and making new conquests, enabling Napoleon to establish his relatives as rulers of states subordinated to France. The other Continental states had no reason to break with France; but should they do so, a united France was prepared for them, whether Prussia, impotent Sweden, or the Russian colossus with feet of clay.[123] Even in 1814 and 1815 Napoleon laid great stress upon the adequacy of the measures taken to defend France and upon the unanimity with which the populace, still not exhausted or even weary, was supporting the government in its determination not to surrender. In fact, at all times the enlightened men had favored Napoleon's plans. Their confidence in the government was as much the result of its financial and other domestic measures as of its military exploits.

A clever means of bolstering French confidence was to emphasize that French civil and military leadership was good and that Napoleon's genius was upholding the glory of France. That genius, as exemplified in the 1805 campaign, was praised by the *Gazette de France*.

[119] Ebbinghaus, *Napoleon, England und die Presse*, 80.
[120] *Moniteur*, 2 Ventôse, Year IX.   [121] *Ibid.*, April 17, 1811.
[122] *Journal*, June 25, 1809.   [123] *Débats*, 13 Fructidor, Year XII.

Military glory appeared exhausted by ten years of triumphs. The French had equalled everything in the military field which ancient and modern centuries offer for the admiration of men. . . . It was reserved to the genius of the Emperor again to astonish the imagination and to surpass all hopes. Who could, in fact, foresee that a campaign of two weeks would suffice to annihilate a plan meditated with as much perfidy as audacity, executed in the most formidable and unforeseen manner, and entrusted to the valor and experience of all the famous generals and war-hardened soldiers of the house of Austria to defend? One finds nothing, even in the military prodigies of recent years, which can stand up to the events of the month which has just ended.[124]

It was pointed out that Fredrick the Great and the Danish minister, Count de Lynar, some seventy years earlier had expressed the belief that France would one day be able to dictate to its neighbors.[125] Thus it could be said that victory was the Gallic destiny. Nor was that all. Not all the news favorable to France was published, because England tried to suppress news unfavorable to itself from such places as Egypt and Denmark.

Closely allied to this confidence was the pride felt by the citizen at being a Frenchman, a member of the "great nation." Several of the points already cited helped support this self-esteem; and Napoleon even went so far as to show that discoveries and innovations claimed by other countries, such as the preservation of potatoes and the fumigation of prisons,[126] were really the product of French genius. France could also be proud of being the most civilized country. Its pre-eminence was illustrated in several ways—the encouragement of the fine arts in celebration of victory, the choice of officials in quiet, truly representative elections, and the constitution given Spain, which allowed colonial representatives in the legislature.

Although most of the foregoing statements indicate to what ex-

[124] *Gazette de France*, October 26, 1805, as quoted in F. V. A. Aulard (ed.), *Paris sous le premier empire: recueil de documents pour l'histoire de l'esprit public à Paris* (Paris, 1912–23), II, 276. Feats such as the march of the army into Italy in 1800 can be attributed to good leadership. The advance was so rapid that the Milanese were unaware even of the army's presence in Italy until twenty-four hours before its entry into their city. Napoleon, *Correspondance*, VI, 329; *Journal*, 22 Prairial, Year VIII.
[125] *Journal*, November 14 and 18, 1806.
[126] *Moniteur*, 29 Messidor, Year X; *Journal*, 11 Vendémiaire, Year IX.

tent the war occupied Napoleon, he did not think it sufficient merely to inspire the French to fight and to show them how well they were doing. It was also important that he show them the positive benefits which he and his government had brought about, and he was not averse to employing Hollywood adjectives in so doing.

The first thing for which the Consulate received praise was the Constitution of the Year VIII and the type of government it had established: a government of laws with an administrative system not "vicious in its principles and corrupt in the means of execution." [127] For this, as for the other domestic measures of the government, the Consulate had received enthusiastic support from the populace. The government was praised for being so liberal. It had held popular elections, an illustration of the equality of citizens before the law. It had retained freedom of conscience— but without the abuse of temporal power by prelates—and inalienability of the property of the poor, and it had refused to tolerate any attempt to restore feudalism. The government was going to establish order, enforce justice, and show moderation. It would likewise assume the task of making the republic dear to citizens, respectable to foreigners, and formidable to enemies.[128] The Additional Act issued during the Hundred Days was the best conceivable guarantee of liberties.

Since the people wanted peace, each treaty the government signed received a great amount of publicity. The religious peace established by the Concordat, which officially reopened the Catholic churches, was also duly extolled. Another achievement toward peace was that the government had forced the Barbary pirates to respect French and Genoese ships.

Each change in the form of government in France and each political rearrangement engineered by Napoleon in another country was adequately publicized. At the time when the life consulate was proclaimed, Bonaparte ordered Joseph Fiévée to point out in the most obvious way the advantages of absolutism.[129] Especially during the Consulate he was concerned that the papers

---

[127] *Moniteur*, Year VIII, *passim*.
[128] Napoleon, *Correspondance*, VI, 37.
[129] Ebbinghaus, *Napoleon, England und die Presse*, 148.

should praise only him. He had worked toward the establishment of unity in France. The civil war in the west had been put down, and *émigrés* had been allowed to return. After Bonaparte had considered the region pacified, he had appealed to the Vendeans to have confidence in the government, as the safety of their families and property and the tranquillity of the region were at stake.[130] He had also helped restore internal peace by greatly diminishing the amount of brigandage.

In Italy, Bonaparte was credited with restoring peace, liberty, industry, commerce, arts, and public credit after the disasters attendant upon rule by England, Russia, and Austria.[131]

In order to further arouse admiration for Bonaparte, newspapers and other publications acclaimed his genius and his moral excellence. The *Journal de Paris* said [132] that he worked eighteen hours a day for the public welfare, had all-inclusive knowledge, got the best possible aides regardless of party, watched over all rights and interests, and never asked the soldiers to endure any hardship he himself would not undergo. Some of the qualities he was said to display were rare talents, intrepidity, constancy of principles, firmness of character, promptness and justness of mind, and modesty. Furthermore, he was invincible, grateful to God, forceful, clever, magnanimous.[133] It was modestly stated by Charles Étienne's ode, "L'Homme du destin," that he combined the qualities of all the great men of history.[134] The *Journal de l'Empire* said that he was "the most active genius ever mentioned in the history of peoples." [135] He had become Emperor merely to safeguard better the interests of France.[136]

---

[130] Napoleon, *Correspondance*, VI, 73, 225.

[131] *Moniteur*, 24 Messidor, Year VIII.   [132] 27 Nivôse, Year VIII.

[133] C. F. A. Fayot (pub.), *Collection complète des discours de M. de Fontanes* (Paris, 1821), 53–63.

[134] *Journal*, January 28, 1807.

[135] November 26, 1805, as quoted in Aulard (ed.), *Paris sous le premier empire*, II, 328.

[136] The interpretation of the British libelist Peltier was somewhat different: "An old Columbine, refuse of all the Clowns of the Revolution, is charged with the care of the heredity of this new dynasty in which already figure with éclat hanged men, butchers, . . . Moslems, . . . operatic danseuses, . . . robbers, . . . poisoners, etc. . . .

"This little monkey of four feet two inches, hereditary Emperor!" Cf. Périvier, *Napoléon journaliste*, 221.

There was great danger that such a superman [137] might be considered aloof from the common people; therefore, an attempt was made to play up his human side. He had granted a pardon, for example, when a man's son had pleaded for him, and had proved unable to resist women's tears. Several papers related the story of a pretty young girl's having been so overcome with emotion upon seeing Bonaparte at Amiens that she had fallen on her knees before him; he and Josephine had both rewarded her, saying kind things and presenting her with pictures of themselves. Despite his greatness, once when in Italy he had removed his hat in honor of unfortunate courage as personified by wounded Austrian prisoners riding by in a cart.[138] He also took great interest in wounded French soldiers.

Napoleon had sponsored the fine arts and the sciences. He had established a yearly prize for work on electricity, awarded a prize for the best essay on croup, and established decennial prizes for achievement in many different fields.[139] The government had paid for publication of the results of the Egyptian expedition in arts and in science. Further proof of Napoleon's scientific bent was that he had encouraged the free vaccination of all citizens.

Napoleon had likewise aided benevolent institutions, and his government had made large contributions to charity. It had founded the first practical school of mining and had established the Imperial University to obtain uniformity of education. Napoleon had also reduced the cost of justice by a third; diminished the number of crimes, so that the courts were handling fewer and fewer cases; improved the prisons, visiting them and other institutions in person; sent medical supplies to the poor in

[137] Benjamin Constant summed up the effulgent praise in a letter to his aunt on November 1, 1802: "You speak . . . of the eulogies which are fashionable; you don't know what eulogies are. You ought to read the *Moniteur*. Four folio columns full of addresses. In one, Providence has created a man to console the earth; in another, one cannot fail to recognize a *monannuelle* [sic] power in the actions of this hero; in the third we shall weep for our nephews who sooner or later will cease to be ruled by him, etc. . . . The eulogies are those of Boileau and Horace minus their poetry and good taste." Henry Benjamin Constant de Rebecque, *Journal intime de B. Constant et lettres à sa famille et à ses amis* (Paris, 1895), 310.

[138] *Empire*, 15 Brumaire, Year XIV; Aulard (ed.), *Paris sous le premier empire, passim.*

[139] *Moniteur*, 6 Brumaire, Year XII; Napoleon, *Correspondance*, XV, 307.

the provinces; ordered and supervised the drafting of the civil, criminal, commercial, and judicial codes; improved the financial system of France by proper legislation; and provided for a better distribution of wealth.

The single aspect of Napoleon's domestic policy which received the most praise was the undertaking of public works— either for utility or for the beautification of Paris and other cities of the empire. In the Year XIII and in 1806 the embellishment of Paris was the subject for the general competition in composition.[140]

Napoleon insisted upon staying in the limelight. Every decoration or other type of reward or compensation was to come from him. Alexandre Berthier's *Relation des campagnes du général Bonaparte en Égypte et en Syrie* received a very lengthy and favorable review. Napoleon figured prominently in the fetes either by his presence or by virtue of their being in his honor; and his every act, especially the trips through the provinces, received a large amount of space in the press.[141]

At all times he had showed that his aim was to work for the welfare of France. He considered the soldiers particularly to be his children and did not waste a single life. The propaganda stressed that it was because Napoleon felt it to be to the best interests of France that he had made the sacrifices of divorcing Josephine, exiling himself on Elba, and abdicating for a second time. Because his dynasty had sprung up under the same circumstances as the new interests the nation had acquired since 1789, it alone was suitable as a form of government for France.

Never once during the entire period of his rule did Napoleon make any miscalculation or commit any errors. He had been forced to leave Egypt, which would have remained French had he stayed there, because of French misfortunes in Europe.[142] Losses sustained by the French had occurred because various subordinates had acted unwisely, because the allies of France had

---

[140] Léon de Lanzac de Laborie, *Paris sous Napoléon* (Paris, 1905-13), II, 86. The public works were undertaken partly to keep the workers quiet. Aulard (ed.), *Paris sous le premier empire*, II, *passim*.

[141] *Moniteur*, 12 Pluviôse, Year VIII.

[142] Napoleon, *Correspondance*, VI, 283-84, 555.

deserted, or because of uncontrollable elements such as the weather or disease.

Napoleon naturally made, from time to time, promises of what the government would do. Immediately after the *coup d'état* of 1799 Bonaparte promised that there would not be any reaction. At the time of his coronation he stated his aims to be stability of proprietorial rights, perpetuity of institutions, respect for law, and the well-being of the nation.[143] To the Italians he promised independence, general laws and national customs under the most favorable constitution, their own army, peace, prosperity, lower taxes, and a reign of justice and social virtues which would protect religion, property, and industry.[144] To the Swiss he stated that France was going to end their internal wars, see to it that the cantonal form of government functioned, and keep taxes low.[145]

These, then, were the points Napoleon wanted people to believe. The manner in which he went about achieving his objective provides one of the most colorful threads in his complicated policy.

---

[143] *Ibid.*, 555.
[144] Prince Murat (pub.), *Lettres et documents pour servir à l'histoire de Joachim Murat* (Paris, 1908–14), I, 229–39; Napoleon, *Correspondance*, VII, 371.
[145] Napoleon, *Correspondance*, VIII, 53.

CHAPTER II

GOVERNMENT MACHINERY FOR CONTROL

SINCE NAPOLEON UTILIZED VIRTUALLY HIS ENTIRE GOVERNMENT organization for propaganda purposes, it would be wise to glance at it at least long enough to obtain a background for understanding its relations with the various mediums of communication.

For the first five years that he was in power, Bonaparte had the title of First Consul. Associated with him, and theoretically just below him in the governmental hierarchy were two other Consuls, Charles Lebrun and Jean Cambacérès, who in reality had no authority. On December 2, 1804, Napoleon became emperor, supposedly in response to the overwhelming demand of the French people.

Directly below him as executives, after he had conquered various territories, were the subordinate rulers whom he established in power. Insofar as possible he selected members of his family for these posts. Among those chosen were his stepson Eugene, as Viceroy of the Kingdom of Italy; his brothers Joseph in Naples and Spain, Louis in Holland, and Jerome in Westphalia; and his brother-in-law Joachim Murat in the Grand Duchy of Berg and in Naples. At times, Joseph as governor of Paris, and Napoleon's wife Marie Louise as regent, also functioned when Napoleon was away on campaign. In addition, we should mention Auguste de Marmont, Governor General of the Illyrian Provinces, and the military governors of various places, particularly in Germany and Austria.

Napoleon had a number of executive departments which carried out certain propagandistic functions. The ministry of police, which attained its status of an independent ministry in 1802, was headed by Claude Regnier, Aimé-Jean Savary, or Joseph Fouché.

One of the specialized tasks assigned it was collecting letters which depicted outrages committed by the allies in 1814. In charge of departmental affairs for some time at the ministry was Pierre Réal. Under him were police commissioners—at least one in each town of 5,000 or more inhabitants, and twelve in Paris. Each city of 100,000 had a commissioner-general of police, and the law of 28 Pluviôse, Year VIII, reorganizing the administrative system, permitted the government to establish prefectures of police in the larger towns. Paris had one, replacing the Central Bureau, headed by François Dubois, Étienne Pasquier, or Réal. The ministry of police also had a press bureau which was headed by Philippe Lagarde.

Three of the ministries had censorship bureaus. The postal administration, under Marie Chamans de Lavalette, had forty employees charged with the censorship of letters. Furthermore, at Napoleon's direction, Joseph ordered the authorities at Burgos to open the letters of the rebels and stop the material they circulated.[1] The information gleaned in this way helped guide the attacks of Napoleon's propaganda machine. The police and interior departments also had censorship bureaus, that of the police primarily for the press and that of the interior for other publications. The latter, designated the Direction Générale de l'Imprimerie et de la Librairie and headed at first by François Pommereul and later by Count Joseph Portalis, reported to the police as well as to its own department.

Heading the department of the interior, as in each of the departments, was a minister. There was a relatively rapid turnover in this department: Lucien had become minister immediately after the *coup d'état* of 18 Brumaire; and there followed him in fairly rapid succession Jean Chaptal in 1801, Champagny in 1804, Emmanuel Cretet in 1807, and Count Jean Montalivet in 1809. From the minister the hierarchy descended through departmental prefects and subprefects in charge of *arrondissements* to the mayors. All of these officials were appointed by Napoleon, with the excep-

---

[1] Stenger, "Histoire de la société française," *loc. cit.*, 196; Joseph (Du Casse, ed.), *Mémoires*, IV, 352. Comtesse Claire de Rémusat, *Mémoires, 1802–8*, pub. by Paul de Rémusat (Paris, 1879–80), III, 482, says she had to write private letters cautiously or they would not have reached their destination.

tion that the mayor of any town under 5,000 was appointed by the prefect.

The ministry of the interior also included special bureaus and divisions which paid a good deal of attention to propaganda. One of these divisions was that of public instruction, the jurisdiction of which extended over the theater and fine arts as well as over the school system. The director of this division, at first Antoine Arnault, was subordinate to the councilor of state in charge of public instruction, the first of whom was Pierre Roederer. The theater bureau, part of the more general division, was headed by Joseph Esménard. At Bonaparte's accession the bureau of education was headed by Jacquemont. He issued instructions on scholastic matters to the prefects, who in turn worked through departmental juries of instruction. After Bonaparte had established the *lycées,* he appointed three inspectors general. They were aided in each *arrondissement* by the president and the government commissioner to the court of appeal and by one of the government commissioners to the departmental criminal court. Later on, of course, he established the University to supervise all education.

The Minister of Foreign Affairs, whether Talleyrand or Champagny or Hughes Maret, worked through French ministers or consuls at the various capitals. Maret, as Minister Secretary of State throughout the period was particularly important in the field of newspaper publicity, even though he held the post of Minister of Foreign Affairs for only three years. Generals aided the Minister of War, Henri Clarke, in propagandizing. He was much more important in Napoleon's propaganda hierarchy than was his naval counterpart, Denis Decrès (who held office from 1801 to 1814), despite the fact that in the military field a large share of the burden was borne by the Major General, Alexandre Berthier, who performed roughly the same functions as a chief of staff does today. The Minister of Public Worship, at first Jean Portalis and later Count Félix Bigot de Préameneu, utilized the church hierarchy and in addition received reports from agents of the police or of the prefects. François Mollien, the Minister of the Public Treasury, and Martin Gaudin, the Minister of Finance, also performed certain propaganda functions, as did the Intendant General of the Extraordinary Domain, Jacques Defermon.

In addition to this regular executive part of the government, Napoleon utilized more-or-less personal functionaries, six of whom were known as Grand Dignitaries. Of these, Cambacérès, the Archchancellor, played the most important role. The Grand Marshal of the Palace, Giraud Duroc, and the Grand Chamberlain, Élisabeth-Pierre, Count of Montesquiou-Fézensac, figured as his personal officials. Cognizance must moreover be taken of Louis Philippe de Ségur, the Master of Ceremonies, and of the Grand Squire, Armand de Caulaincourt. Other personal officials were Auguste de Rémusat, the Superintendent of Spectacles, and the prefects of the palace. Napoleon also entrusted certain propaganda tasks to his aide-de-camp. A special agent, Louis Ripault, submitted a daily report on nonpolitical papers, a statement every five days on such items as placards and posters, and an analysis every ten days of the pamphlets and books which had appeared.[2]

In the field of the arts, the Director General of Museums, Dominique Denon, was charged with paying all painters. The Chapel Master (successively Giovanni Paisiello and Jean Lesueur), the Conservatory of Music, and the Imperial Academy of Music were all important in this field.

In addition to these executive officers, there were also legislative groups, or members of legislative groups, who could be called on. The central legislature consisted of several houses: the Council of State, the Tribunate, the Legislative Body (Louis Fontanes, its president for a time, was the leading orator of the period), and the Senate. Local governing bodies, used to supervise such agencies as the theaters and to deliver public addresses to Napoleon, included councils of prefecture, departmental general councils, district councils, and municipal councils.

In conquered territories Napoleon made use of some of the governmental machinery already in existence or created by him. In addition to the organs of government transplanted from France, the General Confederation of the Poles is a striking example of utilizing governmental organs inherited from the old regime. In Spain the revolutionary Junta, the Council of Castile, and the

[2] Napoleon, *Correspondance*, VII, 201.

Council of Inquisition each played its part. The Governor General and the Director of Police in Holland were admonished for not having fulfilled their functions better.

In fact, while Napoleon never once uttered anything which would lead one to believe that he thought his propaganda machinery insufficient—he ignored completely the confusion among government departments as to the authority of each—his writings are full of criticisms of the way in which the officials functioned.[3] One repeated criticism was that the ministries of foreign affairs and police, the two most active ones, handled publicity so unskillfully that its official character was obvious to the public.

Frequently the way in which material was publicized, or the choice of material itself, was poor. For example, the Municipal Council of Chateau-Thierry, in its address telling of allied atrocities, had inadvertently said of the Russians, "We have heard their talk"; yet the same address had branded as unusual the fact that a priest who had lived in Moscow could make himself understood to the Russians. But no one complained of the discrepancy. Fiévée did criticize, however, the report distributed in Savary's name on the need of repressing the Dutch press: he said that the report had left the impression that Holland longed for its independence and that the French neither read nor discussed political affairs and were not interested in them. In 1805, Napoleon severely rebuked Joseph because, when Austrian plenipotentiaries were sent to negotiate peace, he made known the fact by a military salvo and by announcements at the theaters.

> It was quite useless to announce with so much emphasis the sending of plenipotentiaries. . . . It is a good means of putting the national spirit to sleep, and of giving foreigners a false idea of our internal situation. It is not by crying, Peace! that peace is obtained. I had not wished to put that into a bulletin; it was even more important that it not be announced at the theater. Peace is a word devoid of meaning. What we need is a glorious peace. I find, therefore, nothing more impolitic and more unsound than what was done at Paris on this occasion.[4]

[3] At this point we shall consider only over-all criticisms. Specific complaints regarding the various mediums will be examined in the appropriate sections.
[4] Joseph (Du Casse, ed.), *Mémoires*, I, 341.

Bishop Claude Le Coz claimed that the *Moniteur* had relighted religious dissensions by printing the speech made by the Pope in secret consistory. Leclerc informed Napoleon that since the printed reports of the Minister of Marine appeared in the papers in Santo Domingo it was unwise on the part of this official to insert anything contrary to the ideas of liberty and equality animating all Santo Domingans. Even Napoleon was criticized for portraying the war in 1803 as revolutionary and philosophical, instead of ascribing it solely to the violation of treaties by England.[5]

Another shortcoming of the governmental machinery was the inaccuracy of some of its reports to the authorities. General Henri Bertrand, for one, protested that the news being sent him was inaccurate. Because Fouché stirred up public opinion on the divorce of Napoleon and Josephine and then reported the remarks overheard on it, Napoleon overestimated the preoccupation of the public with the divorce. And police reports were too often based upon personal prejudices.[6]

Most of all, the authorities deplored the lack of energy displayed by their subordinates. Murat complained that his Minister of Police, Dauré, had not obeyed an order to insert certain material, and Napoleon complained that Savary had not co-operated as he should have in portraying the atrocities of the allies in 1814.[7]

The failure of officials to assume greater initiative should not be a source of wonder, however, as they were never sure what Napoleon's reaction would be. In 1814, Napoleon had Berthier bitterly reproach the police for sending out an agent to write up the campaign without first obtaining Napoleon's approval; and

[5] A. Roussel (pub.), *Correspondance de Le Coz évêque constitutionnel d'Ille-et-Vilaine et archévêque de Besançon* (Paris, 1900–1903), II, 9; Paul Roussier (pub.), *Lettres du général Leclerc* (Paris, 1937), 142; *Empire*, February 28, 1814; Joseph Fiévée, *Correspondance et relations de J. Fiévée avec Bonaparte premier consul et empereur pendant onze années (1802 à 1813)* (Paris, 1836), I, 170–71.

[6] Baron de Plancy (pub.), *Souvenirs du comte de Plancy (1798–1816)* (Paris, 1904), 184; Rémusat (P. de Rémusat, pub.), *Mémoires*, III, 596–97; Chaptal (E. A. Chaptal, ed.), *Souvenirs*, 380. The police reported the remarriage of Josephine and Napoleon by the Pope as a false rumor. This gives a hint as to the accuracy of its reports. Ernest d'Hauterive (ed.), *La police secrète du premier empire* (Paris, 1908), I, 220.

[7] Murat (Prince Murat, pub.), *Lettres*, VIII, 205; Napoleon, *Correspondance*, XXVIII, 172.

the Emperor did not like Clarke's acting to make public a cere-mony at Paris without his having ordered it. On several occasions Napoleon criticized Lebrun for printing letters he had written.[8]

To be sure, a few men other than Napoleon shouldered some responsibility. Fouché and the rulers established by Napoleon were probably the most illustrious examples; but Francesco Melzi, Grand Chancellor of the Kingdom of Italy, published a literary paper intended to revive national dignity, and various other offi-cials were allowed to exercise some discretion on what to publicize and on the method of doing so.[9] Had Napoleon permitted them greater latitude, it is possible that the results might have been even more to his liking.

Nevertheless, despite its errors, Napoleon's machinery for ad-ministering propaganda achieved to an impressive extent the aims which he had put before it.

[8] Fiévée, *Correspondance*, III, 107; Napoleon (Lecestre, comp.), *Lettres*, I, 197; Napoleon (Brotonne, ed.), *Lettres*, 49; Napoleon, *Correspondance*, XXV, 263; XXVII, 245.

[9] Lanzac de Laborie, *Paris sous Napoléon*, I, 325-26; Albert Pingaud, *Bonaparte président de la république italienne* (Paris, 1914), II, 382.

CHAPTER III

PAPERS AND BOOKS

A. PAPERS

"I shall never allow the papers to say or do anything contrary to my interests."—NAPOLEON
"I shall not judge on the evil they have done, but on the little good they have done."—NAPOLEON
"Papers must be the first to take cognizance of what the government recognizes."—NAPOLEON

UNQUESTIONABLY, NO OTHER PROPAGANDA MEDIUM PLAYED AS IM-portant a role or received as much personal attention from Napoleon as the press. During the provisional consulate the press enjoyed more freedom than at any time since the fall of the Girondists,[1] but within seven weeks of his accession to power Bonaparte had begun its regulation. One of his first measures along this line, the decree of 27 Nivôse, Year VIII, which reduced the number of daily newspapers in Paris from seventy-three to thirteen, was the outgrowth of his desire to control the papers more easily. Those permitted to continue publication were the *Journal de Paris*, which was of a less propagandistic nature than another survivor, the *Moniteur;* the *Journal des Débats;* the *Journal des hommes libres,* which served Fouché; the *Clef du Cabinet des Souverains* and the *Citoyen français,* which were the last remains of the opposition and were therefore constantly threatened with suppression; the *Gazette de France,* which was concerned primarily with domestic

---

[1] Ebbinghaus, *Napoleon, England und die Presse,* 2. The only paper against which any steps were taken was the notoriously royalist *Aristarque,* according to Albert Vandal (*L'avènement de Bonaparte* [Paris, 1910], I, 460). But the Central Police Bureau reported that it had closed down the presses of the *Defenseur des Droits du Peuple* in Brumaire, Year VIII. Aulard (ed.), *Paris sous le consulat,* I, 21. This suppression may have occurred before Bonaparte's accession to power.

politics; the *Ami des Lois;* the *Décade philosophique;* the *Journal du Soir;* the *Publiciste;* the *Journal des Défenseurs de la Patrie,* which, under Talleyrand's influence was almost as official as the *Moniteur;* and the *Bien Informé.*[2] The only paper which tried to resist the decree, the *Ange Gabriel,* was immediately beaten to its knees and suppressed.[3]

One by one Napoleon found even this number too large and by 1811 allowed only four papers to exist in Paris: the *Gazette de France,* the *Journal de l'Empire,* the *Journal de Paris,* and the *Moniteur.* The *Bien Informé* was ordered to cease on 25 Ventôse, Year VIII; and on 9 Prairial, Year VIII, Lucien had Cambacérès announce the suppression of the *Ami des Lois* because it had criticized the Institute.[4] At the end of Year XIII the *Clef du Cabinet* was suppressed. In 1807, at the order of the government, the *Mercure* (a weekly) absorbed the *Décade philosophique,* and in 1810 Savary instigated merging of the *Publiciste* with the *Gazette de France.* Some of the other papers had been forced by the government to change their names, while still others had amalgamated voluntarily or become bankrupt.[5]

After suppressing various religious papers published in Paris, Napoleon ordered in 1806 that all remaining ones be supplanted by the new *Journal des Curés.* As its predecessors, it was concerned solely with religious news. Furthermore, the number of political papers in the provinces was limited by ministerial circular in 1807 to one per department, edited by the prefect. Even before

---

[2] Ebbinghaus, *Napoleon, England und die Presse,* 10–11. Because those left were the thirteen elite, the suppression did not cause much comment in public. The remaining papers did not dare say anything because their turn might be next, and they did not choose to criticize because they were glad to see papers of the opposite party suppressed. Aulard (ed.), *Paris sous le consulat,* I, 98, 101.

[3] Périvier, *Napoléon journaliste,* 105.

[4] Bonaparte felt that such criticism was insufficient cause for suppression and stated that the greatest liberty should reign. Napoleon, *Correspondance,* VI, 343. It is strange that he allowed Lucien to have his way.

[5] M. van Schoor, *La presse sous le consulat et l'empire* (Brussels, 1899), 13; Lanzac de Laborie, *Paris sous Napoléon,* I, 211; Aulard (ed.), *Paris sous le consulat,* I, ix; Gustave Le Poittevin, *La liberté de la presse depuis la revolution (1789–1815)* (Paris, 1901), 185, 231–33. The *Journal des Débats,* for example, became the *Journal de l'Empire* on 27 Messidor, Year XIII (July 3, 1805). Sometimes Napoleon suppressed a paper merely as a warning to others. During the summer of 1809, for instance, he wrote Fouché, "The papers are going from bad to worse; it is necessary to suppress one." Napoleon (Brotonne, ed.), *Lettres,* 190.

this general order, the government had halted publication of individual papers in the departments, forbidden the establishment of new ones, and required the owners and editors to promise fidelity to the constitution, and to justify the existence of their papers.[6] Among those so terminated were the *Affiches d'Eure-et-Loire* for stressing the sovereignty of the people, the *République démocrate d'Auch* for mentioning the rise in the price of grain,[7] and the *Vedette de Rouen* for stating that a speech by the President of the Institute to Napoleon was inspired by François Fénelon's epic, *Télémaque*. Lucien, Cambacérès, and the Paris prefect of police were the officials who most often decreed the demise of individual journals.[8]

These suppressions of papers were not confined to France proper.[9] After the formation of the Confederation of the Rhine, Napoleon exercised the same authority over the press there as he did in France, being most strict with Baden, which was allowed only one official paper, edited by the foreign minister of Baden. On May 29, 1811, a decree providing that any paper which printed political news not in the *Moniteur* was to be suppressed meant the end of press independence in the states in the Confederation of the Rhine. The more important German papers which Napoleon adjudged valueless or dangerous to his cause were the *Gazette de Fribourg*, the Cologne *Staatsbote* and *Zeitung*, the *Gazette du Bas Rhin*,[10] the *Krefelder Wochenblatt*, the *Aachener Merkur*,

---

[6] Périvier, *Napoléon journaliste*, 267–68; Gershoy, *French Revolution and Napoleon*, 463; Henri Welschinger, *La censure sous le premier empire* (Paris, 1887), 104. There had been 269 departmental papers.

[7] Hamil Grant (*Napoleon and the Artists* [London, 1917], 222) claims that Lucien and Joseph were attempting to get a corner on grain.

[8] Périvier, *Napoléon journaliste*, 111–12; Welschinger, *Censure sous l'empire*, 82–83. Le Poittevin (*Liberté de la presse*, 307) asserts that after 1811 the departmental press, particularly in the newly acquired departments, was suppressed for quoting other Paris papers besides the *Moniteur*. The material in the five 1814 numbers of the Bordeaux *Indicateur* used by the author was primarily extracted from the *Empire;* however, other Paris papers were also used by the Bordeaux paper. The Archbishop of Besançon denounced to the government an impious paper with the result that it was suppressed. Le Coz (Roussel, pub.), *Correspondance*, II, 150.

[9] In general, Napoleon charged the Minister of Foreign Affairs, working through resident agents, with the suppression of inimical papers in non-French territory. Napoleon, *Correspondance*, IX, 299; Salmon, *Newspaper and Authority*, 121.

[10] Suppressed by the prefect.

the *Gazette de Frankfort*, the *Mainzer Zeitung*, the *Gazette de Bayreuth*, the *Gazette d'Erlangen*, and all the papers in Hamburg.[11] In Spain a French paper was suppressed on the ground that it served no useful purpose and that wherever French troops were stationed Napoleon wanted to supervise personally the establishment of French publications. Two Amsterdam papers were stopped at Napoleon's command, and Murat ordered Prime Minister Giulio Mozzi of Etruria to shut down an English paper there.[12]

Officials other than those already designated functioned within the Confederation of the Rhine. In Würzburg, after 1806, the French commandant decided what papers should or should not be authorized to exist. Marshal Louis Davout reported to Duroc that the Frankfurt paper had printed news of French military movements, and Berthier ordered the stoppage of that of Bayreuth, about which the Foreign Minister had complained to Count Christian Haugwitz and to Jerome Lucchesini when Bayreuth was still Prussian.[13] Acting on his own volition in Frankfurt, but with an eye to pleasing the French government, Karl von Dalberg, Prince Primate of the Confederation, on October 10, 1810, ordered all political journals except one to cease publication.[14]

Both in the Confederation and in France many of the papers which were allowed to exist were suspended temporarily for printing some article inimical to the government but not suffi-

[11] Napoleon (Brotonne, ed.), *Lettres*, 284; Ludwig Salomon, *Geschichte des deutschen Zeitungswesens* (Oldenburg, 1906), II, 90; *passim;* Louis Nicholas Davout, *Correspondance du maréchal Davout prince d'Eckmühl, ses commande-ments, son ministère 1801–15*, ed. by Ch. de Mazada (Paris, 1885), III, 514; Karl Obser, "Zur Geschichte der badischen Presse in der Rheinbundzeit," *Zeitschrift für die Geschichte des Oberrheins*, XIV (1899), 132; Léonce de Brotonne (ed.), *Dernières lettres inédites de Napoléon Ier* (Paris, 1903), I, 174; Napoleon (Lecestre, comp.), *Lettres*, I, 225.

[12] Schoor, *La presse sous le consulat*, 32; Murat (Prince Murat, pub.), *Lettres*, II, 341; Albert Du Casse (ed.), *Supplément à la correspondance de Napoléon Ier* (Paris, 1887), 111. La Forest reported that the true reason for the suppression of the French paper in Spain was its failure to exalt the religious feelings of Joseph. Geoffroy de Grandmaison (pub.), *Correspondance du comte de La Forest* (Paris, 1904–13), II, 179.

[13] Napoleon, *Correspondance*, XII, 456, 536; Obser, "Geschichte der badischen Presse," *loc. cit.*, 112. An inspired article in the *Moniteur* acclaimed the loss of another of England's tools with the suppression of the Bayreuth paper. Napoleon (Brotonne, ed.), *Lettres*, 137.

[14] Salomon, *Geschichte des Zeitungswesens*, II, 116.

ciently serious to warrant their absolute suppression. Among the papers so suspended were the *Débats* for printing a brief of the Pope to the *émigré* bishops at London, the *Gazette de France*, the *Wochenblatt* of Kreuznach, which was suspended by the Prefect of Rhin-et-Moselle, and the *Clef du Cabinet* for printing the following article on administrative corruption:

> If there is one virtue necessary in public functionaries in a well-governed republic, it is disinterest; not that disinterest which limits itself to refusing presents, to not loving riches, to not fearing poverty, although even that is infinitely rare, but a universal disinterest which contemns ambition, favor, glory, the desire to be applauded for firmness, and which surmounts, out of fear of going astray, all personal considerations. Yet are those the dispositions which are today found in the men whom one sees placed in posts more or less eminent? Could many be found whose hearts are just and whose hands pure? Heavens! What a frightful picture, that which would unveil the iniquities which have been committed and which are committed daily. The sore which covers the body politic is so universal that there is only one person in whom are combined equally the zeal and genius needed to cure it. Speculations, robberies, cheatings, peculations are common to such a degree that misfortune, for some individuals, lies not in their having to reproach themselves for misdeeds of this sort, but rather in their vainly having to seek the opportunity to make themselves guilty. And with what impudence the ill-gotten goods are displayed! What houses, land, outfits, luxuriousness, tables, mistresses attest the dishonesty of the rich of the day! Such a man as formerly was plunged into indigence and the mud today eclipses the brilliant masters whom he formerly served, and one can now compare his insolence only with his thefts.[15]

Others which were supposedly permanently suppressed were allowed to resume. Thus Fouché was able to win a new lease on life for the *Journal des hommes libres* after a suspension lasting only three days.[16]

---

[15] Aulard (ed.), *Paris sous le consulat*, II, 501.

[16] A. M. Roederer (pub.), *Œuvres du comte P. L. Roederer* (Paris, 1859), III, 369; E. d'Hauterive (ed.), *La police secrète*, III, 160; Welschinger, *Censure sous l'empire*, 270. Even occasional issues of the *Moniteur*, as that printing the bases of peace proposed at Frankfurt in 1814, were suppressed. Napoleon, *Correspondance*, XXVII, 237. Perhaps Napoleon feared they would create too great a popular demand for discontinuance of the war.

The general procedure for halting circulation of a banned paper was for the police, either by command of Napoleon or on its own initiative, to instruct the post office to stop the paper in the mails while the police halted distribution in Paris. Prefects, likewise, suspended papers—witness the *Abeille du Nord*, of neutral Altona seized in the mail by the prefect of Dyle. In Italy Eugene assumed the initiative when suspending the *Gazette de Legnano*, and Napoleon approved his act.[17]

Censorship, both preliminary and punitive, was another method of controlling the press. Preliminary censorship was applied first to the *Journal de l'Empire* when Fouché, acting on orders contained in a letter of May 20, 1805, from Napoleon, appointed Étienne its censor.[18] Étienne was to oversee only the political part of the paper, which paid him a salary of 12,000 francs. His successors were Jean de Lacretelle, the younger, and Esménard. This type of censorship was later extended to other papers; Gabriel Legouvé, for example, became censor of the *Mercure*.[19]

After the establishment of the ministry of general police, there was a definite daily routine for censorship.[20] Attached to the bureaus of the secretary-general of the ministry was the division

[17] E. d'Hauterive (ed.), *La police secrète*, II, 13; Aulard (ed.), *Paris sous le consulat*, I, 123; II, 501; *Journal*, 26 Brumaire, Year VIII; A. Du Casse (ed.), *Mémoires et correspondance politique et militaire du prince Eugene* (Paris, 1858–60), III, 214; Napoleon (Lecestre, comp.), *Lettres*, I, 58. When ordering the suspension of the *Gazette de France*, Napoleon had Minister of Finance Gaudin order that it be stopped at the post office. Napoleon (Brotonne, ed.), *Lettres*, 404.

[18] Napoleon was extremely anxious to control the *Journal de l'Empire* because of its large circulation. In addition to having the first censor and being the first paper to be appropriated by the government, its editors were hounded more persistently than those of any other paper, perhaps because Fouché presented it under false colors. Welschinger, *Censure sous l'empire*, 92. Fiévée (*Correspondance*, II, 262–63) claims that the newspaper was even stopped at the post office by the Minister of Police because it had copied verbatim a *Moniteur* article. The police report stated that it was seized because it had announced the launching of new ships at Antwerp. E. d'Hauterive (ed.), *La police secrète*, III, 291. Périvier (*Napoléon journaliste*, 34) thinks Napoleon's conviction that censorship was necessary arose from his experience with the license of the press, reacting from the censorship under Robespierre, during the Directory.

[19] Périvier, *Napoléon journaliste*, 243; John Charpentier, *Napoléon et les hommes de lettres de son temps* (4th ed.; Paris, 1935), 58, 107. Because Esménard allowed the publication of an article hostile to Russia in 1811, he was exiled from Paris and was forbidden to come within forty leagues of the city, and Étienne, then editor, was suspended for fifteen days. Napoleon (Lecestre, comp.), *Lettres*, II, 123.

[20] Previously Esménard and Étienne had headed censorship of the papers.

of freedom of the press, with Pierre Desmarest censor for the papers. Each morning the imperial censor of a paper received his orders from the Minister of Police, and shortly after supper the next morning's issue was given to the Minister for approval. It was, therefore, not surprising that at ten o'clock one night the police invited the *Journal de l'Empire* to replace a moderate article dealing with Ferdinand by one more virulent.[21] And similar occurrences were frequent.

Even official army news was censored before being published. Napoleon, for instance, wrote Cambacérès on May 11, 1813, to censor news from the Minister of War on Spain, but he ordered that it still be published as extracts from the letters of the Minister.[22]

In Italy a law of May 9, 1801, established complete freedom of the press in the Cisalpine Republic, but on September 27, 1803, preliminary censorship was restored in the Italian Republic. After Eugene became Viceroy of the Kingdom of Italy, he ordered his Minister of the Interior, Felici, to abolish preliminary censorship of the papers once again and merely to punish editors who published inimical news. Topics forbidden to the press were those concerning news hostile to religion, laws of the state, respect and fidelity due the government, and morals.[23] Even though none of the Rome papers wielded much influence, Baron Charles Alquier forbade their printing anything critical of the French.[24]

The French likewise took more and more actions leading to censorship of German papers. Although, so far as is known by the present author, no regular censorship of the Berlin papers was established, Napoleon did have Berthier tell Marshal Victor in 1806 to prevent the *Gazette de Berlin* from publishing articles which would make people think he was building up his arma-

[21] Hippolyte Carnot and M. David (eds.), *Memoirs of Bertrand Barère*, tr. by V. Payen-Payne (London, 1896), III, 92; Welschinger, *Censure sous l'empire*, 20; Comte Pierre François Réal, *Indiscrétions, 1798-1830. Souvenirs anecdotiques et politiques tirés du portefeuille d'un fonctionnaire de l'empire*, ed. by Musnier Desclozeaux (Paris, 1835), I, 126-27; André Fugier, *Napoléon et l'Espagne* (Paris, 1930), II, 445.

[22] Napoleon (Lecestre, comp.), *Lettres*, II, 240.

[23] A. Pingaud, *Bonaparte président de la république italienne*, 347; Eugene (Du Casse, ed.), *Mémoires*, I, 124; *Empire*, August 1, 1806.

[24] Jacques Moulard (pub.), *Lettres inédites du comte Camille de Tournon* (1st Part: *Politics and Public Opinion*) (Paris, 1914), 42. Rome had censorship even before Bonaparte became Consul. *Moniteur*, 21 Brumaire, Year VIII.

ment.[25] In 1809 Napoleon decided to have Berthier establish censorship of the *Gazette de Presbourg* for announcing the surrender of Flushing, and in 1812 Berthier ordered the Duke of Belluno to supervise the press in Prussia to prevent its publishing anything prejudicial to the French or their allied armies. He also ordered authorities of Bavaria and Stuttgart to prevent babbling on military affairs. In Würzburg, the ministry, which was under the direct influence of Napoleon's diplomatic representative, exercised a censorship over and above the regular one. Before suppressing the *Journal politique de Manheim,* the French warned the Baden government to maintain the strictest censorship over it. In Frankfurt, beginning in 1806, Napoleon's envoy Theobald Bacher handled censorship of the press. At Hamburg, Louis de Bourrienne exercised a preliminary censorship, and in the Grand Duchy of Berg under Murat, Hazzi was censor of the papers. In 1810 the *Schwäbische Merkur,* the most important paper in Württemberg, received orders to submit each issue to Minister von Taube for censorship previous to publication. The *Magdebürgische Zeitung* was also instructed to accept orders from the military instead of from the civil authorities; an order of November 22, 1811, required that its publishers show the governor all political articles, which were then to be printed side by side with the French translation. In 1813 Napoleon took complete control of the *Leipziger Zeitung.*[26]

There was a press censor in Amsterdam, and by 1812 there were no longer virulent press attacks against the French in Spain, for the regency closely watched the Cádiz papers.[27]

[25] Napoleon (Picard and Tuetey, eds.), *Correspondance inédite,* II, 203; III, 140, 214; Napoleon, *Correspondance,* XVI, 264, 266; XXIII, 387; Salomon, *Geschichte des Zeitungswesens,* 114, 127, 151, 167, 170–71; Obser, "Geschichte der badischen Presse," *loc. cit.,* 120. In 1810 Hédouville was told to supervise the Frankfurt paper. Napoleon, *Correspondance,* XX, 309.

[26] Though Napoleon ordered Champagny to have Caulaincourt pretend to Russia that Bourrienne could merely express his displeasure after the appearance of certain articles, Metternich wrote that the papers were always submitted to Bourrienne in advance. Bourrienne himself says he often suppressed adverse news. One example was his preventing the Hamburg papers from printing a Russian manifesto to generals and military governors. Louis Antoine Bourrienne, *Memoirs of Napoleon Bonaparte,* ed. by R. W. Phipps, 4 vols. (New York, 1889), I, xi; II, 405; III, 207; Pierre Bertrand (ed.), *Lettres inédites de Talleyrand à Napoléon 1800–1809* (Paris, 1889), 5 Frimaire, Year XIV.

[27] Welschinger, *Censure sous l'empire,* 249; La Forest (Grandmaison, pub.), *Correspondance,* VI, 322.

After the mediation of Bonaparte in 1803, the Swiss press was likewise strictly controlled by the French. The head of the censorship imposed on it was Charles-Louis de Haller; but the French minister, Auguste de Talleyrand, played an active and zealous role until Champagny ordered the suppression of the *Narrateur* of St. Gallen, edited by the most pro-French of all Swiss magistrates, because of its liberalism.[28]

To persuade the average Frenchman that no censorship existed in France, Napoleon ordered the printing of many press articles dealing with the strict foreign censorship, and during the Hundred Days he did abolish all preliminary censorship. Editors then were liable for all articles published, but they were promised that, if they were charged with errors in judgment, they would have trial by jury. Not wanting to surrender all control of the press, Napoleon directed the police to assign to each paper an agent, who was to "inspire" its editing; the agent, of course, often took orders from the Minister of the Interior. In addition, Napoleon once again had the prefects supervise the departmental papers. Minister of the Interior Lazare Carnot was told exactly what tone —one of defending Napoleon against the furious attacks of his enemies—to give to the *Journal général de France*.[29]

In France as well as in other states the censorship was designed to prevent certain types of news from becoming known. Those interdicted as a general rule were the ones mentioning anything derogatory to the Grand Army or the allies of France, to the social pact, or to the sovereignty of the people.[30] A second group was composed of topics on which news stories might be printed or mentioned only if they had previously appeared in the *Moniteur*. These included discussion of religious affairs or the Bourbons and mere mention of the Jesuits, military or naval movements, any of Napoleon's speeches or letters, anything concerning Napoleon personally, and most of the diatribes against Napoleon or his family by the British press.[31] In addition, there were subjects

---

[28] Édouard Guillon, *Napoléon et la Suisse, 1803–1815* (Paris, 1910), 235–38.

[29] Henri Avenel, *Histoire de la presse française depuis 1789* (Paris, 1900), 220; Périvier, *Napoléon journaliste*, 414–15; Napoleon, *Correspondance*, XXVIII, 202. Napoleon also ordered Lavalette to prohibit *Le Censeur des censeurs* from going through the mail. Napoleon (Brotonne, ed.), *Lettres*, 596.

[30] Charpentier, *Napoléon et les hommes de lettres*, 60.

[31] A. L. d'Eckmühl Blocqueville, *Le maréchal Davout prince d'Eckmühl ra-*

temporarily forbidden to the papers because discussion of them was deemed unwise. These included mention of the heavy mortality at Paris or any commentary on the death of the Duke of Enghien. Other internal affairs on which the papers were to remain temporarily silent included the rise in grain prices,[32] the domains awarded in Hanover by Napoleon in 1809, the December 31, 1813, session of the Legislative Body, jokes about the blacks, and anything reminiscent of political parties. Only after the Minister of Justice had given his permission might news of the courts be published. The annexation of Tuscany, the events in Spain and Rome in 1808, the manifesto of the King of Sweden in the same year, and the attempts of England to embroil France with the United States were among the foreign affairs the press was not to discuss for a time. Also on the excluded list was the word "Poland," and Napoleon forbade any discussion of his acts drawn from a foreign source.[33] The papers were instructed not to mention Austerlitz while discussing the commemorative façade of the palace of the Legislative Body, for doing so might humiliate Russia, with which France was once again on good terms. When Joseph was in charge in Paris in 1805, he issued orders to the Minister of Police to prevent the printing of certain articles. As early as the Year IX a ministerial circular forbade publication by the departmental papers of any news which might hamper commerce or make public opinion anxious. In 1804 they were told not to insert anything regarding the police without formal approval by the Minister of Police, and by decree of 1810 the political news in the departmental press was limited to that which had previously appeared in the *Moniteur*.[34]

---

conté par les siens et par lui-même (Paris, 1879–80), IV, 160; Chaptal (E. A. Chaptal, ed.), *Souvenirs*, 349; Périvier, *Napoléon journaliste*, 237; Napoleon, *Correspondance*, XX, 263. Napoleon even refused to let Marie Louise give news to the court in 1813 before it appeared in the *Moniteur*. Napoleon (Lecestre, comp.), *Lettres*, II, 239. *The Journal de Paris* was reprimanded for revealing naval movements in 1805 by reporting that a lot of biscuit was being made at Toulon. Napoleon, *Correspondance*, X, 401.

[32] Order given to the Councilor of State charged with the first police *arrondissement* by the secretary-general of police.

[33] Napoleon told Fouché that use of foreign sources as a basis of French press articles was the cause of half the complaints he had to make about the papers. Napoleon (Lecestre, comp.), *Lettres*, II, 18.

[34] Napoleon, *Correspondance*, XVI, 139; Le Poittevin, *Liberté de la presse*, 146–47; Comte L. Remacle (ed.), *Bonaparte et les Bourbons. Relations secrètes*

Napoleon also banned certain topics from the press in subordinate kingdoms. Joseph was not to mention Sidney Smith, the English Admiral, in the Neapolitan papers; Eugene received instructions not to put purely administrative acts into the papers and to follow the same rule applied to France concerning naval and military news or news of Spain.[35]

In addition to suppressing mention of certain topics, Napoleon ordered that others be spoken of as little as possible. The list included mention of his sister Élisa, suicides and crime,[36] praise of the Austrian court in 1808, Polish affairs in 1810, and Prince Jean Bernadotte in 1811.[37]

By controlling the editors, Napoleon indirectly regulated the news printed by the papers. Very frequently he had some government official, usually the Minister of Police, call various editors in to warn them that they were not running their papers properly and to threaten possible suspension—or the Minister might permit the head of the division of freedom of the press to administer the rebuff. When Savary was Minister, he acted upon reports given him by Esménard. When editors were found ill-disposed toward the government, Napoleon (after perhaps ordering their arrest) would decide on a change in editors—with the Minister of Police again handling the details. When Chateaubriand in 1807 compared Napoleon to Nero, Napoleon ruined him financially by re-

des agents de Louis XVIII à Paris sous le consulat (1802–1803) (Paris, 1899), 249; Leclerc (Roussier, pub.), Lettres, 146; Welschinger, Censure sous l'empire, 105, 110, 122, 294; Périvier, Napoléon journaliste, 109; United States, Department of State, Despatches (France, John Armstrong to Robert Smith, November 26, 1809); Napoleon (Brotonne, ed.), Dernières lettres, I, 313; Napoleon (Lecestre, comp.), Lettres, I, 194; II, 18, 72; Napoleon (Brotonne, ed.), Lettres, 122, 169, 182, 180, 251, 334; Baron Albert Du Casse, "Documents inédits relatifs au premier empire. Napoléon et le roi Joseph," Revue historique, X (1879), 100. It is interesting to note that Napoleon permitted the papers to print Moreau's speech defending himself. Constant, Journal, 43.

[35] Joseph (Du Casse, ed.), Mémoires, II, 255; Eugene (Du Casse, ed.), Mémoires, II, 50; IV, 202; VI, 431.

[36] Partly because the masses did not read the papers. Lanzac de Laborie, Paris sous Napoléon, III, 327.

[37] Napoleon (Lecestre, comp.), Lettres, I, 248. The Moniteur did not describe the ceremony for Napoleon's coronation because it differed from what the Pope had agreed to, and Pius VII would not permit the changes to be revealed in print. Comte Joseph d'Haussonville, L'église romaine et le premier empire (3d ed.; Paris, 1870), I, 358.

moving him as editor of the *Mercure*.[38] Some of the editors whom the government chose were Jean Marignie and Victor de Jouy for the *Publiciste;* Lacretelle, Esménard, and the Chevalier Stanislas de Boufflers for the *Mercure;* Fiévée and Étienne for the *Journal de l'Empire;* Antoine Jay for the *Journal de Paris;* Pierre Tissot for the *Gazette de France;* and Maret and François Sauvo for the *Moniteur.* In addition, the Archbishop of Paris chose the editors of the semiofficial *Journal des Curés.* The only editors who always received a salary were those of the *Moniteur* and *Journal des Curés;* the others, regardless of how chosen, were paid a salary only when their papers showed a profit.[39]

Editors in non-French territories were also strictly controlled. The Minister of Police received orders to arrest the editor of a paper at Speyer, and this same minister appointed the editor of the official Frankfurt paper. He also instructed the Foreign Minister to speak to the French minister in Switzerland about reprimanding an editor and to have his chargé d'affaires at Hamburg demand that some editors be arrested and tried by the laws of the country. Napoleon furthermore had the Foreign Minister order his minister at Cassel to see that politically safe men edited the Westphalian papers, and Baron Bacher was chosen to edit the *Leipziger Zeitung* after Berthier had received orders to shoot Bacher's predecessor if he showed signs of any malevolence.[40]

In considering the financial control of the press by the government, one must remember that during the Napoleonic period the capital invested in a paper was still relatively small, and therefore financial control was simpler and more immediate. As a means to gain such control, the government employed a system of taxation.

[38] The treatment accorded the brothers Bertin, editors of the *Empire,* was the most severe. Périvier, *Napoléon journaliste,* 316, 383; Napoleon (Brotonne, ed.), *Lettres,* 389.

[39] Welschinger, *Censure sous l'empire,* 95, 121-22; Napoleon (Lecestre, comp.), *Lettres,* I, 100, 333; II, 59; Avenel, *Histoire de la presse,* 201; *Journal,* 1 Frimaire, Year VIII; Duke of Rovigo, *Memoirs of the Duke of Rovigo (M. Savary),* 4 vols. (London, 1828), Vol. III, Part I, 14; Joseph Joubert, *Correspondance de J. Joubert* (9th ed.; Paris, 1895), 165. Like Ney's, the *Memoirs* of the Duke of Rovigo are spurious, both having been written by Antoine Bulos.

[40] Napoleon (Brotonne, ed.), *Lettres,* 211; Salomon, *Geschichte des Zeitungswesens,* 117; Napoleon, *Correspondance,* VI, 429; XVIII, 201; Napoleon (Lecestre, comp.), *Lettres,* II, 250. Napoleon sometimes used his military administrators to carry out arrests he had ordered.

One reason for the levies imposed was the desire to so weaken the papers financially that they would be forced to cease publication or to become financially dependent upon the government. Among the burdens each paper had to bear were a stamp tax of three or five centimes per issue [41] and the salary of its imperial censor. In 1805 the government confiscated one sixth or one fourth of the property of the newspapers, partly to obtain funds for pensions to literary men.[42] The *Journal de l'Empire*, whose annual income was 200,000 francs, was compelled to give one fourth to the government, the *Publiciste* only one sixth.[43] The final step in financial control was government seizure in 1811 of the property of all the papers, beginning on February 18 with that of the *Journal de l'Empire*. Of the twenty-four shares into which its stock was divided, eight went to the police and the rest to courtiers and literary men. The decree of September 17 appropriated the property of all the papers to the government, which retained nine seventeenths, an amount worth about 800,000 francs.[44]

Reports on the press were constantly sent to Napoleon to assist him in his control and in his propaganda activities. The police played the primary role in providing information on the conduct of the press—though sometimes Napoleon, in order to arouse the police to greater activity in regulation of the press, beat its officials to the punch and told them that certain papers were not being conducted properly and that they contained inimical articles. In the early days of the Consulate, the Central Bureau—at the orders of the Minister of Police—usually reported on the papers. After the prefecture replaced it, both the prefecture and the ministry reported, praising or censuring, according to what the spirit of

[41] This was paid by the *Moniteur* as well as the rest.

[42] Even the financially weak departmental press had to pay this to the government. Welschinger (*Censure sous l'empire*, 105) says the 260 papers paying it yielded only 2,800 francs. Annual revenue to the government from the Paris papers was in excess of 1,000,000 francs: approximately 200,000 from postal expenses, 250,000 from the present tax, and 575,000 from the stamp tax. Périvier, *Napoléon journaliste*, 374.

[43] Schoor, *La presse sous le consulat*, 51. The salary of the government-appointed editor was another one sixth of the income. Welschinger, *Censure sous l'empire*, 92; Napoleon, *Correspondance*, XI, 69.

[44] Welschinger, *Censure sous l'empire*, 117-19; Avenel, *Histoire de la presse*, 201.

the papers warranted.[45] The Minister of Police, through the prefects and the *gendarmerie*, also supervised the departmental press. Réal was the one who ordered the prefects to report in detail on the press.[46]

When on campaign in 1805, Napoleon had Joseph report on the press in Paris and later had the Minister of Foreign Affairs check on a Spanish paper at Bayonne. Camille de Tournon reported to Joseph Portalis on all the papers printed or circulated in Rome.[47]

Naturally, the hostile foreign papers were not permitted to circulate in France; however, they were often smuggled in.[48] Among those so forbidden were the *Gazette de Leyde* and all the newspapers published in Germany except the Berlin *Minerva*, which, because it was pro-French, Napoleon decided in 1802 might circulate in the Rhenish departments. During the Hundred Days this prohibition on the circulation of foreign papers was renewed for Lille and the northern and Rhenish frontiers.[49]

These channels of control and report did not bring about a completely docile press. The *Journal de l'Empire*, for instance, gave notice of the annexation of Tuscany before the Privy Council even met to decree it, and printed the decree annexing Valais to France in 1810, even though Napoleon did not want it to be published.[50] Napoleon was obliged to renew very frequently his demand to Fouché that the papers should not mention the Bourbons, religion, or military affairs. Indeed, his two most frequent complaints about the press were that it discussed forbidden subjects and that it omitted certain desirable articles. One reprimand

[45] Aulard (ed.), *Paris sous le consulat, passim*. Schoor (*La presse sous le consulat*, 18) says Regnier was quite lenient with the press. For some reason Napoleon relied upon Lavalette to inform Fiévée in 1806 that the *Empire* was badly edited. Napoleon, *Correspondance*, XII, 12.

[46] Schoor, *La presse sous le consulat*, 49; Avenel, *Histoire de la presse*, 199–200.

[47] Napoleon, *Correspondance*, XVII, 31; Joseph (Du Casse, ed.), *Mémoires*, I, 350; Tournon (Moulard, pub.), *Lettres inédites*, 42.

[48] Except *Bell's Weekly Messenger*. In 1811 Napoleon had his aide-de-camp Lemarois stay at Dunkirk a few days to check on the smuggled British papers and to see how much publicity they received. Napoleon, *Correspondance*, XXI, 438.

[49] Napoleon, *Correspondance*, VII, 479; *Journal*, 25 Vendémiaire, Year X; Napoleon (Brotonne, ed.), *Lettres*, 283.

[50] Napoleon (Brotonne, ed.), *Lettres*, 295.

for such an omission was delivered to the *Journal de l'Empire* because it failed to mention the review of March, 1811, and the joy with which the troops had welcomed Napoleon after the birth of an heir.

Yet the press in large measure presented the one-sided view Napoleon desired—in fact, to such an extent that the printing and circulating of underground papers naturally resulted. The royalists at Paris printed *L'Invisible,* and the Jansenists printed *Nouvelles ecclésiastiques,* which lasted until 1803. *L'Invisible* and other papers printed in French, particularly the *Mercure britannique* of Jacques Mallet du Pan, which was printed in Great Britain and had a secret vogue in the early days of the Consulate, were the most popular. The government piqued the curiosity of the Parisians on Mallet's paper by announcing in the *Journal des hommes libres* that copies of it had been seized.[51]

The departmental press was even more servile than that of Paris. The *Journal du Capitole* at Rome was edited under the supervision of the governor general and merely contained news copied from French, Milanese, and Neapolitan papers. The *Gazzetta di Genova* inserted much official material, and the *Oracle* of Brussels was still printing articles on Napoleon's constant victories after the allied armies had entered Belgium in 1814.[52]

There is abundant evidence that the regulatory activity of those in charge of the papers was not always satisfactory to the authorities. In 1804 and 1805 a steady stream of letters complaining about the press flowed from Napoleon to Fouché. Murat wrote Nesselrode in Berg to rebuke Hazzi for the type of articles in the papers, and Davout complained to Eugene in 1813 that the Berlin papers were not supervised closely enough. Joseph complained that Ambassador Antoine de La Forest's agents hindered his propaganda and that the *Gazette de Madrid* had printed acts of the government

[51] A. M. Broadley, *Napoleon in Caricature, 1795–1821* (London, 1911), I, xxxvi; Lanzac de Laborie, *Paris sous Napoléon,* I, 209–10; Salmon, *Newspaper and Authority,* 239. There were also many manuscript bulletins, to one or another of which the entire diplomatic corps subscribed.

[52] Jean Borel, *Gênes sous Napoléon Ier* (Paris, 1929), 34, 120; Édouard Romberg, *Les journaux à Gand en 1815. Une page des cent-jours* (Brussels, 1896), 13. The Paris papers turned against Napoleon on April 1, 1814 (when the allies entered Paris), and June 30, 1815.

succeeding him at Naples in order to harm him. La Forest in turn reported that the *Gazette de Madrid* in 1812 maladroitly repeated news which had been proved false, and he criticized Joseph for not allowing the publication of the *senatus consultum* of March 13 and the minutes of the Senate's two sittings. Napoleon criticized Joseph because the Neapolitan papers concentrated on the details of murders and assassinations rather than on important things. Napoleon thought the censorship unwise when it allowed the papers to berate the *philosophes*, as such criticism would arouse passions and factions once again. Nor could the censorship prevent news unfavorable to France from becoming known at Paris—for example, that of the Battle of Trafalgar.[53] Because of the inaccuracy of the press, which frequently had to contradict articles published only a short time before, even Napoleon was not certain that what he read in the papers was true.[54]

Napoleon's relations with the press also had the very positive aspect of the government's taking steps to make certain that the papers printed what the government desired. The very first such step was to establish, by the decree of 7 Nivôse, Year VIII, the *Moniteur* as the official paper. Part of what it was to publish was

[53] Madame de Rémusat wrote her husband on November 9, 1805: "A piece of sad news on the Cadiz fleet has arrived here. The details, which no official paper has yet given us, are unfailingly added to every day; but, in discounting much, there still remains a rash act of Villeneuve, who wanted to leave before the arrival of his successor, and who conducted this dangerous enterprise very poorly. There was a horrible storm; both sides fought with extreme ferocity. The admiral has been captured; Nelson killed, it is said; Magon also. This last news is certain. Only twelve of our ships returned to port, and the *Bucentaure* was sunk. . . . M. de Lima told Alix yesterday that all the special news items agreed in praising the courage and skill of the French; but they stated at the same time that the wind which was blowing made it impossible to form surely and promptly a line in front of an enemy all drawn up and, moreover, skillful." Paul de Rémusat (pub.), *Lettres de Madame de Rémusat, 1804–14* (Paris, 1881), I, 361–62.

[54] Murat (Prince Murat, pub.), *Lettres*, V, 270; Davout (Mazada, ed.), *Correspondance*, III, 496; Joseph (Du Casse, ed.), *Mémoires*, II, 311; V, 384; La Forest (Grandmaison, pub.), *Correspondance*, VI, 135, 189; Réal (Desclozeaux, ed.), *Indiscrétions*, I, 153; Rémusat (P. de Rémusat, pub.), *Lettres*, I, 361; Napoleon, *Correspondance*, XIII, 526; Périvier, *Napoléon journaliste*, 236–38; Félix Rocquain, *Napoléon Ier et le roi Louis d'après les documents conservés aux archives nationales* (Paris, 1875), 146. It seems to the present author that news and articles reputedly from papers where there was strict censorship—as in Vienna—and composed in a pro-French vein are rather maladroit, even though the correspondents were probably pro-French. See *Empire*, April 1, 1807.

clearly stated: sittings of the constituted authorities, acts of the government, army news, and facts and notions on foreign and internal affairs furnished by ministerial correspondence.[55]

Each of the territories under French control was likewise assigned an official paper, designed to include the same types of information. Included in the list of official papers were: the *Moniteur Napolitain*, the *Moniteur Westphalien*, the *Moniteur de l'île de France*, the *Moniteur Ionien*, the *Journal de Milan*, the *Courrier d'Amsterdam*, the *Gazette de Madrid*,[56] and the *Gazette officielle de Saint-Domingue*.[57] The rulers of the regions generally supervised them, but Jerome allowed Joseph Simeon and Jacques Beugnot to conduct his official paper.[58] When Joseph was in Naples, he himself was to run the *Moniteur Napolitain* as Napoleon indicated, but when he was King of Spain, La Forest was commissioned to edit the *Gazette de Madrid* and to report to France concerning its activities. Murat, Joseph's successor in Naples, frequently requested the Minister of the Police to insert articles in the *Moniteur Napolitain*. It and most of the other official papers were bilingual, while that of the Illyrian Provinces appeared in four languages.[59]

The most important function which Napoleon expected the official press, especially the *Moniteur*, to fulfill was to publish articles which the other papers might extract for reprinting, with or without acknowledgement of the source.[60] Items which the other papers habitually copied were official news and the news

---

[55] *Moniteur*, 7 Nivôse, Year VIII.

[56] Napoleon had earlier ordered Murat to obtain control of it, by force if necessary, and see that it appeared daily. Napoleon (Lecestre, comp.), *Lettres*, I, 188.

[57] Menou also established an Arab paper, *Tambyeh*, in Cairo, but it is unimportant for the purpose of this study. *Moniteur*, 5 Frimaire, Year IX.

[58] A. Du Casse (ed.), *Mémoires et correspondance du roi Jérôme et de la reine Catherine* (Paris, 1861–66), III, 25. Jerome did, however, order his wife to insert articles in it in 1812. Baron Albert Du Casse, "Documents inédits relatifs au premier empire. Napoléon et le roi Jérôme," *Revue historique*, XX (1882), 372.

[59] Joseph (Du Casse, ed.), *Mémoires*, III, 238; Napoleon (Picard and Tuetey, eds.), *Correspondance inédite*, II, 573; Murat (Prince Murat, pub.), *Lettres, passim;* La Forest (Grandmaison, pub.), *Correspondance*, VI, 351; Leclerc (Roussier, pub.), *Lettres*, 29; Marmont, *Mémoires*, III, 435.

[60] In fact, the press copied so many articles that the police thought it worthy of mention when the same news appeared in two papers in different terms. The *Moniteur* also took material from other papers; late in 1810, however, it ceased to do so—or at least ceased to give credit. When it finally did resume quoting

stories which the government demanded appear first in the *Moniteur*.[61] Even in 1815, when the *Moniteur* was theoretically no longer official,[62] the other Parisian papers copied it.

A few of the articles in the *Moniteur*—and sometimes in the other papers—Napoleon personally wrote and inserted. Virtually all of the virulent anti-British articles and the notes refuting British claims were written by him.[63] A report by Philip Stapfer to Swiss Foreign Minister Gottlieb von Jenner stated that all unsigned articles dated from Paris were by Bonaparte when they dealt with foreign affairs. Bourrienne said that Napoleon often dictated articles expounding the need for avenging the spoliation of Poland. An article in the December 15, 1807, *Journal de l'Empire* criticizing the influence of Mme Anna Necker de Staël on Prince August of Prussia was also by Napoleon. In addition he had his own press agency, the Bureau of Public Opinion, which naturally expressed only Napoleon's views.[64]

Able to write only a small portion of the articles he wanted in the papers,[65] Napoleon constantly instructed his subordinates to draw up and insert articles on designated topics, even specifying the number of articles on a topic and the interval between their

them, it confined itself almost exclusively to local news from the departmental press.

[61] At times the *Journal de l'Empire* preceded the *Moniteur* in announcing naval news, but it would then announce that the news was confirmed by the *Moniteur*. See issue of 23 Thermidor, Year XIII. In Year IX, and perhaps later, there was a great deal of military news for which the *Moniteur* received no credit. This may have been because the officials sent the information to all the papers at the same time.

[62] It was still controlled by Maret. *The Substance of Some Letters, Written by an Englishman Resident at Paris during the Last Reign of the Emperor Napoleon* (Philadelphia, 1816), 119, May 24, 1815.

[63] Arthur Beauchesne, "Napoléon journaliste," *Proceedings and Transactions of the Royal Society of Canada*, 3d Series, XIX (1925), Sect. I, 44; Napoleon, *Commentaires de Napoléon premier* (Paris, 1867), I, xiv; Bourrienne (Phipps, ed.), *Memoirs*, II, 89; Remacle (ed.), *Bonaparte et les Bourbons*, 98. Louis Hatin says that Barère long refuted the British papers. *Histoire politique et littéraire de la presse en France* (Paris, 1859–61), VII, 573.

[64] Albert Jahn (ed.), *Bonaparte, Talleyrand, and Stapfer* (Zurich, 1869), 173, 187; Bourrienne (Phipps, ed.), *Memoirs*, II, 67; Paul Gautier, *Madame de Staël et Napoléon* (2d ed.; Paris, 1903), 212; Welschinger, *Censure sous l'empire*, 120. A good many articles by Bonaparte in the *Moniteur* are quoted in Damas Hinard (comp.), *Napoléon. Ses opinions et jugemens sur les hommes et sur les choses* (Paris, 1837–38), *passim*.

[65] When appearing in unofficial papers, particularly the *Empire*, they were frequently listed as "communicated articles."

appearances, the length and type of article, and where it was to appear.[66] Most of these commanded articles, as was to be expected, appeared originally in the *Moniteur*, but Napoleon designated some of them exclusively for the unofficial papers. For example, articles in 1813 telling that a big camp was being formed at Toulon were to appear only in the provincial press. Other such items were an extract from a letter of Marshal Édouard Mortier, the Duke of Treviso, in 1814 and articles on Napoleon's satisfaction with Normandy in 1811.[67]

Several tentative conclusions may be drawn from the orders issued by Napoleon. First, since approximately half of them were given to the Minister of Foreign Affairs,[68] the Major General, the Ministers of War and Marine, and various generals, Napoleon's primary interest in the papers was probably diplomatic and military and naval. Second, the Minister of Police had charge of inserting most of the purely domestic articles. Third, Napoleon paid more attention to directing opinion in Spain and Italy than in any of the other regions subordinate to France.

The single functionary inserting more commanded articles than any other official was the Minister of Foreign Affairs. Without exception these articles dealt with foreign affairs or were designed to influence public opinion in a foreign country; some of them were official reports on the foreign situation, worded so as to affect the attitude of the French. In general, they made their original appearance either in the *Moniteur* or in the small papers of subordinate territories, such as Holland, Spain, Italy, Germany, and Warsaw. Articles on Spain also appeared in the small papers of Paris.

One of the men to whom the Minister delegated the task of actually inserting the articles he drew up was Alexander Hauterive; and Napoleon also told Champagny that the Minister to Holland, François de Rochefoucauld, should insert articles in the

[66] Material for this discussion of articles ordered by Napoleon is drawn, unless otherwise footnoted, from the various editions of Napoleon's correspondence. Napoleon (Lecestre, comp.), *Lettres*, I, 102; Napoleon (Brotonne, ed.), *Dernières lettres*, I, 324; Napoleon, *Correspondance*, XVIII, 203.

[67] Napoleon (Lecestre, comp.), *Lettres*, II, 135.

[68] Exclusive of the fact that he was charged with composing the political articles in the *Moniteur* which the other papers were to copy. Napoleon, *Correspondance*, XII, 157.

Dutch papers. Napoleon personally indicated the tone which should predominate in these articles and checked to see that they were inserted in the proper publications.[69]

To publicize military affairs Napoleon relied both upon the Minister of War and the Major General, Berthier; but the former carried the brunt of the burden, because he remained in Paris while Berthier accompanied the army. Clarke received from Napoleon a few articles to be inserted verbatim. These were accompanied by indications as to how frequently they should appear; Clarke also received instructions to insert a few articles on naval events.[70] And, as in the field of foreign affairs, Napoleon checked to see that his orders, often very detailed, were executed.

The generals acting as military governors of conquered territories were the chief ones to insert articles by command of Napoleon, who was quite explicit as to the publication date. Clarke, as military governor of Austria and later of Berlin, was responsible for such articles in Vienna and Berlin; Davout, and later General Lemarois in Warsaw; Davout in Hamburg; Sextius Miollis in Rome in 1808; Antoine Andréossy in Vienna in 1809; and Marmont in Leipzig and General Pierre Augereau in Frankfurt in 1813. Napoleon also told Clarke to relay to Bourrienne an article for insertion in the Altona paper.[71]

In the field of colonial and naval affairs, Minister of Marine Decrès was the only individual receiving instructions to insert articles, which sometimes got into the papers of Holland. Decrès also received requests from General Leclerc that he insert articles in the *Moniteur*.[72]

Articles inserted by the Minister of Police frequently were not

[69] Albert Vandal, *Napoléon et Alexandre Ier*, 3 vols. (Paris, 1898–1900), I, 26; Napoleon, *Correspondance*, XI, 57; XX, 306; XXIV, 333. According to Hatin (*Histoire de la presse*, VII, 573), articles answering a foreign document were composed by Napoleon's cabinet, the Secretary of State, or the Minister of Foreign Affairs, depending on its importance.

[70] One such time was November 30, 1811 (Napoleon, *Correspondance*, XXIII, 40). Napoleon informed Cambacérès in 1813 that he had erred in appointing Baron Louis Méneval to make extracts for the papers. To Napoleon, deciding what to omit was the function of the Minister of War. Napoleon, *Correspondance*, XXV, 374.

[71] Marmont, *Mémoires*, V, 339; Davout (Mazada, ed.), *Correspondance*, III, 206; Eugene (Du Casse, ed.), *Mémoires*, IV, 256; Napoleon, *Correspondance*, XV, 187.

[72] Leclerc (Roussier, pub.), *Lettres*, 214.

related to police activities as such. In general, the police had charge of inserting articles of castigation,[73] those censuring foreign countries, those denying inconvenient items which appeared in any of the papers, and those dealing with the status of public opinion or with Napoleon's activities. Besides entering the diplomatic sphere, the police trespassed into the military zone with articles on the failure of foreign expeditions and reassurances to the public that the French army was adequately supplied. Fouché also drew up articles to show how much improved was the situation of France under the Napoleonic regime.

Besides the Minister himself, there were other police officials who exercised authority. Philippe Lagarde instructed the *Publiciste* on what articles to insert; Bertrand Barère was in charge of the political articles written under ministerial influence; and Desmarest, commissioned by Fouché, drew up printable reports. The Minister of Police in Spain was in charge of inserting articles in the *Gazette de Madrid*.[74] For the police as for the other ministries, Napoleon carefully issued instructions as to the manner in which the articles should be drawn up, the papers which should publish them (even some in Holland and Germany were included), and other details.

Another individual who inserted many articles was Cambacérès, both as Consul and as Archchancellor. Sometimes when the police inserted articles Cambacérès was ordered to supervise the whole project.[75] Military, personal, diplomatic—there seemed to be no limit to the type of news which Cambacérès handled; but it may be significant that virtually all of his activity took place while Napoleon was on campaign.

After 1811 the Minister Secretary of State, Maret, was entrusted with the actual insertion of all the articles Napoleon desired in

[73] In 1809, Napoleon instructed Fouché in the following terms to censure one man publicly: "The conduct of General Monnet is infamous and unspeakable. It is necessary to make it known in the papers and not to have any consideration for him; it is necessary to have printed to this effect all which comes from the men of the garrison of Flanders who are at Antwerp. This cowardice is unheard of." Napoleon (Brotonne, ed.), *Dernières lettres*, I, 434.

[74] Hatin, *Histoire de la presse*, VII, 428; Alphonse de Beauchamp (ed.), *Mémoires de J. Fouché, duc d'Otrante* (Paris, 1824), 116; Pierre Marie Desmarest, *Quinze ans de haute police sous le consulat et l'empire*, ed. by Léonce Grasilier (Paris, 1900), 293; La Forest (Grandmaison, pub.), *Correspondance*, V, 45.

[75] Arthur Chuquet (ed.), *Inédits napoléoniens* (Paris, 1913–19), II, 484.

the *Moniteur*.[76] Even before that date, in connection with his function—assumed by Cambacérès when Maret accompanied Napoleon in the field—of reviewing the political articles before they were published, Maret had been ordered to draw up and insert a great deal of material. (Some of this Napoleon ordered inserted in the small papers but not in the *Moniteur*.) The articles inserted by Maret included information on military movements, personal activities of Napoleon, governmental affairs, and rewards to the soldiers.[77] Napoleon was not the only person to ask Maret to insert articles: Murat likewise requested him to insert in the *Moniteur* a circular letter to the colonels on Napoleon's coronation.[78]

Joseph served a double role in inserting articles: as governor of Paris in 1805 and 1814, and as King of Naples or Spain. In the two latter places he assumed the initiative, inserting articles in the press before notifying Napoleon.[79] In a letter written in January, 1814, when the military situation was extremely dark, Napoleon admonished Joseph: "Do you want to rally to the throne of a French prince? . . . In that case you must write me a plain letter I can have printed. . . . If this is impossible and you haven't enough good sense, then live in obscurity." [80]

The other ruler established by Napoleon who played an active role in the composition and insertion of press articles was Eugene. He, too, inserted every available type of news and assumed some initiative, in addition to carrying out specific instructions.[81]

The activity of Murat, although not as extensive as that of Joseph or Eugene, was none the less important. While he was in Spain, it was on orders from Napoleon that Murat printed articles or had Marshal Bon-Adrien de Moncey insert news in the papers. In Berg he assumed the initiative as to what articles to insert, although a few of Napoleon's orders did reach him there. In Naples too, Murat frequently decided what should appear in the papers.

[76] Napoleon (Brotonne, ed.), *Lettres*, 360.
[77] Périvier, *Napoléon journaliste*, 127.
[78] Murat (Prince Murat, pub.), *Lettres*, III, 276.
[79] Joseph (Du Casse, ed.), *Mémoires*, V, 127.
[80] Lewis C. Breed (ed.), *The Opinions and Reflections of Napoleon* (Boston, 1926), 132.
[81] Eugene (Du Casse, ed.), *Mémoires*, III, 184.

The official on whom he relied most for the actual inserting was Dauré, though he also used Minister of War Saliceti.[82]

Less important were the other rulers, or their representatives, whom Napoleon established in subordinate states. Though playing only a minor role, those who did function included Élisa, Louis, Jerome, Lebrun as Governor General of Holland, and Grand Chancellor Francesco Melzi, of the Kingdom of Italy.

Other officials whose activity in this field was of only minor importance included the consuls, Louis Otto at Munich, Armand de Caulaincourt at Saint Petersburg, Charles Reinhard at Cassel; the Ministers of Religion, the Interior,[83] and the Public Treasury; Fiévée;[84] Defermon; Marie Louise when she was regent; and Bernard de Lacépède.

Besides being a source from which various organs of propaganda took articles, the *Moniteur* served other purposes. If the other papers displeased Napoleon, he used the *Moniteur* to correct the impression left by their articles. In 1810, for example, he had Fouché order articles severely criticizing the Spanish monks after the *Publiciste* had published an article favoring them. Similarly, he used it to thunder against attacks on himself which appeared in pamphlets and speeches. When Napoleon said something he thought likely to influence public opinion in his favor, he was careful to have his bon mot inserted in the *Moniteur*. The *Moniteur* also kept him apprised concerning current events, and he sent it to various officials so that they, too, might be informed.[85]

In the early days of the nineteenth century, it was quite normal for a paper to have, by present-day standards, an extremely limited number of subscribers. In part this was the result of the limited financial investment; in part it sprang from the fact that the papers had to rely for patronage on the *bourgeoisie,* since the lower

[82] Murat (Prince Murat, pub.), *Lettres,* V, 5, 336; VIII, *passim.*

[83] Comte Alfred Boulay de la Meurthe (ed.), *Documents sur la négociation du concordat et sur les autres rapports de la France avec le Saint-Siège en 1800 et 1801* (Paris, 1891–1905), IV, 357. The Archbishop of Besançon requested de Gerando, secretary-general of the ministry of the interior, to insert material in the *Moniteur.* Le Coz (Roussel, pub.), *Correspondance,* II, 262.

[84] Gautier, *Madame de Staël,* 117; Fiévée, *Correspondance,* II, 77.

[85] Napoleon (Lecestre, comp.), *Lettres,* II, 6; Napoleon, *Correspondance,* VI, 295; Fouché (Beauchamp, ed.), *Mémoires,* 221; Gautier, *Madame de Staël,* 35; Remacle (ed.), *Bonaparte et les Bourbons,* 97.

classes could not have afforded them even had they been literate.[86] Napoleon, however, set his government machinery into motion to encourage the widest possible distribution of the papers, especially of the *Moniteur*, because it and the other papers directly at his beck and call could naturally exert greater influence as they became more widely known. But the number of subscribers to the *Moniteur* lagged far behind that of the *Journal de l'Empire*, the lists of which included nearly half of all the subscribers to Paris papers.[87]

Setting the example for other rulers, Napoleon personally sent a thousand copies of the *Gazette de Bayonne* to Murat and additional ones to Marshal Jean Bessières and Berthier for distribution. In Naples Murat ordered the Intendant of Further Calabria, Colette, to reprint articles from the *Moniteur*. Joseph received orders from Napoleon to print twelve to fifteen thousand copies of the *Gazette de Madrid* and scatter them everywhere. When Clarke was military governor of Berlin in 1806, he distributed copies of the Berlin papers.[88]

Supplementing the rulers in meeting Napoleon's wishes for a wide distribution was the military organization. Decrès was charged with sending copies of the *Moniteur* to Barcelona and with dispatching ships carrying papers to the colonies. In 1808, Berthier was to distribute at least a thousand copies of the *Gazette*

[86] The price of the average Parisian paper was approximately fifty francs a year.

[87] 1810 subscription figures as given by Le Poittevin (*Liberté de la presse*, 239) are: *Courrier de l'Europe*, 3,150; *Feuille économique*, 3,000; *Gazette de France*, 5,150; *Journal de l'Empire*, 20,885; *Journal de Paris*, 2,380; *Journal du Soir*, 2,242; *Publiciste*, 2,352. The *Moniteur* had approximately 6,000 subscribers. It was estimated that for each subscriber there were ten readers (*Conspiration anglaise*, 2 vols. [Years IX and X], I, 10). Though on the whole a very fine study, Ebbinghaus (*Napoleon, England und die Presse*)—as well as Périvier—follows the error of Hatin (*Histoire de la presse*, VII, 6) in assuming that the number of copies sent into the departments through the mail was the total number of subscriptions. For the original report see Roederer (A. M. Roederer, pub.), *Œuvres*, VII, 241. Just as a basis of comparison, it might be noted that the London *Times* in 1814 had 5,000 subscribers and cost eighteen cents a copy.

[88] Napoleon (Lecestre, comp.), *Lettres*, I, 186; Murat (Prince Murat, pub.), *Lettres*, VIII, 319; Napoleon (Picard and Tuetey, eds.), *Correspondance inédite*, II, 195; Napoleon (Brotonne, ed.), *Dernières lettres*, I, 232; Napoleon, *Correspondance*, XVIII, 177. Although making reprints from the *Moniteur* was common practice, the officials at times felt that special authorization was necessary before using it. La Forest (Grandmaison, pub.), *Correspondance*, III, 273.

de Madrid each day, to see that the *Moniteur* reached the army, and to have the generals scatter the *Moniteur* throughout the regions where they were located. The Minister of War also sent copies of the *Moniteur* to the generals for distribution, and even had the commandant at Brest send several scores of copies of the February 16, 1810, issue into England.[89]

The *Moniteur* reached the schools as well as the army camps, and was read aloud in the dining halls of the *lycées*. In Paris every paper was read in public gatherings and there were many reprints of the *Moniteur* in handbill form.[90]

Various means were utilized to assure distribution of government-inspired articles and papers in subordinate territories. For example, copies of a Spanish-language gazette were sent to prefects of departments bordering Spain; from these the prefects could print additional copies, which would be distributed in Spain, partly by generals stationed there and partly by Spanish authorities.[91] Otto received directly from Napoleon instructions to send to Hanover, Hamburg, Cassel, and Frankfurt the articles he had ordered inserted in the Munich papers. Napoleon had Lavalette send French papers to Joseph in Naples, and Fouché was obeying his orders in instructing the prefects of those regions to spread in Piedmont, Genoa, Parma, and Corsica one thousand copies of the Italian paper printed at Paris. Copies of this paper even went by courier to Milan and Naples.[92]

Important numbers of the *Moniteur* were sent gratuitously to all the other European countries, where it was read in political

---

[89] Napoleon (Brotonne, ed.), *Dernières lettres*, I, 377; Napoleon, *Correspondance*, XVIII, 112; XX, 403; XXI, 338, 340, 525; XXIII, 52; XXVIII, 54; Napoleon (Picard and Tuetey, eds.), *Correspondance inédite*, III, 452.

[90] Périvier, *Napoléon journaliste*, 139; J. M. Thompson (ed.), *Letters of Napoleon* (Oxford, 1934), 96; Aulard (ed.), *Paris sous le consulat*, I, 349.

[91] Napoleon (Brotonne, ed.), *Dernières lettres*, I, 316. Azanza and Urquijo informed Joseph of the news in the *Moniteur* of September 11, 1808—an instance which reveals the working of the French government in Spain. Napoleon, *Correspondance*, XV, 557.

[92] Napoleon, *Correspondance*, XII, 405; XVIII, 518; Aulard (ed.), *Paris sous le premier empire*, III, 367. Aulard said he did not know the title. It was *Il Corriere d'Italia*. See Napoleon, *Correspondance*, XV, 557; Joseph (Du Casse, ed.), *Mémoires*, V, 75. Originally the French government paid for 2,000 subscriptions at 30 francs each, but within 7 months it reduced the number of its subscriptions to 500. Napoleon (Brotonne, ed.), *Lettres*, 109.

circles,[93] and beginning in July, 1813, Maret dispatched a weekly ship to carry the *Moniteur* and the Copenhagen papers to Danzig. During the peace following the Treaty of Amiens, Talleyrand was charged with having five hundred copies of the *Argus* scattered in the various island colonies of Britain. It is certain that the *Argus* also entered Ireland, and that the *Journal de l'Empire* reached Austria.[94]

Napoleon was also journalistic godfather to papers other than official ones. Mention has already been made of the establishment of the *Journal des Curés* in 1806.[95] By the very next year it had incurred the anger of Portalis, who co-operated with the police in supervising it, and of Napoleon because its policy seemed contrary to the liberties of the Gallican Church. Though it continued to exist until 1811, the *Journal des Curés* contained but little news which it did not extract from the *Moniteur*. It therefore fulfilled no really useful function.[96]

Interested much more in the political than in the religious sphere, Napoleon established the *Argus, Bulletin de Paris,* and *Mémorial anti-britannique* as semiofficial papers which could be directed more closely than ordinary ones. Each of these papers disappointed Napoleon's expectations as to what it would accomplish, perhaps largely because it was common knowledge that they were edited by order of the government.[97] Though the *Argus*, at first edited by the Briton Lewis Goldsmith, was frequently quoted by the other papers,[98] Napoleon complained fre-

[93] The London papers published excerpts from it, and it was read even by opponents of Napoleon. Léon-G. Pelissier (ed.), *Lettres inédites de la comtesse d'Albany à ses amis de Sienne (1797–1820)*, 3 vols. (Paris, 1912–15), III, 106.

[94] Napoleon, *Correspondance*, VIII, 110; XXV, 456; Ebbinghaus, *Napoleon, England und die Presse*, 41; *Journal des Curés, ou Mémorial de l'Église gallicane* (hereafter cited as *Curés*), April 19, 1809.

[95] Cf. page 45.

[96] Napoleon, *Correspondance*, XV, 497–98; Napoleon (Brotonne, ed.), *Lettres*, 80.

[97] Salmon, *Newspaper and Authority*, 322; Hendrik Van Loon, "Napoleon as a Propagandist," *Nation*, CVIII (1919), 501. Van Loon makes the incorrect statement that the number of papers was reduced from seventy-three to thirteen in France. These figures apply only to Paris.

[98] Of those used by the author, the *Journal de Paris* was the most regular in making excerpts. By 1807 the *Journal de l'Empire* quoted it less frequently than earlier.

quently that it was not worth the fifty thousand crowns which
it cost the government every year, and threatened to suppress it
unless it were more effectively edited. Talleyrand defended it
as being better than the English-language papers it combatted and
claimed that the fault lay in the lack of distribution rather than
in the paper itself. It had the longest life of the semiofficial papers,
lasting from 1802 through 1810.[99] The *Bulletin de Paris,* established March 11, 1802, was a purely personal organ edited by
Michel Regnault and designed for home consumption. Even a
change in name could not prevent its demise after a run of not
quite fifteen months.[100] In 1803 Barère undertook publication of
the *Mémorial anti-britannique,* as anti-British as the English-language *Argus.* It never had over 1,500 subscribers, virtually none
of whom lived in Paris, and after a number of changes in name
it was finally absorbed by the *Courrier de l'Europe* in 1810.[101]

The rest of the press was subjected to various types of "per-
suasion" to print what Napoleon wished. Those papers which
were not so subservient as Napoleon desired were placed at a
disadvantage. Official news was so important that a paper was
seriously handicapped in its struggle for existence if the government refused to give it handouts. Fiévée therefore denounced the
government's giving foreign news to the other papers earlier than
to the *Journal de l'Empire,* and Roederer said the *Journal de Paris*
was going to be ruined by the prohibition of announcements. On
the other hand, the government did everything possible to promote the more servile papers. Because it was "well edited," Napoleon favored the *Gazette de France* by ordering Fouché to send

[99] Talleyrand (Bertrand, ed.), *Lettres à Napoléon,* 31; Napoleon (Lecestre,
comp.), *Lettres,* I, 106; II, 47. Perhaps Talleyrand defended it partly because it
was almost wholly drawn up in the foreign office. Ebbinghaus, *Napoleon, England und die Presse,* 171.

[100] Périvier, *Napoléon journaliste,* 197-98.

[101] Aulard (ed.), *Paris sous le premier empire,* I, x; Barère (Carnot and David,
eds., Payen-Payne, tr.), *Memoirs,* III, 120-55. Barère claims he was never paid,
as Napoleon promised he would be; but Schoor (*La presse sous le consulat,* 48)
says the police did support the paper financially, and a statement that Barère
received 500 francs a month is found in Baron Claude-François de Méneval,
Memoirs of Napoleon Bonaparte, ed. by Baron Napoleon de Méneval (New
York, 1910), II, 433. It is true, however, that the government did not pay Chau-
sseblanche, official printer at Rennes. Gilbert A. Thierry, *Conspirateurs et gens de
police. Le complot des libelles (1802)* (Paris, 1903), 64.

it all the information coming to his knowledge.[102] In addition to favoring papers with news, the government might even subsidize them, generally in the form of subscriptions.[103] The police [104] also set the tone of the press by translating foreign papers, publishing official news, and encouraging literary men.

Even the foreign press in conquered countries was worked on by Napoleon's agents, for he was not content merely to prevent the publication of disadvantageous articles [105] and the circulation of inimical papers. Primarily he was interested in having it perform the useful function of reprinting news from the Paris papers, particularly the *Moniteur,* which were too expensive to be widely circulated outside of France.[106] Bourrienne ordered the Hamburg papers to print nothing from the Austrian papers unless it had first appeared in the *Moniteur.* Davout reported to Clarke that he had instructed the *Gazette de Bamberg* to insert only articles from the *Moniteur,* and early in 1813 he called upon Józef Poniatowski to insert articles in the Warsaw papers. The official Frankfurt paper merely copied the *Moniteur* and the *Journal de l'Empire.*[107]

[102] Napoleon (Lecestre, comp.), *Lettres,* I, 48; Fiévée, *Correspondance,* II, 265; Roederer (A. M. Roederer, pub.), *Œuvres,* VIII, 560. To force discontinuance of the press feature, "News or Various Facts," a decree of 1 Frimaire, Year VIII, forbade the police to give notes to the journalists. Welschinger, *Censure sous l'empire,* 82.

[103] The Italian-language paper printed at Paris has already been mentioned. Napoleon was willing in 1810 to buy 1,000 subscriptions to the *Mercure de France,* but only after it carried out his plans for it. Napoleon, *Correspondance,* XXI, 242–44.

[104] Although Tournon reported to the Minister of the Interior on the *Journal du Capitole* at Rome (*Lettres* [Moulard, pub.], 67), Welschinger's statement that the ministry of the interior set the tone of the departmental press (*Censure sous l'empire,* 34) is contradicted by most of the evidence. He seems to have overlooked the fact that the prefects received orders from both the police and interior departments, and that they were acting under orders from the police when they regulated the papers in the departments. It was the police who reported the suppression of papers by the prefects and who instructed the prefects to have articles written—at least before 1810. Cf. E. d'Hauterive (ed.), *La police secrète,* I, *passim;* Plancy (Baron de Plancy, pub.), *Souvenirs,* 515–16.

[105] If hostile articles got into the papers, they were corrected. Murat (Prince Murat, pub.), *Lettres,* VIII, 302; Napoleon, *Correspondance,* XII, 366.

[106] Fiévée, *Correspondance,* II, 127; Napoleon (Brotonne, ed.), *Dernières lettres,* I, 511; Napoleon (Lecestre, comp.), *Lettres,* II, 213; H. E. Bourne, *The Revolutionary Period in Europe* (New York, 1916), 283.

[107] Bourrienne (Phipps, ed.), *Memoirs,* III, 207–208; Davout (Mazada, ed.), *Correspondance,* II, 358; III, 472; IV, 445; Salomon, *Geschichte des Zeitungswesens, passim.* As early as 1803 the German papers copied the *Moniteur* so

The attempt to control the foreign press met with varying success. Bourrienne reported that he was able to prevail upon the Hamburg press to insert any article he wished. Davout in Warsaw experienced somewhat more difficulty; he had to exert authority before the papers—other than the one established by the French —would insert desirable articles.[108] Napoleon vainly tried to win over some British journalists by sending Fiévée to England in 1802. By fulminating against the British press, Napoleon hoped to persuade the British government not to allow diatribes against France, and he actually did obtain the prosecution of the libeler Peltier. Furthermore, Napoleon attempted to influence the foreign press by having the Minister of Foreign Affairs complain to the ministers resident at Paris about the Stuttgart, Vienna, and Pressburg papers. He also promised Lange, the editor of the pro-French *Telegraph* in Berlin, a subsidy when the war was over if his paper proved useful—but the paper had gone out of existence before he saw fit to start paying.[109]

Napoleon utilized even the foreign press hostile to him, primarily by obtaining the information it afforded. Although he held a low opinion of the press in foreign countries other than England and Germany, he wanted copies of the principal papers of all his opponents. English papers he received from Marmont, Fouché, Louis, Davout, and from the Minister of Foreign Affairs, whom he reproached for sending British papers to other individuals. This latter official also forwarded German papers, as did Eugene in the spring of 1813.[110]

---

extensively that Constant (*Journal*, 327) wrote that all the papers of Germany resembled the *Moniteur* because their aim was to avoid suppression. Or, as Salomon (*Geschichte des Zeitungswesens*, 119) expresses it, the German papers swam in French channels.

[108] What these Warsaw papers printed was frequently not known to Napoleon, yet Russia held him responsible for what they said. Vandal, *Napoléon et Alexandre Ier*, II, 382.

[109] Davout (Mazada, ed.), *Correspondance*, II, 72; Harold C. Deutsch, "Lunéville to Pressburg: a Study in Napoleonic Diplomacy, 1801–05" (unpublished Ph.D. thesis, Harvard, 1929), I, 179–80; Napoleon (Brotonne, ed.), *Dernières lettres*, I, 231. The statement of Périvier (*Napoléon journaliste*, 255) that Napoleon established the *Telegraph* is therefore erroneous.

[110] Napoleon, *Correspondance*, XVIII, 349; XIX, 107; XXV, 472; Eugene (Du Casse, ed.), *Mémoires*, IX, *passim*; Napoleon (Picard and Tuetey, eds.), *Correspondance inédite*, I, 72; Napoleon (Lecestre, comp.), *Lettres*, I, 82; Davout (Ma-

These hostile, smuggled-in papers went to the ministry of police where Jay—until his appointment as editor of the *Journal de Paris* —translated the news of political interest for Napoleon.[111] Napoleon's royal brothers, after having a translation of the political news in the foreign papers made for themselves, might forward to him the information they had obtained. Much of what Napoleon knew on Spanish affairs he learned from the British papers. Knowledge of this fact evoked from Arthur Wellesley, the Duke of Wellington, a complaint about the "babbling of the English newspapers, from whose columns the enemy constantly drew the most certain information of the strength and situation of the army." Two years later, in 1812, Wellington said of the British papers: "While deceiving the public with stories of victories never gained, battles never fought, enthusiasm and vigor which had no existence, they did assiduously enlighten the enemy as to the numbers, situation, movements, and reinforcements of the Allies." [112] Napoleon also sent the British newspapers to Spain to keep officials there informed, and acquainted Decrès with news on naval events gleaned from them. As a result of reading English papers, Napoleon was able to advise his subordinates, principally Joseph, Clarke, de Caulaincourt, Champagny, and Jerome, of the news against which they should direct propaganda.[113]

Exploiting the foreign papers as a source of extracts for the French press, Napoleon made them render service in still another way. According to Talleyrand's statement to John Armstrong,

zada, ed.), *Correspondance*, II, 358; Napoleon (Brotonne, ed.), *Dernières lettres*, I, 92.

[111] Beginning on March 1, 1806, the Minister of Foreign Affairs also sent Napoleon translations, with just a note on the date and arrival if the papers contained nothing important. Napoleon, *Correspondance*, XII, 113. How long this practice continued it is impossible to state definitely, but in 1809 Napoleon was sending Champagny translations made by the police. *Ibid.*, XIX, 401, 485. Napoleon also exploited the press of subject kingdoms to keep himself informed. Hatin, *Histoire de la presse*, VII, 574.

[112] Aulard (ed.), *Paris sous le consulat*, I, 258; Fouché (Beauchamp, ed.), *Mémoires*, 205; Joseph (Du Casse, ed.), *Mémoires*, III, 113; Rocquain, *Napoléon et Louis, passim;* Eugene (Du Casse, ed.), *Mémoires*, I, *passim;* Napoleon, *Correspondance*, XII, 405; Salmon, *The Newspaper and the Historian*, 198–99. Napoleon (*Correspondance*, XVIII, 131) corroborates the statement that they contained information on the position of the British.

[113] Napoleon, *Correspondance*, XVII, 419; XXII, 146; Napoleon (Brotonne, ed.), *Dernières lettres*, II, 86.

each French paper—even the *Moniteur*—could reprint what it chose, and there was nothing official in the reprinting; however, one doubts the veracity of the statement, since in 1812 Napoleon ordered Savary to have the police "continue" to make extracts from the British and American press for the *Moniteur*. In 1813 parts of treaties specifically designated by Napoleon were extracted by the Minister of Foreign Affairs for publication in the *Moniteur*.[114]

Napoleon likewise had plans regarding the ways in which the unofficial French press might serve his purposes. It is noteworthy that the papers, particularly the *Journal de l'Empire*—though it managed to keep its *feuilleton* independent, and like the *Publiciste*, retained partial independence longer than other papers—[115] did become increasingly subservient. Knowing that the *Journal de l'Empire* and the *Gazette de France* were read by many partisans of the Bourbons, Napoleon used them for the insertion of conciliatory notes.[116]

Napoleon also insisted that the police direct papers so that they would attack the usages, literature, and constitution of England. His plans for the *Mercure* therefore included the copying of extracts from the British papers and the refuting of "false rumors"; in addition it was to give a résumé of the week's news and supplant all other papers in the distant departments.[117] He also intended to have Joseph print a Spanish-language paper in Paris in 1815, but Waterloo thwarted his plans.[118]

In general, except for the semiofficial press, which did almost nothing but copy other papers, the governmental machinery fulfilled Napoleon's expectations with regard to the positive effect of its propaganda; nevertheless, Napoleon sometimes found it necessary to complain to Cambacérès: the Emperor was displeased

[114] Department of State, *Despatches* (France, Armstrong to Madison, March 21, 1806); Napoleon (Brotonne, ed.), *Dernières lettres*, II, 281, 485.

[115] The *Empire* even dared criticize the execution of the Duke of Enghien by translating a fragment of a Latin poem opposing assassination. The poem was called *Second Punic War*, by Silius Italicus. Avenel, *Histoire de la presse*, 184–92. The *Empire* was also rather impartial in reporting parliamentary debates.

[116] Vandal, *Napoléon et Alexandre Ier*, III, 135–38; Lanzac de Laborie, *Paris sous Napoléon*, 78.

[117] Napoleon, *Correspondance*, X, 467; XXI, 242.

[118] Napoleon (Du Casse, ed.), *Supplément à la correspondance*, 210.

that papers disobeyed his order not to publish anything until the arrival of the official bulletin, and he complained that Cambacérès should not have assigned to Méneval the task of deciding what to eliminate before publishing news.[119]

That is not to imply, however, that opportunity for more complaints was lacking. Many government-inspired articles were, according to Fiévée, poor; especially articles which Decrès caused to be inserted were so inept as to particularly irritate Napoleon. Decrès also called forth rebukes for not carrying out a general order by Napoleon to insert all the little naval events and for not putting into the papers an article on the departure of Admiral Charles Magon. Bonaparte informed Lucien that Félix Desportes wrote too much to the Berlin journalists, and he rebuked Joseph for having Roederer insert an article in the *Journal de Paris* in 1806 and for praising in the *Gazette de Madrid* the brigands defending Saragossa.[120]

Definitely, the policy of having the press exist solely to serve the government, though largely effective, had its serious drawbacks.

B. BOOKS

To Napoleon, virtually the only worth-while function of newspapers was that of developing the sort of public opinion he wanted. He expected some books to be written merely to fulfill the same purpose, but he also desired books of a high literary quality. Therefore he took various steps to encourage both types.

Many authors received regular pensions in return for writing the types of books he desired. Why did Napoleon continue these pensions when his own words reveal his realization that the results were poor? "These fellows are good for nothing under any government. I will, however, give them pensions because, as Head of

[119] Napoleon, *Correspondance*, XIV, 424; XXV, 374.
[120] Fiévée, *Correspondance*, II, 381–86; Napoleon, *Correspondance*, X, 430; XXII, 350; Lady Mary Loyd (tr.), *New Letters of Napoleon I Omitted from the Edition Published under the Auspices of Napoleon III* (London, 1898), 17; Napoleon (Lecestre, comp.), *Lettres*, I, 292; Aulard (ed.), *Paris sous le consulat*, I, x. Joseph informed Napoleon that he and Roederer had had nothing to do with the article which provoked Napoleon's reprimand of the two.

the State, I ought to do so." [121] One reason was that a tax levied on the press defrayed most of the cost; another reason was that he felt the pensions were essential arguments in persuading creative writers to defend the Imperial throne and celebrate its glory. Such authors, he believed, could fulfill their tasks better by inspiring heroic sentiment in youth, the army, and the nation, than they could by praising him directly. If works appeared meritorious in Napoleon's eyes, he awarded their authors additional sums; for example, the entire net proceeds from the accounts of the battles of Marengo and Lodi went to the authors, and the compiler of the *Dictionnaire géographique et topographique des treize départements réunis* received 3,000 francs. [122] Writers could also add to their income by winning one or more of the various prizes offered by the government, including the decennial ones [123] and a yearly prize for Italian literature.

Money alone did not prove sufficient inducement to the literati. Napoleon, therefore, gathered authors around himself at Saint-Cloud and charged Fontanes with locating writers susceptible of being influenced by the Emperor. [124] Frequently the government issued direct orders that a book be composed on a specified topic, and sometimes it suggested the author. Subordinates to whom Napoleon entrusted the details on such occasions included Eugene, the Archchancellor, and the Ministers of Foreign Affairs, Interior, Religion, or Police. Fouché had writers under his influence publish antidotes to the bad impression left by dangerous works which had escaped the investigation of his agents, and the censorship was responsible for many of the anecdotes, songs, and stories adapted to the maintenance of patriotism and devotion to Napoleon and his dynasty found in the almanacs. [125] Most of the ordered works

[121] Napoleon (Breed, ed.), *Opinions and Reflections*, 309–10.

[122] Napoleon, *Correspondance*, IX, 318; X, 3; Napoleon (Chuquet, ed.), *Inédits napoléoniens*, II, 69.

[123] These were never paid, partly because Napoleon was irritated at the failure of the committee to select Chateaubriand's *Génie du christianisme*. Napoleon, *Correspondance*, XXI, 311. The nine first prizes were to cover a wide range of activities.

[124] Napoleon, *Correspondance*, XX, 124; Charpentier, *Napoléon et les hommes de lettres*, 22, 38.

[125] Welschinger, *Censure sous l'empire*, 60; Hippolyte A. Taine, *The Modern Regime (The Origins of Contemporary France)*, tr. by John Durand (New York, 1890–94), II, 203. Félix Nogaret was one of Fouché's aides in the task of counteracting undesirable impressions.

were of a historical nature,[126] and they were above all to deal with military affairs and were to have a political, moral, and patriotic aim rather than a philosophical or religious aim. Of course, the instructions indicated the bias of these works, frequently anti-papal—ostensibly because of the temporal tendencies of the popes —and anti-British. Sometimes the instructions also contained orders on the method of distribution.[127]

Sometimes a government functionary encouraged a book without directly subsidizing or ordering it. After the establishment of the censorship bureau in 1810, the censors assumed as one of their tasks that of raising the reading level of the public by promoting books of a higher standard; these were designed to arouse love for and loyalty to the rulers and a spirit of bravery, honor, and generosity. Napoleon or some important official might accept the dedication of a suitable book, which may have been published under his auspices, or the *Moniteur* might state that the book was honored by the subscription of certain dignitaries.[128]

In order to purge or prohibit undesirable books,[129] the Consular government permitted arbitrary arrests and established a commission to review books prior to publication.[130] During the first part of the Empire, such examination was a duty of the Prefect of Police. After the Prefect had made a recommendation, the Minister of Police issued orders on the disposition of the books. He reported to Napoleon on what works he had revised or seized, occasionally receiving in exchange a rebuke for unwise suppres-

[126] Concluded from a study of the various editions of Napoleon's correspondence.

[127] Napoleon, *Correspondance*, VI, 459; XIV, 89; XVIII, 303; XIX, 506; XXI, 385; Victor Coffin, "Censorship and Literature under Napoleon I," *American Historical Review*, XXII (1916–17), 299; Charpentier, *Napoléon et les hommes de lettres*, 189.

[128] *Journal typographique*, V (1810), 110; Napoleon, *Correspondance*, IX, 540; *Moniteur*, 16 Floréal, Year IX.

[129] The government forbade obscene as well as politically undesirable books. Morally offensive books sometimes passed the censorship, politically offensive ones rarely if ever did. Napoleon, *Correspondance*, XXIV, 261–62. Coffin says he was unable to find that on December 12, 1812, Pommereul repeated to the censors Napoleon's statement that censorship should eliminate only such items as were obscene or tended to disturb public calm; but Welschinger cites it. Napoleon (Chuquet, ed.), *Inédits napoléoniens*, II, 61; E. d'Hauterive (ed.), *La police secrète*, III, 234.

[130] Welschinger, *Censure sous l'empire*, 132; Lanzac de Laborie, *Paris sous Napoléon*, I, 216. The present writer is accepting the statement of Welschinger instead of that of Lanzac de Laborie that there was not any censorship.

sion. Napoleon himself often determined what should be altered or suppressed, basing his decision on reports by the prefecture and ministry of police, both of which agencies analyzed the books published and perhaps stated how the public had received them, and on the analyses of books by Ripault. Or he might refer to the Ministers of the Interior or of Public Worship—or even to Baron Denon, the Director-General of Museums, for a volume on the engravings of various columns—the altering of a book in order to make it acceptable.[131]

In February, 1810, a special censorship bureau officially entitled the Direction Générale de l'Imprimerie et de la Librairie was established in the ministry of the interior.[132] The bureau was originally headed by Pommereul and later by Count Joseph Portalis. It sent the Minister weekly reports on nonperiodic publications, basing its observations on the reports of the censors and inspectors and of the departmental prefects. These latter officials were relatively unimportant, as only rarely were books published in the provinces. In general, the duties of the inspectors were somewhat vague, but they did supervise distribution of the books.[133] To protect himself, the author or printer of a book could submit it to the government for approval prior to publication; after being approved by the censor, it was seizable only on Napoleon's orders. If an author had not taken the precaution of submitting his book and was dissatisfied with the report of the bureau, he could appeal to the Minister of the Interior to order a new perusal. Then the Director General plus as many censors as he deemed wise would make a decision, final except for recourse to the Senate commission on freedom of the press, which consisted of seven men, one of

[131] E. d'Hauterive (ed.), *La police secrète, passim;* Napoleon, *Correspondance,* XII, 95; XVII, 278; Napoleon (Brotonne, ed.), *Lettres,* 219; Napoleon (Thompson, ed.), *Letters,* 81, 145; Aulard (ed.), *Paris sous le consulat, passim.* One rebuke to Fouché was the result of his suppressing Geoffroy's commentary on Racine.

[132] Its function is described in Welschinger, *Censure sous l'empire,* and in Coffin, "Censorship," *loc. cit.* The present study will omit from consideration, insofar as possible, any materials this book and article cover. The police retained its censorship bureau under Étienne, which supervised the theaters, papers, and the printing and selling of books. It included one censor especially for plagiarism and another for works hostile to the liberties of the Gallican Church. But prefects in the departments no longer reported to it. Welschinger, *Censure sous l'empire,* 70–72.

[133] Coffin, "Censorship," *loc. cit.,* 288–93.

whom retired every four months. The commission was to deal with works not published periodically or sold by subscription, but it never functioned.[134] Interestingly, the only appeal ever made to the Minister was decided in favor of the author.[135]

Even approval by the censors was no guarantee that the book would not be seized if it displeased the police or Napoleon, as in the case of Mme de Staël's *De l'Allemagne*.[136] Apparently there was no effort to conceal the seizure of a book. It is extremely doubtful, though, that the public knew military works were forbidden unless previously approved by the Minister of War.[137] When no reason could be found to suppress books they disliked, the authorities attempted to restrict their sale and influence by forbidding announcement or mention of them in posters or in the literary and political papers. A decree of October 14, 1811, moreover provided that no book might be announced until a notice on it had been printed in the *Journal général de l'imprimerie et de la librairie*, which was edited in accordance with documents furnished by the censorship bureau. Furthermore, publishers and booksellers upon whose political attitude Napoleon could not rely lost their licenses.[138]

The functioning of the censorship was far from perfect. Funds were inadequate, and the censors and their clerks were not always

---

[134] The decree establishing the senatorial commission provided that it should function in the following intricate and ineffectual manner: writers would petition the commission, which could ask the Minister of the Interior to revoke the order; if he had not done so after three invitations at one-month intervals, the commission was to ask for a meeting of the Senate, which would declare, "There are strong presumptions that the liberty of the press has been violated." Then the case would go to the Imperial High Court. *Moniteur*, 30 Floréal, Year XII.

[135] Baron Jean Locré (ed.), *Discussions sur la liberté de la presse, la censure, la propriété littéraire, l'imprimerie et la librairie qui ont eu lieu dans le conseil d'état pendant les années 1808, 1809, 1810 et 1811* (Paris, 1819), 249–50.

[136] Welschinger, *Censure sous l'empire*, 179–82. The few phrases suppressed by the censorship were innocent, but the general spirit of the book was hostile to despotism. The seizure by Savary of the 10,000 printed copies was illegal, although the police had long indulged in the practice of seizing copies, breaking the forms, and sealing the presses. Duc de Broglie and Baron de Staël (pubs.), *Mémoires de Madame de Staël*, 2 vols. (New ed.; Paris, 1882), II, 89; Gautier, *Madame de Staël*, 261; E. d'Hauterive (ed.), *La police secrète, passim*.

[137] *Journal*, 28 Brumaire, Year IX; Napoleon, *Correspondance*, XVI, 165.

[138] Welschinger, *Censure sous l'empire*, 155, 203–204; *Journal typographique*, XIII, 321; Charpentier, *Napoléon et les hommes de lettres*, 129. Because of his anti-Napoleonic bias, Charpentier misinterprets Napoleon's statement on the guilt of heroes of tragedy. Napoleon (Loyd, tr.), *New Letters*, 213.

of the highest caliber. Besides these two factors, it was unquestionably difficult to decide what to prohibit.[139] Napoleon expected his censorship to do no more than prevent the publication of ideas troubling the peace, interests, or good order of the state, or arousing disrespect for the Christian religion. Books were therefore not allowed to include praise of the Bourbons, England, or the papacy; anything contrary to the glory of the army; reactionism; and other items thought inopportune.[140] However, in their efforts to please the Emperor, the censors were often so severe that Napoleon had to intervene to obtain leniency.[141]

Napoleon made at least a gesture toward abolishing the censorship of books in Italy. However, the instructions which he sent Eugene show clearly enough what he meant by suppression of censorship. The following order must have been confusing to Eugene. "I want you to suppress completely the censorship of books. This country already has a narrow-enough mind without straitening it more. Of course the publication of any work contrary to the government would be stopped. Demand only that when the bookstores have a work to put on sale, they send a copy of it to the police seven days beforehand." [142] Eugene received from Napoleon a second and similar order:

> The intention of His Majesty is that the magistracy of review be suppressed and that no kind of censorship be exerted on the press, and that, in case of the author's being unknown, the seller be responsible for anything contrary to public order or to the interest or the honor of private citizens. His Majesty thinks it proper, however, that seven days before putting a work on sale a copy of

---

[139] Coffin, "Censorship," *loc. cit.*, 289; Napoleon (Hinard, comp.), *Opinions et jugemens*, I, 218; Aulard (ed.), *Paris sous le consulat*, I, 660. These facts may have partially influenced Napoleon's decision to abolish all preliminary censorship during the Hundred Days. At that time five copies of each printed and engraved work had to be deposited. One copy went to the Minister of the Interior, and one went to the Minister of Police. Napoleon (Chuquet, ed.), *Inédits napoléoniens*, II, 398; *Bulletin des lois* (Series 6), 35.

[140] Napoleon, *Correspondance*, XII, 358; Charpentier, *Napoléon et les hommes de lettres*, 128; Vicomte Hervé de Broc, *La vie en France sous le premier empire* (Paris, 1895), 250; Welschinger, *Censure sous l'empire*, 207.

[141] They may have prohibited a game of lotto familiarizing children with the history of France because the game tended to trouble the peace of the state by referring too much to the immediate family of Louis XVI. Taine, *Modern Regime*, II, 203.

[142] Eugene (Du Casse, ed.), *Mémoires*, I, 145.

it be sent to the Minister of the Interior so that, if it contains something contrary to public order, the publication of it can be stopped;
the work may be stopped each and every time it is recognized as
being contrary to the government and to the public good. Present
me, therefore, with a project of a decree to attain this goal.[143]

Thus, one is not surprised that Eugene failed to fulfill properly
the demands of his superior. Napoleon wrote him that "Article 5
of your decree on the abolition of censorship is a little too strong.
Every man is free to write and publish his thoughts, but with
many restrictions." [144]

Elsewhere in Italy concern was shown for the "public good."
Tournon in Rome promised Portalis to prevent the importation
of any harmful books. He also gave assurance that he would report any works which might influence public opinion either for
or against France.[145]

Governmental control may have been partially responsible for
the lack of much noteworthy literature and for the great number
of translations; but even with complete freedom for writers, the
Napoleonic period would not have been a favorable one for literature, and the censorship was, relatively, not bad.[146] Napoleon
blamed much of the literary sterility on the prevailing spirit of
criticism, designed to discourage rather than to encourage and
guide nascent but inexperienced merit.[147] The primary reason for
the inadequacy of literary criticism was really that it had perforce
become the tool of the government. To modify this spirit he eventually proposed the establishment of a paper with enlightened and
impartial criticism which contained no injurious brutality striking
down youthful, but meritorious, writers.[148]

But this desire to encourage literary output was superseded in
Napoleon's mind by matters more pressing, so that it did not bring
about any positive achievement.

[143] *Ibid.*, 158. The government still retained effective control.
[144] *Ibid.*, II, 206.
[145] Tournon (Moulard, pub.), *Lettres inédites*, 28. Napoleon also attempted
to control the publication and selling of books in Germany, Spain, Portugal,
Holland, and Switzerland. "Napoleons gänzliche Unterdrückung der Pressfrei-
heit," *Miscellany*, 2.
[146] Broc, *Vie en France*, 478; Coffin, "Censorship," *loc. cit.*, 307.
[147] Welschinger, *Censure sous l'empire*, 159; and see Chapter VIII.
[148] Napoleon, *Correspondance*, XIV, 406.

CHAPTER IV

POLITICAL AND MILITARY PUBLICATIONS

A. PAMPHLETS, HANDBILLS, AND POSTERS

ALTHOUGH THE NAPOLEONIC PERIOD WAS FAR FROM BEING A golden age of literature, there was no lack of writers. Unable to produce works of literary merit, these men were yet able to write creditable polemical pamphlets, and they were urged to do so by numerous government officials.

When Lucien was Minister of the Interior, he had Louis Fontanes write *Parallèle entre César, Cromwell, Monck et Bonaparte*.[1] A plea for the establishment of a monarchy in France, it proved to be premature. Because of Lucien's connection with this pamphlet, in fact, public opinion became so hostile to him that Bonaparte was forced to remove him and appoint him Minister to Spain.[2]

Le cri d'honneur, ou: un jeune volontaire à ses compagnons was an official pamphlet written in 1800 urging the French to fight England.[3]

The official pamphlet, *De l'état de la France à la fin de l'an 8*, by Alexandre Hauterive, the head of a division in the department of foreign affairs, was very well received and ran into several editions. Its purpose, to urge all Continental powers to unite against

---

[1] There is still some doubt as to whether Bonaparte was involved in the scheme. Iung (*Lucien Bonaparte*, I, 431) thinks the initiative was solely that of Lucien; the police reported on the pamphlet in rather great detail to Bonaparte; and Bonaparte ordered Fouché to stop its distribution openly. Mme de Staël (*Mémoires* [Broglie and Staël, pubs.], 220) says Lucien knew Napoleon's plans perfectly, and Welschinger (*Censure sous l'empire*, 135) claims that Napoleon never forgave Fouché for discovering the plot.

[2] Maurice Vitrac (ed.), *Autour de Bonaparte. Journal du comte P.-L. Roederer* (Paris, 1909), 40.

[3] The *Moniteur* of 23 Germinal, Year VIII, said this pamphlet was in answer to a request of the Prefect Demousseau of l'Ourthe for such a work.

the commercial predominance of England, was even more forcefully pressed by *Du Jacobinisme des Anglais sur les mers*. Again in 1804 Hauterive was ordered to draw up a pamphlet, *Changements survenus en Europe depuis vingt-cinq ans*, primarily to show that Austria and England had each gained more than had France, who had moreover suffered from the defeat of its natural allies, Poland and Turkey.[4]

Notice sur la mort de Paul Ier empereur de Russie was probably written upon command from Napoleon, by an author described in the *Journal de Paris* as an "experienced writer." [5] There is no doubt about the official inspiration for *Réponse d'un républicain français au libelle de Sir Francis d'Yvernois, naturalisé Anglais, contre le premier consul de la république française* by Barère, whose *Lettre d'un citoyen français en réponse à lord Grenville* was written at Bonaparte's command. Barère also translated pamphlets favorable to Napoleon, such as *Better Late Than Never; or, the Necessity for Making Peace Between France and England*.[6]

In 1800 Talleyrand was asked to supervise the printing in German as well as in French of the pamphlet *Lettre d'un membre patriote du corps germanique sur la politique de la maison d'Autriche* to show that the growth of Austria was at the expense of, and to the detriment of, the Holy Roman Empire. In 1805 he was instructed to have someone draw up a pamphlet on the right of wreckage, recapitulating the principles which guided Napoleon, particularly that the right to a wreck belonged to the ruler.[7] When Napoleon ordered pamphlets, his care for detail was amazing. For example, in July, 1800, Napoleon, having advised Talleyrand to print *Lettres d'un envoyé à la Diète germanique*, reminded him to use German paper and type and to date the pamphlet from Frankfurt.[8]

In order to arouse hatred against England, Méhée de la Touche

---

[4] *Débats*, 1 Frimaire and 27 Ventôse, Year IX; Ebbinghaus, *Napoleon, England und die Presse*, 126–28; Napoleon, *Correspondance*, IX, 437.

[5] *Journal de Paris*, May 31, 1810; Duchesse Laura d'Abrantès, *Mémoires de madame la duchesse d'Abrantès*, 10 vols. (Paris, n.d.), IV, 443.

[6] Barère (Carnot and David, eds., Payen-Payne, tr.), *Memoirs*, I, introduction; III, 164–65.

[7] Napoleon, *Correspondance*, VI, 331; X, 257.

[8] *Ibid.*, VI, 395.

wrote *Alliance des Jacobins de France avec le ministère anglais,* describing how he had purposely deceived England and had received 192,000 livres from the British agent Drake, in Munich, to aid in the plot against Bonaparte.[9]

In 1806 Napoleon ordered Cambacérès to print, in less than a week, *Ms. trouvé dans le cabinet du roi de Prusse à Berlin,* and ordered that it be accompanied by a précis—by a literary man—showing the indignity of the partition of Poland. The same official was supposed to draw up a well-made, ten-page pamphlet entitled *Un vieil Ottoman à ses frères* to be an appeal against the Russians.[10]

Fouché in 1804 assumed the initiative in ordering brochures for the coronation, and in 1809 he drew up *La France en 1709 et en 1809* to point out how greatly the situation of France had improved during the last century. In 1807 Napoleon postponed his decision as to how many copies to publish of Fouché's collection of General Louis St. Hilaire's letters, whose general tone was one of unmasking British intriguers, until he had some idea of their value.[11]

As Napoleon's lieutenant in Spain, Murat, at Napoleon's order, directed that pamphlets be written to stress Napoleon's recognition of Charles IV and his willingness to aid him, his guarantee of the integrity of Spain, and the exile of Manuel de Godoy. When he was King of Naples, Murat ordered pamphlets which, in addition to their distribution in Naples, were scattered profusely throughout Sicily. Melzi tried to remove the political torpor gripping the Italian Republic by publishing official pamphlets. Two such pamphlets were *Raisonnement sur les destinées de la république italienne* and *Saggio sulla genealogia natura ed interessi politici e sociali della republica italiana.*[12]

Count Antonio Aldini, resident minister of the Kingdom of

[9] *Débats,* 5 Floréal, Year XII. Méhée was in the pay of the French government.

[10] Napoleon, *Correspondance,* XIII, 528; XIV, 64. The pamphlet on Prussia had not yet been printed three weeks later. Perhaps Napoleon was truthful in saying he had found the manuscript.

[11] *Ibid.,* IX, 546; *Empire,* March 21, 1809; Napoleon (Lecestre, comp.), *Lettres,* I, 129.

[12] Napoleon (Lecestre, comp.), *Lettres,* I, 176; A. Pingaud, *Bonaparte président de la république italienne,* II, 381–82; Murat (Prince Murat, pub.), *Letters,* VII, 422. After having a pamphlet written by Fonvielle, Murat sent it to Napoleon with the statement that if Napoleon found it satisfactory, he could have it reprinted at Bayonne and distributed in Navarre and Biscay.

Italy at Paris, was one of the diplomatic agents who was set to work. He wrote a historical memoir on the popes and their preponderant power in Italy; Otto supervised the drawing up by the Bavarians, and the distribution throughout Germany, of pamphlets against the Hapsburgs as an antidote to publications of the Austrian house.[13]

Many pamphlets on Spanish affairs were written in 1808 at Napoleon's express command. One of these made the claim that Europe was watching with interest France's handling of Spain. Others were *Précis des événements qui ont amené un changement de dynastie en Espagne* (which was soon suppressed because its effectiveness was nullified by its silence on well-known facts), *Notice sur l'affaire du prince des Asturies,* and *Précision sur les derniers événements de la cour de Madrid.*[14]

On the basis of an account sent him by Napoleon in the same year, the Minister of the Interior ordered the printing of pieces criticizing the Pope, and the composition of a pamphlet for distribution in Spain on events there. This latter work, which was to have the appearance of being written by a Spaniard, pointed out why Ferdinand was unfit to rule, stressed de Godoy's faults, and realistically portrayed the King and Queen. In 1810 the Minister personally wrote a pamphlet on neutral countries. In 1814 the Minister of the Interior was ordered to send auditors to the communes from which the invaders had been beaten back, in order to draft printable procès-verbaux of the atrocities committed by the allied armies. The same Minister was also told to instruct the prefects that their answers to communal deputations should be such that, when printed, they would impress the enemy with the good morale of the French.[15]

Many speeches made in the legislature and first printed by the *Moniteur* were reprinted in official pamphlets, generally by

[13] Napoleon, *Correspondance,* XVIII, 518; XX, 16.
[14] Department of State, *Despatches* (France, Armstrong to Madison, January 22, 1808); Don Pedro Cevallos, *Exposé des moyens employés par l'empereur Napoléon, pour usurper la couronne d'Espagne* (Paris, 1814), 121; Fugier, *Napoléon et l'Espagne,* II, 424.
[15] Fugier, *Napoléon et l'Espagne,* II, 422–23; Napoleon (Brotonne, ed.), *Lettres,* 270; Napoleon, *Correspondance,* XX, 126. The Minister of Police also sent commissioners to obtain details on enemy crimes in 1814. Napoleon, *Correspondance,* XXVII, 236.

order of the legislative body concerned. Among them were the *Exposés of the Situation of the Empire*, which appeared in pamphlet form. In 1813 the Legislative Body ordered the printing of three thousand copies,[16] but we cannot state whether it was the customary procedure to reprint all these annual reports for so wide a distribution.

The entire governmental organization was utilized in the distribution of these official pamphlets. Eugene was ordered to distribute them in the Kingdom of Italy.[17] A bundle of Lucien's pamphlets, accompanied by the distribution orders, was sent to every prefect; and Lucien himself profusely distributed a pamphlet entitled *Dialogue entre un député des Anciens et un député des Cinq-Cents*. It was his decision that fourteen thousand copies of Barère's *Lettre . . . en réponse à lord Grenville* should be printed. Pamphlets designed to agitate the populace were thrown on the coasts of Sweden by Berthier. Napoleon ordered Savary to print in Spanish and spread everywhere the "seventh number" of news from Spain. Talleyrand took charge of spreading a pamphlet in Germany. For distributing the ten thousand copies, half in Arabic and half in Turkish, of the pamphlet *Un vieil Ottoman à ses frères*, Napoleon's orders were clear-cut and definite. He himself, his ministers at Vienna and Constantinople, ships leaving Marseille for the Levant, and Eugene (for circulation in Dalmatia) were each to receive a thousand copies in each tongue. Napoleon also ordered Murat to send all the pamphlets appearing at Madrid to General Andoche Junot and to have the provisional government print and distribute the protest of Charles IV against the decision of a commission of Spaniards to establish a regency. The masses could afford these pamphlets, for the sales price was designed to cover merely the cost of printing. Then too, the semi-official press was used for reviews and excerpts, and even for complete insertions of short pamphlets.[18]

[16] *The Empire: Government Publications 1804-1815*, 2 vols., in Boulay de la Meurthe collection of pamphlets.

[17] There is frequent mention in Napoleon's correspondence of his sending pamphlets to his brothers, but there is no indication as to what further use they made of them.

[18] Fouché (Beauchamp, ed.), *Mémoires*, 121; Napoleon (Lecestre, comp.), *Lettres*, I, 169; Iung, *Lucien Bonaparte*, I, 308; the Hamburg *Le Spectateur du Nord*, February, 1801; Barère (Carnot and David, eds., Payen-Payne, tr.),

The government's machinery functioned to check on the publication of pamphlets with which it had had nothing to do and on the effect of those it had ordered. The ministry of police and the prefecture of police sent regular reports to Napoleon on the authors, contents, publishers, and sellers of pamphlets, regardless of whether they were illegal or friendly; the Minister of Justice took over this function and the other police duties when the ministry of general police was temporarily suppressed, from 1802 to 1804.[19] Departmental prefects reported to the Minister of Police on hostile pamphlets.[20]

In addition, Napoleon sought information on nongovernmental publications in subordinate regions from the Minister of the Interior, the Minister of Police, his royal brothers, and military

---

Memoirs, III, 88; La Forest (Grandmaison, pub.), *Correspondance*, VI, 231; Napoleon, *Correspondance*, VI, 331; XIV, 64; XVII, 59, 333; XXI, 237. Even before receiving orders from Napoleon, Murat had sent pamphlets to Junot and Bessières (to whom Napoleon also wrote to distribute pamphlets) with the order to have them reprinted and spread in Andalusia and Galicia. Murat (Prince Murat, pub.), *Lettres*, VI, 21–23, April 27 and 28, 1808. There were so many political pamphlets that Madame de Genlis said they alone saved publishers and booksellers from ruin. Mme Stéphanie de Genlis, *Mémoires inédites de madame la comtesse de Genlis, sur le dix-huitième siècle et la révolution française, depuis 1756 jusqu'à nos jours*, 10 vols. (Paris, 1825), VI, 55. After France had become an empire, there were many pamphlets expressing opposition to the Bourbons and the republic. Fiévée, *Correspondance*, II, 25.

[19] Abrantès, *Mémoires*, IV, 84. Rather interestingly, the signed pamphlets for the Year VIII are more hostile to the government than are the anonymous ones. Most of these latter are in fact favorable to the Consulate, with no indication that they are official or semiofficial. One such semiofficial pamphlet was *Aurons-nous la paix? ne l'aurons-nous pas? est-il possible de la faire avec l'Angleterre?* (Ebbinghaus, *Napoleon, England und die Presse*, 23). These conclusions are based on *Consulate: Contemporary Pamphlets Year 8: Authors; Consulate: Contemporary Pamphlets Year 8: Anonyms*, in Boulay de la Meurthe collection. The flyleaves of some of the hostile pamphlets listed London or Hamburg as the place of publication. If they were actually printed there, the pamphlets are evidence that smuggling went on rather effectively. In any case they show that some people feared the consequences of what they wrote or published; also, perhaps they were unable to find a printer for an anonymous work. The *Journal* of 13 Vendémiaire, Year X, announced a pamphlet by G. Feydel to combat one by Gentz on the status of France, but again there was no indication as to whether it was government-inspired.

[20] Aulard (ed.), *Paris sous le consulat, passim;* E. d'Hauterive (ed.), *La police secrète*, I, *passim*. One reason for Napoleon's insistence on publicity for his every move was a belief that such a practice would deprive hostile pamphleteers of some of their thunder. The Duchesse d'Abrantès (*Mémoires*, IV, 74–80) thought that many of the hostile pamphlets circulating under the Consulate were composed by foreigners of the diplomatic corps at Paris.

men to whom he had given the rule of certain territories temporarily or permanently. Napoleon likewise kept his officials informed of pamphlets, telling Davout, for example, of pamphlets by August von Kotzebue and the English. Davout ordered his subordinates to concert with the civil authorities in seizing the copies—and especially the sellers—of hostile pamphlets.[21]

All pamphlets were subjected to censorship. The police punished the publication of unfriendly pamphlets by seizing all the copies and arresting the printers and sellers.[22] If an unfriendly author or printer continued turning out pamphlets, the Minister of Police ordered the prefect to forbid any of his future works. At the request of the Minister of Police, Bourrienne, who had claimed he did nothing to restrict freedom of the press in Hamburg, even prosecuted the author of *Prophéties remarquables que la guerre française* . . . , which appeared in that city. Napoleon told Fouché that hawkers were not to cry out the titles of pamphlets without a police permit, and that the posting of anything on the Paris walls required preliminary authorization. Because of Fouché's personal biases, the police were more lenient with Jacobins than with the royalists.[23]

Sometimes Napoleon himself intervened, ordering the seizure of pamphlets, commanding Talleyrand to tell the Senate of Nuremberg to burn all the libels published and arrest the sellers or suffer the consequences, or telling one of his royal brothers to prevent the circulation of a hostile pamphlet in his state. In addition, he might instruct Fouché to prevent the circulation of Barère's *Lettre à l'armée* because soldiers did not read the vain

---

[21] Napoleon (Brotonne, ed.), *Lettres*, 175; Joseph (Du Casse, ed.), *Mémoires*, IV, 84; Davout (Mazada, ed.), *Correspondance*, I, 254; II, 184; Napoleon, *Correspondance*, XXIII, 44.

[22] There is evidence that the "corrections" of the police did have an effect on the sellers. Aulard (ed.), *Paris sous le consulat*, I, 266, and *passim*. However, Remacle ([ed.], *Bonaparte et les Bourbons*) and Abrantès (*Mémoires*) both claim that pamphlets were circulated in manuscript if the printing of them was watched too closely.

[23] Aulard (ed.), *Paris sous le consulat*, I, 276; E. d'Hauterive (ed.), *La police secrète*, III, 204; Napoleon, *Correspondance*, VI, 211; Welschinger, *Censure sous l'empire*, 14, 136. Hence there may be some basis of truth in the statement of the Duchesse d'Abrantès (*Mémoires*, IV, 84) that the agents of the prefect of police were more active than those of Fouché, even though the reports in Aulard (ed.), *Paris sous le consulat* and *Paris sous le premier empire*, do not necessarily substantiate this claim.

prattling of pamphlets, or forbid a Spanish pamphlet to be made known at Paris. Montalivet's order to the Director General of Printing not to allow any pamphlets on ecclesiastical affairs, inasmuch as some bad ones had been produced, was the result of Napoleon's prodding.[24] Napoleon ordered the Minister of Police to have the Archtreasurer and the Director of Police see that pamphlets appearing in Holland—after its annexation by France—were censored and that those men trying to corrupt public opinion were arrested and punished.[25]

The functioning of the censorship met with very little complaint, but Joseph did reprimand his Minister of Police in Naples for approving Catalani's *Mémoire pour les Napolitains Bourbons, par un ami de la vérité,* as its circulation would have aroused hatreds.[26]

Viewing the practice of placarding as a sign of weakness,[27] Napoleon very seldom ordered the composition of materials solely for posters or handbills. The Central Bureau, however, was authorized to use placards to deny rumors. The only other occasions which have come to the notice of the present author were an order to Fouché to post the sentence of an executed spy, because the public should be kept informed of the reasons for extraordinary events, and an order to General Antoine Drouot in the Hundred Days to make posters for recruiting the Young Imperial Guard.[28]

Materials which were placarded were primarily designed for some other medium such as the press, bulletins, or charges of the bishops. Thus in 1808, Murat received the order to distribute materials as handbills only if there were no papers, which Napoleon looked upon as the best of all mediums.[29] Realizing, however,

---

[24] Napoleon, *Correspondance,* VI, 546; IX, 511; XIII, 37; XVII, 66; Jerome (Du Casse, ed.), *Mémoires,* III, 376; Napoleon (Lecestre, comp.), *Lettres,* II, 144. The Minister of the Interior also had to approve all publications by the chambers of commerce and the *Bulletin* of the Society for the Encouragement of National Industry. *Journal typographique,* XIII(1810), 57. At times the government used the press to inveigh against hostile pamphlets. Remacle (ed.), *Bonaparte et les Bourbons,* 98.

[25] Napoleon (Brotonne, ed.), *Lettres,* 312.

[26] Joseph (Du Casse, ed.), *Mémoires,* III, 08.

[27] Napoleon, *Correspondance,* XIV, 80.

[28] *Ibid.,* XV, 79; Napoleon (Lecestre, comp.), *Lettres,* II, 351; Lanzac de Laborie, *Paris sous Napoléon,* I, 18.

[29] Napoleon, *Correspondance,* XV, 79; XVI, 396.

that the press did not reach everybody, Napoleon did frequently order the placarding of bulletins, addresses, and accounts of ceremonies. Those to whom he issued the commands included Montalivet, Joseph, and Maret.[30] But his chief reliance still remained the press.

B. ORDERS OF THE DAY, BULLETINS, PROCLAMATIONS

Whereas pamphlets and broadsides were supposed to reach all classes of the civilian population, orders of the day were designed essentially to speak to the soldiers. Not confined merely to routine regulations, as one might expect, they played a role in Napoleon's propaganda.[31] Generally speaking, they contained three sorts of propagandist material. Some censured negligent or unheroic soldiers.[32] Others contained expressions of satisfaction with the army, including a listing of those who had especially distinguished themselves and of the captures they had made. Still a third category inspired the army to greater deeds, exhorted the inhabitants of territories under French control to support Napoleon's military measures, or, while warning of the dire consequences of continued opposition, assured the inhabitants of newly conquered territories that the French were not to be feared.

Good examples of the third category of material are found in the orders of the day of October 23, 1805, to the Grand Army and the Bavarian Army:

> Soldiers, your Emperor is with you. You are only the advance guard of the great people; if necessary, it will rise as one to confound the new league woven by England's hatred and gold.
> But, soldiers, we have forced marches to make, fatigues and pri-

---

[30] Ibid., XVII, 233, 236; Napoleon (Brotonne, ed.), Lettres, 540; Aulard (ed.), Paris sous le consulat, passim; E. d'Hauterive (ed.), La police secrète, passim. Regnaud, ardently pro-Bonaparte, addressed a placard to the new government of 1799 telling what France expected of it, but there was no indication that it was official. Moniteur, 23 Brumaire, Year VIII. If hostile placards appeared, it was naturally the police who removed them.

[31] Murat (Lettres [Prince Murat, pub.], VI, 69) thus said that he deemed an order of the day necessary so as to relieve the general consternation.

[32] Criticisms such as that of a divisional quartermaster for not clothing his men properly (Napoleon [Picard and Tuetey, eds.], Correspondance inédite, V, 409) tended to show the soldiers that Napoleon was on their side.

vations of every kind to endure: whatever obstacles may be set in our way, we shall overcome them, and we shall rest only when our eagles are on the territory of our enemies.

Bavarian soldiers, I put myself at the head of my army to deliver your country from unjust aggressors.

The House of Austria wants to destroy your independence and incorporate you into its vast estates. You will be faithful to the memory of your ancestors, who, though sometimes oppressed, were never beaten and always kept their independence and political existence, the first blessing of nations, just as fidelity to the Palatine House is the first of your duties.

As your sovereign's good ally, I have been touched by the marks of love you have shown him in this important circumstance. I know your bravery; I flatter myself that after the first battle I shall be able to say to your prince and my people that you are worthy of fighting in the ranks of the Grand Army.[33]

Although usually only a commander in chief was permitted to issue orders of the day, Napoleon, who utilized the reports of subordinates to obtain materials for the orders, sometimes delegated to Berthier the task of drawing up his orders. Others who issued orders included Napoleon's brothers, Murat, and various marshals, while General Jean Rapp issued one at Strasbourg.[34]

Such orders received publicity in several ways. They were always read to the men by divisional officers, and they were published and distributed in the army corps in accordance with the general rule that they be printed, signed by the Major General, and published at 9:00 A.M. The papers, in conquered territories as well as in France, published many of them, and they were frequently posted as placards.[35] Napoleon often utilized his administrative hierarchy for the publicizing of these orders. His representatives in territories with autonomous governments such

[33] Napoleon, *Correspondance*, XI, 294; Napoleon (Picard and Tuetey, eds.), *Correspondance inédite*, I, 114-15. The *Correspondance* lists the order to the Bavarian soldiers under the date of October 7.

[34] Alexander L. Kielland, *Napoleon's Men and Methods* (London, 1937), 140; Napoleon (Picard and Tuetey, eds.), *Correspondance inédite*, I, 154; Napoleon, *Correspondance*, XVI, 23; *Gazette de France* (hereafter cited as *Gazette*), April 13, 1815.

[35] *Journal*, August 8, 1809; *Empire*, July 25, 1807; Napoleon (Picard and Tuetey, eds.), *Correspondance inédite*, I, 114.

as Spain and the Kingdom of Italy ordered their subordinates, at Napoleon's behest, to make them known to all the civil, military, and religious authorities, and to print them for general distribution. At home Napoleon told Clarke to publish some of the orders and commanded Cambacérès to have that of May 12, 1809, containing news of the army's entrance into Vienna and urging the soldiers to maintain discipline, distributed in printed form simultaneously with its being read aloud from the stages of the theaters.[36]

Napoleon was not, however, always satisfied with the orders of the day as they appeared. Those by his brothers seemed especially to displease him: he rebuked Joseph for an order expressing satisfaction with the army, which had not merited it; one of Jerome's orders he said made him the laughing stock of Germany, Austria, and France; and Murat was curtly informed that three orders of the day such as his would demoralize the army.[37]

The civilian counterpart of the orders of the day was the bulletins, expected to produce a favorable impression among the civilians, to whom they spoke about the army. The few bulletins which Napoleon himself did not compose (though he insisted that the source be kept secret) [38] he expressly ordered.[39] In 1809 Camba-

[36] Napoleon, *Correspondance*, XIV, 319; XVIII, 552–53; Napoleon (Lecestre, comp.), *Lettres*, I, 171; Murat (Prince Murat, pub.), *Lettres*, VI, 45. After becoming King of Naples, Murat ordered his administrators to print and distribute his own and Napoleon's orders of the day without awaiting special instructions from Napoleon. Murat (Prince Murat, pub.), *Lettres*, VII, 249; VIII, 319. In conquered regions the orders were generally translated. Napoleon, *Correspondance*, XVI, 397.

[37] Joseph (Du Casse, ed.), *Mémoires*, VI, 262; Napoleon (Breed, ed.), *Opinions and Reflections*, 111 and 170. Because of Napoleon's displeasure, the order by Murat never appeared in the *Moniteur*.

[38] Napoleon (Brotonne, ed.), *Lettres*, 154. Mme de Rémusat (*Mémoires* [P. de Rémusat, pub.], II, 289) says that Napoleon used Maret as author in chief. According to Bausset, the day after every battle was spent in gathering reports from the army corps in order that Napoleon might draw up the bulletin with which the army became acquainted only through the Paris papers. L. F. J. de Bausset, *Mémoires anecdotiques sur l'intérieur du palais et sur quelques événemens de l'empire depuis 1808 jusqu'au 1er mai 1814 pour servir à l'histoire de Napoléon* (Paris, 1827–29), I, 90–91.

[39] This statement does not apply to subordinate kingdoms. In Italy, Masséna issued bulletins which Eugene forwarded to Napoleon and his brothers and to various places in Italy, and Napoleon's representative Reinhard in Westphalia drew up a bulletin based on the courier's recital. Eugene (Du Casse, ed.), *Mémoires*, I, 425–50; Jerome (Du Casse, ed.), *Mémoires*, III, 365. The only com-

cérès was commanded to print an official bulletin every day on Walcheren affairs, and in 1811 Decrès was charged with publishing a little daily bulletin on the movement of the squadrons of Toulon, Antwerp, Lorient, and Brest in order to encourage the sailors without disclosing the strength of the French forces.[40]

The topics treated by the bulletins varied. Although political reflections and heated answers to enemy claims found their way into them, by far their most important contents were accounts of army accomplishments, with special stress on victories won. A few nonmilitary bulletins also appeared: for example, those Talleyrand was ordered to draw up in 1802 to explain Santo Domingan affairs and the amnesty of the *émigrés*.[41]

Believing that the bulletins, intended to be merely rapid sketches of events, were insufficient by themselves to satisfy the conceit of the officers, Napoleon ordered Berthier to make an abstract of the generals' reports.[42]

It is impossible to state that the bulletins appeared at some certain interval—there was no set rule. Generally, a bulletin appeared after every battle—sometimes even two in a day—but there were also bulletins announcing important progress made by the army without a struggle.[43] Though the only safe statement that one can make is that Napoleon wanted bulletins printed often enough to quiet the people's fears and prevent adverse rumors,[44] it may be accurate to say that they appeared less frequently during the Russian campaign than during any other, and that after 1806—except for 1814—they appeared more and more rarely.[45]

---

plaint of Napoleon on the issuance of bulletins was made in 1806 against one by Lebrun in Holland, which he ordered Fouché to keep out of the papers. Napoleon, *Correspondance*, XI, 554–55.

[40] Napoleon, *Correspondance*, XIX, 334; XXII, 393.

[41] Marie Joseph Adolphe Thiers, *Histoire du consulat et de l'empire* (Paris, 1845–62), VII, 176; Napoleon, *Correspondance*, XI, 436.

[42] Napoleon, *Correspondance*, XVIII, 513.

[43] If news was deemed too unimportant for a bulletin, it was merely inserted in the *Moniteur*. Napoleon, *Correspondance*, XI, 436.

[44] Napoleon, *Correspondance*, XIX, 334; Baron Agathon Fain, *Manuscrit de mil huit cent quatorze* (3d ed.; Paris, 1825), 141.

[45] Based on the author's own comparison of frequency during the different campaigns. The time at which bulletins appeared depended somewhat on circumstances other than the army and public opinion. In 1813, for example, Napoleon had to await the return of Caulaincourt from Prague. Napoleon, *Correspondance*, XXVI, 62.

Various officials and officers were in charge of publishing and distributing the bulletins. Cardinal Joseph Fesch at Lyon printed and distributed profusely the bulletins he received, and while on campaign in 1800 Bonaparte ordered his fellow Consuls to print the bulletins he sent them. Napoleon authorized the prefects to publish them and post them on town halls and even on the churches, but the curés were forbidden to publish them. Fouché and Portalis agreed, in accordance with a practice which had gradually developed, that the priests should read bulletins from the pulpit; Napoleon at first voiced no objection, but later he ordered the discontinuance of such reading.[46] Cambacérès or the Minister of Police sometimes ordered Dubois to print and placard bulletins, and in 1805 Joseph also had bulletins posted and read in the theaters and streets. Napoleon gave the Minister of War permission to publish the bulletins of Eylau on condition that he give them a different form, and in 1814 the same official used bulletins extensively for publicizing French victories.[47]

All bulletins—until 1812, when more careful selection of them was exercised—appeared in the *Moniteur*. The Minister of Foreign Affairs himself inserted the bulletins, or sent them to Cambacérès for insertion. The purpose of this latter method was primarily to cause a delay of five or six days, thus preventing the bulletins from being of aid to the enemy.[48] The other papers copied the *Moniteur* or merely summarized the news contained in the bulletins. Talleyrand even ordered that until bulletins had appeared in the *Moniteur* they were not to be made public in Italy and Naples; when Eugene and Joseph complained to Napoleon about the ruling, they were authorized to print the bulletins immediately upon receipt.[49]

[46] Napoleon, *Correspondance*, XIII, 469; Haussonville, *Église et empire*, II, 240. Although Napoleon had forbidden this procedure in 1805, priests read bulletins in all the communes of Doubs in 1806. E. d'Hauterive (ed.), *La police secrète*, III, 51.
[47] Lanzac de Laborie, *Paris sous Napoléon*, I, 93; Napoleon (Brotonne, ed.), *Lettres*, 154; Joseph (Du Casse, ed.), *Mémoires*, I, 343–44; Napoleon, *Correspondance*, VI, 338; XIV, 319; XXVII, 272; Albert Du Casse, *Histoire des négotiations diplomatiques relatives aux traités de Morfontaine, de Lunéville, et d'Amiens, pour faire suite aux Mémoires du roi Joseph précédée de la correspondance inédite de l'empereur Napoléon Ier avec le cardinal Fesch*, 3 vols. (Paris, 1857), I, 45.
[48] Napoleon, *Correspondance*, XIII, 338; XVI, 14.
[49] *Ibid.*, XI, 304; Aulard (ed.), *Paris sous le premier empire*, III, *passim;* Eugene

The bulletins were apparently very widely read. In 1812 the *Journal de l'Empire* reported that in one day 35,000 copies of Bulletin 18 had been sold. Another indication of their popularity is revealed in one of Napoleon's orders. In 1814, he ordered Savary to have the bulletins published in small format to the number of 40,000 for distribution throughout all France.[50] Sometimes, however, the bulletins were not printed. Napoleon often sent them to the King of Spain or Holland with the definite order not to print them. Eugene in 1805 made public from one of Napoleon's bulletins only the brilliant deeds of some officers, because he felt that publishing the entire bulletin might attenuate the effects of the previous bulletin, which had announced a victory. This shows that Napoleon allowed at least Eugene to use some initiative, as he had also done in 1800 when permitting General Martin Vignolle, the military commandant of Lombardy, to have a bulletin printed.[51]

Rulers of subordinate kingdoms, who received the bulletins from the Minister of Foreign Affairs, took charge of distribution within their own realms. In Spain the usual procedure was to reprint them hastily in the army print shop and have them distributed before they appeared in the *Gazette de Madrid* of the following day. When war first broke out between France and Spain in 1808, Decrès was charged with sending bulletins to Barcelona and with dispatching huge quantities of them to the colonies of France, in order that they might be forwarded into Spanish colonies for distribution. The Minister of War had Bulletin 26 of the Army of Spain printed a second time and ordered the curés of the leading communes in Spain to comment on it. Eugene inserted the bulletins in all his papers and forwarded copies to General André Masséna and to Rome, Genoa, Lucca, and Piedmont. Murat also disseminated French bulletins profusely.[52]

(Du Casse, ed.), *Mémoires*, I, 420; III, 200, 213; Joseph (Du Casse, ed.), *Mémoires*, III, 225, 232. At the end of 1808 Murat was still complaining (*Lettres* [Prince Murat, pub.], VI, 432) that bulletins were delayed because they were sent via Paris.

[50] *Empire*, October 1, 1812; Napoleon, *Correspondance*, XXVII, 240–41.

[51] *Moniteur*, 19 Prairial, Year VIII; Eugene (Du Casse, ed.), *Mémoires*, I, 419.

[52] Napoleon, *Correspondance*, XVIII, 82; XI, 304, 366; *Empire*, March 1, 1809; La Forest (Grandmaison, pub.), *Correspondance*, II, *passim;* Talleyrand (Bertrand, ed.), *Lettres à Napoléon*, 270. Davout also translated them into Polish and German in Warsaw.

Napoleon was quite anxious that the bulletins reach territory not under French control, and therefore had the Minister of Foreign Affairs send them to various places in Germany. Murat sent bulletins into English-dominated Sicily, where they were placarded at Messina, and some bulletins even appeared in the British newspapers. In 1814 the police were entrusted with the task of introducing bulletins into French territory occupied by the enemy.[53]

The papers also published enemy bulletins, often with annotations. Napoleon used these bulletins to obtain information on the strength and movements of the enemy, and printing them gave him another opportunity to berate the enemy for lying.[54]

The handling of proclamations was much more flexible than that of either bulletins or orders of the day. Many of the proclamations were military, thanking the troops for what they had done, inspiring them to further efforts, and delivering just about the same type of message to the civilian population. Others were intended to justify acts of the leaders and to denounce the enemy.[55]

Napoleon personally composed a great many of these proclamations, but they were also issued by other officers, including virtually all of Napoleon's generals. In addition there appeared proclamations by rulers whom Napoleon had established,[56] by Poles to their fellow countrymen and by confederations of Frenchmen to their fellow citizens, by Joseph [57] and Marie Louise at the time of the invasion of France, by the soldiers and the Imperial Guard upon Napoleon's return from Elba,[58] by defeated enemies urging their followers to submit, by the Landamman of Switzerland when Swiss troops were incorporated into the French

[53] Napoleon, *Correspondance*, XIX, 177; *Empire*, August 12, 1812; Murat (Prince Murat, pub.), *Lettres*, VI, 498; VII, 205, 224; Napoleon (Brotonne, ed.), *Lettres*, 535; *Journal*, February 17, 1807.

[54] Napoleon, *Correspondance*, XXV, 100–101; Thiers, *Histoire du consulat*, XI, 231. Sometimes these enemy bulletins circulated against Napoleon's desires.

[55] Eugene (Du Casse, ed.), *Mémoires*, X, 74.

[56] Each territory over which the French gained control received proclamations from its new administrators.

[57] Although Joseph's name appeared on this proclamation, Pasquier claimed that he had drawn it up. Duc d'Audiffret Pasquier (ed.), *A History of my Time; Memoirs of Chancellor Pasquier*, tr. by Charles E. Roche (New York, 1893–94), II, 266.

[58] Actually, Napoleon had drawn these up himself.

army, and by Count Charles Decaen to the Île de France.[59]

Proclamations in a similar vein by persons whose plans were consonant with those of Napoleon also received publicity in France. The proclamations of Prince Christian, commander in chief in Norway, the one urging the Norwegians to oppose England and the other urging them to follow the maritime trade, appeared, respectively, in the *Journal de l'Empire* of October 5, 1807, and in the *Journal de Paris* of February 15, 1808. When the Tyrolese were restless, General Karl Wrede issued a proclamation urging them to remain loyal.

Many other proclamations dealt with civil affairs. In addition to the categories of officials already listed, several other officials issued proclamations of this type. Among them were Chaptal,[60] Fouché, the prefects of police, departmental prefects, and the councilors of state sent out by Napoleon in 1814 as special commissioners for military affairs, charged with the *levée en masse*. In specific subordinate territories proclamations were issued: in the circles of Hof and Wunsiedel by the Intendant, Camille de Tournon, at Bern by Auguste de Talleyrand, and in Spain by the Spanish Junta, the Council of Castile, the Council of Inquisition, and the Biscayans. Eugene permitted his ministers of war, justice, and finance to issue proclamations only upon his order and after a preliminary censorship.[61] More of the proclamations, such as that urging the four departments of the Left Bank of the Rhine to be faithful and to forget all the bonds tying them to the Germanic body,[62] appeared when there was a change of government than for any single other type of event. Napoleon and Eugene also used proclamations to say their adieus.

Those to whom the proclamations were addressed included the army or some of its units, the national guard, residents of various countries and of smaller governmental units, and fairly large groups of functionaries.

[59] Sources in which these proclamations were found include newspapers, memoirs, and correspondence of the individuals issuing the proclamations.

[60] Chaptal (*Souvenirs* [E. A. Chaptal, ed.], 138) says that he received the power to issue proclamations in 1814. The one proclamation of his located by the author was addressed to the youth of the department of the Rhône. *Empire*, January 17, 1814.

[61] This list of persons issuing proclamations on civil affairs naturally is not concerned with those who issued proclamations which were merely orders.

[62] *Bulletin des lois* (Series 3), III, 159, 29 Messidor, Year IX.

Even for those proclamations not issued by himself, Napoleon assumed a great deal of initiative. Eugene reported that his proclamation to the Tyrolese contained only what Napoleon had ordered him to say. Napoleon ordered Berthier to have the clergy and leading magistrates of Toro and Zamora issue proclamations. In 1815 Davout received the command to have Marshal Guillaume Brune issue proclamations and to reach an agreement with Decaen on the contents of the proclamation to the latter's troops. When planning to install Joseph as King of Naples, Napoleon instructed him to inform the Neapolitans, after the first battle, of all that Napoleon had done to keep war away from them and of everything the Queen had done to attract it. He also told Joseph that when he entered Naples, he must issue another proclamation containing liberal promises.[63] After Joseph had moved to Spain, he received instructions to dispatch intendants to issue proclamations for the provinces. Bessières in the same country was commissioned to order the court of appeal, the metropolitan with jurisdiction over Santander, and Gregorio de la Cuesta, Captain General of Old Castile, to issue proclamations after the French troops had been on the march for two days. In 1809, Napoleon wrote the Kings of Bavaria and Württemberg to issue proclamations and asked the rulers of Darmstadt and Baden to do likewise. He frequently relayed orders to the generals and prefects, and even to his sister Élisa, through the Minister of War. Others issuing proclamations at the express command of Napoleon were Berthier, Murat, all the marshals and generals, especially in 1814, Lazare Carnot (to the Corsicans during the Hundred Days), and Fouché.[64]

Proclamations about which Napoleon did not know in advance were usually reported to him. Generally this was done by the

[63] Joseph (Du Casse, ed.), *Mémoires*, II, 38, 55. Yet Driault merely says Joseph's proclamations probably were inspired by Napoleon. Édouard Driault, *Napoléon en Italie (1800–1812)* (Paris, 1906), 494. These ideas were combined into one proclamation, issued by Joseph on February 21, 1806.

[64] Eugene (Du Casse, ed.), *Mémoires*, VI, 104; Napoleon (Lecestre, comp.), *Lettres*, I, 268; Napoleon, *Correspondance*, XVII, 265; XVIII, 481–82; XXVII, 306; XXVIII, 33, 89, 193, 219; Napoleon (Chuquet, ed.), *Inédits napoléoniens*, I, 436; Napoleon (Brotonne, ed.), *Lettres*, 522; Murat (Prince Murat, pub.), *Lettres*, VI, 30; Napoleon (Picard and Tuetey, eds.), *Correspondance inédite*, III, 221; Napoleon (Loyd, tr.), *New Letters*, 344.

person issuing the proclamation, but the Minister of War reported those proclamations issued by French generals in Spain. The mere fact that they were allowed to make proclamations before telling him shows that Napoleon's subordinates were allowed to assume some initiative—illustrated by General Jacques de Lauriston's offering his opinion to Admiral Siniavin on the type of proclamation to make, and General Jean Reynier's giving Joseph a proclamation to issue.[65]

Some people, however, received definite orders against indulgence in this type of propaganda. Davout in Hamburg wrote General Friant not to make any proclamations himself or allow any to be promulgated. The Minister of Commerce instructed the Prefect of Nevers not to make any proclamations. When Napoleon ordered Eugene to seize the cantons of Italian Switzerland, he included a demand that the generals Eugene sent should not issue proclamations, and that General Lemarois was not to do so while chasing the brigands out of the Kingdom of Italy. Napoleon had Berthier order General Marc Beaumont not to issue absurd proclamations, and Joseph reported to Napoleon that he had forbidden General Étienne Radet to print any addresses to the people. Though at other times he published proclamations, General Pierre Lefebvre was forbidden to print any at Innsbruck. Napoleon advised Decrès that the governor of Batavia, rather than he, should issue proclamations in order to adapt them to local circumstances, and he told Joseph that nominating his ministers and grand officers would be better than any proclamation.[66]

Distribution of some proclamations was made more widespread by their insertion into the orders of the day. Others—dealing with civil affairs—appeared in the *Bulletin des lois,* and many were circulated through the *Moniteur* or other papers. Those proclamations intended for the *Bulletin des lois* had to pass through several hands before being published: at Napoleon's order, Maret

[65] Marmont, *Mémoires,* III, 77; *Journal,* November 11, 1806; Joseph (Du Casse, ed.), *Mémoires,* II, 58; VII, 66 and 77; Eugene (Du Casse, ed.), *Mémoires,* I, 405; Murat (Prince Murat, pub.), *Lettres,* V, 488; Plancy (Baron de Plancy, pub.), *Souvenirs,* 505.

[66] Davout (Mazada, ed.), *Correspondance,* III, 302; Napoleon, *Correspondance,* XVI, 107; XVII, 311; XIX, 268; XXI, 191, 283; Joseph (Du Casse, ed.), *Mémoires,* II, 218.

sent them to the Minister of Justice, who published them, in compliance with orders included at the end of the proclamations themselves or with a separate set of instructions.[67] For those which appeared as leaflets or placards, Napoleon assigned the duty of distribution to various subordinates.

Berthier played a very important role in the distributive process, ordering various generals, and even Eugene, to follow his example of having proclamations printed and disseminated. Some of the generals so used were Marmont, Ney, Davout, Bessières, Lauriston, and Pierre Lapisse.[68]

The Minister of Marine did not play as important a role as Berthier. He did, however, send some proclamations to the commandants at leading bases in order that they might make them known in port or among the fleet, and he did send others to the colonies for distribution.[69]

Rulers of subject kingdoms also figured prominently in publicizing this medium of propaganda. As King of Naples, Joseph had a proclamation by Napoleon printed in French and Italian. Murat received the order to publish Napoleon's proclamations in Spain and send them everywhere by special courier, even to the Council of the Indies to be forwarded to America, and ordered Generals Pierre Dupont and Georges Frère to spread profusely the proclamation of the Junta. After leaving Spain for Naples, he had his Chief of Staff, General Paul Grenier, insert a proclamation in the order of the day and had General Louis Partouneaux print and spread profusely Napoleon's proclamation to the soldiers. Eugene also received repeated orders to spread outside as well as inside the Kingdom of Italy the proclamations which Napoleon sent him.[70]

Napoleon used a variety of other people for the purpose of

---

[67] *Moniteur*, 21 Messidor, Year X; Napoleon, *Correspondance*, VII, 306.

[68] Davout (Mazada, ed.), *Correspondance*, III, 43; Napoleon (Brotonne, ed.), *Lettres*, 158; Napoleon (Brotonne, ed.), *Dernières lettres*, I, 334; Eugene (Du Casse, ed.), *Mémoires*, VII, 378; Napoleon, *Correspondance*, XVIII, 61; XIX, 51.

[69] Leclerc (Roussier, ed.), *Lettres*, 280; *Moniteur*, 7 Frimaire, Year VIII.

[70] Murat (Prince Murat, pub.), *Lettres*, VI, 205-206; VII, 205; VIII, 460; Napoleon, *Correspondance*, XVII, 213; XVIII, 19; Joseph (Du Casse, ed.), *Mémoires*, II, 64.

propagating his proclamations. While Josephine was visiting in Strasbourg in 1809, she received the order to have a proclamation to the Army of Italy translated into French and German and disseminated throughout Germany. Otto, Napoleon's minister at Munich, was to do likewise with Napoleon's proclamation and with those of his allies at the start of the 1809 campaign. The Minister of the Interior was commissioned to distribute a proclamation on the celebration of July 14, 1801. Carnot's proclamation to the Corsicans was made known by the auditor Napoleon had sent to Corsica. The brigades of Generals d'Avenay and Maupetit were instructed to conquer Toro and Zamora and publish Napoleon's proclamation there, and proclamations by Napoleon to the Hungarians and by Eugene to the Tyrolese were also spread by military detachments.[71]

While it is impossible to say exactly how successful the French were in reaching with proclamations such hostile forces as the Tyrolese, there are a few indications as to speed and extent of their distribution. Though Eugene's proclamation to the Tyrolese was spread in profusion among them, he complained that the tardiness of dissemination interfered with its effectiveness. Proclamations by General Gabriel Hédouville in the Year VIII reached the rebel chiefs in France and several copies of Bonaparte's proclamation to the Swiss in 1802 reached the rebel leaders, in accordance with a decree of the Helvetic Senate; yet at Bern all possible means were used to prevent circulation of Bonaparte's proclamation, and the public was not allowed to speak of the few copies it did see. Napoleon's proclamation to the Hungarians was almost unknown outside French territory and the lack of print shops in

[71] Lazare Carnot, *Correspondance inédite de Carnot avec Napoléon, pendant les cent jours* (Paris, 1819), 98; Eugene (Du Casse, ed.), *Mémoires*, VI, 212–20; Napoleon, *Correspondance*, VII, 193; XVIII, 176, 481–82; XIX, 47, 142; Napoleon (Lecestre, comp.), *Lettres*, I, 267. At least one proclamation was read aloud in the main cities. Napoleon, *Correspondance*, XVII, 520. In Paris the proclaiming for such occasions was done by the prefect of police. At these ceremonies he was accompanied by the twelve mayors of Paris and their deputies, police commissioners, officers of the peace, officers of the general staff of Paris, and officers of the *gendarmerie* of the Seine. *Débats*, 28 Germinal, Year X. In departmental capitals the prefects and police commissioners proclaimed peace or other important events, and in other communes the mayors were responsible for such duties. Napoleon, *Correspondance*, VII, 82.

Spain and Naples prevented Murat from distributing proclamations, directed respectively at the rebels and the Sicilians, as widely as the government desired.[72]

The number of copies of these proclamations frequently ran into the thousands. For example, Napoleon caused to be printed six thousand copies of the proclamation urging the Poles in the service of Russia to desert and telling them they were never better adorned than when covered with the blood of their enemies. The proclamations published by Napoleon at Gap reached several thousand copies, and Napoleon ordered Auguste de Talleyrand, his minister to the Swiss Confederation, to print several thousand copies of a proclamation analyzing political and military events.[73]

Those addressed to the soldiers were read to them by the commanding officers. This meant that the marshals read them to the different corps after receiving them from the Chief of Staff. In 1806 Napoleon ordered that a proclamation be read every day the army was on the march, and in 1812 he sent specific orders that a proclamation be read aloud by a delegation composed of the general staff and the heads of corps to the sound of the drum and fife or some other kind of music to attract attention.[74]

Those who distributed proclamations, as well as those who issued them, were allowed some freedom. Bernadotte was left free to decide how to print one of Napoleon's proclamations to the army. In Naples, early in 1806, Joseph decided to publish Napoleon's Proclamation Number Four but to omit Number Three for fear of inciting the Queen's rage. Telling Arias, President of the Council of State, that he had not sent enough copies of

[72] Léon de la Sicotière, *Les conférences 1799–1800* (Angers, 1885), 37–40; Eugene (Du Casse, ed.), *Mémoires*, VI, 93, 165; *Journal*, 21 and 27 Vendémiaire, Year XI; Murat (Prince Murat, pub.), *Lettres*, V, 48; Joseph (Du Casse, ed.), *Mémoires*, II, 187; Davout (Mazada, ed.), *Correspondance*, III, 40; *Débats*, 18 Vendémiaire, Year XI. Those proclamations destined for non-French territories were naturally in the native tongue of the region for which they were destined and were usually bilingual. Even in Santo Domingo they were in French and Creole. Eugene (Du Casse, ed.), *Mémoires*, I, 405; Leclerc (Roussier, ed.), *Lettres, passim.*

[73] Napoleon, *Correspondance*, XXIV, 68–70; *Gazette*, March 24, 1815; Napoleon (Brotonne, ed.), *Dernières lettres*, I, 419. Naturally some proclamations had a smaller distribution.

[74] *Moniteur*, 22 Fructidor, Year IX; Napoleon (Picard and Tuetey, eds.), *Correspondance inédite*, I, 101–106, 153; Napoleon (Chuquet, ed.), *Inédits napoléoniens*, I, 190.

the order of the day and of his proclamation, Murat left it to his discretion as to how many more should be printed.[75]

Napoleon took great care that "D-Day" for the publication of any one proclamation should be so selected as to enhance its effectiveness. His representatives at foreign but subject courts reported to him on the proper time for the issuance of proclamations. One he wrote at Schönbrunn late in 1805 he did not allow to appear in the *Moniteur* until February 1, 1806, as he wanted to be certain that Joseph actually was going to Naples. Eugene's proclamation to the Hungarians Napoleon ordered postponed until after a battle, and to King Maximilian Joseph of Bavaria Napoleon wrote in 1809 that speed would be the chief merit of the proclamation he wanted issued.[76]

The method of handling proclamations did not always satisfy the government authorities. Joseph complained that the proclamations of the French generals in Spain were designed to discredit him. And, although he did not complain about them, in some villages, forged proclamations had been posted in his name. Murat reported to Napoleon that a certain proclamation had merely aroused unrealizable hopes. La Forest reported that the language Joseph used was not suitably dignified for a king, and late in 1807 Napoleon reproved Jerome for the same shortcoming.[77]

In fact, Napoleon was frequently critical of his subordinates. Joseph had stationed Negro troops in front of Gaeta, where they might possibly see the proclamations thrown on the coast by the British, who were making the claim that Toussaint L'Ouverture had been betrayed. Napoleon therefore rebuked Joseph for affording these proclamations an opportunity to be effective through his disposition of the troops. Talleyrand received a reprimand for not having informed Napoleon of a false proclamation by Haugwitz, whose publication he had failed to stop, and Talley-

---

[75] Napoleon, *Correspondance*, XVIII, 488; Joseph (Du Casse, ed.), *Mémoires*, II, 58; Murat (Prince Murat, pub.), *Lettres*, VI, 58.

[76] Driault, *Napoléon en Italie*, 385; Jerome (Du Casse, ed.), *Memoires*, IV, 457; Napoleon, *Correspondance*, XIX, 197; La Forest (Grandmaison, pub.), *Correspondance*, I, 17.

[77] Joseph (Du Casse, ed.), *Mémoires*, II, 164; VII, 260; Murat (Prince Murat, pub.), *Lettres*, V, 498; La Forest (Grandmaison, pub.), *Correspondance*, I, 164; Napoleon, *Correspondance*, XVI, 226; Jerome (Du Casse, ed.), *Mémoires*, III, 82–83.

rand was moreover ordered to declare publicly that it was contrary to Napoleon's dignity and engagements. Because Napoleon wanted to spare the feelings of Turkey, he criticized, through Joseph, Berthier's proclamation welcoming Corfu into the "Grand Empire." To Eugene he wrote that a proclamation by General Jacques Menou was nonsensical, and on the same day ordered Menou not to issue any more. Napoleon reported to Carnot that the subprefect of Vitry-le-François had made a very unwise proclamation, and rebuked Lebrun for inconveniencing him by issuing numerous proclamations on topics not even serious enough to mention. The *Journal de Paris* stated that the prefects also were making too many proclamations.[78]

Another complaint of Napoleon's was that the Paris papers printed his French proclamations from German translations. If the press was disinclined to wait until it had received the proclamations from the government, Napoleon said, it could make an analysis of the translation, in good French and without using his name. This hasty press policy sometimes led the papers into the more serious error of copying false proclamations.[79] The only instances known to the author in which Napoleon praised a proclamation not his own were the issuance of Masséna's proclamation at Marseille in April of 1815 and the publication in 1808 of the following proclamation by the Spanish Junta:

> Spaniards, the supreme junta of the government . . . speaks to you to dissipate . . . fatal errors. . . .
>
> At the moment when Spain, . . . impoverished, exhausted, dishonored in the eyes of all Europe by the vices and disorders of its government, was reaching the time of its complete annihilation, . . . Providence offered us a means of raising our country to a degree of happiness and splendor it had reached only in the most brilliant epochs of its history. . . . The most powerful prince of Europe has received the renunciation of the Bourbons . . . so as

[78] Joseph (Du Casse, ed.), *Mémoires*, II, 294; Napoleon, *Correspondance*, XII, 192; XVI, 460; Napoleon (Lecestre, comp.), *Lettres*, I, 256; II, 126; *Journal*, 15 Germinal, Year VIII; Carnot, *Correspondance avec Napoléon*, 21; Driault, *Napoléon en Italie*, 475; Eugene (Du Casse, ed.), *Mémoires*, IV, 246, November 28, 1808; Davout (Mazada, ed.), *Correspondance*, II, 198. Toussaint L'Ouverture was the leader of a successful uprising of the Haitian Negroes against French rule. He was, however, made prisoner and brought to France.

[79] Napoleon, *Correspondance*, XVIII, 526; Fiévée, *Correspondance*, II, 171-73.

to establish the Spanish monarchy on new bases. . . . Brave Spaniards, will you let yourselves be seduced by the deceitful promises of the secret agents of the enemy nation? . . . What is the goal which these vile promoters of agitation and disorder propose to themselves? . . . Misled inhabitants of the provinces, . . . do you think that a tumultuous *levée* of inhabitants . . . will be able to resist experienced armies? . . . The junta wishes to make known to you the intentions of the new sovereign who comes to govern you. Listen and judge.

The Cortes . . . are going to be re-established. . . .

The annual expense of the royal house will be fixed. . . .

The Catholic religion will be exclusive in Spain.

. . . The taxes levied for the present war will be considerably diminished.

. . . Gradual reforms will be brought about in all branches.

. . . Unite sincerely with your government and your local authorities. . . . If you contemn this salutary advice, fear the just anger of a monarch who is as severe when it is necessary to punish . . . as he is generous and prompt to pardon a moment of error. Do you not know that large French armies have already entered Spain? Do you not know that other armies equally as large are on the way toward our frontiers?[80]

The last aspect of the proclamation phase of Napoleon's propaganda was an endeavor to check on enemy proclamations that reached France. He ordered Fouché to have Müller arrested for sending out the proclamations of Louis XVIII from Frankfurt, informed his Minister of Police that the proclamations of Ghent were mailed at Noyon, and told him to stop all the apocryphal proclamations and orders of the day published over his, Napoleon's, name. Eugene received the order to counteract any incendiary proclamations the Austrians might scatter on his side, as they had done at Stuttgart, by a lively one telling how they had mistreated Italy.[81]

At the very end, Napoleon was still vigorously waging the war of the pamphlet, as well as that of the sword.

[80] Napoleon, *Correspondance*, XVII, 279–80.
[81] Napoleon (Brotonne, ed.), *Lettres*, 52; Napoleon, *Correspondance*, XIV, 29; XVIII, 473; Napoleon (Lecestre, comp.), *Lettres*, II, 350.

CHAPTER V

PUBLIC GATHERINGS

A. FESTIVALS

Music, poetry, speeches, and free performances at the theaters constituted the highlights in the pageantry of the festivals, of
which there was a regular series. During the Consulate the national
festival days were limited to July 14 and September 21, the anniversary of the establishment of the Republic, because Bonaparte
wanted "only those festivals retained which belonged to periods
when public opinion was unanimous." [1] But with the change to
an imperial regime these gradually fell into disuse and were replaced by the annual celebration of Napoleon's birthday on
August 15, the Battle of Jena, the 18 Brumaire, and the coronation
of Napoleon and the Battle of Austerlitz on the first Sunday in
December. [2]

Various foreign territories under Napoleon's control also regularly celebrated events pertaining specifically to those regions.
The Kingdom of Italy, for example, observed the anniversaries
of the Battle of Marengo and of Napoleon's royal coronation. [3]

There were also festivals which did not recur regularly. On
this list, those for the celebration of victories, treaties of peace,
constitutional changes, and important events affecting the imperial family, such as Napoleon's marriage and the birth of his

[1] Napoleon (Barral, ed.), *Messages,* 27.
[2] Lanzac de Laborie, *Paris sous Napoléon,* III, 2, 13. The press had been instructed not to mention the revolutionary fetes. In 1813 the fete of August 15
was advanced five days because of military operations and was designed to cheer
the soldiers. Napoleon (Lecestre, comp.), *Lettres,* II, 276; Charles Pelleport-
Burête (ed.), *Souvenirs militaires et intimes du général v^te de Pelleport* (Paris,
1857), II, 74. The annual industrial exposition was also a type of fete, designed
to show French industrial progress. Rémusat (*Mémoires* [P. de Rémusat, pub.],
III, 419) says Portalis suggested August 15 as the proper date to celebrate
Napoleon's birthday.
[3] Napoleon, *Correspondance,* VI, 382; XV, 340.

son, played a prominent part. Other celebrations honored the army and the hoisting of the flag of Elba.[4]

The type of ceremony varied according to the celebration. One favorite of Napoleon was that accompanying the sending of captured flags to some constituted body such as the Senate or Legislative Body at Paris. Such an occasion usually featured a parade, followed by one leading, and perhaps several minor, speeches and a *Te Deum*. In 1814, a review of the national guard was added to the ceremony. Earlier, in 1807, Napoleon planned a variation of the same ceremony, when he sent the sword and decorations of Frederick the Great to Cambacérès at Paris. Napoleon wrote Cambacérès the details of his plan:

> I think the sword and decorations of Frederick should be presented to the Invalides without further delay. That can serve as the purpose of a little fete in a room of the Invalides, where can be placed a throne, which will remain vacant. You will represent me there and in front of the assembled Invalides will deposit this trophy. This little fete, announced a few days in advance, cannot fail to arouse curiosity. You might have an ode composed in honor of the brave men of Jena. This would be a natural occasion to have the flags taken in the campaign which number, I think, about four hundred, carried in front of you to the Invalides to be deposited there. . . .
>
> . . . Have Marshal Moncey carry the sword and decorations of Frederick.[5]

Until 20 Ventôse, Year IX, the civic fetes were philosophic— held to celebrate such virtues as tolerance, beneficence, good households. Although the religious element was important after this date because of the influence of the Catholic Church on the populace, the fetes became increasingly and primarily military. Many began with an artillery salvo and ended with a general illumination, usually ordered by the prefect, and fireworks. The pyrotechnic displays were one of the amusements upon which the government placed special stress, others being concerts, free dramatic performances, horse races, and balls. Sometimes, especially at celebrations honoring the army, there were special fea-

---

[4] Lanzac de Laborie, *Paris sous Napoléon*, III, 14.
[5] Napoleon, *Correspondance*, XV, 122.

tures such as public weddings with dowries furnished by the government.[6] Generally, too, the government furnished food, so that the entire program of national fetes was reminiscent of the "bread and circuses" of the Roman emperors. What could have been more appropriate for Napoleon, this Caesar and classicist?

Special funeral ceremonies were also staged for French national heroes. Those so honored were Generals Henri de Turenne, Sébastien de Vauban, Louis Desaix de Veygoux, and Jean Lannes. The central ceremony took place in Paris, but the provinces were expected to celebrate, to the best of their ability, simultaneously with the capital.

At times Napoleon would take the initiative and supervise the details: in 1807, he even required that the answer in behalf of the Imperial Guard to the municipal body of Paris be submitted to preliminary censorship; in 1814, he dictated the answer of Marie Louise when Clarke presented captured flags to her. Lucien, while Minister of the Interior in 1800, received a letter from Napoleon which stated:

> I saw in the *Moniteur* . . . the prospectus of the fete for July 14.
>
> You will find annexed a decree concerning the honors to render General Desaix. Perhaps it would be fitting to have his funeral oration pronounced by Garat, Fontanes, or some other. You know that this bit must be extremely well done.
>
> You will find enclosed a copy of a letter I have just written to General Berthier [at that time commander in chief of the army of reserve at Milan, and told to invite two of the best virtuosos in Italy to sing a duet in Italian for the fete of July 14]. I should like to have these virtuosos perform, with choirs, an Italian piece on the deliverance of Cisalpine and Liguria, and on the glory of our arms, which will have been composed at your behest. It is a supplement to make to your prospectus.
>
> General Berthier informs me that he expects to send either Mme Billington or Mme Grassini, who are the two most famous virtuosos in Italy. Therefore, have a fine piece composed in Italian, with good music. The tone of voice of these actresses is surely known to Italian composers.[7]

[6] *Ibid.*, XVI, 90; *Curés*, August 24, 1810.
[7] Napoleon, *Correspondance*, VI, 382.

Two years later, Napoleon issued a proclamation explaining why everybody should celebrate July 14. In 1805, the Minister of the Interior received permission to decide what celebrations to order in keeping with the customs of each district [*pays*]. Napoleon also arranged for the presentation of four hundred flags from Prussia and of Frederick's sword, as described above. Berthier was also commissioned to provide, with Napoleon's approval, for the presentation of captured flags. Ségur, the official Master of Ceremonies, was permitted to take to the Legislative Body the flags Junot had captured. At Napoleon's command, the Minister of War also presented captured flags and arranged that the entry of prisoners into Paris be accompanied with suitable pomp. Joseph received instructions to celebrate French successes against the British if the enemy made a move on Aranjuez, and the Minister of Foreign Affairs was charged with regulating the funeral arrangements for Lannes.[8]

At other times some government official would take the initiative. The Minister of Foreign Affairs and the Minister of War each gave a fete celebrating the Treaty of Lunéville, and Cambacérès gave one to celebrate the first anniversary of Bonaparte's return from Egypt. At Lyon the prefect generally assumed the initiative. Though Chaptal suggested reviving the celebration for the liberation of Orléans by Jeanne d'Arc, no other Minister of the Interior assumed as much initiative in arranging for fetes as did Lucien. Other relatives of Napoleon also acted of their own volition: Joseph arranged the first celebration, in 1805, for the victory at Austerlitz; and Murat, as King of Naples, did not await or expect Napoleon's authorization for fetes he ordered.[9]

Though not many exact figures are available on the amounts appropriated for these fetes, the sums were evidently quite im-

---

[8] Napoleon (Picard and Tuetey, eds.), *Correspondance inédite*, III, 381; Napoleon, *Correspondance*, VI, 382; VII, 518; XVI, 134; XX, 193; XXVI, 404; XXVII, 153; Charles de la Roncière (ed.), *Napoleon's Letters to Marie Louise* (New York, 1935), 197; Joseph (Du Casse, ed.), *Mémoires*, V, 297, December 27, 1808; Napoleon (Chuquet, ed.), *Inédits napoléoniens*, I, 37.

[9] Iung, *Lucien Bonaparte*, I, 406–407; Murat (Prince Murat, pub.), *Lettres*, VII, 44; Joseph (Du Casse, ed.), *Mémoires*, I, 346; François Dutacq, "Fêtes lyonnaises de l'empire," *Revue des études napoléoniennes*, XL(1935), 21; *Journal*, 18 Vendémiaire, 30 Pluviôse, and 3 Germinal, Year IX; *Moniteur*, 2 Floréal, Year XI.

pressive. The Prefect of Rome, Tournon, reported that at the elaborate celebration of the birth of the King of Rome, 50,000 francs had been given for relief of the poor; yet in 1811 the status of Rome's finances was rather poor.[10] Napoleon had Minister of Foreign Affairs Champagny chide Otto for having a niggardly fete in honor of Napoleon's marriage; Otto had spent only 10,000 francs when, in the Emperor's opinion, he should have spent 100,000 francs, since it was better to give no fete at all than to stage one which failed to win public approbation because it was obviously underfinanced.[11] The fete at Lyon on the same occasion cost 50,000 francs plus charity appropriations of 60,000 francs.

The fetes received more than local prominence through published accounts of them. Since the departmental press was composed largely of extracts from Parisian papers, the items published at Paris about the celebrations there and elsewhere reached all parts of the territory under Napoleonic control. Some accounts also appeared in pamphlet form.[12]

The government occasionally experienced some difficulty in obtaining the type of celebration it wanted and proper co-operation from its administrators. Cretet was ordered to reprimand the Prefect of Troyes for authorizing a fete in honor of Count Thibaut of Champagne. Napoleon reproved Duroc, the Grand Marshal of the Palace, because he had not illuminated the Amsterdam palace when the King of Rome was born. He also reproved the Grand Chamberlain, Comte de Montesquiou, because he had kept the public waiting:

> I was dissatisfied to learn that the fete of August 15 had been so badly planned and carried out that the Empress spent an infinite time at a bad concert, with the result that the public had to wait two hours for the fireworks. . . . Nothing could have been more

[10] Tournon (Moulard, pub.), *Lettres inédites*, 28, 137, 165. For this fete the complete hierarchy of minister, prefect, and subprefect functioned.

[11] Dutacq, "Fêtes lyonnaises de l'empire," *loc. cit.*, 21; Napoleon, *Correspondance*, XXI, 418. French ministers to other courts were likewise expected to give fetes celebrating the marriage. Napoleon (Brotonne, ed.), *Dernières lettres*, II, 36.

[12] *Church and Religious Affairs during the Consulate and Empire: Contemporary Pamphlets 1805–1806*, in Boulay de la Meurthe collection. Hereafter, all pamphlets concerned with religious affairs are from this collection.

inconvenient and it was really very simple at the hour set for the fireworks to notify the Empress, who would have left the spectacle; . . . finally, there was a very little inconvenience in having the Empress leave a little sooner from a spectacle at which she was choking with heat, while there was a very great one in making wait a whole population accustomed to retiring at nine P.M.[13]

Joseph complained that the ceremony to proclaim him King of Spain went off in mediocre fashion, and the police reported that the fete at Marseille for the Italian coronation had been unworthy of its subject.[14] The soldiers had not attended the *Te Deum*, and the authorities found it difficult to obtain musicians because the latter had not been paid for playing at the celebration of the imperial coronation.

Whether they went off well or not, the festivals strikingly illustrated the emotional attitude and manner of thinking desired by the government.

B. RUMORS AND MEETINGS

Since large numbers of people in a favorable mood were in the streets or other public places for these fetes, they furnished one excellent opportunity for a whispering campaign by Napoleon's agents. Such a campaign obviously spread only rumors favorable to the government's point of view. Napoleon exploited this method, especially when he felt that proclamations or press articles would seem too official, because it afforded the government an opportunity to influence public opinion without seeming to have a hand in it.

Frequently members of the governmental hierarchy received instructions to instigate and disseminate rumors. Napoleon directly commanded Ministers of Police Fouché and Savary to circulate rumors. Eugene in Italy, Clarke when he was governor of Vienna, Joseph as governor of Paris, the Major General, Berthier, Élisa, Davout, Masséna, the Duke of Valmy, Louis in Holland, Maret, General Philippe Duhesme, Josephine, and various

---

[13] Napoleon, *Correspondance*, XXVI, 113; Napoleon (Brotonne, ed.), *Lettres*, 320.
[14] Joseph (Du Casse, ed.), *Mémoires*, IV, 385; E. d'Hauterive (ed.), *La police secrète*, I, 456.

French ministers and ambassadors—all received commands to spread news without printing anything or giving it an official character.[15]

At times some of the above people acted only as intermediaries, passing along to their subordinates rumors which Napoleon wanted planted. Champagny received orders to send French ministers and agents in foreign countries a circular on the basis of which they could belie rumors. Eugene was informed of rumors that Élisa in Piombino, Fesch, and General Lemarois were to propagate unofficially. Mollien was to have his treasury agents start favorable reports at the Bourse. Jerome received the order from Napoleon, via Berthier, to spread the rumor that he was awaiting 6,000 troops which would enable him to attack.[16]

Men other than Napoleon occasionally seized the initiative. Davout reported to Napoleon that he had already told General Louis Montbrun to start a rumor, and Eugene ordered General d'Anthouard to spread favorable rumors concerning troop movements.[17]

By various means, rumors were made to sound plausible. The government might regulate its own activities in such a manner that the rumors would seem valid, or it might print articles in the papers. The police reported that private letters tended to bear out what rumors said.[18]

These rumors served three important purposes. First, they

[15] Eugene (Du Casse, ed.), *Mémoires*, I, 473; III, 177, 218, 231; Napoleon, *Correspondance*, XI, 424; XIV, 121; XVIII, 280, 478, 522; XXII, 336; XXVI, 111, 530; XXVII, 191; Napoleon (Brotonne, ed.), *Lettres*, 375; Napoleon (Brotonne, ed.), *Dernières lettres*, II, 476; Jerome (Du Casse, ed.), *Mémoires*, II, 77; Fugier, *Napoléon et l'Espagne*, II, 432; Joseph (Du Casse, ed.), *Mémoires*, III, 221; Léon Cerf (comp.), *Lettres de Napoléon à Josephine* (Paris, 1928), 124.

[16] Jerome (Du Casse, ed.), *Mémoires*, II, 177; Eugene (Du Casse, ed.), *Mémoires*, I, 473; Napoleon (Brotonne, ed.), *Dernières lettres*, II, 476; Napoleon, *Correspondance*, XXI, 96; XXVII, 259.

[17] Eugene (Du Casse, ed.), *Mémoires*, X, 73; Davout (Mazada, ed.), *Correspondance*, II, 502; Fiévée, *Correspondance*, III, 227; Napoleon, *Correspondance*, XXI, 315. It is interesting to note that in 1811 Davout received these orders: "Spread pacific rumors—the return of the troops to France, the decrease of the Danzig garrison, etc. Everything which can tend to diminish the alarms of Russia is part of my system." Napoleon, *Correspondance*, XXII, 336.

[18] Fugier, *Napoléon et l'Espagne*, II, 63; Czartorysky, Despatch of March 19, 1804, *Sbornik, Die Berichte der russischen Gesandten aus Paris (1801-4)* (St. Petersburg, 1890-91), LXXVII, 515; E. d'Hauterive (ed.), *La police secrète*, III, 108.

bolstered public morale. An illustration would be the instruction Joseph received from Napoleon in October of 1806 that until news of the first events arrived, he should spread the rumor that peace had been made.[19] Second, they aided the government's military tactics and strategy. Thus a rumor spread by de Marmont in 1805 that an armistice had been made helped delay the destruction of a bridge, and Napoleon had Junot insinuate to the Portuguese—hoping he could use them to restrain the Spaniards in 1808 —that French differences with Spain arose from Napoleon's desire not to divide Portugal.[20] Third, they enabled the government to get some indication of whether public opinion was favorable. For example, Reinhard wrote Champagny that he had deliberately started the rumor that he was leaving Westphalia, in order to ascertain the effect of his departure. The relative alacrity with which the public accepted favorable or unfavorable rumors was evidence of its state of mind.[21] Persons well-inclined toward the Napoleonic regime would obviously be less likely to believe in the authenticity of rumors criticizing the government or reporting bad news than would persons opposed to the course that events were taking.

Napoleon had at times to restrain as well as encourage his subordinates. He ordered Murat not to circulate ridiculous rumors, and, upon withdrawing from Paris in 1805, instructed Joseph to allow ample time for the arrival of news and not to insert anything concerning rumors in the *Moniteur*. He also found it necessary to warn Davout in Hamburg that his activities were angering the Germans.[22]

In conquered territories as well as in France proper, the most important function of the *Moniteur* and other papers with regard

[19] Joseph (Du Casse, ed.), *Mémoires*, III, 221.

[20] Napoleon was to some extent guided in his military actions by rumors which the enemy spread. If these rumors were uncertain and contradictory, he was rather certain that the enemy was still distant; and he assumed the news in a deliberately circulated rumor was false. Marmont, *Mémoires*, II, 334; Napoleon (Brotonne, ed.), *Dernières lettres*, II, 457.

[21] Marmont, *Mémoires*, II, 336; Napoleon (Lecestre, comp.), *Lettres*, I, 161; Jerome (Du Casse, ed.), *Mémoires*, IV, 88; Fiévée, *Correspondance*, I, 200. Napoleon sometimes used rumors reported to him as a means of checking on his functionaries.

[22] Joseph (Du Casse, ed.), *Mémoires*, I, 304; Napoleon (Lecestre, comp.), *Lettres*, I, 250; Napoleon, *Correspondance*, XXIII, 44.

to rumors was counteracting hostile ones.[23] Papers forestalled rumors merely by printing news, as rumors tended to spring up when news had been lacking for some time. They warned their readers to exercise the utmost care in sifting rumors, and, by telling who was spreading rumors and by what means, they put the people on their guard.[24] When rumors had already been spread, the papers endeavored in various ways to discredit them. At different times they announced that the government had received more recent news, refuted the rumors point by point, showed that the enemies of France would benefit if certain rumors were believed, and ridiculed the statements by asking rhetorically whether (since Parisian papers copied foreign ones) distant places were better informed or by sneering contemptuously at the quality of the press in countries other than France. Sometimes, they merely issued a flat denial. Articles of this nature might be inserted by Maret, the prefect, some police agent, or the person designated by Napoleon to govern a subordinate territory.[25]

The handling of rumors by the papers was not entirely satisfactory. Any they did not deny were deemed valid, even though the papers refused to confirm them, because people assumed the press had been ordered to remain silent. Furthermore, activity by the papers could not prohibit people from making remarks in public.[26]

The task of directing conversation at public or secret gather-

[23] Statements made about the relation of the press to rumors also apply to items in the foreign papers which the French called false. The papers (and couriers) were also used to propagate rumors, with Clarke and Eugene acting in accordance with Napoleon's orders. Joseph (Du Casse, ed.), *Mémoires*, IV, 160; Eugene (Du Casse, ed.), *Mémoires*, IX, 148.

[24] *Moniteur*, 3 Thermidor, Year X; *Journal*, 30 Prairial, Year IX. This seems to the author the most effective way to deal with hostile rumors through the press. A clever article in several newspapers in 1804 told the readers how much credence they might give to the phrases *on dit*, *on parie*, and *on assure*. *Mercure*, 3 Frimaire, Year XII.

[25] Aulard (ed.), *Paris sous le premier empire*, I, 96; E. d'Hauterive (ed.), *La police secrète*, III, 166; Murat (Prince Murat, pub.), *Lettres*, V, 411; Davout (Mazada, ed.), *Correspondance*, II, 40, 355; Napoleon, *Correspondance*, XVI, 176; *Journal*, 11 Germinal, Year XI; *Moniteur*, *passim*. For a time, beginning on April 18, 1806, the *Moniteur* ran a monthly article specifically dealing with rumors.

[26] Aulard (ed.), *Paris sous le consulat*, I, 274; Lanzac de Laborie, *Paris sous Napoléon*, III, 15; Fiévée, *Correspondance*, II, 357; A. Pingaud, *Bonaparte président de la république italienne*, II, 415.

ings devolved upon the police. Fouché had three hundred men who attempted to make the conversation of the Paris *salons*, cafés, secret societies, and public groups flow in proper channels. Their accounts were the basis of the reports which Napoleon received almost daily from the police, while his own agent reported on the literary assemblies.[27]

In general, the *salons* were hostile to Napoleon and the remarks exchanged there were characterized by partisan feeling. In fact, Napoleon was obliged to order even Josephine to see that hostile remarks were not bandied in her *salon*. To correct the *salons* where hostile remarks were numerous—such as those of Mesdames Jeanne Marie Tallien, Jeanne Françoise Récamier, and Françoise Marie de Chevreuse—Fouché would summon the patroness of the *salon* and order a better supervision of the guests.[28]

Both the police of the general ministry and that of the prefecture reported on public gatherings and on cafés and gaming houses, using them as sources of information on public opinion and checking to learn whether they were distribution centers for materials hostile to the government. Remarks overheard in these places sometimes formed the basis of newspaper articles designed to combat unfriendly rumors.[29]

Because the press alone had proven inadequate to cope with such rumors, the police included rumors in its reports on public gatherings. The Central Bureau used printed placards to deny rumors which tended to counteract the measures taken by the government. Dubois, the Prefect of Police, was zealous in gathering and reporting anticlerical rumors. Departmental prefects working under Fouché counteracted reputedly false rumors, about which they had warned the populace, by contrary ones,

[27] Aulard (ed.), *Paris sous le consulat* and *Paris sous le premier empire, passim;* Fouché (Beauchamp, ed.), *Mémoires,* 246; Duchesse Laura d'Abrantès, *Histoire des salons de Paris* (Paris, 1837–38), I, 73; Napoleon, *Correspondance,* II, 201.

[28] George S. Hellman (ed.), *Memoirs of the comte de Mercy Argenteau. Napoleon and the Empire* (New York, 1917), 11; Abbé Dominique de Pradt, *Histoire de l'ambassade dans le grand duché de Varsovie en 1812,* Napoleon *Pamphlets,* XVII, 45, in Boulay de la Meurthe collection; Aulard (ed.), *Paris sous le premier empire,* I, 312; Napoleon, *Correspondance,* XIV, 437; Rémusat (P. de Rémusat, pub.), *Mémoires,* III, 507; Charpentier, *Napoléon et les hommes de lettres,* 77.

[29] Napoleon (Picard and Tuetey, eds.), *Correspondance inédite,* I, 402; Aulard (ed.), *Paris sous le consulat, passim.*

and they reported to Fouché himself on rumors in their departments. The men who spread malevolent rumors the police might
arrest or exile to some small commune where they could be easily
watched, while the police itself took steps to dispel such rumors
by a favorable whispering campaign.[30]

Tab was kept on the private meetings of groups such as the
Chouans and Masons. Though favoring the Masons—because of
their opposition to the Pope—sufficiently to allow the number of
lodges to increase from 300 to 900 between 1804 and 1814, Napoleon controlled them strictly; after 1805 all meetings were forced
to begin and close with the triple cry of *"Vive Napoléon le Grand
et son auguste famille"*; members of Napoleon's circle—officers,
magistrates, and court—and confidants of the police joined the
lodges; and Napoleon appointed the heads of the Masonic organizations.[31]

At times Napoleon gave vent to his dissatisfaction with the
handling of rumors by his agents. It was not unusual for him to
tell the police where to check on rumors or which ones to counteract. He accused it of cleverly trying to enhance its standing with
him by reporting on dangerous rumors it had deliberately sown.
The police—especially the commissioners at Hamburg, Antwerp,
and Amsterdam—felt the sting of his displeasure for passing on
to the generals all the false rumors spread from London.[32]

Mollien's administration also combatted damaging rumors and
false news. The syndic of the stockbrokers reported on rumors
from foreign sources at the Bourse on the French political situation. In return, Napoleon advised what news was to be denied, by
giving Mollien notices to be written up and published separately

[30] Lanzac de Laborie, *Paris sous Napoléon*, I, 19; IV, 50; Napoleon, *Correspondance*, XV, 310; *Journal*, 8 Germinal, Year VIII; *Moniteur*, 2 Prairial, Year
X; Aulard (ed.), *Paris sous le premier empire*, III, 652. The prefect at Lyon
even issued a proclamation to destroy a rumor that Bonaparte had been poisoned.
Journal, 8 Floréal, Year IX. Murat, as King of Naples, likewise ordered (*Lettres*
[Prince Murat, pub.], VII, 226) arrests of bearers of malevolent news. If rumors
on a certain topic displayed a uniformity, they were adjudged to be from the
same source. Aulard (ed.), *Paris sous le consulat*, III, 466.

[31] Aulard (ed.), *Paris sous le consulat* and *Paris sous le premier empire, passim*;
Napoleon, *Correspondance*, XXXII, 317; Hector Fleischmann, *Napoléon et la
franc-maçonnerie* (Paris, 1908), *passim*.

[32] Napoleon, *Correspondance*, XXI, 315, 362; Napoleon (Lecestre, comp.),
Lettres, II, 247; Fiévée, *Correspondance*, III, 227.

as formal announcements. The Emperor thought that such a method of refuting false news would be more effective than insertions in the *Moniteur*. The notices were drawn up according to the general pattern suggested by Napoleon: "We know from a certain source that such and such a rumor is false." [33] All notices were, of course, signed by the syndic.

Continuing the check on hostile rumors was Cardinal Fesch, who naturally reported largely on religious affairs.[34] All the French ministers in the foreign courts were to belie false rumors upon command from the Minister of Foreign Affairs, and—after de Caulaincourt in Russia had set the example—they were ordered to send home an unsigned bulletin of rumors to inform Napoleon on the spirit of the moment outside France.[35]

An important role in checking on rumors was that of the military. Liébert reported to the Major General on the accuracy of rumors, and Joseph, Eugene, Jerome, and Davout each sent out reconnoitering parties to ascertain the accuracy of rumors. General Jean Baptiste Jourdan wrote de Marmont in 1812 that Joseph wanted to know whether a certain rumor was true, and generals were to report on rumors from wherever they were stationed. Sometimes the organizational setup was more complex, so that the actual check was made by men receiving secondhand or even third-hand orders. For example, on one occasion, General Paul Thiébault reported to de Marmont that he had ordered the prefect to send some men to verify the facts in a certain case.[36]

The ministry of the interior acted principally by counteracting rumors, especially after 1810. Beginning in that year, it ordered the central administrations of the departments to counteract the effect of various rumors, some of which Napoleon himself

---

[33] Napoleon, *Correspondance*, IX, 395; XVIII, 238. These same brokers had to be restrained because speculation caused by rumors they circulated affected public opinion. Napoleon, *Correspondance*, XIX, 241.

[34] Du Casse, *Négotiations diplomatiques*, I, 91, 120.

[35] Napoleon (Lecestre, comp.), *Lettres*, I, 277; Napoleon, *Correspondance*, XXI, 96, 222; XXV, 214.

[36] Joseph (Du Casse, ed.), *Mémoires*, IX, 145; Eugene (Du Casse, ed.), *Mémoires*, II, 227; VIII, 352; Jerome (Du Casse, ed.), *Mémoires*, II, 76; Davout (Mazada, ed.), *Correspondance*, II, 54; Marmont, *Mémoires*, IV, 282, 406; E. d'Hauterive (ed.), *La police secrète*, III, 63. If the rumors were too improbable, it was suggested that no one bother to refute them. Davout (Mazada, ed.), *Correspondance*, I, 111.

had singled out for special treatment. It informed the prefects about the truthfulness of these rumors in circulars that Élisa and the governors general of Turin and Rome also received. Tournon, at the latter place, saw to it that rumors he attributed to idleness were denied.[37] Archchancellor Cambacérès caused the rumor that Russia had allied with England to be denied and in 1808 ordered Fouché to end the remarks in his *salon* on the impending divorce of Napoleon and Josephine.[38]

Rulers Napoleon had established reported to him on rumors in their states, in which they were charged with contradicting those hostile to French interests. They in turn received reports from their own and Napoleon's functionaries.[39] Fiévée often dealt with the matter of rumors in the notes he sent Napoleon. When Napoleon was away on campaign, he frequently left Joseph in charge at Paris. Joseph would then report to the Emperor on Parisian rumors and receive orders from Napoleon on how to deal with them. For example, the command of March 4, 1814, had Lavalette punish those in the postal administration who spread false rumors. Letters, such as that which Binot sent home from Egypt, also were used to deny enemy claims.[40]

Napoleon's final problem regarding hostile rumors was to prevent his subordinates and allies from believing them. He personally warned Jerome and Joseph not to let their acts be determined by enemy reports and informed various generals and the Kings of Württemberg and Denmark that no British news was to be believed. It was at his order that Champagny, Berthier, and Eugene each told men under his jurisdiction that all British rumors, plus certain other specifically designated ones, were false.[41]

[37] Tournon (Moulard, pub.), *Lettres inédites*, 86; *Moniteur*, 18 Frimaire, Year VIII; Napoleon (Lecestre, comp.), *Lettres*, II, 77, 88; Napoleon (Brotonne, ed.), *Lettres*, 292.

[38] Napoleon, *Correspondance*, X, 445; XVII, 318.

[39] Jerome (Du Casse, ed.), *Mémoires*, VI, 277, 298; Eugene (Du Casse, ed.), *Mémoires*, VI, 259; Joseph (Du Casse, ed.), *Mémoires*, III, *passim;* Napoleon (Lecestre, comp.), *Lettres*, I, 82; Napoleon, *Correspondance*, XV, 280; Murat (Prince Murat, pub.), *Lettres*, V, 418; VIII, 98. Joseph especially was active with regard to reporting rumors.

[40] Joseph (Du Casse, ed.), *Mémoires*, II, 365; III, 114; X, 194; Napoleon, *Correspondance*, XXVII, 280; *Journal*, 24 Germinal, Year IX.

[41] Joseph (Du Casse, ed.), *Mémoires*, V, 83; Jerome (Du Casse, ed.), *Mémoires*, IV, 120; Marmont, *Mémoires*, V, 339; Eugene (Du Casse ed.), *Mémoires*, IX, 4;

Some difficulties in the handling of rumors the authorities were unable to surmount. It was obviously impossible to attempt to counteract all rumors they deemed inimical. Yet it was dangerous not to do so, for if the authorities were silent, the rumors would be mentioned more consistently. With regard to rumors, as well as in other respects, the officials displayed a servile dependence upon Napoleon. When he was distant from Paris so that couriers required some time to make the round trip, the result of the government's denying a rumor was often that it reprovoked public thought on a matter which had already been relegated to minor importance. Still a third difficulty was that the officially inspired rumors did not always coincide with statements in the semiofficial press.[42]

C. SPEECHES

Many of the gatherings mentioned in the preceding section were relatively exclusive. In addition to these, Napoleon utilized general, open meetings at which speeches were delivered. Even now an influential means of mobilizing public opinion, the public meeting 130 or 140 years ago was relatively more important and was utilized more frequently than today. Besides influencing those actually hearing the addresses at the time of delivery, these discourses could reach many more through publication [43] and by word of mouth.

On the whole, addresses were made to Napoleon rather than by him. The great majority were delivered on behalf either of governmental units and agencies or of bodies of soldiers. Primarily these addresses pointed out how pleased the constituents of these groups were with the government or promised to aid in

Napoleon, *Correspondance*, XVIII, 111; XXI, 125; XXIV, 368–69; XXV, 126, 133, 167, 205; XXVI, 279, 282, 286. The letter to Eugene is printed on both pages 125 and 225 of Volume XXI, under the dates September 17, 1810, and October 17, 1810. For present purposes it is unimportant which date is correct. At other times Napoleon merely kept the men informed of what rumors were circulating, without indicating whether they were true or false. Napoleon, *Correspondance*, XXVI, 270.

[42] Fiévée, *Correspondance*, II, 70, 340; Aulard (ed.), *Paris sous le consulat*, III, 498.

[43] Sometimes they were censored before being printed. Napoleon (Lecestre, comp.), *Lettres*, II, 20.

whatever Napoleon happened to be undertaking at the moment. In 1814, however, deputations from various municipalities exploited the new topic of the atrocities being committed by the allies. Deputations from virtually every possible governmental unit, many of them sent by the prefects upon instructions from Napoleon, made addresses. On each occasion for an address, the *Moniteur* (whose excerpts were the most complete) could print, because of lack of space, the addresses of only a few delegations, and thus was forced merely to list most of the groups which sponsored speeches.[44] The lists were made as extensive as possible, in order to convey the impression that all the influential people supported Napoleon, who acted upon the same theory of the value of extensive listing in urging Joseph to print all the speeches addressed to him as King of Spain by Spanish deputations.

Napoleon also caused to be published addresses from groups which were not in the governmental hierarchy. In order to impress people in the interior of France with the popularity of the practice of burning British merchandise, the *Moniteur* printed addresses of thanks from numerous economic organizations. Early in 1811, addresses of cathedral chapters [45] pledging support to Napoleon filled the same paper.

Such addresses did not occur at regular intervals but generally appeared when Napoleon arrogated more power to himself, changed the status of non-French regions,[46] or made peace. Events important to Napoleon personally, such as his escapes from assassination,[47] his marriage to Marie Louise, and the birth of the King of Rome, also occasioned innumerable public addresses. The awarding of prizes and the ending of the school year were other excellent occasions for speechmaking. Warned in advance of what was to be said to him, Napoleon was able to answer the deputations he received with an array of carefully chosen, pompous, and sterile phrases suitable to the occasion. His speeches always thanked the delegates for what they had done and at the

---

[44] Napoleon, *Correspondance,* XVIII, 236; XXV, 360; Léonce Pingaud, *Jean de Bry (1760–1835)* (Paris, 1909), 328. Some of the addresses by Italian delegations were printed only in the original; others were followed by a French translation.

[45] A cathedral chapter is the assembly of the canons of the home church of a bishop.

[46] Each new region brought under French control would decree addresses.

[47] At these times the diplomatic corps also delivered addresses.

same time cleverly implied that more was expected of them. Generally his other speeches were made before some legislative body or to the soldiers.[48]

There were times, however, when Napoleon utilized individuals rather than deputations to drive home his point.[49] When George Washington died, the official eulogy of him by Fontanes was designed primarily to stress Bonaparte's greatness:

> Washington began it [the American Revolution] with energy and carried it through with moderation. . . .
> . . . Today military glory shines with a greater brilliance. . . .
> The mourning which the First Consul has ordered for Washington announces to France that the examples he gave are not lost. It is less for the illustrious general than for the benefactor and friend of a great people that funeral crepes have covered the flags of victory and the uniform of our warriors. . . .
>
> . . . The military prodigies of the French troops have weakened the fame of every prior illustrious military achievement. . . .
> The emotions of a magnanimous soul . . . carry out and maintain revolutions more surely than trophies and victories. . . .
> . . . A people in revolution has no friends or allies. . . . It is usually necessary in the wake of great political crises for an extraordinary person to arise who, by the mere ascendance of his glory, compresses the audacity of all parties and brings back order out of confusion. . . .
>
> . . . He [Washington] had triumphed over England; he undertook against the license of parties a struggle no less painful or less glorious. . . .
> . . . He had fled authority when the exercise of it could have

---

[48] Charles Doris, *Mémoires secrets sur Napoléon Bonaparte*, 2 vols. (Paris, 1815), I, 89. Many of his addresses were never delivered in person, but were merely published. The generals in charge of the various corps also harangued the soldiers. Napoleon, *Correspondance*, XXIV, 378; *Courtier de l'Europe et des spectacles*, January 6, 1811.

[49] The uniformity of the addresses offers some evidence of government initiative. In 1814 Napoleon's correspondence proves that he ordered the addresses on allied atrocities. And Murat's emphasis (*Lettres* [Prince Murat, pub.], II, 419) on the fact that he had not influenced his troops to write an address to Bonaparte illustrates that the government often—or even usually—did assume the initiative in army addresses.

been arbitrary; he wished to bear the burden of it only when it was restricted within legitimate limits. . . .

He is one of the prodigious men who appear from time to time . . . with the character of greatness and domination. . . . It is in vain that these men, designated in advance, remain aside or mingle in the crowd; the hand of fortune raises them suddenly and carries them from obstacle to obstacle and from triumph to triumph up to the summit of power. . . .
. . . None of his compatriots loved liberty more ardently, none feared more the exaggerated opinions of a few demagogues. . . .

. . . It seems to me that . . . Washington cries to all France, "Magnanimous people, who know so well how to honor glory, I conquered for independence; but the happiness of my country was the reward of the victory. Do not be content with imitating the first half of my life; it is the second which recommends me to posterity."
Yes, your counsels will be heard, oh Washington! . . . He who, while still young, surpassed you in battles will, as you, close the wounds of the country with his triumphant hands.[50]

Though Fontanes was the most celebrated orator of the period, others were also important. Arnault, head of the Division of Public Instruction, in a speech to the Spanish Academy, urged closer co-operation of France and Spain. When the President of the Court of Appeals administered the oath to the Legion of Honor, he expressed sentiments appropriate to the occasion. Marie Louise in 1813 expressed to the Senate her confidence in France and the French. The Archchancellor and the Minister of War, at Napoleon's command, chose orators to deliver generals' funeral orations.[51] Various government functionaries delivered addresses in the course of their duties, and the legislative bodies contained many speechifiers, naturally almost always favorable to the government, who hoped to have their speeches published. Those with that desire in mind were doomed to disappointment in the fall of 1813, because Napoleon said then that it was no longer opportune

[50] Fontanes (Fayot, pub.), *Discours*, 3–17.
[51] Napoleon, *Correspondance*, XXV, 360.

to publish speeches. They caused harm but did no good.[52] Or did
he fear the unknown factor, that potential danger lying dormant
in the center of every censored speech?

[52] *Moniteur*, 16 Pluviôse, Year IX; October 8, 1813; and *passim*. The address
of Roederer to Joseph on behalf of the French Senate did not appear in the
Moniteur because its praise of Joseph was too lavish to please Napoleon.
Similarly, the *Moniteur* did not publish the address of the Duc de l'Infantado,
because it did not express formal recognition of Joseph, and contented itself
with printing the speech of Azanza, which did express such recognition. Driault,
Napoléon en Italie, 401; Bausset, *Mémoires*, I, 266; Napoleon (Lecestre, comp.),
Lettres, II, 291.

CHAPTER VI

EDUCATION AND RELIGION

A. EDUCATION

"Young people can hardly avoid accepting whatever version of the facts is presented to them."—NAPOLEON
"Public instruction should be the first object of government."—NAPOLEON

THE FIRST OF THE ABOVE REMARKS EXPLAINS FULLY WHY NAPOleon should have made a statement such as the second. To him instruction meant molding the pupils who were exposed to it and thus training the type of public servant he wanted. Therefore, since his educational system was, like that of the revolutionary period, to a large degree propagandistic in purpose,[1] Napoleon controlled the schools very closely.[2]

When the Consulate was established, education was in the hands of a bureau under Jacquemont in the ministry of the interior, and freedom of teaching was limited by departmental juries of instruction appointed by the prefect after he had received the approval of the Minister of the Interior. During the Year IX, education, fine arts, and theaters were consolidated into a division under Arnault, who by a decree of 21 Ventôse, Year X, was subordinated to a councilor of state in charge of public instruction.[3]

[1] In fact, Aulard goes so far as to say that Napoleon was interested in schools only as a source of power. François V. A. Aulard, *Napoléon Ier et le monopole universitaire* (Paris, 1911). Perhaps a government must stress the propaganda side of education when there is a sudden change in the type of government. Certainly Nazi Germany and Soviet Russia in our own day, to mention only two states, have not overlooked the importance of this aspect of schooling.

[2] Many of the details have been omitted. Aulard (*Monopole universitaire*) and Louis Grimaud (*Histoire de la liberté d'enseignement en France depuis la chute de l'ancien régime jusqu'à nos jours* [Paris, 1898]) treat them adequately.

[3] Léon de Lanzac de Laborie, "La haute administration de l'enseignement sous

A law of 11 Floréal, Year X, effected a complete reorganization of primary and secondary education. Thenceforth the mayors and municipal councils were to select the teachers for the elementary schools on which the subprefects were to report monthly to the prefects. All private schools which offered courses above the primary-school level and all secondary schools, which could be established only with government approval,[4] were to be under the supervision and special inspection of the prefects. An administrative council appointed by the First Consul and consisting of a principal, a censor, and a fiscal manager [*procureur-gérant*] was to be in charge of each *lycée*. There was to be at least one *lycée* per *arrondissement*, and each *arrondissement* was to have an administrative bureau consisting of the prefect, the president of the court of appeal, the governmental commissioner to the court of appeal, one of the governmental commissioners to the criminal court, the mayor, and the principal. Lastly, the law provided for three inspectors general, selected by the First Consul, to visit each *lycée* at least once a year.[5]

Napoleon felt very strongly the desirability of teachers trained to believe as he prescribed, for they were the ones who were to indoctrinate the pupils with a true national spirit. He expressed the belief that "there never will be a fixed political state of things in this country until we have a corps of teachers instructed in established principles. So long as the people are not taught from their earliest years whether they ought to be Republicans or Royalists, Christians or Infidels, the State cannot be properly called a nation, for it must then rest on a foundation which is vague and uncertain and be forever exposed to disorders and fluctuations." [6] Napoleon's demands regarding teachers were em-

---

le consulat et l'empire," *Revue des études napoléoniennes*, X(1916), 186–87; Aulard, *Monopole universitaire*, 3.

⁴ Thus special decrees were issued for all *lycées* established later.

⁵ *Bulletin des lois* (Series 3), V, 217 ff.; René Simon, "Un lycée sous l'empire; le lycée de Poitiers," *Revue des études napoléoniennes*, VII(1915), 324. According to Roederer (*Autour de Bonaparte* [Vitrac, ed.], 112) this law was the work of Bonaparte. Its silence on primary schools showed that the government intended to allow them while obtaining a monopoly on *lycées* and special schools. Grimaud, *Liberté d'enseignement*, 77. One inspector general was Marie Joseph Chénier. *Le Citoyen français*, 17 Ventôse, Year XI; Gilbert Stenger, *La société française pendant le consulat* (Paris, 1903–1908), VI, 399.

⁶ Napoleon (Breed, ed.), *Opinions and Reflections*, 303.

bodied in the law of May 10, 1806, which decreed that a special teaching body was to be formed in order to offer a uniform and complete education. This teaching body, the University, was actually established by a decree of March 17, 1808. Among other things this latter decree provided that no educational institution was to be established outside the University or without the approval of its chief and that persons opening schools must belong to the University and hold a degree from one of its faculties.[7] Seminaries, dependent on the bishops, who in turn were to conform to the rulings authorized by the Emperor, constituted the only exception. If any private school taught principles contrary to those professed by the University, it was to be closed by the Grand Master of the University.[8] No printed piece concerning private schools was to be made public without the approval of the rectors and the academic councils.[9]

Private schools were later restricted further by an impost levied in accordance with a decree of September 17, 1808, which provided that private schools would pay the University 5 per cent of what each student was supposed to pay (even if he was admitted free), that there would be a charge for authorization to establish a school, and that annually a sum equal to one fourth of this charge would be paid to the University. In December of the same year all unalienated real and personal property belonging to the old educational institutions was given to the University, which was to retain a *lycée* or college in each place where there had been a university.[10]

The government regulated the ecclesiastical as well as the lay schools. A decree of April 9, 1809, seemed to suppress the little seminaries, but departments, cities, and bishops were authorized

---

[7] Fontanes, the Grand Master of the University, interpreted these clauses to mean that no person could teach without his permission. *Curés*, April 5, 1810. From top to bottom the University hierarchy, a branch of the ministry of the interior, was composed of the Grand Master and the University Council; inspectors general; special inspectors; the directors and teachers in the special schools, the principals, censors, and teachers in the *lycées*, and the teachers and directors in the colleges; the tutors; and the fellows.

[8] Grimaud, *Liberté d'enseignement*, 92.

[9] Each academy had a council of ten chosen by the Grand Master of the University and presided over by the rector. "Enseignement," *La Grande encyclopédie*, 31 vols. (Paris, n.d.), XV, 112.

[10] *Bulletin des lois* (Series 4), IX, 259–60; Grimaud, *Liberté d'enseignement*, 94.

to establish schools to train children for the clergy.[11] Finally, a decree of November 15, 1811, was designed to make a reality of the University monopoly by limiting the number of secondary schools to one ecclesiastical school per department and by requiring that all teachers be members of the University, which would act through the prefects or subprefects to supervise all educational establishments. Napoleon appointed the seminary directors and teachers from nominees of the bishops. Since the Protestant seminaries recognized Napoleon as head of the church, there was no need to supervise the doctrines taught in them.[12] Thus all the schools—private and public, seminarial and secular—were subject to control by Napoleon's government. This same educational system was re-established in the Hundred Days, though with fewer establishments and pupils.[13]

Higher education did not escape direct control by the government. The University of Genoa, for example, was examined weekly by a commission of three chosen by the administrative bureau from the bureau's own membership.[14]

By means of its financial power the government also exercised indirect control, even of the Catholic seminaries. Each member of the University received a pension of at least 500 francs. The government encouraged education by giving sites for schools, by paying the expenses of 6,400 students in the *lycées,* and by rewarding the schoolmasters who had the most pupils admitted into the *lycées.*[15]

[11] Aulard, *Monopole universitaire,* 300.

[12] *Ibid.,* 306–308; Taine (Durand, tr.), *Modern Regime,* II, 148–49. Previous to this time public and private schools had each had approximately 30,000 pupils. Yet, at least during the Consulate, many boarding schools directed by priests or directly under their influence absolutely escaped supervision by the civil authorities. Louis Benaerts, *Le régime consulaire en Bretagne. Le département d'Ille-et-Vilaine durant le consulat (1799–1804)* (Paris, 1914), 323.

[13] Carnot, *Correspondance avec Napoléon,* 128. His report a month later, however, stated that the number of pupils had not dropped. *Gazette,* June 14, 1815.

[14] *Bulletin des lois* (Series 4), IV, 17.

[15] *Curés,* May 30, 1810; *Bulletin des lois* (Series 3), V, 218; *Moniteur,* 30 Germinal, Year X. Only 3,000 of the 6,400 scholarships were conferred. Taine (Durand, tr.), *Modern Regime,* I, 195. Although the government did not give any financial aid to the primary schools, which were supervised by the rector and an ecclesiastic, the prefect had to authorize their establishment. Taine (Durand, tr.), *Modern Regime,* II, 171–72. Financial penalties were imposed on those attending private schools rather than *lycées. Ibid.,* II, 195.

Immediate control was again exercised in the appointment of teachers, who agreed to stay in the teaching body at least five years after graduation from the normal school. Those in the primary schools were appointed in accordance with the law of 11 Floréal, Year X. For the *lycées*, the inspectors general and three members of the National Institute chosen by Napoleon were to recommend two persons for each teaching post, while Napoleon was to recommend one. Napoleon alone could select teachers to fill vacancies in other, nonspecialized schools. These teachers were chosen from nominees of the inspectors general, the bureau, the council, and the established teachers.[16] The inspectors general proposed all promotions.

Other spheres of control were studies, activities, and texts. The plan of studies of a communal college was to be in accordance with the regulations proposed by the administrative bureau and was to be approved by the minister of the interior, who would approve or disapprove on advice of the prefect. History was viewed by the authorities, who expressly stated that people could learn it by themselves, as potentially dangerous, and therefore was not taught as a separate topic. Even in the Collège de France the history chairs were limited to the military history of France, the history of legislation in France, and critical literary history. Napoleon also favored mathematics and science over foreign languages, though he insisted that inhabitants of provinces incorporated into France learn French. Rulers rather than men of letters or science being the focuses of the pupils' interest, *Abrégé des actions de Napoléon-le-Grand* became an integral part of the course of studies in 1811. Pupils in the normal schools were required to read Caesar's *Commentaries*, Pierre Corneille, and Jacques Bossuet, so that they might be taught to enter into the established order, to fortify it, and to embellish it. Instruction in

---

[16] *Bulletin des lois* (Series 3), V, 217–20. The system for special schools was somewhat different, but it still left the final choice to Napoleon. Louis Liard, *L'enseignement supérieur en France 1789–1889*, 2 vols. (Paris, 1888–94), II, 55, confuses the method for schools in general with the one for special schools, which provided for Napoleon's selecting one of three nominees proposed by the teachers, the corresponding class in the Institute, and the inspectors general. Until 1808 the principals had been allowed some latitude in selecting teachers. Simon, "Lycée de Poitiers," *loc. cit.*, 334.

the higher schools was designed to afford the minimum essentials necessary to practitioners in the various professions or trades, without any philosophical background for them.[17]

Competitions of various sorts tended to promote patriotism. The elevation of Bonaparte to the imperial throne was the topic of the prize competition at the *lycée* of Dijon in the Year XII, and the pupils at Louis-le-Grand in 1807 wrote about the Battle of Jena. A decree of 30 Fructidor, Year X, provided that all prizes be awarded at the same time, and that the occasion be made a regular national celebration.[18]

Whether it followed the advice of Fiévée [19] it is impossible to say, but the government did both inspire texts and decide which ones were to be used exclusively, while the police prevented any competitors. Napoleon stated in the Council of State in May, 1804: "The minister of public worship must determine what classical works shall be placed in the hands of young men; and I desire that he will print a small volume for each class, containing passages selected from ancient as well as modern writers, and which shall have a tendency to inspire the rising generation with opinions in conformity with the principles of the new empire." [20] In 1802 Montelle wrote *Cours d'histoire, seconde année* by order of the Minister of the Interior. In 1809 *Histoire de France* by Paul François Velly, Claude Villaret, and Jean Jacques Garnier, with a continuation demanded by Napoleon and written by Antoine Fantin-Désodoards, was adopted. Napoleon sent Minister of the Interior

[17] *Bulletin des lois* (Series 4), IV, 80; Napoleon, *Correspondance*, XV, 8; *Moniteur*, 11 Floréal, Year X; Grant, *Napoleon and the Artists*, 207; *Empire*, November 20, 1811; Napoleon, *Vues politiques*, comp. by Adrien Dansette (Paris, 1939), 238; Taine (Durand, tr.), *Modern Regime*, II, 185. Rather interestingly, Napoleon forbade the teaching of French at Elba. Léon G. Pelissier (ed.), *Le registre de l'île d'Elbe. Lettres et ordres inédits de Napoléon Ier* (Paris, 1897), 46.

[18] Taine (Durand, tr.), *Modern Regime*, II, 168; *Napoleon I: Contemporary Pamphlets*, in Boulay de la Meurthe collection; Léon de Lanzac de Laborie, "L'enseignement secondaire à Paris au début du consulat: les écoles centrales (an VIII–an X)," *Revue des études napoléoniennes*, XII (1917), 269. What was written on such occasions might form a partial index of the effect the teaching had on the pupils.

[19] For eleven years he sent a secret bulletin of advice to Napoleon, making the suggestion about textbooks in November, 1802.

[20] Baron Joseph Pelet, *Napoleon in Council*, tr. by Basil Hall (London, 1937), 198.

Cretet the following instructions regarding the continuation in a letter of April 12, 1808:

> . . . The principles enunciated in the note of the minister [21]
> . . . were true twenty years ago, they will be true in sixty, but
> they are not today. Velly is the only author who has written in
> some detail on the history of France. The *Abrégé chronologique*
> of President Hénault is a good classical book. It would be very use-
> ful to continue them both. Velly ends with Henry IV, and the
> other historians do not go beyond Louis XIV. It is of the greatest
> importance to assure yourself of the spirit in which the continua-
> tors will write. The manner in which facts are presented to youth
> determines the only method by which it can judge them. To de-
> ceive it while retracing memories is to prepare future errors for it.
> His Majesty has charged the Minister of Police with supervising
> the continuation of Millot; he wants the two ministers to get to-
> gether and have Velly and President Hénault continued. This
> work should be entrusted not only to authors of a true talent, but
> also to devoted men who will present facts in their true light and
> who will prepare a sound instruction by taking up where these
> historians left off and bringing their histories to the Year VIII.
>
> His Majesty does not care about the expense. He even wants the
> minister to make it understood that no work can merit the
> Emperor's protection more.
>
> With each line the effects of the court of Rome, of the notes of
> confession, of the revocation of the Edict of Nantes, of the ridicu-
> lous marriage of Louis XIV with Madame de Maintenon, etc. must
> be made felt. The weakness which precipitated the Valois from
> the throne, and that of the Bourbons, who let the reins of govern-
> ment escape from their hands, must arouse the same sentiments.
> One must be just to Henry IV, Louis XIII, Louis XIV, and Louis
> XV without being adulatory. The massacres of September and the
> horrors of the Revolution must be painted with the same touch as
> the Inquisition and the massacres of the Sixteen. All reaction must
> be carefully avoided in speaking of the Revolution. . . .
>
> Attention must be directed to the perpetual disorder of the
> finances, the chaos of the provincial assemblies, the claims of the
> parlements, the lack of rule and energy in the administration, this
> motley France, without unity of laws and of administration, rather

---

[21] The note, dated April 6 and sent to Napoleon, stated that the government would neither intervene in the continuation nor pay for it.

a union of twenty kingdoms than a single state. Thus the reader will breathe freely on arriving at the time when the benefits due to the unity of laws, of administration, and of territory are enjoyed. The constant weakness of the government under even Louis XIV, under Louis XV and XVI must inspire the need of supporting the newly accomplished work and the newly acquired preponderance. The re-establishment of religion and of the altars must inspire fear of the influence of a foreign priest or of an ambitious confessor who could succeed in destroying the peace of France.

. . . But such a work as Velly or the *Abrégé chronologique* . . . must have only one continuator. When this work, well-done and written in a good spirit, has appeared, no one will have the will and the patience to make another, especially when, far from being encouraged by the police, he will be discouraged by it. . . .

The only questions to examine regarding any individual who presents himself are whether he has the necessary talent and a good mind, and whether the sentiments which would guide his research and lead his pen can be counted on.[22]

This type of instruction from Napoleon to his minister shows rather clearly that even those books which the government did not inspire were judged according to their attitude on absolute power. The censors examined all books, drawings, and engravings entering the *lycées*, to prohibit those which might be antagonistic to social customs. In 1804 *Huitième et dernière livraison de l'Atlas historique*, by A. V. Sage, was adopted for the *lycées* by the Commission on Public Instruction. A decree of 10 Fructidor, Year X, charged a commission of Fontanes, Champagny, and Louis Domairon with selecting the classical works to be used for Latin and literature courses in every communal and secondary school. Other books adopted were *Tables chronologiques de l'histoire ancienne et moderne etc.* and *Épitomé de l'histoire de France* by A. Serieys, censor of the *lycée* of Cahors; *Elémens raisonnés de lecture à l'usage des écoles primaires*, by Jean Baptiste Maudru; *Instruction élémentaire, à l'usage des écoles primaires du départe-*

---

[22] *Moniteur*, 2 Germinal, Year X; 11 Prairial, Year XII; *Journal typographique*, XII(1809), 545; Napoleon (Thompson, ed.), *Letters*, 216; Napoleon, *Correspondance*, XVI, 489–91; Napoleon (Dansette, comp.), *Vues politiques*, 232. The phrase "one law, one land, one government" might be viewed as the early nineteenth-century equivalent of Hitler's *"Ein Volk, Ein Reich, Ein Führer."*

ment de L'Oise; and *Tableau comparatif de l'histoire moderne* by Ch. S. Leprevost d'Iray.[23]

The educational system described in the first part of this chapter was for boys. As one would expect, the primary function of the educational institutions was to produce military men. In addition, the government thought it advisable to train men to be public functionaries, artists, savants, writers, and priests—all to be inspired with a love of country and of the Napoleonic dynasty. Because Napoleon stressed the militaristic side of education, the best pupils of the *lycées* were sent at government expense to a special military school. They were prepared for such a step by the strict military discipline maintained in the *lycées*. There the pupils were required to wear uniforms; and the rolling of drums, living in barracks, simulating the position of "carry arms," and marching at command constantly reminded them that they were preparing to serve France and their Emperor. The government further required that the pupils regularly pledge allegiance to Napoleon, and the University regulated even their games. The teachers, moreover, constantly read the army bulletins.[24]

It is rather interesting to note that Napoleon devoted considerable thought to the education of women. At Napoleon's order Madame de Rémusat wrote *Essai sur l'éducation des femmes,* but it was published only after his death. Because he thought women's place was in the home, their education was largely manual; and one year there was a prize offered for the best essay on the topic, "What type of education for women will best promote the happiness of men in society?" The literature they read was to be such as would not awaken their imagination, and particularly for them

[23] Broc, *Vie en France,* 144; *Moniteur,* 8 Brumaire, Year XI; 24 Frimaire and 19 Nivôse, Year XIII; *Journal typographique,* VII (Year XII), 106. In addition to controlling the texts, the ministry of the interior authorized and censored the education annual. Napoleon (Dansette, comp.), *Vues politiques,* 232–33. Note that this ordering and approval of history books does not contradict the statement made earlier in this chapter that history was not a separate course.

[24] *Archives parlementaires,* IX, 403; Napoleon (Chuquet, ed.), *Inédits napoléoniens,* II, 47; Broc, *Vie en France,* 140; Napoleon (Thompson, ed.), *Letters,* 216; F. M. Kircheisen (comp.), *Memoires of Napoleon I Compiled from His Own Writings,* tr. by Frederick Collins (New York, 1929), 246; Pelet (Hall, tr.), *Napoleon in Council,* 198; Louis R. Gottschalk, *The Era of the French Revolution* (New York, 1929), 350; *Moniteur,* 30 Germinal, Year X; Taine (Durand, tr.), *Modern Regime,* II, 168; Stenger (*Société française,* VI, 412) asserts that the stress on the military aspect made the *lycées* unpopular.

—though also for the boys—he stressed the need of religion in the school curriculums.[25]

The amount of attention paid to education in the regions under French control varied greatly. In Santo Domingo, in accordance with Bonaparte's instructions, there was no educational system. Marmont merely had time in the Illyrian Provinces to open a few schools, send a few pupils to France, and encourage the Croat tongue. In the Grand Duchy of Warsaw, on the other hand, the French extended and completely revised the system of government control of education. For Naples Murat decreed a system as similar to the French organization as circumstances permitted. In the Italian Republic (later the Kingdom of Italy) the creation of a public educational system, which Napoleon expected to contribute to the moral unification of the country, was almost entirely the result of his initiative. A law of September 8, 1802, established an educational hierarchy, but the article on elementary schools remained a dead letter, and not much was done in regard to the *lycées*. In fact, the state paid only the teachers of the universities, academies, and technical schools, who were selected from lists presented by their colleagues.[26]

Because the education offered in 1799 was poor and the exposition of the situation of the republic at the beginning of the Year X admitted that education was languishing, the Institute was ordered to propose once every five years means of improving public instruction. The greatest obstacle in the way of such better-

[25] Napoleon (Dansette, comp.), *Vues politiques*, 240–41; Napoleon, *Correspondance*, XV, 110; Paul Lacroix, *Directoire, consulat et l'empire. Moeurs et usages, lettres, sciences, et arts* (Paris, 1884), 39. One of the criticisms of the schools in the anonymous religious pamphlets for 1801 was the lack of provision for religious education in the private schools. The government admitted that the principles of religion were practiced feebly or not at all in many schools. But it later claimed that the University had remedied many of the abuses by making the precepts of the Catholic religion, the maxims and liberties of the Gallican Church, the maxims on which the Organic Articles rested, and fidelity to the Emperor, the Imperial monarchy, and the Napoleonic dynasty, the common basis of teaching. Aulard, *Monopole universitaire*, 187; *Moniteur*, July 1, 1811; *Church and Religious Affairs during the Consulate and Empire: Contemporary Pamphlets 1801: Anonyms*.

[26] Leclerc (Roussier, pub.), *Lettres*, 274; *Moniteur* February 15, 1812; Édouard Driault, *Le grand empire (1809–1812)* (*Napoléon et l'Europe*) (Paris, 1924), 649; A. Pingaud, *Bonaparte président de la république italienne*, II, 333–38; Murat (Prince Murat, pub.), *Lettres*, VIII, 157; Édouard Driault, "Napoléon Ier et l'Italie," *Revue historique*, LXXXIX (1905), 54.

ment was a lack of resources. The necessary financial backing was absent, and Napoleon was unable to obtain the personnel requisite for achieving his goal of a monopoly on education by the University. The lack of teachers especially accounts for his failure to issue at an earlier date the decree of November 15, 1811, which required that all teachers be of the University. Furthermore, the prefects were none too eager to carry out instructions, and Fontanes, the Grand Master of the University, became the accomplice of private teaching.[27]

B. RELIGION

"I was Mohammedan in Egypt; I shall be Catholic here, for the good of the people. I do not believe in religions."
—NAPOLEON

Despite his stated disbelief in religion, Napoleon recognized that it and education could complement one another in the services that they could render him. It could aid in the proper development of French youth, help inculcate correct ideas of citizenship in adults, and assist in public celebrations which played up Napoleon and his regime.

In these festivals the role of the church was primarily that of singing a *Te Deum*. Although this is an established part of the Catholic ritual, it was often embellished with music that was more than incidental and with a speech appropriate to the occasion.[28] *Te Deums* were quite generally featured in victory celebrations [29] as well as in the fetes. There were also special ones for Napoleon's escape from death on 3 Nivôse, Year IX, the discovery of the Cadoudal plot in 1804, the re-establishment of re-

[27] Napoleon, *Correspondance*, VIII, 402; *Débats*, 15 Ventôse, Year X; Aulard, *Monopole universitaire*, 167, 302–306; Joubert, *Correspondance*, 211.

[28] *Church and Religious Affairs in Rouen 1799–1806: Contemporary Pamphlets;* John Julian, *A Dictionary of Hymnology* (London, 1892), 1130; *Débats*, 25 Germinal, Year X.

[29] There was not one for Eylau because Napoleon thought that would leave insufficient time between them. Lanzac de Laborie, *Paris sous Napoléon*, III, 53. Napoleon was also careful to tell Marie Louise (*Correspondance*, XXV, 367) that *Te Deums* are effective only if they are rare. That for Austerlitz was to be held annually.

ligion in 1802, Napoleon's wedding, and the birth of the King of Rome. As a rule, the *Te Deum* celebrating any event was performed on the Sunday following the reception of the news of that event. This practice made it unlikely that news of a defeat would arrive in the meantime to lessen the effect of the *Te Deum*.[30]

Usually the civil authorities took the initiative in proposing a *Te Deum*. Napoleon himself might act; he might commission some official to order it; or someone else, such as the head of a region subordinate to France, or Marie Louise when she was regent, might put forth the plan. Among those so delegated were Joseph, Marie Louise, Cambacérès, Jean Portalis, Eugene, Talleyrand, and Lebrun. In the departments the prefects acted after carefully awaiting an order from someone higher in the religious or governmental hierarchy.[31] As early as 1800 people were sufficiently suspicious of the role of the government in the *Te Deums* for the *Gazette de France* of June 24 to include in the announcement of a *Te Deum* that "the government does nothing and prevents nothing; it wants all cults to be free, and they are."

There were instances, however, of the clergy's acting without any positive order from the government. A case in point was the singing of a *Te Deum* to celebrate the re-establishment of religion. In 1806 the Archbishop of Naples requested General Reynier to grant permission for a *Te Deum* for the happy arrival of Joseph's army. Yet such instances were sufficiently rare for the police to consider them worthy of mention.[32]

In addition to ordering the ceremony and setting the time, the government decided what the services should be like. The speeches were to be delivered by the ecclesiastic in charge. Generally they praised Napoleon, eulogizing his tolerance, self-sacrifice, and

[30] Napoleon, *Correspondance*, XI, 469; XXV, 367; Napoleon (Lecestre, comp.), *Lettres*, II, 249.

[31] *Church and Religious Affairs during the Consulate and Empire: Contemporary Pamphlets: Agen-Le Mans;* G. Fraikin (comp.), "Sept lettres inédites de Napoléon Ier," *Miscellanea Napoleonica*, ed. by Alberto Lumbroso (Rome, 1899), 13; Jerome (Du Casse, ed.), *Mémoires*, I, 368; Joseph (Du Casse, ed.), *Mémoires*, I, 306, 329; L. Pingaud, *Jean de Bry*, 270; Aulard (ed.), *Paris sous le consulat*, I, 450.

[32] *Church and Religious Affairs in Paris during the Empire; Church and Religious Affairs during the Consulate and Empire: Contemporary Pamphlets, Meaux-Vannes; Church Affairs: Agen-Le Mans;* E. d'Hauterive (ed.), *La police secrète*, III, 41, October 30, 1806.

moderation in the midst of victory, and emphasizing that he was essential to the welfare of religion, the Empire, and Europe. Quite naturally, too, they claimed that God was on the side of the French.[33]

Recognizing the influence the church exerted on the masses,[34] Napoleon utilized it to perform the additional service of encouraging dutiful citizenship. Able to control most of the clergy as a result of the Concordat of 1801, he had the bishops direct their subordinates to obey the commands of the government because the Bible exhorted Christians to "render unto Caesar that which is Caesar's." [35] On 19 Prairial, Year X, Portalis, the Minister of Public Worship, outlined to the archbishops the duties which the clergy was expected to perform. In return for re-establishing religion the government expected all ministers to use every effort to unite the citizens; to inspire a love for laws, respect for social institutions, and obedience to the magistrates; and to direct grateful piety to the prosperity of the Republic and the welfare of the people.[36] The two campaigns in which the clergy proved most valuable were those promoting vaccination and urging that conscription be carried out smoothly.[37]

Episcopal charges to the pastors, who read them from the pulpit, were the most common means of reaching the people. Since many of these charges, after approval of the bishop had been obtained, were put in the papers or printed in leaflets which might be posted, they received wider publicity than would appear on the surface to be the case. Circular letters by the bishop to his

---

[33] Napoleon, *Correspondance*, XV, 340; XX, 29; Eugene (Du Casse, ed.), *Mémoires*, I, 430; III, 189; VI, 84; Napoleon (Lecestre, comp.), *Lettres*, II, 236; *Church and Religious Affairs in Paris 1802–13: Contemporary Pamphlets;* Joseph (Du Casse, ed.), *Mémoires*, II, 156.

[34] The Minister of the Interior wrote to the Bishop of Orléans, "Your influence is incalculable."

[35] *Church Affairs: Meaux-Vannes.*

[36] *Concordat: Pièces.* The Council of 1801 of the constitutional clergy composed a letter to all the Catholics of France on the submission due to the temporal powers. Among other things it stated: "The submission to existing powers is to be frank and sincere. . . . It is not enough to avoid evil—you must do good. The country is our common mother. . . . No matter what distress you may be in, obey its laws. . . . One duty is fidelity, to procure the welfare of the country."

[37] *Church Affairs: Agen-Le Mans; Church Affairs: Meaux-Vannes.*

clergy sometimes replaced these charges, but they fulfilled the same purpose.[38]

Although more leeway was granted with regard to who might propose pastoral charges or letters, in general the government machinery functioned as it did for the *Te Deums*. The most important difference was that for the latter the civil authorities took the initiative, whereas for the pastoral letters the Minister of Public Worship usually assumed responsibility, although the Minister of Interior did so occasionally. A case in point is shown in one of Napoleon's letters: On April 21, 1807, he wrote to Portalis asking him to have a bishop in the West draw up a charge denouncing the persecution of Catholics in Ireland and ordering prayers that they might enjoy religious freedom. The letter further instructed Portalis: "Write a fine article for the *Moniteur* to serve as a text for the charge. No bishop ever dared not heed these recommendations."

As was to be expected, these charges contained extravagant praise of Napoleon—of the same type as that mentioned earlier. For example, the pastoral letter of the Bishop of Bayeux written on April 28, 1807, to encourage the 1808 draft class to report six months early gave his clergy the following instructions: "In your public instructions and private relations you are to seize every opportunity to make known Napoleon's paternal intentions (as our previous orders have repeated); he makes war only to get peace and wants peace so that he can assure the happiness of his subjects and the calm of Europe; encourage agriculture, sciences, and art; enliven commerce; and return to religion its empire." [39]

---

[38] Some of them are addressed to both the clergy and the people. At the end of each charge Napoleon's circular letter to the bishops was to be printed as it was really directed to the people. Napoleon, *Correspondance*, VII, 481; XIX, 414; *Church and Religious Affairs in Paris during the Empire*. The same means were used to point out to citizens their duty to vote, and in Spain to urge the populace not to hate or fear the French, as the war was not one of religion. *Actes du second concile national de France*, 3 vols. (Paris, Years IX and X), II, 201; *Curés*, February 3, 1809. The order of the Cardinal-Archbishop of Paris regarding Easter sold for seventy-five centimes. In order that nothing might recall the recent divisions among French Catholics, the government in 1802 ordered all bishops to use the formula, "By the divine mercy and by the grace of the Apostolic Holy See."

[39] *Church Affairs: Agen-Le Mans.*

If the bishops were remiss in including laudatory remarks, some government official would probably remind them to eulogize Napoleon more: witness the instructions received in 1810 by Abbé de Broglie, Bishop of Ghent, from the Prefect of Police, Réal.[40]

In addition, many pieces written by lay authorities were read from the pulpit. During 1805 bulletins were publicized in that way in order to reach the departments where they were not well-enough known; in December of that year Napoleon had Fouché end this practice because it gave the priests too much importance. "I see some difficulties on the subject of reading bulletins in the churches; I find this reading completely unsuitable, it is fit only to give the priests more importance than they should have; for that gives them the right to comment, and, when there is bad news, they will not fail to comment on it. . . . Mr. Portalis has acted very wrongly in writing his letter without knowing whether it was my intention." [41] This order followed close upon the advice of the Bishop of Tours, that, instead of a dry reading of the whole bulletin, the priests and curates should read the parts interesting to the parishioners, stressing Napoleon's "traits of humanity, genius, intrepidity, and prudence" and his love for peace and his enemies. However, it is impossible to deduce from the prevailing evidence whether the Bishop's advice caused Napoleon to stop the practice of reading entire bulletins from the pulpits. In any event, in 1809 the government, in ordering the priests to comment on the bulletins and to read only the passages of interest, did an about-face and followed the earlier lead of the Bishop of Tours. Napoleon's address to the Senate and the *senatus consultum* establishing the life Consulate were also read upon the order of Portalis, who had in turn received his instructions from Napoleon.[42]

Article VIII of the Concordat provided that the priests were

[40] Haussonville, *Église et empire*, II, 239.

[41] Napoleon, *Correspondance*, XI, 500. But in 1809 the Italian Minister of War ordered the curés of the leading communes to comment on the twenty-sixth bulletin of the Army of Spain.

[42] *Church and Religious Affairs in Clermont during the Consulate and Empire;* "Pastoral Letter," December 8, 1805, *Church and Religious Affairs in Tours during the Consulate and Empire.* Portalis was especially anxious to give various items publicity, and the fact that the government had taken the initiative was generally indicated. Boulay de la Meurthe (ed.), *Documents sur la négociation du concordat,* IV, *passim.*

to say a prayer for the nation and its rulers at the end of mass; but in 1809, Napoleon instructed Bigot de Préameneu that without orders from the government, the public should not be told to pray for anybody. In accordance with these regulations, the bishops ordered their clergy, who might not act without their authorization, to hold public prayers, those for the success of the armies and for the birth of the King of Rome being among the more important ones.[43]

At some times there are indications, both in France and in non-French territories under Napoleon's control, that the government had ordered these prayers, at other times not. In France itself, the general practice, if it followed that in the diocese of Clermont, was for municipal authorities to ask the priests and curates for special and public prayers; these members of the lower clergy would then ask the bishop, who would grant permission in an order.[44]

Thus far, only activities of the Catholic church have been considered. But the Protestants and Jews also served. Placing less emphasis upon ceremonialism than did the Catholics, but faithfully celebrating Napoleon's birthday on the Catholic fete day of August 15, the Protestants favored the government in sermons, carefully pointing out that only with the Reformation did churches begin to look upon themselves as supports for the government. Especially useful sermons the authorities—e.g., Dubois when secretary of the Central Bureau—might order published. Also published in the *Moniteur* were speeches by the consistories of the reformed churches throughout France. These speeches were mainly concerned with the subject of religious peace. The Protestants also used circular letters and conducted services of thanksgiving, and the Organic Articles for the Protestant Sects provided that pastors were to pray and have their people pray for the nation and its rulers.[45] Not much material is available on the

[43] *Concordat: Reprints;* Napoleon (Thompson, ed.), *Letters,* 234; Eugene (Du Casse, ed.), *Mémoires,* VII, 46; Aulard (ed.), *Paris sous le consulat,* IV, 178.

[44] Napoleon, *Correspondance,* XV, 280; "Order of Organization of the Diocese," *Church Affairs in Clermont,* 17. The municipal authorities would naturally not take such a step without having received orders from higher government officials.

[45] Frank Puaux, "La prédication protestante," *La revue chrétienne,* 33d year, Vol. XI of new series, 333; *Protestantism in France during the Consulate and*

activities of the Jews, but they did at least offer thanks and hold celebrations on suitable occasions, such as Napoleon's birthday.[46]

The actions of both Catholics and Protestants were subject to strict government control. Napoleon, for example, had Chaptal order the prefects of Geneva and of five departments in France where Protestants were numerous to send one minister each to Paris in order to reach an agreement with the government on how to keep "good order" in religion. Indirect control of the Catholics could be exercised through the right granted Napoleon by the Concordat to appoint bishops and through government control of church finances.[47]

More direct control was made manifest when in 1808 the government ordered the bishops to have Napoleon's message to the Senate printed. Government authorities also gave bishops the outlines for their charges and, after the bishops had added the customary ecclesiastical verbiage, censored the charges before allowing them to be submitted to the priests. As a final step the police had agents (who might be the prefects) in the congregations to report on whether the clergy executed the orders it received and whether the performance was a success.[48] Hence Napoleon could express his displeasure with the sermon preached on his birthday in 1805 by Robert, a priest at Bourges.

Napoleon expected the church to supplement the University in the proper training of youth. Perhaps the most important single step in this direction was the drawing up of a new catechism—ostensibly on the initiative of Portalis, though he was probably following orders—to be used exclusively. This catechism contained the following section on the duties of the Chris-

Empire: Contemporary Pamphlets 1802–13; Acts of Local Synods 1800–1801; Concordat: Reprints; Lanzac de Laborie, Paris sous Napoléon, IV, 365.

[46] Aulard (ed.), Paris sous le premier empire, III, 698, 821; Empire, May 22, 1813.

[47] Chaptal (E. A. Chaptal, ed.), Souvenirs, 58; Napoleon, Correspondance, VII, 222; XXI, 395; Débats, 21 Floréal, Year XI. Napoleon likewise refused to permit the ordination of any priests without his permission in the departments of Rome and Trasimeno. Haussonville, Église et empire, III, 353; Napoleon (Chuquet, ed.), Inédits napoléoniens, II, 255.

[48] Napoleon (Thompson, ed.), Letters, 130; Aulard (ed.), Paris sous le consulat, I, 200; Church and Religious Affairs in Bordeaux during the Consulate and Empire; Du Casse, Négotiations diplomatiques, I, 18; Broc, Vie en France, 208.

tian toward the state and, more particularly, toward Napoleon. This section, especially if properly stressed, as it probably was by the constitutional clergy,[49] could be relied on to impress children:

Q: What are the duties of Christians with respect to the princes who govern them, and what are in particular our duties toward Napoleon I, our Emperor?

A: . . . love, respect, obedience, fidelity, military service, tributes ordered for the preservation and defense of the Empire and of his throne; we also owe him fervent prayers for his safety and for the spiritual and temporal prosperity of the State.

Q: Why do we have these duties towards our Emperor?

A: First, because by bountifully bestowing talents on our Emperor both in peace and war, God has established him as our sovereign and has made him the minister of His power and His image on earth. To honor and serve our Emperor is therefore to honor and serve God himself. Secondly, because our Lord Jesus Christ . . . has taught us what we owe to our sovereign . . . ; He has ordered us to give to Caesar what belongs to Caesar.

Q: Are there not special motives which must attach us more strongly to Napoleon, our Emperor?

A: Yes: for he is the one whom God has given us in difficult times to re-establish the public worship of the holy religion of our fathers and to be the protector of it. He has re-established and maintained public order by his profound and active wisdom; he defends the State with his powerful arm; he has become the Lord's anointed through the consecration which he received from the pontifical Sovereign, head of the universal Church.

Q: What must one think of those who may fail in their duty towards our Emperor?

A: According to the apostle Paul, they would resist the established order of God himself and would be worthy of eternal damnation.

Q: Do the duties towards our Emperor bind us equally towards his successors?

A: Yes, undoubtedly; for we read in the Holy Scripture that God.

---

[49] Grant, *Napoleon and the Artists*, 210–11; *Church Affairs in Tours*.

Lord of heaven and earth, . . . gives empires not only to one person in particular, but also to his family.[50]

In light of what had happened to religion since the outbreak of the French Revolution, it would not have been surprising if the clergy had used its influence to work against the republican tradition during the Consulate and to seek restoration of at least part of the domain confiscated from it by the government. Any attempt to do so, however, was an important item on the list of things forbidden to the church. Another prohibition, contained in a letter from Napoleon to his uncle, Cardinal Fesch, dealt with giving the appearance of meddling in politics. No priest could conduct religious services in a private house without the consent of the government or in a church without that of the bishop, and no missionary could go to the colonies without express authorization from the Minister of Marine. The Organic Articles for the Protestant Sects provided that "no doctrinal or dogmatic decision or formulary or change in discipline may be published or taught before the government approves it"; the Organic Articles for the Catholics provided that no writing from Rome might be received or printed without the approval of the government and that decrees of foreign synods might be published only after the government had examined them. Perhaps the main reason for these provisions was Napoleon's fear that the clergy might arouse hatreds which would trouble public tranquillity.[51]

Such governmental control was difficult and did not always function smoothly. In so vast a program of control there was bound to be trouble. In Turin, Italy, several of the episcopal orders and clerical speeches were read in French, a fact which canceled any effect they might have had on the Italian-speaking people. At home, too, there was trouble. Fouché once repri-

[50] Charpentier, *Napoléon et les hommes de lettres*, 135–37. Haussonville (*Église et empire*, II, 253) says Napoleon and Cardinal Caprara wrote this catechism section. It was merely a translation, with variations, of similar catechisms exalting the Republic. Gottschalk, *French Revolution*, 350.

[51] *Concordat: Reprints;* Alberto Lumbroso (ed.), *Cent quatre-vingt-trois lettres inédites de Napoléon* (Rome, 1899), 16; *Débats*, 8 Brumaire, Year XI; Napoleon (Thompson, ed.), *Letters*, 89; Aulard (ed.), *Paris sous le consulat*, I, 14; *Church and Religious Affairs during the Consulate and Empire: Contemporary Pamphlets, 1802.*

manded the *Journal des Curés* for printing a sermon by Napoleon's almoner, the Abbé Étienne de Boulogne, in which he had rebuked the policy of conquest; yet the paper declared it had not felt justified in correcting a sermon by Napoleon's own almoner. At another time only the presence of Portalis in the crowd prevented the infliction of penalties on Abbé Denis Frayssinous, who, the police reported, had preached superstitious practices. Portalis himself fell into disgrace and was exiled forty leagues from Paris in 1811 for permitting the circulation of a printed piece tending to provoke disobedience and contempt for authority.[52]

Since, perfect or not, there was control, two things are deserving of mention. First, freedom of conscience, which the prefects had been ordered to maintain, did subsist rather well, and the expression of opinion on religious matters remained relatively free.[53] Second, a large proportion of the priests and bishops remained refractory and ultramontane. In France at the time of the Concordat the majority of priests refused to resign, even though opposed to the government, but the new clergy appointed by the government did gradually consolidate itself. In Rome, despite strict control, only a few clerics favored Napoleon in his struggle with the Pope. General religious opposition, already aroused by Napoleon's treatment of the Pope, became especially strong when he married Marie Louise, because thirteen cardinals held that his marriage with Josephine was still valid. Some of the refractory priests insisted upon celebrating religious festivals suppressed by the Concordat; others flatly refused to execute orders of the government; still others obeyed the orders only in a manner designed to spoil the effect. Some instances of clerical refractoriness reported by the police were the refusal by the priests of Loire-Inférieure to read the bulletins on the ground that religious ceremonies were for things exclusively religious; [54] the refusal of the

[52] Aulard (ed.), *Paris sous le premier empire*, III, 432; *Curés*, April 16, 1809; J. Latappy, "L'église et l'université sous Napoléon Ier," *Le Correspondant* (1901), 1036; Napoleon, *Correspondance*, XXI, 353.

[53] Concluded from a thorough perusal of the Boulay de la Meurthe collection of religious pamphlets at Harvard University. Hostile discussion of political affairs by the clerics was, however, not tolerated. Napoleon, *Correspondance*, XXI, 353.

[54] In November, 1806—after the time at which Napoleon had ordered that reading bulletins in the churches be discontinued.

Bishop of Finistère to use the new catechism; and the failure of the priests in the four Rhenish departments and Antwerp to say the required prayers for the government.[55]

In short, Napoleon's use of religion in disseminating propaganda, although a powerful means of influencing the public, was not wholly satisfactory because the clergy refused to become 100 per cent servile.

[55] Haussonville, *Église et empire*, V, 143; *Local Church and Religious Affairs during the Consulate and Empire: Contemporary Pamphlets: Aix-Lyon;* Remacle (ed.), *Bonaparte et les Bourbons*, 201, 442; Eugene (Du Casse, ed.), *Mémoires*, V, 226; *Church Affairs: Agen-Le Mans; Church and Religious Affairs in Besançon during the Consulate and Empire;* Napoleon (Brotonne, ed.), *Lettres*, 201; E. d'Hauterive (ed.), *La police secrète, passim.* Refractory priests were the ones who refused to take an oath of allegiance to the government; ultramontane ones were those who looked "beyond the mountains" to the Pope, whom they wanted to have considerable influence in French domestic affairs. In some places where the constitutional clergy was well disposed to the government, the people stayed away in droves. Such a spot was the department of Hérault, the prefect of which ordered the mayors to close the cabarets during divine service.

CHAPTER VII

THE ARTS

A. THEATER

ALTHOUGH NAPOLEON CONCERNED HIMSELF WITH ALL THE ARTS, he paid particular attention to drama and the theater because he realized their potential attraction for the people.

In fact, at the start of the Consulate the theaters in Paris and the other cities of France were very well patronized because they expressed public opinion so vehemently.[1] This was true of both the big theaters such as the Opéra and the unpretentious, but extremely popular, boulevard theaters.

To a Napoleon desirous of controlling every phase of public life, however, whether or not the theater was popular was a secondary matter. The important thing was that it render him two services: it was to glorify him indirectly by performing the classical works (particularly tragedies, with stress on those by Pierre Corneille), and it was to perform patriotic pieces voluntarily or upon request of the government. An idea of the importance he attached to the influence of the theater may be gathered from the amount he was willing to lavish on it and from the strictness of governmental control.

Largely in order to achieve these aims, he heavily subsidized the large theaters, which were unable to compete with the little ones.[2] The Opéra alone cost the government 800,000 francs a year, and in 1811 it received a special subsidy of 186,176 francs.[3] Nor was Napoleon niggardly with the other theaters. Beginning in 1801

---

[1] Vandal, *Avènement de Bonaparte*, I, 406.

[2] Bausset, *Mémoires*, I, 93–94. The prefecture of police of the Seine furnished further proof. It reported that the leading stockholder in the Opéra Buffa had disappeared, leaving many debts. Aulard (ed.), *Paris sous le consulat*, IV, 286, August 4, 1803. Bausset was a prefect of the palace.

[3] Napoleon (Brotonne, ed.), *Dernières lettres*, II, 142.

the Opéra Comique received 50,000 francs a year, and the amount was raised in 1805 to 100,000.[4] Another theater which had its subsidy doubled in 1805, receiving a second 100,000 francs yearly, was the Théâtre Français, until 1803 called the Comédie Française.[5] Until it closed for lack of funds, the Opéra Buffa received a regular subsidy of 50,000 francs. In addition, it received 40,000 francs in 1804 from a special fund of 100,000 given to Rémusat, the Superintendent of Spectacles.[6] The 1807 budget called for allotting 1,500,000 francs to the theaters. In 1815 Napoleon established a special coffer which was to give the Grand Marshal of the Palace 100,000 a month for theater expenses.[7]

A second way of subsidizing the theaters was to give pensions to the actors. The casts of the Théâtre Français and the Opéra received 88,000 francs yearly from the government, with the share of each performer ranging from 2,000 to 5,000 francs; an additional 32,000 francs went to actors in other theaters. A decree of 6 Messidor, Year X, set aside 300,000 francs which the Minister of the Interior was to use for pensions, and in 1806 the actors received 180,000 francs from the government.[8]

The theaters received financial support from the government in another form, the prohibition of complimentary tickets by decree of 13 Messidor, Year X. This measure was worth 60,400 francs annually to the Opéra alone for boxes occupied by government authorities.[9] Special subsidies were also awarded for plays of circumstance.[10] Partially raised by an income tax of from 5 to 20 per cent levied on the secondary theaters and on curiosities after August, 1811, the subsidies yielded about 300,000 francs a year.

A second means of promoting the large theaters was to diminish

[4] Lanzac de Laborie, Paris sous Napoléon, VIII, 89, 94.

[5] August Fournier, "Napoleon I und das Theater," Bühne und Welt, 3d year (1901), 543; Eugene Laugier, Documents historiques sur la comédie française pendant le règne de S. M. l'empereur Napoléon Ier (Paris, 1853), 63.

[6] Napoleon, Correspondance, IX, 420.

[7] Ibid., XVI, 106; Chuquet (ed.), Inédits napoléoniens, II, 516.

[8] Lanzac de Laborie, Paris sous Napoléon, VII, 34; Napoleon, Correspondance, XII, 402; Chaptal (E. A. Chaptal, ed.), Souvenirs, 95.

[9] Arthur Chuquet (ed.), Ordres et apostilles de Napoléon, 1799–1815 (Paris, 1911–12), I, 175.

[10] L.-Henry Lecomte, Napoléon et le monde dramatique (Paris, 1912), 122; Castil-Blaze [François H. Blaze], Mémorial du Grand-Opéra (Paris, 1847), 41.

the competition. One step in this direction was a decree of August 6, 1806. This forbade the establishment of any theater without authorization from Napoleon and limited the number of theaters, to be authorized by the prefect, to two in the main cities and to one in the lesser cities of France. Ambulatory groups were thenceforth required to obtain the approval of the Minister of the Interior and of the Minister of Police. The approval of this latter functionary was necessary before any play could be performed, and the Minister of the Interior was entrusted with the task of selecting for the Opéra, Opéra Comique, and Théâtre Français repertoires from which other theaters might select a work only with the approval of the theater to which the play had been originally allotted.[11] In accordance with the terms of this decree the Opéra was to present only music and dance, the Théâtre de l'Impératrice only comedy, the Opéra Comique only plays written in Italian. Each of the other Parisian theaters was limited to a specific category of performance by another decree of April 25, 1807: Vaudeville—little pieces with couplets to well-known tunes; Variétés—jolly, vulgar, and rustic pieces with some couplets; Porte-Sainte-Martin—melodrama, with songs to popular airs; Variétés Étrangers—translations; Gaîté—pantomines without ballets. The Gaîté theater disregarded the decree but was not troubled because the Minister of Police reported that its melodramas were useful to public opinion. A ministerial decree of July, 1808, forbade owners of curiosities to stage dramatic pieces of any type,[12] as they might be competition to the established theaters.

Although the little theaters eulogized Napoleon effectively, a decree of July 29, 1807, reduced the number of theaters in Paris from thirty-three to eight, probably in order to facilitate the supervision and improve the chances for financial success of those which remained: Opéra, Opéra Comique, Théâtre Français, Théâtre de l'Impératrice, Vaudeville, Variétés, Gaîté, and Am-

[11] Georg Storost, *Napoleons I Stellung zur zeitgenössischen und klassischen französischen Literatur* (Schönebeck, 1914), 89.

[12] Maurice Albert, "Napoléon et les théâtres populaires," *La revue de Paris,* IX (1902), III, 806; Maurice Albert, *Les théâtres des boulevards, 1789–1848* (Paris, 1902), 213–18; Lecomte, *Napoléon et le monde dramatique,* 116. The Théâtre de l'Impératrice was the same as the Odéon and was considered an annex of the Théâtre Français.

bigu. Exceptions were allowed, however. The Jeunes Artistes gave fairy tales. The Théâtre de la Porte-Sainte-Martin, the only one to protest the decree, was permitted to reopen as the Théâtre des Jeux Gymniques, but in 1812 it was again suppressed for continuing to perform dramatic works. And by 1813 Cirque Olympique, Théâtre des Fabulistes, Jeux Forains, Théâtre de Madame Saqui, and Funambules had all come into being.[13]

All of these theaters were subject to governmental regulation designed to obtain in the theater that order which Napoleon's mind seemingly prized above all else in every sphere of activity. As early as Nivôse, Year VIII, the police commissioner attached to the central administration of the department of the Seine reported to the Minister of Police:

> The spectacles have almost always been in opposition to the spirit of the government, always too far or not far enough, thus announcing that they are without principles and have no other consideration than their own interest. . . . After the last event of brumaire they showed cowardice, but the government's prohibition of plays which would revive animosities has put them back in their place and produced an excellent effect. These different oscillations and this lack of principle in management unquestionably seem to require a change in their organization and their mode of existence. Does not the management of spectacles, as an agency of public instruction, belong incontestably to the government? Does not national honor place upon it the duty of seizing them, of representing to a grateful public the traits of devotion, courage, and genius which are worthy of being offered for the admiration of our contemporaries and for the instruction of posterity?[14]

Napoleon acted upon this recommendation that the government should direct the theaters; and in accordance with it the Division of Public Instruction under Arnault in the ministry of the interior did include, except momentarily under the Consulate, the Bureau of Theaters.[15]

By 1801 the government had acknowledged its control of the

---

[13] Albert, *Théâtres des boulevards*, 235; Lacroix, *Directoire, consulat et l'empire*, 190; L.-Henry Lecomte, *Histoire des théâtres de Paris 1402-1904* (Paris, 1905-10), I, 7; Broc, *Vie en France*, 460, 463.
[14] Aulard (ed.), *Paris sous le consulat*, I, 106-107.
[15] Lanzac de Laborie, *Paris sous Napoléon*, VII, 7.

Théâtre de la République (later the Théâtre Français) and had announced that the artists of this theater should not have exclusive jurisdiction over its plays and debuts because the theater was supposed to "purge morals, conserve taste, and form opinion." On December 11, 1802, the Opéra Buffa, Opéra Comique, and Louvois theaters also became government controlled, each administered by a prefect of the palace, while the Superintendent of Spectacles supervised the Théâtre Français. A decree of November 1, 1807, directed the latter official to supervise the four big theaters so that they would be more serious.[16] Even as early as 1803 the gay *Carnaval de Beaugency* had been forbidden as being beneath the dignity of the theater. Because of the increasing governmental supervision, the years 1800–1802, before the government played its role in the theater too seriously, were the gayest theatrical ones of the whole period from 1789 to 1815.[17]

That the government did play a role was evidenced by Chaptal's forbidding the Théâtre Français on 28 Ventôse, Year IX, to stage vaudeville or comic opera simultaneously with awarding it the exclusive right to perform tragedy and high comedy. In 1803 Roederer, who was now Director of Public Instruction, sent a circular to theater owners ordering them to remit their repertoires to the Minister of the Interior. When Regnier was Minister of Police, he ordered the owners to submit their repertoires, which they had to abide by, to the Minister of the Interior every three months.[18] The decrees of 1806 and 1807 dealing with repertoires have already been mentioned, and that dated from Moscow on October 15, 1812, which governed the Théâtre Français for a hundred years, finally provided that the reading committee which was to decide whether to perform a play was to be chosen by the Superintendent of Spectacles rather than elected by fellow actors.[19]

[16] Minister of the Interior, Chaptal de Chanteloup, quoted in the *Moniteur*, 10 Germinal, Year IX; Lecomte, *Napoléon et le monde dramatique*, 66, 116. Since giving charge of various theaters to the palace prefects was primarily to obtain a monarchical organization rather than to disseminate propaganda, their role is not discussed in detail in this book.

[17] Abrantès, *Mémoires*, III, 441; Remacle (ed.), *Bonaparte et les Bourbons*, 262.

[18] Fournier, "Napoleon und das Theater," *loc cit.*, 545; Lecomte, *Napoléon et le monde dramatique*, 428.

[19] Lanzac de Laborie, *Paris sous Napoléon*, VII, 159.

There was also very strict preliminary censorship of plays.[20] In 1800 the Minister of the Interior wrote all the theater directors that no play could be performed without his previous approval, a written order of which was to be shown to the Prefect of Police in Paris or the departmental prefect in the provinces before the play was announced.[21] One type of play automatically banned was that based on the Scriptures, just as the government proscribed all plays referring to the Bourbons, the person of Napoleon (after 1810), usurpation of a throne, punishment of a tyrant, or a victory over France.[22] In addition, certain plays or types of plays might be temporarily prohibited or suspended because they were judged inopportune. A decree issued 4 Frimaire, Year VIII, forbade all plays dealing with Brumaire; [23] *Phèdre*, a classical tragedy by Racine, was suspended during the trial of Moreau because the public found in it allusions damaging to the government; and at the time of the Russian campaign all plays with passages favorable to Russia or its rulers were suspended.[24]

It is interesting to note, however, that a play deemed unfit for performance might receive permission to be printed.[25] Any of a number of reasons might explain the granting of such permission. It is possible that the authorities realized that the illiterate play-going public would not be adversely affected by the printed word. Sometimes, too, Napoleon desired to salve the feelings of the authors. Or, horrible thought to a dictator like Napoleon, there might even have been lack of co-ordination among the censorship agencies.

There really was no excuse for faulty co-ordination because the Bureau of Theaters, headed by the poet Joseph Esménard after Frimaire, Year IX, had received specific instructions to co-

[20] As much as possible of the material contained in Welschinger, *Censure sous l'empire*, is omitted from this discussion.

[21] *Journal*, 21 Germinal, Year VIII.

[22] Chaptal (E. A. Chaptal, ed.), *Souvenirs*, 385; Napoleon (Lecestre, comp.), *Lettres*, II, 11; Napoleon, *Correspondance*, XXI, 241.

[23] This merely formalized the action of the Central Bureau of the Canton, to which Fouché had entrusted censorship of the theaters. It in turn had commissioners of police report on the various theaters. Aulard (ed.), *Paris sous le consulat*, I, 50; II, 606.

[24] Lecomte, *Napoléon et le monde dramatique*, 437; Lanzac de Laborie, *Paris sous Napoléon*, I, 18.

[25] Aulard (ed.), *Paris sous le consulat*, III, 600.

operate with the press bureau under Lagarde. Although responsibility for the censorship of plays lay with Esménard's agency,
Lagarde demonstrated his willingness to co-operate by removing
Mérope and *La Mort de César* from the repertoire of the Théâtre
Français.[26] Some of the other plays prohibited by the theater
bureau were *La Journée de Saint-Cloud* for fear it would arouse
factionalism; *La Partie de Chasse d'Henri IV* because it praised the
Bourbons; [27] and *William the Conqueror* lest a speech about the
death of Roland be interpreted as referring to Napoleon.

Even approval by the censors was no guarantee that a play
could be performed without any hindrance. The police had agents
in the audience to check on the plays and their reception; if
a play created a disturbance, it was banned.[28] The attempt of
the police to prevent signs of disapproval or approval on the
ground that such activity savored of disloyalty was, however,
criticized by Napoleon: "It is extremely ridiculous not to grant
the Piedmontese the right to whistle at shows,[29] and to make a
national affair out of it. If the Piedmontese are not to be permitted
to applaud the danseuse they want, one should not raise the standards of the Emperor, but should have one hundred gibbets raised
in the city. Moreover, I shall never be made to think that to whistle
at or applaud dancers can be an act against France." [30]

A play was prohibited if Napoleon decided it contained something disadvantageous, a conclusion he might reach on the basis
of a report submitted by his agent, Ripault, who analyzed all
plays within forty-eight hours of their first performance.[31] Napoleon, for example, stopped the comedy *L'Antichambre ou les
valets entre eux* after the first performance, dismissed the censor,

[26] Lanzac de Laborie, *Paris sous Napoléon*, VII, 143.

[27] This was played three times at Nantes to discover who was attached to
the Bourbons, and then it was forbidden. As the audience was indifferent, this
governmental stratagem failed. E. d'Hauterive (ed.), *La police secrète*, I, 137,
24 Vendémiaire, Year XIII.

[28] Lew Rosen, *Napoleon's Opera-Glass* (London, 1897), 65; Lanzac de Laborie,
Paris sous Napoléon, I, 217–21. The *Gazette de France* defended this type of
censorship on the ground that it mutilated the work rather than the author.
Aulard (ed.), *Paris sous le premier empire*, III, 264.

[29] It is interesting to note that in America, whistling is a sign of the highest
approbation, in Europe, of profound dissatisfaction and discontent.

[30] Napoleon, *Correspondance*, X, 10.

[31] *Ibid.*, VII, 201. This same agent reported on all other types of mediums
which might have political importance.

François Campenon, and exiled the author, Louis Dupaty, to the colonies because he deemed the following dialogue insulting to the army:

> First Valet: I have served.
> Second Valet: And I, I am still serving.[32]

He also prevented the performance of *Pinto ou la journée d'une conspiration* by forcing repeated leaves upon the leading man in order to save the dignity of the authors. Étienne's *L'Intrigante* was not allowed to continue, and Lucien caused the production of *Édouard en Écosse*, which had been examined five times and had been returned, approved, by the Minister of Police on the very morning of its first performance, to be halted because of similarities in the circumstances of the Bourbons and the Stuarts. Cambacérès also dabbled in controlling the theaters, suspending the performance of *Molière chez Ninon*.[33]

In addition, the censorship often altered plays—usually by eliminations, less frequently by additions—before allowing them to be presented. The classic example was Jean Roger's having to eliminate from his comedy, *Caroline, ou le Tableau*, the phrase *"mille louis"* because it might remind people of the King. Censorship mutilated even Corneille, deleting passages or adding praise of Napoleon. Esménard, for instance, composed twenty verses alluding to the establishment of the Empire for insertion into *Heraclius*.[34]

Such additions illustrate how the theater, while prevented from damaging Napoleon's cause, was made to serve him positively. Impromptus and *à-propos* were given to celebrate such important occasions as the 18 Brumaire, important victories, peace,[35] Napoleon's marriage, the birth of the King of Rome. In fact, at least one half of the plays produced between 1804 and 1815 depended on the circumstances they depicted for their success.[36] Plays of

[32] Chaptal (E. A. Chaptal, ed.), *Souvenirs*, 387.
[33] Broc, *Vie en France*, 464; Napoleon, *Correspondance*, VII, 91; Charpentier, *Napoléon et les hommes de lettres*, 64; Remacle (ed.), *Bonaparte et les Bourbons*, 35.
[34] Broc, *Vie en France*, 459.
[35] After the Treaty of Lunéville, the *Moniteur* announced that every theater had given one or more plays relative to peace.
[36] This conclusion was reached after a thorough study of L.-Henry Lecomte, *Napoléon et l'empire racontés par le théâtre 1797–1899* (Paris, 1900).

this type were *Le Rêve ou la Colonne de Rosbach* by Pierre Barré, Jean Radet, and François Desfontaines, and *Inauguration du Temple de la Victoire*, an opera with words by Pierre Baour-Lormian and music by Pierre de Winter, Louis Persuis, and Jean Lesueur, to celebrate the victory of Jena. After the Treaty of Tilsit, appeared *Un Diner par Victoire* by Marc Antoine Désaugiers and *Les Bateliers du Niémen* by the same author, Francis, and G.-F. Moreau de Commagny. At the time of the birth of the King of Rome, 170 works (not all of them plays) were written, for which the authors received 88,400 francs.[37] Three causes account for the composition and performance of such circumstantial works: a sincere admiration of Napoleon; a fear that unless such plays were staged, the theaters would be forcibly closed; and a desire on the part of the theaters for subsidies and on the part of the playwrights for pensions.

These financial gratifications to playwrights were an important means of inducing them to write the types of plays Napoleon desired. Barré, Radet, and Desfontaines, the founders of the Vaudeville, each received a pension of 4,000 francs. A decree issued in 1802 stating that the authors of every operatic or dramatic work should receive an official subsidy placed the minimum at 300 francs a night for the first 20 nights, 200 for the next 20, and then a special bonus of 500 francs. In Italy, as well as in France, the government paid playwrights.[38]

Napoleon, who expressed a preference for tragedies because they afforded the best opportunity for the expression of elevated thoughts and tended to produce heroes, also suggested topics to be worked into plays or other types of drama. It was he who directly suggested the ballet *Le Retour d'Ulysse* and he who proposed that tragedies be written on the themes of Frédégonde, Clovis, and other national themes, which would play upon the patriotic sentiments of the French. He recommended to Jean Luce

---

[37] Theodore Muret, *L'histoire par le théâtre, 1789–1851* (1st series, *La révolution, le consulat, l'empire*) (Paris, 1865), 242–45.

[38] Grant, *Napoleon and the Artists*, 270 (Grant's figures are respectively £12, £8, and £20); Méneval (Baron de Méneval, ed.), *Memoirs*, II, 46; A. Pingaud, *Bonaparte président de la république italienne*, II, 350. Such grants as these explain why Napoleon supported even the bad works of men whom he was favoring, such as Paisiello's *Proserpine*. Remacle (ed.), *Bonaparte et les Bourbons*, 366.

de Lancival and Victor de Jouy that they write *Hector* and *Tippo-Saïb*, respectively. And he suggested to Fouché that he take steps to get the proper type of play for the French to see: "There is talk of a tragedy about Henry IV—that is not distant enough not to arouse passions. . . . Without interfering with the theater too much, you ought to veto this particular play; but do not make your intervention public. . . . Could you not commission him [François Raynouard] to write a tragedy on the transition from the Valois to the Bourbons? . . . the successor would be the savior of the nation. . . . Have the same idea in the oratorio *Saul* —a great man succeeding a degenerate King." [39] The Ulysses ballet and the opera *Le Triomphe de Trajan*, by Esménard, Lesueur, and Persuis, with the proper type of allusions to make the audience think of Napoleon when Trajan was mentioned, were —to the knowledge of the writer—the only actually successful performances Napoleon proposed.[40]

Oftentimes the government used more than mere suggestion. On March 2, 1810, Napoleon told Rémusat exactly what plays were to be performed and when, after having instructed him earlier in the year to produce only historical and mythological ballets which were analogous to the circumstances of the day. At a theater party at Saint-Cloud, after the curtain went down, an actor read for the benefit of the diplomatic corps, which was present, an ode by Fontanes bitterly attacking England. André Miot de Melito says that this was written and recited at Bonaparte's express command. Whether or not Miot is correct, it is known that in 1803, to form a public opinion favorable to an invasion of England, the government ordered plays for the theaters, some of them including scenes from the life of that successful invader, William the Conqueror.[41] At the time of the invasion of France the police ordered the theaters to exercise their influence on public thinking by presenting suitable plays. Needless to say, there were many pieces urging resistance to the invaders, espe-

[39] Napoleon (Thompson, ed.), *Letters*, 118.

[40] Paul Gaffarel, "L'opposition littéraire sous le consulat," *La révolution française*, XVI(1889), 431; Chaptal (E. A. Chaptal, ed.), *Souvenirs*, 384; Napoleon (Thompson, ed.), *Letters*, 48.

[41] Rémusat (P. de Rémusat, pub.), *Mémoires*, I, 76; Rosen, *Napoleon's Opera-Glass*, 42.

cially the Cossacks, and the nationalistic opera *L'Oriflamme* with words by Étienne and Baour-Lormian and music by Henri Berton, Ferdinando Paer, Konradin Kreutzer, and Étienne Méhul was performed at the Opéra as late as March 20, 1814.[42]

Beginning on November 25, 1805, Napoleon also used the theaters as a means of publicizing his bulletins, which were always followed, at least in the little theaters, by enthusiastic odes or improvised scenes from the pens of such favorite boulevard playwrights as Jean Gabiot, Augustin Prévost, or René Pixérécourt. As early as 1800 Joseph had had favorable news such as that of the Battle of Marengo read in the main theaters, and in 1805 he debated the advisability of again following this practice. Archchancellor Cambacérès, who in 1807 had relayed to the prefect of police the command from Josephine to read bulletins, again ordered their reading in 1809. As regent in 1814, Marie Louise ordered the Minister of Police to have current bulletins read.[43]

Napoleon realized the effect which the drama can have on people. In order to arouse the sentimental attachment of the lower classes to historical anniversaries and important events, he had the theaters give free performances, beginning on August 15, 1802, with the celebration of his birthday. During the Consulate there were eleven such celebrations—during the Empire twenty-eight—important enough to include free theatrical performances.[44] It was because of his realization of the power of the drama that at Erfurt, in 1808, Napoleon had command performances of heroic tragedies carefully selected to impress the German nobility. For the benefit of the troops he ordered Minister of Marine Pierre Laplace to send a troupe of comedians to Egypt to prevent the soldiers from becoming nostalgic after the assassination of General Jean Kléber,[45] sent actors of the Vaudeville

---

[42] Lecomte, *Napoléon et le monde dramatique*, 432; Rosen, *Napoleon's Opera-Glass*, 42–43; Welschinger, *Censure sous l'empire*, 258; Napoleon (Lecestre, comp.), *Lettres*, II, 11; Muret, *Histoire par le théâtre*, 171–73; Napoleon, *Correspondance*, XX, 252; Lecomte, *Napoléon et l'empire racontés par le théâtre*, 260. The oriflamme was the ancient national standard of France.

[43] Joseph (Du Casse, ed.), *Mémoires*, I, 288; Aulard (ed.), *Paris sous le premier empire*, III, 64; Albert, *Théâtres des boulevards*, 189, 202; *Empire*, February 12, 1814; *Mercure*, July 15, 1809.

[44] Muret, *Histoire par le théâtre*, 192; Lecomte, *Napoléon et le monde dramatique*, 45.

[45] Kléber was the general whom Bonaparte had left to succeed him in Egypt.

theater to the Grand Army to sustain morale (especially among the officers), took a troupe of actors to Russia, and had actors come to Dresden in 1813. At the request of the Grand Squire, Rémusat chose the actors, and Napoleon's aide-de-camp Antoine Drouot devised the plan for paying them.[46] That Napoleon was willing to spend lavishly to achieve his end is shown by the expense accounts for the Erfurt and Dresden trips: 26,000 francs plus wages for Erfurt, and 111,500 francs to pay the actors who came to Dresden.[47]

Even though the government recognized the value of provincial theaters, they were hard put to it financially. The theater at Marseille, for example, was forced to close early in 1806 because its receipts were 3,000 francs and its expenses 18,000 francs a month; the police urged that it be opened as soon as possible to assist in maintaining order. Other cities with their own theaters included Amiens, Toulouse, Douai, Nîmes, Brest, Rouen, Grenoble, Valenciennes, Flushing, Riom, Ostend, Caen, Bayonne, Lyon, and Lille.[48]

All these provincial theaters were controlled as strictly as those at Paris, despite the fact they were not so popular. This control was exemplified by the mayor of Amiens, who forbade the tragedy *Athalie* because he feared hostile demonstrations. The Prefect of Lyon, the theaters of which were directed by Lainé, a pensioner of the Imperial Academy of Music, named Laurent Bérenger dramatic censor to eliminate licentiousness, and the one at Tours forbade *Fénélon* because certain passages were hostile to the Catholics. The decree of 1806 (supposedly based on information reported by the prefects, who in turn relied on the mayors) substituted control by the minister of the interior for local control.[49]

---

[46] Rosen, *Napoleon's Opera-Glass*, 44; Napoleon, *Correspondance*, XXV, 374; XXVI, 22; Lecomte, *Napoléon et le monde dramatique*, 167; Lanzac de Laborie, *Paris sous Napoléon*, VII, 303–305. At Dresden the aim was primarily to impress England and Spain with French morale, so the hitherto-contemned comedians received more than the tragedians. The troupe sent to Egypt never reached that country.

[47] Laugier, *Documents sur la comédie française*, 187.

[48] Lacroix, *Directoire, consulat et l'empire*, 173; E. d'Hauterive (ed.), *La police secrète*, II, 262; III, 255, 416.

[49] Baron A. de Calonne, *Histoire de la ville d'Amiens: Amiens au XIXe siècle* (Amiens, 1906), 18; *Débats*, 6 Thermidor, Year X; Adolphe Crémieux, "Un théâtre de province pendant le premier empire. Le théâtre de Nîmes, de 1807 à 1815," *La révolution française*, XXXVII (1899), 144.

Theatrical affairs did not always move more smoothly at Paris than in the departments. The *Moniteur* of 9 Vendémiaire, Year XII, remarked that the comic repertory of the Théâtre Français needed new pieces and that there should be more variety in the tragedy. Napoleon complained of the censorship, even writing the Minister of the Interior to examine personally all the plays, ordering Savary in 1813 to revise his censorship committee as "only stupid or ill-disposed people . . . could approve such a play [as *l'Intrigante*]," and telling Chaptal that the censor who had barred *Tancred* and *Le Tartuffe* should be a market inspector.[50] On the whole, however, Napoleon's theater censorship was relatively good, as censorships go, from the standpoint of both the public and the authors.[51]

B. MUSIC AND POETRY

As was the case with the theater, the government considered music and poetry sufficiently important branches of communication to support and control them. The Conservatory of Music received a regular stipend, and the Imperial Academy of Music —from which a member could be dismissed only by order of Napoleon—was associated with the subsidized Opéra.[52]

A wide variety of rewards was offered individual poets and composers. They might receive government positions or cash payments, or become members of the Legion of Honor (as did Nicholas Dalayrac and Maria Luigi Cherubini), Tribunes, or Senators. Among those receiving actual money pensions ranging from 1,200 to 6,000 francs were Louis Jean Lemercier, Joseph Treneuil, Charles d'Avrigny, Esménard, Pierre Piis, Étienne, Lesueur, Étienne Méhul, Charles de Chênedollé, Antoine Arnault, Paer, Niccolò Piccini, Cherubini, Nicolas Zingarelli, Baour-Lormian, Luce de Lancival, Marie Joseph de Chénier, Pierre Lebrun, Louis Picard, Monge, and Mme de Genlis. The last seven received the top figure. Poems or translations which were successful won for their authors additional pay. Picard, for in-

[50] Charpentier, *Napoléon et les hommes de lettres*, 115; Napoleon (Lecestre, comp.), *Lettres*, II, 223; Storost, *Napoleons I Stellung zur Literatur*, 92.
[51] Lecomte, *Napoléon et le monde dramatique*, 438.
[52] Napoleon, *Correspondance*, VI, 508; X, 112.

stance, received 6,000 francs for "Marionnettes," and Lebrun 3,000 and de Jouy 4,000 francs for the opera *La Vestale*. In addition Napoleon had his own chapel orchestra and dance troupe which cost up to 350,000 francs per annum. It was the task of this organization, directed successively by Paisiello and Lesueur, to set the high standard in music which would make the regime noteworthy for that art.[53]

The government tried to raise the standard of poetry, not only by the rewards already mentioned, but by suggesting the topics most acceptable to the regime. Time and again articles in the *Moniteur* encouraged the use of national subjects and heroes.[54]

With the exception of Chénier, all of the above-named poets were paid to celebrate at fixed times the main events of Napoleon's reign—such as victories, peace, Napoleon's coronation, his marriage with Marie Louise, and the birth of the King of Rome—and the exploits of the French heroes of the period. Lebrun, for example, received a bonus of 1,000 crowns in 1803 for an ode on the project of invading England.[55] Even if such pieces were not directly ordered,[56] they were rewarded: in 1804, for instance, Napoleon wrote the Minister of the Interior, Champagny, to present gifts in proportion to the value of their works to the poets and musicians composing pieces for his coronation. He also

[53] Chaptal (E. A. Chaptal, ed.), *Souvenirs*, 385; Victor Jeanroy-Félix, *Nouvelle histoire de la littérature française pendant la révolution et le premier empire* (Paris, 1886), 457, 463; Maurice Allem (ed.), *L'épopée napoléonienne dans la poésie française* (Paris, 1912), 21; Lecomte, *Napoléon et le monde dramatique*, 444–49. Storost (*Napoleons I Stellung zur Literatur, passim*) has a list, which must be virtually, if not entirely, complete, of literary men receiving pensions. Though the writer could find no definite statement in regard to them, it is probable that Charles Millevoye and Désaugiers, both of whom composed many patriotic pieces, received government gratifications. It is instructive to compare the figures on the income of poets and composers with that of some of Napoleon's generals: Ney, 728,000 francs; Davout, 900,000; Berthier, 1,350,000. Charpentier, *Napoléon et les hommes de lettres*, 176. Perhaps one reason for the smallness of the amounts was, as Storost (*Napoleons I Stellung zur Literatur*, 40–47) stated, Napoleon's feeling that good poetry could not be commanded and that these payments, at the expense of the newspapers, aimed merely at preventing the poets from becoming dangerous.

[54] 21 Germinal, Year VIII; February 28, 1812.

[55] Bernard Jullien, *Histoire de la poésie française à l'époque impériale*, 2 vols. (Paris, 1844), I, 72, 83.

[56] Merlet says that most of the dithyrambs and cantatas were ordered by the government. Gustave Merlet, *Tableau de la littérature française, 1800–15*, 3 vols. (Paris, 1878–83), I, 183.

worked through the Institute, which proposed patriotic themes for poetry competitions.[57]

In general, no new idea was propounded in these works. They merely reiterated in a variety of forms, generously sprinkled with classical allusions, the two favorite themes of exaltation of Napoleon and opposition to the enemy, either in a serious or jocular vein.[58] One exception might be the poem by "T." in the *Mercure de France* of March 5, 1814, entitled "A S.M. l'empereur de Russie," which pointed out that all the greatest rulers of history limited the benefits of their rule to the subjects of their own empire.

Various means were used to get these official works before the public. The Imperial Print Shop published *Odes sur la guerre d'Autriche* by Manvel, the secretary of Cambacérès; the papers printed innumerable poems, and there was a special collection of poems celebrating the birth of the King of Rome.[59] Official music and songs might be presented in some theater, performed by the strolling singers whom the police encouraged, distributed by the prefect of police, or used for a *Te Deum* or some other fete.[60]

The music for the fetes was very elaborate, designed to impress by its brilliance and mass effects rather than to become popular.[61] But songs destined for popularity were also composed on order. Thus in 1800 Napoleon ordered Lucien as Minister of the Interior to have Lebrun and Claude Rouget de l'Isle compose a battle hymn, to some well-known tune such as the latter's *Marseillaise*, which was to include statements applicable to all the circumstances of war and show that peace could come only after

[57] Napoleon, *Correspondance*, X, 72; Aulard (ed.), *Paris sous le consulat*, II, 531.

[58] *Poésies révolutionnaires et contre-révolutionnaires* (Paris, 1821), II, 139.

[59] *Moniteur*, 25 Frimaire, Year XIV; J. J. Lucet and Eckard (comps.), *Hommages poétiques à leurs majestés impériales et royales sur la naissance de S. M. le roi de Rome* (Paris, 1811). Though these eulogies were not by any means all ordered, the vast majority were written either by government functionaries or by poets on the official payroll. Most of the functionaries were teachers, but the remaining ones held a wide variety of posts.

[60] Lanzac de Laborie, *Paris sous Napoléon*, III, 60; VIII, 223; Aulard (ed.), *Paris sous le consulat*, II, 184; *Poésies révolutionnaires*, II, 65.

[61] Constant Pierre, *Musique des fêtes et cérémonies de la révolution française* (*Ville de Paris: Publications relatives à la révolution française*) (Paris, 1899), *passim*; Alfred Bruneau, *La musique française* (Paris, 1901), 52.

victory.[62] In 1803 Napoleon ordered Minister of the Interior Chaptal to see to the composition of several songs about the invasion of England, with at least one to the tune of the *Chant du Départ* by Méhul; one song in accord with the latter part of this mandate was a new *Chant du Départ* by Pierre Crouzet. The army which was going to depart—the brave army of Boulogne— was the recipient in 1805 of a heroic march composed by the Chapel Master, Lesueur, at the direct order of Napoleon. Although the army never did sail against England, it campaigned well enough from 1805 to 1807 for Napoleon to desire in 1808 the composition of songs mentioning the glory the troops had acquired and would acquire and the freedom of the seas which would result from their exploits. To obtain these songs, which were to be sent to the various cities, he worked through Cretet, and in the following year he ordered Fouché to have songs written. When *La Lyonnaise*, which urged resistance to the invader, became popular in January, 1814, the government provided that it be played by public orchestras and arranged as a marching song.[63]

There was an element of government control as well as one of government inspiration. The police tried to prevent the singing in public places and on the streets of songs hostile to Napoleon or relative to current events. In 1810 the head of the censorship bureau, Count Joseph Portalis, had the Minister of the Interior send a circular to the prefects charging them rather than the censors with supervising popular musical works and with revising them in the interests of order and decency by substituting glorious deeds from the history of the Empire. The Minister of the Interior also had to see that songs at the Opéra were worthy of that theater. Napoleon's personal role in this control

---

[62] Napoleon, *Correspondance*, VI, 160. The result was probably the *Chant de guerre* inserted in the *Moniteur* of 28 Pluviôse, Year VIII, said to have been written by a general. Some of the ideas expressed by this *Chant de guerre* to the tune of the *Marseillaise* were urging the French to fight for liberty, glory, and victory, as they were the great people. The song also cast aspersions on the enemy as being cowardly and refusing a peace; promised that the enemy would not return home; gave a description of the battle and the joy at the victory; and expressed a desire for peace.

[63] Napoleon, *Correspondance*, XVII, 518; Charpentier, *Napoléon et les hommes de lettres*, 70; Napoleon (Lecestre, comp.), *Lettres*, I, 260; *Débats*, 17 Frimaire, Year XIII; *Empire*, January 31, 1814.

may be glimpsed from his permitting the presentation of Mozart's *Don Juan* only after asking Fouché what its effect on public opinion would probably be.[64]

Censorship likewise functioned for poetry. Abbé Jacques Delille's *Poème de la Pitié* was seized and revised twice, the second time because the new edition contained the suppressed verses. Even though the motives of the composer of *Invitation à partir pour l'Angleterre* were satisfactory, the results did not quite measure up to his intentions, and the police were charged with discovering his identity.[65]

Inspiration, compensation, interdiction—each played a role in Napoleon's policy on poetical and musical composition.

C. DECORATIVE ARTS AND CARICATURE

Napoleon intended that the decorative arts, partly as a result of measures of prompting and control similar to those used for music and poetry, should glorify him in two ways. They were to do so directly by commemorating his outstanding achievements, indirectly by setting a new standard of excellence which would make his epoch unique.[66]

Especially useful for commemorative purposes were medals, which were produced principally in the medal mints established by the government at Paris and Milan. Though the types of events which they depicted varied greatly, it is safe to say that there were medals for all the important victories of the French.[67] Distribution of Legion of Honor crosses; the establishment of new schools, museums, lodges, or similar institutions; vaccination; the civil code; the important domestic events in Napoleon's immediate family; the various political changes Napoleon effected in Europe; and even the invasion of England were all honored by

[64] Aulard (ed.), *Paris sous le consulat*, I, *passim*; Coffin, "Censorship and literature," *loc. cit.*, 292–94; Napoleon, *Correspondance*, XIII, 561; Rosen, *Napoleon's Opera-Glass*, 57.

[65] Welschinger, *Censure sous l'empire*, 141–42; Charpentier, *Napoléon et les hommes de lettres*, 72.

[66] Napoleon, *Correspondance*, XVI, 389.

[67] Edward Edwards (ed.), *The Napoleon Medals: a Complete Series of the Medals Struck in France, Italy, Great Britain, and Germany from the Commencement of the Empire in 1804 to the Restoration in 1815* (London, 1837–40), I, *passim*.

the striking of special medals. Hercules, undoubtedly representing French strength, was a favorite among the anti-English medals: in one he is strangling a fish; in another he is holding an English leopard which he is preparing to chain. In addition to these medals celebrating important events, there were official medals to commemorate Napoleon himself and French heroes such as Desaix and Lannes; various virtues such as justice, good faith, and friendship; imperial stage-coach offices; or such occurrences as official visits to the medal mint. Many unofficial medals were also produced.

As early as 1800 a consular decree charged the Minister of the Interior with producing a medal to commemorate the conquest of Bavaria, and others on successes of the Egyptian campaign. The first one ordered by Napoleon after becoming Emperor was in honor of the Battle of Jena, and he later commissioned the Class of History and Ancient Literature of the National Institute to prepare *Histoire métallique de Napoléon le Grand*.[68] Encouragement for a high standard of workmanship included a *Prix de Rome* and two seats in the Institute.

It is impossible to say just how many medals were struck of each design or to be certain what distribution was made of them, but it is known that the generals, officers, and noncommissioned officers of the army received those celebrating the Egyptian campaign. By being impressed into public monuments or reported in the press, many medals received a wider distribution than might superficially appear to be the case.[69]

Engravings, some allegorical, some portraying Napoleon or members of his family, were encouraged. At Napoleon's express command some portrayed the King of Rome in the uniform of the national guard with the inscription, "I pray to God for my father and France," in preference to "May God watch over my father and France." An announcement in the papers often added to the importance of an engraving, which could be sold by hawkers after they had obtained police permission.[70]

---

[68] Jean Babelon, "La médaille et les médailleurs sous le premier empire," *Revue des études napoléoniennes*, XXIX (1929), 199–202; Napoleon, *Correspondance*, VI, 413, 453. In 1810 Napoleon ordered an antiregicide medallion to warn revolutionaries.

[69] Napoleon, *Correspondance*, XXV, 511.

[70] *Ibid.*, XXVII, 262; Welschinger, *Censure sous l'empire*, 14; *Moniteur, passim.*

In order to arouse patriotic interest, Napoleon frequently had maps of battles and campaigns published and distributed.[71] Although the Minister of War occasionally performed this task, Cambacérès usually received the assignment.

The erection of monuments was another way in which outstanding events or men were commemorated. Such edifices might be statues, columns, arches of triumph, fountains, or temples; and frequently Napoleon ordered them as much to subsidize artists as for propaganda reasons.[72]

In 1800 Bonaparte ordered a column erected in each departmental capital in memory of the soldier dead and of those who had received marks of distinction. A national column was to be erected in Paris, and for quite a long time the papers were filled with discussions as to the proper location and design for it. There were also monuments to celebrate famous battles, and several monuments to the Grand Army. One of these Napoleon paid for from his personal coffers, locating it on the Place de la Madeleine and giving very specific directions as to the design. The statues, usually of generals, were sometimes paid for by public subscription, with the papers listing the names of the donors and the amounts they had contributed.[73] When statues of bishops were permitted, the Minister of Public Worship chose the sculptors. There were various other monuments, all designed to promote patriotism and some even to humiliate the enemies of France. Inscriptions on the different triumphal arches were particularly jingoistic. That on the Arc de Triomphe at the Pantin barrier read: "The Emperor said, 'Soldiers, you will return home only under triumphal arches.' 'I am satisfied with my Grand Army!' 'Crowns of valor to the children of victory—your eagles will not let their crown be torn away.' 'Soldiers, come receive the embraces of your brothers, come place your laurels in the bosom of your families.' 'Soldiers, your courage has confounded the enemy, and

[71] Based on the various editions of Napoleon's correspondence. Napoleon, *Correspondance*, XIV, 89; XV, 224.

[72] Napoleon, *Correspondance*, XII, 372. In Italy, too, the government favored architects and decorators with orders. A. Pingaud, *Bonaparte président de la république italienne*, II, 351.

[73] Napoleon, *Correspondance*, VI, 194; X, 378; XII, 116, 480, 487; XIV, 14; XV, 84; XX, 197; *Moniteur*, 15 Messidor, Year VIII; Aulard (ed.), *Paris sous le premier empire*, II, 621.

your constancy has braved the climates; eternal gratitude.' " [74]

The Minister of the Interior executed the decrees for departmental columns and for a monument to the Grand Army. For this latter monument the National Institute selected the winning architectural design from the entries in a contest ordered by Napoleon. Monuments were placed on Italian battlefields under the supervision of Eugene, Napoleon's viceroy.[75]

Napoleon spent colossal sums on monuments. The Arc de Triomphe de l'Étoile cost 4,500,000 francs, exclusive of the ornaments. Another monument, a temple to the Grand Army on Montmartre, involved the expenditure of between thirty and forty million francs, but members of the electoral colleges were each to contribute from one hundred to three hundred francs a year for a ten-year period to defray the cost.[76]

Painters also received governmental gratifications, plus the hint that they choose important men and events in French history, especially contemporary history, as topics.[77] The painter most favored by Napoleon was Jacques David, who in 1800 received the title "Painter of the Government" with a yearly stipend of 12,000 francs. Except when some established painter such as he was doing the government work, Napoleon left the choice of the artist to Denon, Director General of Museums, who paid all the painters. Those receiving pensions—of 2,000, and later 4,000 francs—included Antoine Gros, François Gérard, Charles Thévenin, Pierre Prud'hon, Mme Marie Benoist. For work performed they received added compensation, and the government might pay them for pictures it had not ordered by buying the best can-

[74] Aulard (ed.), *Paris sous le premier empire*, III, 420; Napoleon, *Correspondance*, XII, 373; *Moniteur, passim*. When the prefect of La Roer proposed a monument in honor of the Chevalier d'Assas, Napoleon vetoed the suggestion. Napoleon (Picard and Tuetey, eds.), *Correspondance inédite*, IV, 405. He also vetoed a proposed monument to himself, preferring to let posterity build it. He did, however, allow equestrian statues of himself, and he commissioned Antonio Canova to carve a large, nonequestrian one. Aulard (ed.), *Paris sous le premier empire*, II, 621; Napoleon, *Correspondance*, VII, 352.

[75] Napoleon, *Correspondance*, XV, 336.

[76] *Ibid.*, XVI, 346; XVIII, 79. These contributions were not at all voluntary. Original plans called for the expenditure of only fifteen million francs, with each elector paying one hundred francs a year.

[77] *Moniteur*, 22 Frimaire, Year X.

vases displayed at the annual or biennial *salons*, for which paintings were selected by a commission of artists established by Lucien when he was Minister of the Interior.[78] Although painters received less for historical pictures than for portraits, worth 3,000 or 4,000 francs for originals and 1,500 francs for each copy, Napoleon did pay 12,000 francs each for eight large historical paintings.[79]

Napoleon found other ways to encourage the decorative arts. Among the prizes awarded for works of merit were prizes to celebrate the Treaty of Amiens and the religious peace, and an architectural one for drawings to publicize the Grand Army and Napoleon.[80] Lucien selected the artists who were deliberately publicized as the ten best. Finally, certain artists, who received recompense according to their age and services, were allowed to live at the Louvre.[81]

The cartoons which Napoleon encouraged naturally directed their barbs primarily at the enemy, especially England. One series, showing that Britain would not keep the Treaty of Amiens, included the "Pâté d'Amiens," which stressed that England did not have to be afraid to break such trifles as treaties. Another series poked fun at the precipitance with which the British left Hanover. One of the cartoons, "Retour du duc de Cambridge à la maison paternelle," shows the Duke receiving a prize for agility. Of a third series, on the invasion of England, the Bourbon agents reported that the number of anti-British caricatures was growing daily. The last of the anti-British series, all of which displayed

---

[78] Lanzac de Laborie, *Paris sous Napoléon*, VIII, 367, 383–414, 430; Napoleon, *Correspondance*, X, 110–11; Charpentier, *Napoléon et les hommes de lettres*, 197; François P.-G. Guizot, *De l'état des beaux-arts en France et du salon de 1810* (Paris, 1811), *passim*.

[79] One of these may have been that by Callet, *La France considérée à l'époque du 18 brumaire. Moniteur*, 24 Messidor, Year IX.

[80] Aulard (ed.), *Paris sous le consulat*, II, 840; *Moniteur*, 28 Fructidor, Year XI. The provisional government of the Italian Republic also offered a prize to the Italian painter who produced the best historical or allegorical work depicting Bonaparte and the Republic's gratitude to him. *Moniteur*, 15 Prairial, Year X.

[81] Napoleon, *Correspondance*, VI, 457; X, 323. Outstanding artists were also exempt from military service. Napoleon (Picard and Tuetey, eds.), *Correspondance inédite*, I, 63.

much coarseness, used as its theme the perfidy of England and its practice of buying coalitions. Regarding such cartoons Napoleon wrote Fouché on May 30, 1805: "Have some caricatures made: an Englishman, purse in hand, begging different powers to receive his money, etc. That is the true slant to give this. The immense attention which the English direct to gaining time by false news shows the extreme importance of this work." [82]

More personal cartoons were directed against William Pitt, the Younger, than against any other Englishman. These appeared primarily after 1803. In various cartoons he was portrayed as warlike, dreaming of the success of his military plans while being rocked in a cradle by his partisans, or frightened at French victories.[83] Other caricatured Britishers included Lord Morpeth [George Howard], Drake, George III, Charles James Fox, Wellington, Queen Charlotte, the Dukes of York and Cambridge, Lord Horatio Nelson, and Sir John Acton. One cartoon on Drake, for example, pictured him, characterized by eagle feathers and claws to indicate speed, with his secret inks and codes, fleeing while clad in a fox in front of whose mouth was a swarm of flies (*mouches*) with the caption, "No, Mr. Drake is not a *gobemouche* [prattler]." [84]

Napoleon personally suggested cartoons pointed at many of these personages and at the Queen of Naples and the Prince of Hesse-Cassel. Usually he suggested the subjects to Fouché, who relayed them to the artists. In 1800, however, he ordered Talleyrand to commission a caricature representing Baron Franz Thugut between the doge of Venice and a Cisalpine director, the allusion being that the Austrian Thugut robbed the one by the Treaty of Campoformio and imprisoned the other for not recognizing that

[82] Broadley, *Napoleon in Caricature*, I, 254; Aulard (ed.), *Paris sous le consulat*, IV, 158, 205, 282; Remacle (ed.), *Bonaparte et les Bourbons*, 346–48. For specific titles of more cartoons see André Blum, "La caricature politique en France sous le consulat et l'empire," *Revue des études napoléoniennes*, XIII (1918), 296–312. There were also many fans, covered with satirical designs, showing scenes of invasion. Harold F. B. Wheeler and Alexander M. Broadley, *Napoleon and the Invasion of England, the Story of the Great Terror* (London, 1907), II, 309; Napoleon (Lecestre, comp.), *Lettres*, I, 51.

[83] Blum, "Caricature politique en France," *loc. cit.*, 301.

[84] Aulard (ed.), *Paris sous le consulat*, IV, 765; Broadley, *Napoleon in Caricature*, I, ix–x. John Holland Rose wrote the introduction to this latter book.

treaty.[85] Napoleon also evolved the idea of the "Father Violet" in 1814 and 1815.[86]

Several cartoons, including some appearing in subject lands, poked fun at the enemies of France. In one, Queen Louise of Prussia was pictured as an Amazon getting news from Alexander, while her husband, standing by halting on a wooden leg, thanked himself that he had enough rope left to hang himself. One of 1807 showed the deluge of Napoleon's power (the Continental System) flooding the mainland and leaving John Bull far off in a stormy sea on which cotton was floating. The four regal figures in the foreground of the caricature were in anything but regal positions: Alexander was clinging to a breaking tree on the edge of a cliff; Queen Louise was grasping his waist; Frederick William III was clinging to her; and his frame was holding up the half-drenched Elector of Hesse.[87]

There were also cartoons lauding the French, instead of belittling the opposition. Some dealt with French victories such as Ulm and Austerlitz, and different long series of cartoons represented Napoleon as a Gallic cock (the symbol of French courage) or stressed his invincibility, the folly of those opposing him, and the doom of England. One, entitled "The Triumph of the French Eagle," showed the Napoleonic bird seizing in its talons the double-headed eagle of Austria and driving in ignominious flight the Prussian eagle and the Russian goose.[88]

Even under the Consulate the English in France had experienced difficulty in obtaining caricatures produced in England and had been able to procure them only via Hamburg. After becoming Emperor, Napoleon tightened still more the reins on inimical cartoons. He experienced great difficulty locating the editors of

[85] Napoleon, *Correspondance*, VI, 395. Hence the statement in Broadley (*Napoleon in Caricature*, I, xxxiii) that the first documentary evidence of Napoleon's ordering a cartoon is a letter of May 30, 1805, not found in the official correspondence, is inaccurate. There were also other cartoons against Austria, Russia, and Prussia. Blum, "Caricature politique en France," *loc. cit.*, 303–305.

[86] Broadley, *Napoleon in Caricature*, I, xxxii; II, 26–27, 106; Napoleon, *Correspondance*, VI, 395. "Father Violet," who returns in the spring, was the symbol of the Bonapartists during the first restoration.

[87] Broadley, *Napoleon in Caricature*, I, xliii, lviii.

[88] *Ibid.*, I, xliii, lvii; II, 33–34.

political caricatures jibing him, one of the more amusing being that of a Boulogne tailor who was trying a garment on Bonaparte. Bonaparte admired the garment's quality and workmanship, but in putting it on he could not get his arm into the sleeve (*passer son bras dans la manche*). The caption was, " 'Never,' says the legend, 'shall I pass that *manche*.' " [89] Under both the Consulate and the Empire, the police regularly reported on caricatures, but there is no indication whether the favorable ones were officially inspired.[90]

Some of the important caricaturists in France were Philippe Hennequin, V. M. Picot, Ruotte, Forestier, Chasselat, Desrais, and Tassart. Works of these men were sold by various publishers, of whom Martinet was the most prolific. Other cartoons were signed by le Campion, le Campion frères, and Pierre Rolland.[91] In order to give greater circulation to the cartoons, Napoleon ordered Fouché to send caricatures into Italy and Germany. Cartoons, such as the one showing a British squadron sailing up the Rhine without being able to gain the aid of any of the peasants, regularly received publicity in the press.[92]

In such fashion did Napoleon make use of the arts. Although he definitely crippled them in many respects, it is only fair to note that there were times—as in the case of the theater and of architecture—when his interest was occasionally something more than that of the mere propagandist.

[89] Blum, "Caricature politique en France," *loc. cit.,* 302. "*Manche*" in French means both sleeve and English Channel.

[90] Broadley, *Napoleon in Caricature,* I, xxxix; Aulard (ed.), *Paris sous le consulat,* IV, 266; and *passim*; E. d'Hauterive (ed.), *La police secrète, passim.*

[91] Broadley, *Napoleon in Caricature,* II, 29-30; Wheeler and Broadley, *Napoleon and the Invasion of England,* II, 274. One of the cartooning Campions was probably Charles Philippe, the engraver.

[92] Napoleon (Lecestre, comp.), *Lettres,* I, 260; Aulard (ed.), *Paris sous le consulat, passim; Journal,* 2 Brumaire, Year XI.

CHAPTER VIII

DEVICES

GRANTED A MASTERLY GOVERNMENTAL ORGANIZATION WHICH completely utilizes the mediums of expression, the propagandist still has several tricks up his sleeve. They are devices which help bring the unwitting victim around to the desired frame of mind.

INITIATIVE

Because of the psychological impact of an original impression, a propagandist must try to drive home his arguments before the other side swings into action to influence public opinion. For Napoleon, the British, who were able to get their material into France, constituted the most important element in that "other side" whose charges he had to counteract. According to some of the British allegations, Napoleon was a bloodthirsty tyrant who deliberately murdered his sick soldiers at Jaffa and who encouraged his soldiers, unwillingly forced into the army to further his desire for world dominion, to commit atrocities. He forbade any personal freedom. A religious opportunist, he disregarded all laws of morality in his personal life. Some of his acts violated all international law: for instance, imprisoning the British within his grasp upon resumption of hostilities in 1803, and seizing the Duke of Enghien in Baden.[1]

---

[1] John Grand-Carteret, *Napoléon en images* (Paris, 1895), 18; Ebbinghaus, *Napoleon, England und die Presse*, 61; John Ashton, *English Caricature and Satire on Napoleon*, 2 vols. (London, 1884), *passim; Atrocities of the Corsican Daemon; or a Glance at Bonaparte* (London, 1803), *passim*. William Sotheby, *A Song of Triumph* (London, 1814), 6; Napoleon (pseud.), *Proclamation of the First Consul, intended to be Issued Immediately on the Landing of the French Army in England, with a Copy of the Original Letter, in which it was Inclosed, Addressed to Sir ——, Bart.* (London, 1804); Galgacus (pseud.), *The Anti-Corsican* (London, 1804), *passim*. Evjen, "English Propaganda against Napoleon," 91, 113; Baron de Guilhermy, *Papiers d'un émigré, 1789–1829*, ed. by Col. de Guilhermy (Paris, 1886), 232; Broadsides, De Paul University collection.

While defending himself against these attacks,[2] Napoleon drew up a series of indictments against England. These have been mentioned in another connection in Chapter I, but the more important will bear repetition: as England was ambitious and aimed at universal monopoly of the sea, it did not respect neutral rights or other aspects of international law; it was mercenary and perfidious; it stooped even to participating in assassination plots; and its press was licentious.

The royalists, Jacobins, and papists in France also caused some trouble by asserting that Napoleon had usurped the throne, that he was reactionary, and that he utilized religion merely to further his own interests.[3] Against each of these arguments he defended himself, at the same time taking the fight into the enemy camp by accusing the Jacobins of being anarchists and the Bourbons of plotting civil war and fighting alongside the enemies of France. Whether or not he succeeded, he always attempted to forestall arguments of hostile elements by charges of his own.[4]

OPPOSITION SOURCES

Such charges against the enemy could attack more vulnerable spots after France had discovered, by the methods discussed in the preceding chapters, what the enemy was thinking. One such means was the use of the enemy press, which could also fulfill the role played by all opposition sources of lending added authority to French statements. Because the rabid opposition press in England was allowed great freedom, it was particularly easy for Napoleon to quote British papers criticizing their government. Those London papers most frequently cited were the *Morning Chronicle*, the *Statesman*, the *Pilot*, the *Alfred*, and the *Independ-*

[2] The charges were made and answered primarily in the press, rumors, pamphlets, and handbills. The British used this last method much more extensively than did Napoleon. Naturally Napoleon answered other opponents as well.

[3] *Consulate: Contemporary Pamphlets, passim,* esp. *Manifesto des royalistes des provinces de l'Ouest de la France* and *La vérité au Corse usurpateur du trône de Louis XVIII.* They also used songs and spectacles for defamatory purposes. Aulard (ed.), *Paris sous le consulat* and *Paris sous le premier empire, passim.*

[4] One *Moniteur* article which the British answered was that entitled "A Capitulation in Time of Peace."

ent Whig.[5] He also exploited opposition spokesmen in Parliament, quoting them in the French papers.

The French also cited enemy sources not in opposition to their own government. Intercepted letters were quoted, and Napoleon publicized favorable material extracted from the archives of conquered countries. One example of citing a hostile source was Mallet du Pan's admission that factions had disappeared in France. Among other foreign material reprinted in France were the London *Times*'s confession that the attack on Boulogne had accomplished little and an enemy bulletin which admitted heavy losses on its side. During the Year VIII the *Moniteur* quoted letters supposedly from the Cardinal of York to the King of England criticizing the British war policy. Even more effective was the citing of publications which the enemy had designed to bolster its own views. Thus *War in Disguise, or the Fraud of Neutral Flags*, written by Samuel Rogers under ministerial influence, pointed out just what France had been trying to tell the powers.[6]

Although people are prone to accept enemy statements favorable to their own side, they tend to be skeptical about those advantageous to their opponents. Napoleon therefore permitted bad news, such as the loss of Santo Domingo or the Trafalgar disaster, to leak out via citation of the enemy so as to attenuate the impact of the revelation.[7]

PRESTIGE

Another way to lend authority to one's claims is to cite people recognized as authorities in their own fields or as having influence with the people. That is why Napoleon ordered in 1814 that the appropriate executives demand statements on allied atrocities by

[5] *Moniteur, passim.* In order to lend credit to French statements, Napoleon tried to use mediums in the tongue of the region he wanted to influence, regardless of whether those mediums were pro-French. Napoleon, *Correspondance*, XVIII, 202. In this chapter, when papers are cited for general statements, it is merely to indicate examples of those statements.

[6] *Empire*, 19 Frimaire, Year XIV; March 24, 1814; Napoleon, *Correspondance*, XVI, 446; *Débats*, 18 Germinal, Year VIII; 3 Brumaire, Year XIII; *Moniteur*, 23 Pluviôse, Year VIII; *Curés*, May 17, 1809. Another use of hostile sources was to test public opinion by quoting them, in order to propose measures which Napoleon desired. Thiers, *Histoire du consulat*, V, 66.

[7] *Moniteur*, 11 Prairial, Year XI; *Empire*, January 29, 1806.

bishops, canons, and curés; by prefects and mayors; by post-masters and other governmental employees; by judges, justices of the peace, and notaries; and by former lords, bourgeois, and men of affairs.[8]

It is obviously impossible to cite all the men (in addition to those above) who spoke with authority, but at least some indication can be given of the variety of fields covered by French propaganda. Cardinal Ercole Consalvi praised the French agents for having been obliging and courteous to the Pope. The faculty of the school of medicine at Paris denied the rumor that there were more deaths than usual. Whenever possible Napoleon used natives of foreign territories to speak to their populations: German savants said all their universities desired the success of the French in Egypt because the French greatly favored the arts and sciences. A chief of brigade reported that the Maltese regretted the departure of the French, and a French officer analyzed the Russian report on Austerlitz.[9]

UNIVERSALITY

Asserting that one's propaganda claims are the general belief of the public is another means of lending them prestige. Napoleon therefore tried to persuade the French that only a small part of the Spanish nation was resisting in 1808 and that in reality most of the populace were disposed to submit. He also maintained that all nations were supporting France in its opposition to absolute control of the seas by Britain, and, to make his assertion seem valid, gave considerably more space to those nations supporting the French stand than to those siding with England or even remaining neutral.[10]

At home he refused to admit the differentiation between his interests and those of France as a whole, a differentiation which foreign propaganda sought to make. Once, during a speech, he

[8] Napoleon, *Correspondance*, XXVII, 245–46.

[9] *Moniteur*, 14 Germinal and 19 Thermidor, Year VIII; 1 Ventôse, 1 Prairial, and 29 Messidor, Year IX; April 21, 1806; Marcel Handelsman, *Napoléon et la Pologne, 1806–1807* (Paris, 1909), 17.

[10] *Débats*, 28 Pluviôse, Year XI; 22 Fructidor, Year XII; *Empire*, November 5, 1809; *Journal*, September 28, 1808; May 3, 1809; Joseph (Du Casse, ed.), *Mémoires*, V, 186.

assured his audience that his every move was for the good of France: "Frenchmen, my will is that of the people; my rights are its own; my honor, my glory, my happiness can be none other than the honor, glory, and happiness of France." [11] The large number of addresses filling the papers, as well as the favorable articles which the press published, tended to convey the impression that all the people perceived that their interests and his were one and the same.

RHETORICAL QUESTIONS

Such identity of interests heightened the usefulness of rhetorical questions, which assumed that the public was favorably enough disposed to the questioner to respond in the desired way. In answering enemy accounts of military events, Napoleon would query: "Who remained master of the villages . . . ? Who lost two regiments of cuirassiers and five hundred cavalry prisoners?" [12] In other than the military field, rhetorical questions figured most largely in criticisms of Great Britain and her policies and in the notes of the *Moniteur* answering British statements. "Is it not pleasant to see a government justify violation of a treaty on the presumed intention of another government also to violate it?" After criticizing the British attack on Copenhagen in 1801, the *Moniteur* asked the well-chosen rhetorical question, "Powers of Europe, what would have happened to your independence and order if England had the half million soldiers France does?" [13]

SARCASM, IRONY, RIDICULE

Since prestige is a purely relative matter, Napoleon was able indirectly to increase that of his own propaganda by lessening that of his enemies through the use of the potent weapons, sarcasm, irony, and ridicule. In 1807 the *Journal de l'Empire* declared that England respected the neutrality of Austria—by firing on its ships. The British waged a glorious campaign in Spain in

[11] *Empire*, June 3, 1815; *Archives parlementaires*, XIV, 390, on the *Champ de Mai* celebration of May 31, 1815.
[12] Napoleon, *Correspondance*, XXVI, 397.
[13] *Débats*, 8 Prairial, Year XI; *Moniteur*, 12 Ventôse, Year VIII; 16 Germinal, Year IX.

1809, the French newspaper sarcastically claimed: outnumbering an unprovisioned French army three to one, they were unable to capture it and were reduced to offering thanks because some of the débris of the British army returned to England. The British ministers' plans of campaign were flawless on paper; all they lacked was that the enemy's fortifications should also be of paper. They sent Nelson once more against Boulogne, a *"burnt city* whose *bell tower* no longer exists, whose *port is destroyed,* whose hospitals are full of *wounded,* whose shore is covered with *dead and drowned,* and when our fleet . . . is sunk." [14] These and many other press articles illustrate the use of sarcasm and irony to attack the enemy.

Ridicule was employed even more frequently, and very effectively. The Russians were said to have started a new school of war: that of beating the drums of retreat after their victory, the *Te Deum* for which was always interrupted by the arrival of French troops. The Russian declaration that ports occupied by French troops were in a state of blockade was likened to the ancient prince who whipped and chained the sea for thwarting his plans. Russian bulletins killed many French soldiers who were well and revived Russians who had been dead three or four months. And Prussia was made to look ridiculous by French quotation, after the news of Jena had reached Paris, of an article in the London *Star* that Prussia would surely win because it had the finest soldiers in the world.[15]

The answers to British statements contained a good deal of ridicule, employed in place of reasoned arguments. Britain's various military activities on the Continent were the butt of ridicule, the French press even charging that the British forces left the island of Avemakoë because they thought the regular troops were there when the men donned their wives' red aprons. Parliament had to vote thanks to the volunteers before they had done anything, inasmuch as it was afraid there would be no opportunity to do so later. It seemed that the English had a thousand horses

[14] *Empire,* September 14, 1807; *Journal,* April 8, 1806; February 20, 1809; *Moniteur,* 4 Vendémiaire and 1 Fructidor, Year IX; 12 Thermidor, Year XI. The London *Ambigu* effectively used sarcasm against France.

[15] *Mercure,* September 19, 1812; *Journal,* April 8, 1806; October 31, 1806; March 26, 1807.

brought so they could run away faster; if the French troops were in the bad plight depicted by the English government, why were they so successful against the British? England was still talking about the *levée en masse*, propaganda claimed; we thought it was completed ages ago. The *Moniteur* commented that England used its espionage money very poorly to know so little about French affairs. The *Journal des Débats* ridiculed the London *Times*'s report of Kléber's assassination by pointing out that the *Times* had often had Bonaparte killed. The announcement of the London *Courier* that on 1 Vendémiaire, Year IX, the French clergy was to be recalled was ridiculous, as the sixth of that month had already arrived.[16]

Individuals opposing France were likewise made to appear absurd. Antirepublicans were portrayed as being foolish. A story was circulated of an officer who ran better than the French soldiers marched. General Karl Mack was made fun of for his proclamation that the soldiers should eat horseflesh rather than surrender, and in 1813 it was hinted that Bernadotte was crazy. The *Moniteur* recommended that, in judging the present acts of all such individuals, their past conduct should be considered.[17]

LETTERS

Letters (which were often used as a means of announcing news) tended to give authenticity to statements of the government because they were individual and usually relatively simple, dealing with only one topic. Papers constantly printed actual or forged letters,[18] many of which Napoleon had ordered his government officials to write.[19]

Napoleon himself wrote letters for publication and instructed various generals and naval officials, the Helvetic executive com-

[16] Ebbinghaus, *Napoleon, England und die Presse*, 104; *Moniteur*, 6 Prairial, Year VIII; 25 Ventôse, Year X; February 5, 1809; June 6, 1810; *Débats*, 6 Frimaire, Year VIII; *Empire*, October 12, 1809; October 17, 1810; *Journal*, 6 Vendémiaire, Year IX; 7 Fructidor, Year XI; September 13, 1807; May 26, 1808; Napoleon (Lecestre, comp.), *Lettres*, I, 260.

[17] *Empire*, October 22, 1813; *Moniteur*, 10 Messidor, Year VIII; 20 Floréal, Year IX; *Gazette de Hamburg, passim*.

[18] The forged ones will be considered in the last section of this chapter. It is possible that private letters were seized by the post office, opened, and used.

[19] *Journal*, 23 Floréal, Year VIII.

mission, his wife during the regency, and Ferdinand to write others for publication. Though there is no proof that they were written at its request, the government publicized many other letters. Two such letters were those of Secretary of State Pedro de Cevallos in Spain and of the Divan of Cairo. There are also letters from various army corps asking to serve in the Grand Army rather than in the Army of the Interior.[20]

Private letters were particularly effective when they were at least reputedly intercepted from members of the opposition, such as one telling about English losses in Egypt and said to have been written by a British naval officer, or when they mentioned events affecting the correspondent, such as the numerous ones describing the pillaging of the writer's own goods by the allies in 1814.[21] A capitalist who had just started a business in France wrote several letters (which appeared in various papers) complaining to a London banker about England's policy. Napoleon in 1814 ordered the police to collect and print letters received in Paris from places where the enemy had been forced to withdraw. There were many letters with no indication of author or place, or with a statement so general (as that of "a capitalist") that it gave no clue as to the person of the author, even though he was said to be so situated that he might particularly know about the situation his letter described.[22]

HISTORICAL AND RELIGIOUS VOCABULARY

In pointing up certain events in European history and in relating French history to Biblical writings, the propaganda machine used

[20] Napoleon, *Correspondance*, VI, 338; XVII, 197; XXVII, 213; *Moniteur*, 6 Prairial, Year IX; December 27, 1812; Murat (Prince Murat, pub.), *Lettres*, V, 492.

[21] Napoleon (*Correspondance*, XXVII, 247) told Savary to leave in the French faults so as to show that the bare and complete truth was being given to the public.

[22] *Moniteur*, 25 Messidor, Year IX; *Citoyen français* and *Journal*, Ventôse, and Germinal, Year XI. The letter of a Russian to a friend at Hamburg, appearing in the *Moniteur* of 9 Ventôse, Year IX, was not written very cleverly. The author of the letter was apparently confused as to the person whom he was addressing. After saying "England recognized only its own rights," he later wrote as if he were addressing England: "You [England] have the most flourishing commerce." Some of these letters contained puns—for example, "*bal*," meaning "bullet" or "dance." *Journal*, 20 Ventôse, Year VIII.

a vocabulary of words and phrases designed to appeal to the people's sense of patriotism. If God and history were on the side of the government, naturally more influence would accrue to statements of the government's position. The French therefore cited history to show that England had not been faithful in observing its treaties even in the past, that—as in the case of Carthage and Holland—commerce gave a temporary ascendancy only, that the same complaints made against England now were repetitions of former complaints. There was also a great deal of historical argument in connection with naming Napoleon Emperor, and the *Moniteur* reminded the Poles in 1812 that Napoleon was leading them into the same regions in which their ancestors had won brilliant victories.[23] In addition to claiming divine support and guidance, government propaganda indicated that Jeremiah had prophesied Napoleon as a savior of the world.[24]

EMOTIONAL VOCABULARY

Even more powerful than the emotional connotation of the religious and historical vocabularies was that of certain words repeated so frequently that they might be termed catchwords. These naturally simplified issues in order that the people might understand them more easily.

One series of these phrases depicted what a wonderful man Napoleon was.[25] Not content with being a "conquering hero" who "liberated" [26] subject peoples, this "genius," [27] a "second

[23] *Moniteur*, 23 Pluviôse, Year VIII; 8 Vendémiaire, Year XII; September 13, 1812; A. Hauterive, *De l'état de la France*, 72. Yet the government was not averse to saying that historical comparisons, such as Caesar with Bonaparte or Athens with France, did not necessarily hold, because of circumstantial differences. A. Hauterive, *De l'état de la France*, 310–44.

[24] *Prophétie qui n'a été jamais imprimée*, in *Church Affairs: Contemporary Pamphlets: 1805–6.*

[25] Unless otherwise indicated, all of the words and phrases mentioned in this section appeared in the newspapers. Addresses to Napoleon, poems, and music were particularly replete with them. These phrases are presented thus as a compromise between listing them all and merely telling about them, because they were much more effective in their contexts than they would be in a list.

[26] Citoyen Letournel, "Ode à Bonaparte, premier consul de la république française," *Napoléon jugé par lui-même, par ses amis et ses ennemis*, ed. by Baron Nicolas Massias (Paris, 1823).

[27] *Napoléon libérateur*, in *Church and Religious Affairs during the Consulate and Empire: Contemporary Pamphlets 1810–1815.*

Charlemagne," [28] became the "savior" [29] of France. "Generous" as a "pacifier," his "noble goodness" proved "benevolent" to France. "Brave and intrepid" on the field of battle, "moderate in triumph," "faithful" to his obligations, he bore with "dignity" the burden of a "just, strong, liberal, and wise" government which would win "immortality" for its "paternal and humane" chief.

Among the many benefits bestowed upon the country by this government were the "abolition of factions"—but there was to be "no reaction" even though the "revolution was ended." All "patriots" might now rally to a government based on the "principles" of "national representation, equality, morality, civil liberty, individual liberty"—including "religious freedom." This "stable" government "ruling by law" has "restored order" [30] and will restore "peace and prosperity" [31] and protect property. "Harmony and unity" will characterize the support given to an "equitable" government working "salutary changes" for the "welfare" and "enlightenment" of the French people, partly by "encouraging the arts and sciences." One of these changes is the "constitution," another is the "code."

It is no wonder that the "great nation joyfully expressed" its "admiration and love" for and "confidence" in a government to which it was duly "grateful." Displaying "ardor and constancy" in making "sacrifices" to obtain "honor and glory" like that of their "ancestors" in the eyes of "posterity," its members desired to demonstrate their "patriotism" by obtaining "vengeance." Its soldiers during this "national war" have shown themselves "heroic, magnanimous, and loyal" in a "just cause—defense" of their "hearths and their families," the "glory and independence" of their country, and "freedom of the seas."

The enemies against whom they must fight represent only "despotic" governments which stoop to any "odious crimes: assassination, pillage, piracy, massacre, and atrocities." In addition to this "brutality," worse than that of the "Huns and Vandals," they rely upon "corruption, libels, perjury, and perfidy" to at-

[28] *Church Affairs: Agen-Le Mans.*
[29] Volland, *Vers à l'honneur de Bonaparte* (n.p., n.d.).
[30] *Ode to Buonaparte* (Cork, 1817).
[31] P. F. Malingre, *Ode sur le premier consul* (Paris, Year X), 3.

tain their "mercenary and ambitious ends." All acts of these "mad scoundrels" are characterized by a "rapacious cupidity" striking "terror" in the hearts of all but their "sycophants." Any territory they conquered immediately became the victim of the "spoliation" and "enslavement" marking their "tyrannical" rule. "Proud Albion," which is after all only a "sacrilegious nation of shopkeepers," especially desires "carnage" and "perpetual war." It even hires and "plots" with "brigands," and allies with the "barbarous hordes" of Russia.

While catchwords thus praised Napoleon and the government of France, discussed the French, and blasted the enemy, there was a slight change in the stress given them. Gradually the words "republic" and "liberty" disappeared, and in 1801 the government ordered suppression of the epigraph "Liberty, Equality, Fraternity" in official acts.[32] When fortune ceased smiling upon France, more and more stress was laid upon the need for unity and sacrifice. Illustrative of this trend was the adoption late in 1813 of the new slogan "Emperor, country, and honor." Imminent danger of loss called forth the catchword that France should "forget about its conquests and think only of national boundaries," and this plea—with the addition that France would not meddle in the affairs of other states and would not allow them to intervene in its internal affairs—was conspicuous during the Hundred Days. After France had lost, one rallying cry, similar to that of the Germans after 1918, was that its armies had never been conquered, that they had merely been betrayed.

REASONING

Wherever possible, the heated type of argument described in the preceding section was supplemented by rational explanations. The papers printed many statistical articles on the different departments. The financial reports contained voluminous tables which the thoughtful reader might analyze, and to a large extent the annual expositions of the state of the nation were rational. Naturally these were reassuring and stressed the benefits derived from the government.

[32] Stenger, *Société française*, VI, 30; *Journal*, 5 Frimaire, Year X.

At times even actual, logical reasoning was done. This type of argument was used most frequently in discussions regarding the probable authenticity of news, as in the *Journal de Paris* article of 4 Prairial, Year VIII, on Egyptian affairs.

APPEAL TO VARIOUS CLASSES

Evidence of Napoleon's intentions to appeal to diverse groups, as well as to make different types of appeals, is contained in a letter to the Archbishop of Malines: "Every day [propaganda] pieces of every type, of every style, tending to the same goal but addressing themselves to sundry sentiments and minds, must be published. It is thus that a whole nation is successfully put into a kind of intoxication." [33] Carrying out these instructions naturally entailed stressing the type of emotional or rational argument most suitable for the group toward which a particular bit of propaganda was aimed. To win the workers, Napoleon placarded large numbers of the bulletin on the Battle of Marengo in the Paris *faubourgs*,[34] and there can scarcely be any doubt that the fetes—with attractions such as brilliant fireworks and gifts to the populace—were intended primarily to cater to the masses. Much of Napoleon's propaganda was also designed specifically to influence the soldiers.[35]

The Catholics received more attention in Napoleonic propaganda than did any other one civilian group. Much of the stress on how poorly England treated the Irish was designed to arouse French Catholics against the British.[36] Even the abasement of the Catholics in England received a fairly large amount of space. In this campaign Fouché and Jean Portalis co-operated: Fouché inspired suitable press articles, and Portalis instructed the bishops as to what was required of them.[37]

[33] Napoleon, *Correspondance*, XXIII, 444.
[34] Vandal, *Avènement de Bonaparte*, II, 430.
[35] See Chapter IV. Before publishing the Milan Decree, Napoleon ordered Minister of the Interior Cretet to circularize all the chambers of commerce to point out the necessity for answering the legislation of England and to arouse them to following the proper course.
[36] There seems to be no other reasonable explanation for the order that this type of argument should be stressed especially in the departments of Brittany, Vendée, Piedmont, and Belgium. Napoleon (Lecestre, comp.), *Lettres*, I, 93. In the Duchy of Warsaw, Napoleon inveighed against the Russians as schismatics. Broc, *Vie en France*, 208.
[37] Napoleon, *Correspondance*, XV, 29; Haussonville, *Église et empire*, II, 238.

DEVICES   181

Other means of catering to the Catholics were tried. In December, 1802, Bonaparte gave the Pope two sloops with which to defend his interests against the Barbary pirates. Even earlier, Bonaparte had taken steps designed to win the Italian Catholics. These included a *Te Deum* at Milan for the deliverance of Italy from the heretic British and infidel Turks, and a speech to the Milan curés on the importance of the Catholic religion. The Pope's activities received a great deal of favorable publicity during his trip to France in 1804 and 1805. In 1812 the papers were forbidden to appear on the five fete days established by the Concordat.[38]

While attempting to win the Catholics, Napoleon was careful not to alienate the Protestants. He therefore issued orders that press articles berating treatment of Catholics by England should always speak of the "Anglican Church" rather than of "Protestants" because there were Protestants in France.[39]

At all times Napoleon was very mindful of the phrasing used. It was not until the day before his coronation that he employed the expression "my people." In 1807 Cretet received the order to motivate the fete of December 2 as the anniversary of the coronation rather than of the victory at Austerlitz. Clarke received a reprimand for speaking of "hostages" instead of "prisoners of war," and Napoleon issued orders that the King of Sweden should merely be called "head of the Swedish nation." German and Polish divisions of the army in Spain were always referred to as the divisions of the Grand Duchy of Warsaw and of the Confederation of the Rhine, and at various other times the words "Poland" and "Germany" were banned. In the fall of 1813 Maret was instructed never to use the terms "court" or "house," when referring to Austria, but to say "cabinet."[40]

Material was so worded as to appeal to the class at which it was directed, for Napoleon felt that the true ruler should give to each utterance "the style and character" of the people con-

[38] *Moniteur*, 18 Nivôse, Year XI; Driault, "Napoléon et Italie," *loc. cit.*, 38–40; Welschinger, *Censure sous l'empire*, 317; Aulard (ed), *Paris sous le premier empire*, I, *passim.* Just as a matter of interest, it might be noted that Napoleon also finished the front of Milan cathedral.

[39] Napoleon (Lecestre, comp.), *Lettres*, I, 94.

[40] Lanzac de Laborie, *Paris sous Napoléon*, III, 86; Napoleon, *Correspondance*, XVI, 90, 433; XX, 134; XXII, 406; XXVI, 185; Napoleon (Picard and Tuetey, eds.), *Correspondance inédite*, III, 359.

cerned.[41] Many press articles were designed for the lower classes, and financial dealings were simplified in order to be comprehensible to the general public. Lucien was informed that the masses did have wit and judgment, and that therefore more ideas and less pathos were necessary in addressing them. So painstaking was Napoleon that he even applied a different adjective to each nationality.[42]

CHANGE OF OBJECTIVE

French propaganda changed not only its methods, but also its appeals, with the most rapid changes in objectives occurring in the case of Russia. When Paul showed himself friendly in 1800, the Paris papers stopped insulting Russia. During the early part of the Russo-Turkish War beginning in 1806, the French press claimed that Turkey was faring splendidly; but as soon as the Peace of Tilsit was signed, the papers printed only news of the constant successes of Russia.[43]

SPACE

The amount of publicity given various topics indicated Napoleon's attitude toward them. Those items mentioned in the section on papers as being played down, plus others such as court expenses or the sentences inflicted on Frenchmen who had borne arms against France, were minimized.[44] On the other hand, such items as the assassination of Kléber and the Cadoudal plot against Napoleon's life, the Irish rebellion in 1803, British affairs, the plebiscites, the various treaties made by Napoleon, important battles, Napoleon's marriage and the birth of his son, and the fetes received emphasis. British affairs gradually took up more and more space in the *Moniteur*, being treated most fully during the Hundred Days.

[41] Napoleon, *Correspondance*, XV, 73.

[42] La Forest (Grandmaison, pub.), *Correspondance*, VI, 215; Jeanroy-Félix, *Littérature française*, 393; *Débats*, 7 Germinal, Year X; Napoleon (Du Casse, ed.), *Supplément à la correspondance*, 60. Napoleon also tried to win various nationalities to support him by giving them credit for military victories. Napoleon, *Correspondance*, XVIII, 128.

[43] *Débats*, 15 Germinal, Year VIII; Napoleon, *Correspondance*, XV, 381; *Empire*, September 3, 1807; *Journal*, April 11, 1807. Similar though not such precipitant changes occurred when other countries came to terms with France.

[44] Napoleon (Chuquet, ed), *Inédits napoléoniens*, I, 150.

The French also exploited this space device to present one side of controversial questions in a light favorable to the government. In making excerpts from parliamentary debates, French papers gave the greatest spread to antiministerial members, often quoting their speeches *in extenso* and merely summarizing those of the government speakers. Similarly, anti-British declarations by Presidents Thomas Jefferson and James Madison were cited verbatim. With one exception, only the Russian bulletins on the Russo-Swedish War received publicity in the French press.[45]

REPORTING AS NEWS

What has been said earlier in this chapter should indicate that news items, as well as the many unsigned press articles advocating the viewpoint of the government, also served Napoleon. One additional way to arrange for publication of desired material as news was to hold an inquest which would justify printing the pieces. There are two outstanding instances in which this method was used. One of them occurred when a commission of senators and marshals investigated the treatment of French prisoners; the other when the affair of Generals Pierre Dupont, Armand Marescot, and Dominique Vedel was taken to the high court.[46]

DIVERSION

By stressing certain topics, Napoleon hoped to prevent preoccupation of the people with other matters. He is quoted as saying that his only aim in encouraging the sciences and arts was to prevent men from occupying themselves with more serious things.[47] The intrigues against the opera *Trajan* furnished a means to divert interest from rumors of impending war, and Napoleon recommended other literary and musical controversies to distract the people from politics. One such controversy—instigated directly by the police—concerned the relative merits of Italian and French music.[48]

[45] *Moniteur, passim.* See also the other papers, particularly the *Empire.*
[46] Napoleon, *Correspondance*, XX, 101; XXV, 481.
[47] Napoleon (Hinard, comp.), *Opinions et jugemens*, 359.
[48] E. d'Hauterive (ed.), *La police secrète*, III, 398; Lanzac de Laborie, *Paris sous Napoléon*, VII, 246; Broc, *Vie en France*, 248. This desire to divert attention from politics may have been the motive for Napoleon's allowing the many doctrinal disputes, illustrated by those in the religious pamphlets used by the author.

REVIEWS

Even literary criticism was so presented as to serve Napoleon's ends. Books favorable to the government received lengthy, flattering reviews without any delay; books deemed disadvantageous were either criticized harshly or ignored completely.[49]

When Russia, under Paul, had become friendly with France, a volume entitled *Mémoires secrets sur la Russie*—giving a black picture of the Russian government—was criticized because the author had been led astray by the revolutionary spirit; but when Napoleon desired to arouse sentiment against the Russians in 1807, the papers received orders to exalt Claude de Rulhière's *Histoire de l'anarchie de Pologne et du démembrement de cette république.* Napoleon ordered Fouché to have J.-T. Bruguière du Gard's *Napoléon en Prusse* criticized harshly. In 1810, after Napoleon had arrested Pius VII, the *Journal de l'Empire* received an order from the Secretary-General of the ministry of police to praise *Essai historique sur la puissance temporelle des Papes*. The four-volume *Cornelius Népos français* was reviewed favorably because it was dedicated to the glory of the armies and designed to nourish the courage of youth.[50]

TECHNICAL DEVICES

In addition to attracting attention to certain topics by playing them up, the papers used various technical devices. In order to give British affairs the prominence Napoleon felt they deserved, the press always placed them on the front page. Observations on foreign material being refuted were always in type of different size from that of the foreign statement, and sometimes they and the foreign claim occupied parallel columns, each extending halfway across the page. The use of large type was not confined to these observations, and capital letters and exclamation points—even in series—were employed extensively. When the Dutch surrendered the Cape of Good Hope to Great Britain after the sign-

[49] Le Poittevin, *Liberté de la presse*, 211. *Débats*, 8 Prairial, Year VIII, criticized judging writers by their political opinions rather than the worth of their work.
[50] Fiévée, *Correspondance*, II, 255; *Débats*, 25 Prairial, Year VIII; *Moniteur* and *Empire, passim*; Le Poittevin, *Liberté de la presse*, 211; Rosen, *Napoleon's Opera-Glass*, 68; *Moniteur*, 15 Pluviôse, Year VIII.

ing of the Treaty of Amiens, the *Moniteur* billed it as "Une CAPITULATION EN TEMPS DE PAIX!!!!!" [51]

SPECIFIC AND GENERAL STATEMENTS

Such devices were intended to assist the reader to the proper beliefs on various topics. Napoleon, who realized that specific statements are more readily believed than general ones, was extremely clever in his decisions as to when to be vague and when to be specific in order to produce the desired result. Losses of the enemy were generally related in detail while those of the French were merely stated to be "considerable" or "unimportant"— though if they were really insignificant, the actual figures were sometimes given.[52] The French were also specific in reciting captures by privateers. Ships captured were listed by name, and the weight of each ship was given. In 1814 Napoleon also insisted that the pieces recounting allied atrocities contain detailed facts.

> It is not by a general picture that people will be convinced . . . but only by facts narrated simply and in detail. . . . It is impossible that the citizens of Paris and the government men do not receive letters from all regions where the enemies have been forced to withdraw. Cannot these letters be collected and printed? It is then, after all these particular details have been noted, that well-written articles will have a good result. They will be pictures composed of elements about which everybody will know the truth. The prefects are in general men known and esteemed; they ought to write to the Minister of the Interior, who would have their letters printed.[53]

There were times, usually related to the military and naval resources of France, when Napoleon desired that the printed information be less specific. In 1808 he inquired of Decrès, "Why do the papers say the *Oreste* returned to Bayonne? It is necessary to give the news to the public; but you must make it more vague." [54] If the picture was not so favorable as desired—for ex-

[51] Périvier, *Napoléon journaliste*, 153; *Moniteur*, 10 Germinal and 23 Prairial, Year XI; 10 Prairial, Year XII; October 5, 1813; June 2, 1815.
[52] Napoleon, *Correspondance*, XI, 400; XIII, 353.
[53] *Moniteur*, January 10, 1811; *Empire*, April 17, 1807; *Moniteur* and *Empire*, *passim*; Napoleon, *Correspondance*, XXVII, 215–16.
[54] Napoleon (Brotonne, ed.), *Dernières lettres*, I, 364.

ample, with regard to discharging draft classes from the army—
it was not to be detailed, and perhaps not even mentioned. Napoleon forbade the utterance of any but vague statements in advance
of the official announcement, which he wanted to be as effective
as possible, and in 1807 he instructed Talleyrand to mention the
"peoples of Prussia" without giving the exact number.[55]

PERSONALIZATION

Stressing the actions of individuals, either by directing attacks
at them or by praising deeds of valorous Frenchmen, was a means
of making propaganda effective by being specific, and French
accounts of individual acts covered a wide compass. They ranged
from the case of a French prisoner who refused to lose confidence
in Napoleon even when threatened with perpetual slavery by
England, to that of a French grenadier and a Bavarian soldier
who responded contemptuously to Russian proclamations urging
them to desert, to examples of individual French ships which escaped from or beat superior enemy naval forces with which they
dueled. Accounts of individual bravery too numerous to mention
were constantly reported by the press, and activities of Napoleon
were of course duly chronicled.[56]

Individuals bore the brunt of many of the propaganda attacks
against the enemies of France because the French found them
something tangible to hate. During his lifetime, Pitt was the object
of more official French odium than any other individual. Others
attacked by the French included Windham, Grenville, and other
British ministers; George III; Wellington; Nelson, who, it was
suggested, had perhaps found another Lady Emma Lyon Hamil-
ton in Sicily; Cadoudal; Bernadotte; Johann Cobenzl; Freiherr
Heinrich vom Stein, the object of contempt of all honest men;

[55] Napoleon, *Correspondance*, XIV, 544; XV, 69; XVIII, 244; Napoleon (Picard
and Tuetey, eds.), *Correspondance inédite*, V, 88; Napoleon (Lecestre, comp.),
Lettres, II, 311; Joseph (Du Casse, ed.), *Mémoires*, 301; *Moniteur*, 19 Nivôse,
Year XIV.

[56] *Moniteur*, 17 Ventôse, Year XII; *Débats*, 11 Brumaire, Year XI; *Empire*,
August 7, 1812; September 10, 1812; *Journal*, 12 Messidor, Year XI; *Moniteur*,
passim; Napoleon, *Correspondance*, XIV, 117. Cummings says the simple story
is the classic lie of newspaper war propaganda. Arthur John Cummings, *The
Press and a Changing Civilization* (London, 1936), 27. Vandal (*Avènement de
Bonaparte*, II, 403) points out that the army bulletins contained simplified and
dramatized accounts of military operations and were replete with anecdotes.

Prince Karl von Hardenberg; Toussaint L'Ouverture; and Louis XVIII and the other Bourbons.[57]

TIMING

Napoleon was careful to have his propaganda appear at the most opportune time to assure its potency. News was not made public too early for fear it might endanger Napoleon's plans, and news of an unfavorable nature, such as the refusal of Russia to ratify the peace in 1806 or the departure of Napoleon from Spain in 1809, was postponed in order to mitigate its effects.[58]

On some occasions events influenced the type of propagandizing; one instance was Napoleon's delayed publication of his proclamation to the soldiers, postponed so as not to precede Joseph's entry into Naples. Bonaparte timed his return from Egypt so that the bulletins on the victory of Aboukir would precede him. On other occasions, Napoleon timed publications so that they might influence events. The *Moniteur* announced the Concordat before it had even been concluded. One aim in announcing the impending recall of Louis was to influence negotiations begun in England by the Dutch.[59]

The state of public opinion influenced the decision on when to publish some items. If the public was famished for news, an announcement was made; if it was too excited by recent events, publication was delayed. By announcing future events, Napoleon hoped to prepare opinion for them. Delay sometimes prevented the opposition press from protesting against the government's policy. In order to mitigate the possible effect of his moving to the Tuileries, Napoleon postponed the official eulogy of Washington to coincide with his change of residence, and the same issue of the *Moniteur* which contained parliamentary debates complain-

[57] *Moniteur*, 27 Floréal, Year XIII, and *passim*; *Empire*, July 25, 1807; August 15, 1811; October 14, 1813; May 23, 1815; *Journal*, 1 Nivôse, Year XI.

[58] Napoleon (Du Casse, ed.), *Supplément à la correspondance*, 195; Napoleon, *Correspondance*, VI, 369; XVII, 94; XVIII, 227; Joseph (Du Casse, ed), *Mémoires*, III, 181. Rather surprisingly, there were many notices on sick French prisoners even after the preliminaries of peace had been signed with England. *Moniteur*, 20 Brumaire, Year X.

[59] Napoleon, *Correspondance*, X, 359; XI, 509; XVI, 398; J. Crétineau-Joly (ed.), *Mémoires du cardinal Consalvi*, 2 vols. (Paris, 1864), I, 359; Rocquain, *Napoléon et Louis*, cii. There was a noticeable slackening of propaganda during peace. *Moniteur*, *passim*.

ing of the seizure of Switzerland by France contained Swiss expressions of gratitude. Napoleon advocated set speeches during the campaign rather than at the moment of battle and recommended that the body of Lannes should leave Strasbourg May 22 and reach Paris June 6 because those were the anniversaries of the French victories at Essling and Wagram.[60]

REPETITION

One of the devices which Napoleon understood best and utilized most effectively was repetition. The French hammered away on the various items mentioned in Chapter I, and Napoleon's recommendations that there be variation in the form of this repeated material are in keeping with the best present-day thought on propaganda. It is, of course, unnecessary to cite examples of the use of this device; suffice it to say that the entire message, and especially the emotional parts of it, did appear again and again.

FALSIFICATION

Most of all, however, did Napoleon specialize in the device which has done most to give the term "propaganda" a malodorous connotation: falsification. He did not even desire to be truthful, despite his protestations that his official propaganda was accurate and true. He himself stated that bulletins and the press were designed to influence the public and not to be historical accounts. At other times he told Marmont and Clarke to be certain that, regardless of what they told the public, he learned the truth from them. He had Clarke tell Joseph that the art of war lay in exaggerating one's own forces and depreciating those of the enemy and informed Clarke himself on what sort of publicity to put out. "Nothing is more contrary to military rules than to make known the strength of the army in the papers or orders of the day; . . . if you speak of it, you must exaggerate by doubling or trebling the number; . . . when you speak of the enemy, decrease his strength by one half or one third; the mind of man is

[60] Joseph (Du Casse, ed.), *Mémoires*, I, 346; Napoleon, *Correspondance*, XVII, 83; XX, 193; XXVI, 185; *Moniteur*, 11 Prairial, Year XI; Bourrienne (Phipps, ed.), *Memoirs*, I, 370; Vandal, *Avènement de Bonaparte*, II, 204; *Napoleon's Maxims of War* (New York, 1861), 152.

such as to believe that in the long run a small number will be beaten by a big one." [61] In similar vein Fouché was told to reduce the size of the Russian armies or keep still about them, and Napoleon told Savary: "One of the first principles of war is to exaggerate and not depreciate one's forces. How are you going to make poets, who want to flatter me and national pride in place of doing good, understand that?" [62]

Articles written by public officials, generally the minister of police or of foreign affairs, and labeled as news coming from some distant place, were a favorite form of falsification. Napoleon had Fouché insert in the *Moniteur* notes purportedly translated from an English paper—being careful to choose an obscure one. Fouché was to print letters as coming from St. Petersburg, but he was severely reprimanded at the end of 1806 for trying to influence the Poles by printing a letter supposedly written by Thaddeus Kosciuszko. At another time Napoleon asked Fouché whether the arrest of an English agent was little enough known to warrant saying that it had happened at Valençay. Napoleon personally sent news which ostensibly came from Constantinople and wrote and inserted in the *Moniteur* letters which he claimed had been written by subordinates.[63] In order to convince the Swedes that the French government was well informed, the Minister of Foreign Affairs was to insert news under the rubric of Denmark, and Napoleon had Maret write for the little papers a letter which was supposedly from London.

Evidence does not support Napoleon's claim that if he erred, it was on the side of understatement.[64] In the spring of 1809 he had Berthier tell Marshal François Kellermann to announce that his corps, really to consist of 14,000 men, would be 50,000 strong. In 1812 he ordered Maret to double, for purposes of publicity, the number of reinforcements actually sent for the campaign against Russia; and announcements inserted in the Berlin, Vienna, and

[61] Napoleon (Dansette, comp.), *Vues politiques,* 304.

[62] Napoleon (Lecestre, comp.), *Lettres,* I, 371; Napoleon, *Correspondance,* XII, 157; XIX, 378, 419; XXVII, 206, 239.

[63] Napoleon, *Correspondance,* IX, 490; X, 445; XIV, 126; XVII, 327; XX, 429; Jerome (Du Casse, ed.), *Mémoires,* II, 476; Napoleon (Lecestre, comp.), *Lettres,* II, 24, 136; Napoleon (Brotonne, ed.), *Dernières lettres,* I, 532.

[64] Napoleon (Cerf, comp.), *Lettres à Joséphine,* 110; Joseph (Du Casse, ed.), *Mémoires,* X, 129; Napoleon, *Correspondance,* XIV, 437.

Warsaw papers stated that 30,000 Spanish troops were coming, although the number actually sent was 14,000. On June 21, 1813, the very same day on which Napoleon told Eugene to speak of his army as three corps and nine divisions, he wrote Eugene, "I am glad to see in your letter of June 14 that by July 1 your six divisions will be organized." [65] In the same letter saying, "You must have 14,000 men," Jerome was ordered to spread the rumor that he had 40,000. Clarke was told to exaggerate the strength of Napoleon's division and of the Spanish troops, and he was also to exaggerate the size of the cavalry and to treat the twenty-four missing infantry regiments as though they existed. Even though the British knew of the departure, Decrès was to say that Magon left with four vessels instead of two. Marshal Augereau in 1813 commanded only an observation corps, but Napoleon had him play it up as though it were an army. Napoleon also criticized Marmont for surrendering Paris in 1814, claiming that the city was able to defend itself until aid arrived; yet the capitulation was made by order of Joseph, the redoubts announced by the papers did not exist, there were only 42,000 men (partly national guardsmen) to oppose 100,000 veterans, and the Minister of War was said to have refused arms to the national guard.[66]

Reporting of enemy and French military losses [67] was no more

[65] Eugene (Du Casse, ed.), *Mémoires*, IX, 172.

[66] Napoleon, *Correspondance*, X, 430; XV, 256; XVIII, 456, 520; XXI, 205; XXIV, 268; XXV, 377; Eugene (Du Casse, ed.), *Mémoires*, IX, 107; Napoleon (Brotonne, ed.), *Lettres*, 70; Auguste de Marmont, *Réponse du duc de Raguse à la proclamation datée du golfe de Jouan, le 1er mars 1815* (n.p., n.d.), 1–4; Pelleport (Pelleport-Burête, ed.), *Souvenirs*, II, 114; Fugier, *Napoléon et l'Espagne*, II, 173; John Holland Rose, *The Life of Napoleon I* (7th ed.; London, 1919), II, 420–21; Boulay de la Meurthe (Paris, 1868), 226; Jean Hanoteau (ed.), *Mémoires du général de Caulaincourt duc de Vicence, grand écuyer de l'empereur*, 3 vols. (Paris, 1933), III, 286.

[67] For this type of falsification, only instances proved by contemporary sources or by the standard works of Gershoy (*French Revolution and Napoleon*) and Rose (*Napoleon*) will be indicated, as they will be illustrative of the trend. Enemy bulletins, as printed by Frédéric Schoell, *Recueil de pièces officielles, destinées à détromper les françois sur les événemens qui se sont passés depuis quelques années*, 9 vols. (Paris, 1814–16), proved almost valueless for this purpose as they, too, exaggerated blatantly. The Prussian and Russian reports on Lützen (Schoell, *Recueil de pièces officielles*, I, 49–54) treated it as a victory; Württemberg laid claim to having captured 30,000 of their enemies and stated that the French had left behind 12,000 wounded men—for a battle the French actually won (Schoell, *Recueil de pièces officielles*, III, 91). Part of the reason for this exaggeration was that officers wanting advancement sent in false

accurate than the accounts of French military power. In letters to
Count Pierre Daru and Cambacérès on the same day, Napoleon
told the one that there were 3,000 wounded and the other 8,000,
although the true number was three times the latter figure. After
the Battle of Austerlitz Napoleon claimed that the allies had lost
50,000, exclusive of a column drowned in the lake, and the French
4,000; the French actually lost 9,000 and the allies 30,000. The
Moniteur reported that on August 15, 1806 (the day on which
Napoleon's birthday was celebrated), the naval squadron to which
Jerome was attached had made captures worth 20,000,000 francs;
the report of Jerome to Decrès said that the prizes were worth
3,000,000 francs and were seized on August 18. The French reported that the Prussians had had 150,000 troops at the city of Jena
and had lost 40,000; actually the main body of the Prussians, at
near-by Auerstädt, was only 40,000. The bulletin of the Battle of
Eylau reported that the French lost 7,500 and the Russians 22,000;
each side really lost about 25,000. Although the entire Russian
force at Friedland was only 45,000 and its losses were not over
15,000, Napoleon reported there were 60,000 Russians *hors de
combat*. The French claimed that the war with Austria in 1809
had slowed the French conquest of Portugal, but their claims often
stated that not one man had left Portugal for the eastern front.[68]
At Wagram each side lost about 25,000; the French claimed the
Austrians admitted over 30,000. Marshal Jourdan's report that he
had captured 5,500 prisoners was changed to 10,000 in the bulletin.
A letter from Marshal Mortier to Marshal Nicolas Soult reported
the capture of 20,000; the British report printed in the *Moniteur*
admitted 15,000; and an order of the day said the number was
25,000. At Dresden in 1813 the allies lost 35,000; the figure given
by the French was 60,000. Would not the five French generals
lost at Lützen have loved the claim that nobody of importance

---

reports. Jean Morvan, *Le soldat impérial (1800–1814)*, 2 vols. (Paris, 1904), II,
290. Napoleon indirectly admitted that the bulletins were not accurate by ordering Berthier to eliminate the statements recognized to be false. Napoleon, *Correspondance*, XXIII, 42.

[68] Similarly, Napoleon had stated that the Boulogne preparations were false
demonstrations, and that he would have been able to invade England but for
Austria's actions. Napoleon, *Correspondance*, IX, 216; *Empire*, January 4,
1814.

was lost there? The French losses at Leipzig were 35,000, but they admitted only 2,500—losses which they blamed on an overly hasty destruction of the bridges by the rear guard. The *Moniteur* never made any mention of a large body of French troops being captured, yet England and her allies had 70,000 French prisoners. As late as October 13, 1813, the exposition of the military situation was completely false. It was likewise in 1813 that Napoleon ordered Clarke to exaggerate the number of prisoners in order to deceive Europe. The notices in the French papers on the allied forces during the Hundred Days were most inaccurate regarding strength and position.[69]

Another claim made by Napoleon was that French soldiers were very well disciplined, whereas allied soldiers pillaged terribly; the truth seems to be, however, that the conduct of the two sides was very similar, and Napoleon even claimed that looting was a right of war. The first column of the reserve army in 1800 was said to have committed excesses toward the people. In 1806 Murat reported to Napoleon that the lack of discipline of his troops, who later did a great deal of pillaging after the Battle of Jena, was having a grievous effect on the enthusiasm of the Poles. Once they had acquired from the Neapolitans a taste for looting, the Swiss and French, who until then had maintained good discipline in Spain, subjected Burgos to pillage and worse atrocities. Marshal Victor's corps became the least disciplined, and its march through Germany was marked by disorderly acts. The Bavarians also committed every kind of excess in the Tyrol in 1809. Marshal Emmanuel de Grouchy had to order that the hussars stop doing vexatious things, and even the very pro-Napoleonic Countess Auguste Charlotte Kielmannsegg reported that the Italians plundered her estates in June, 1813.[70]

[69] Salmon, *Newspaper and Authority*, 321; *Moniteur*, December 18, 1809; September 6, 1813; Rose, *Napoleon*, II, 99, 114, 124, 196, 346, 365; *Empire*, October 26, 1806; Napoleon, *Correspondance*, XI, 463; XIV, 293–95; XV, 363; XXVI, 367; Gershoy, *French Revolution and Napoleon*, 401; Joseph (Du Casse, ed.), *Mémoires*, I, 332; V, 231; *Mercure*, December 16, 1809; *Journal*, February 1, 1810; Jerome (Du Casse, ed.), *Mémoires*, I, 470; Napoleon (Lecestre, comp.), *Lettres*, II, 277. Vasile Gh. Luta, *Die deutschen Volkslieder auf Napoleon I von seinen Anfängen bis zum Beginn der Befreiungskriege* (Berlin, 1931), 36, claims that the Russian column (of 20,000 men, according to Napoleon) which drowned at Austerlitz proved (when Marshal Louis Suchet had the lake searched four days later) to be only three soldiers.

[70] Pierre Conard, *Napoléon et le Catalogne 1808–1814* (Paris, 1910), 65, 88;

Nor were the accounts of resources other than man power any more accurate. The troops were always pictured as being plentifully provided with supplies; yet they lacked shoes, food, pay, and even ammunition. "The army is horribly fatigued. . . . It has needs of every kind." Thus did Napoleon write the Duke of Bassano on November 30, 1812.[71] It is strange that although affairs in Egypt and the colonies were always "progressing splendidly," Decaen and Leclerc constantly pled for more supplies, Leclerc reported an overwhelming amount of disease; and the minutes of the final council of war called by General Menou showed that much of the preceding publicity on Egypt had been false. Although the French navy was supposedly being built up to match Great Britain's, Napoleon informed Decrès in 1813 that French frigates shortly would not dare appear any place.[72]

There is evidence that the bright outlook of the government in domestic, as well as in military and naval, affairs was not always justified. In 1806 commerce was stagnant at Marseille and Bordeaux, and Fesch wrote that two thirds of the population at Rome was financially ruined. The Spanish government was poverty-stricken, as was the government of France in 1802—though by 1809 it had an abundance of specie. The price of grain continued to rise because of the flour shortage; and the military establishments on the English Channel, after renewal of the war in

---

Pasquier (Audiffret-Pasquier, ed., Roche, tr.) *Memoirs*, I, 366; A. Rambaud, *L'Allemagne sous Napoléon Ier* (3d ed.; Paris, n.d.), 327; A. G. Macdonnell, *Napoleon and His Marshals* (New York, 1934), 213; Napoleon (Thompson, ed.), *Letters*, 225; George de Grouchy (ed.), *Mémoires du maréchal de Grouchy* (Paris, 1873–74), II, 385; H. Butterfield, *The Peace Tactics of Napoleon 1806–1808* (Cambridge, 1929), 3; G. Aretz (ed.), *Memoiren der Gräfin Kielmannsegge über Napoleon I* (Dresden, 1927), 177; Comtesse de Beaulaincourt-Marles (pub.), *Journal du maréchal de Castellane 1804–1862* (2d. ed.; Paris, 1895), I, 33; *Débats*, 9 Germinal, Year VIII; Murat (Prince Murat, pub.), *Lettres*, IV, 460.

[71] Morvan, *Soldat impérial*, I, 367–443, 388–90; Marshal Laurent Gouvion Saint-Cyr, *Mémoires pour servir à l'histoire militaire sous le directoire, le consulat et l'empire*, 4 vols. (Paris, 1831), IV, 476; La Forest (Grandmaison, pub.), *Correspondance*, VI, 340; Grouchy (G. de Grouchy, ed.), *Mémoires*, II, 340; Camille Rousset (ed.), *Recollections of Marshal Macdonald*, 2 vols. (London, 1892), I, 56; II, 4; Murat (Prince Murat, pub.), *Lettres*, V, 424.

[72] Leclerc (Roussier, pub.), *Lettres, passim*; *Débats*, 7 Pluviôse, Year VIII; Henri Prentout, *L'île de France sous Decaen* (Paris, 1901), 155, 205; Aulard (ed.), *Paris sous le consulat*, III, 534; *Moniteur*, 28 Ventôse, Year VIII; Napoleon, *Correspondance*, XXVI, 7. Similarly, the press ridiculed London reports of Kléber's assassination until the Paris papers had to admit the truth. *Débats*, 6 Frimaire, Year VIII.

1803, raised the price of every necessity of life to unprecedented heights.[73]

In the field of international relations the French were no more truthful. They would place all the blame for grievous events, even when there was doubt as to who was responsible, solely upon the enemy: France, for example, never offered the least provocation to war. Similarly, France privately accused Sweden of not supporting the Continental System at the same time that it publicly asserted that Sweden was co-operating fully with French plans; when the French later publicly charged Sweden with violating its agreements, the decline in Swedish customs revenue showed the French charge to be at least partly false. The guilt in the controversy over prisoners was by no means all on one side.[74]

Simultaneously with praising the zeal of the Poles, Napoleon wrote Murat: "The Poles . . . ask so many guarantees . . . ; they are egotists whom love of country does not fire. . . . My greatness is not based on my alliance with a few thousand Poles." [75] He asserted that only the death of Fox prevented peace with England in 1806, yet he had been unwilling to accept Fox's condition that Russia be included in the negotiations. The *Moniteur* ran several articles on the triumphal entry of Joseph into Spain after he had been forced to flee Madrid. During the Hundred Days, Marseille was said to have accepted the tricolor voluntarily, but the truth was that Marshal Masséna had threatened to

[73] E. d'Hauterive (ed.), *La police secrète*, III, 4; Department of State, *Despatches* (France, Robert Livingston to Madison, January 13, 1802; Joel Barlow to James Monroe, December 21, 1811); *Copies des lettres originales et dépêches des généraux, ministres, grands officiers d'état, etc.* (Paris, 1814), 294; La Forest (Grandmaison, pub.), *Correspondance*, IV, 242; Rose, *Napoleon*, II, 378; P. Coquelle, *Napoleon and England, 1803–13* (London, 1904), 238; Remacle (ed.), *Bonaparte et les Bourbons*, 91, 209, 381; Du Casse, *Négotiations diplomatiques*, 42.

[74] *Moniteur, passim;* Coquelle, *Napoleon and England*, 241–45 and *passim;* R. B. Mowat, *The Diplomacy of Napoleon* (New York, 1924), 129; Department of State, *Despatches* (France, Livingston to Madison, March 24, 1803); Verfasser des Napoleon, *Napoleon und Pitt, oder Wer wird siegen* (Hamburg, 1805), 16–21; Edward Fraser, *Napoleon the Gaoler* (New York, 1914), 34, 54, *passim;* Oscar Browning (ed.), *England and Napoleon in 1803* (London, 1887), *passim;* Rose, *Napoleon*, I, 395; Schoell, *Recueil de pièces officielles*, II, 350; M. Bail (ed.), *Correspondance de Bernadotte, prince-royal de Suède, avec Napoléon, depuis 1810 jusqu'en 1814* (Paris, 1819), 70–79. Napoleon actually believed the charges against Sweden to be true.

[75] Rosen, *Napoleon's Opera-Glass*, 86.

force his way in if it had not accepted this flag by the following night.[76]

Another type of event in which falsification produced an erroneous effect was that involving changes in the government of conquered territories. Desiring that the initiative appear to come from the region itself, Napoleon used his subordinates to have some responsible group request a change of rulers. An Italian delegation asked Napoleon to be King of Italy after Napoleon had demanded such a deputation; Napoleon had the Dutch ambassador ask him to allow Louis to be king; and, at Murat's instigation, the Council of Castile—along with other organizations later—requested Joseph for king. Although Joseph had already left Naples, presumably temporarily, at Napoleon's command, Napoleon assured the Spaniards that his brother would leave that kingdom immediately upon receipt of their request.[77]

There were also many instances of absolute prevarication. In 1808 Napoleon ordered Soult to blow up Spandau and say it was an accidental explosion of stored powder. On the same day on which he wrote his French minister to Würzburg to deny that the King of Saxony was no longer loyal, Napoleon reproached the King for his lack of friendship. Upon leaving the army in 1812 he deliberately deceived it for over a week as to where he was going, and when Murat deserted it, said that he had left because of ill health. Jerome spread the rumor that Napoleon was coming to Warsaw in 1812 even though, as he admitted, "I knew positively the contrary." Desaix was shot through the heart and died immediately, without making the patriotic statement ("Go tell the First Consul that I die regretting not having done enough to live in posterity.") ascribed to him by the bulletin. At the start of the 1805 campaign Napoleon ordered Eugene to make a proclamation that Napoleon would be back in less than a month. And Napoleon deliberately stated that Louis, in accepting the crown of Holland, had announced his intention of renouncing it if the colonies

[76] Schoor, *La presse sous le consulat*, 72; *The Hundred Days: Secondary Material*, in Boulay de la Meurthe collection of pamphlets; Lord John Russell (ed.), *Memorials and Correspondence of C. J. Fox* (London, 1853–57), IV, 156–59; Butterfield, *Peace Tactics of Napoleon*, 37–38.

[77] Joseph (Du Casse, ed.), *Mémoires*, IV, 229; A. Pingaud, *Bonaparte président de la république italienne*, 423–27; Napoleon, *Correspondance*, XVII, 111; *Moniteur*, June 6, 1806.

were not restored at the general peace; Louis had never made any such declaration.[78]

Even when apparently frank, Napoleon deliberately conveyed a false impression by suppressing part of the unfavorable information. The most famous example cited by Napoleon's followers as illustrative of his truthfulness, Bulletin 29 in 1812, did not tell the whole truth. Notes on Bulletin 9 of the Austrian army at Turin, omitting mention of captured munition wagons and large amounts of baggage, pointed out that the total results of a big Austrian victory were one cannon and one drugshop. In order to better influence the spirit of the French sailors, Napoleon ordered Decrès not to mention any mistakes in his report. Of the letters sent to India in 1803 and captured by a privateer, the *Moniteur* printed only those dreading invasion most and left out all but one abusing Bonaparte or France. Fouché was charged with eliminating parts of letters which it might be inconvenient to publish in the *Moniteur*. In publishing an account of British funds, Napoleon reduced the amounts by 8 per cent, because of the depreciation of their bank notes. Napoleon ordered Eugene to omit from his proclamation mention of the fact that the newly established dukes in Italy would not participate in the government of the state. Considering General Joseph von Alvinczy his most skillful opponent, Napoleon omitted all mention of him in bulletins, while praising the generals he did not fear. Though mention was made of the suppression of military commissions in Naples, no mention was made of those retained. The press gave only tendentious information on the assembly of the Jews in 1806, and it never once referred to the letter of the Pope to Archbishop Jean Maury of Paris. In requesting Berthier to insert in the *Moniteur* the jour-

78 Napoleon (Thompson, ed.), *Letters*, 226; Napoleon, *Correspondance*, VI, 362; XXIV, 336; XXV, 214; Jerome (Du Casse, ed.), *Mémoires*, V, 409; Count Charles Labédoyère, *Memoirs of the Public and Private Life of Napoleon Bonaparte* (London, 1837), I, 220; Rocquain, *Napoléon et Louis*, xxxi; *Moniteur*, January 27, 1813. Count François Mollien, *Mémoires d'un ministre du trésor public, 1780–1815*, 3 vols. (Paris, 1898), contains, in the introduction by Ch. Gomel, xvii, the statement that Napoleon did nothing to discourage the prevalent belief that most of the contributions imposed on conquered peoples flowed to the treasury. Napoleon was probably lying when he said that he never had intended to invade England; more than likely he adopted this stand so as to avert admitting failure in an enterprise. David Hannay, "Did Napoleon Mean to Invade England?" *Macmillan's Magazine*, LXXXV (1902), 285–87.

nal of the siege of Cádiz, Napoleon ordered him to suppress anything inconvenient. The repulse of Marshal Bon-Adrien Moncey
in Valencia did not reach the papers as the complete defeat that it
was, and while purporting to keep the public informed on the
gradual retreat from Spain—which it ascribed to lack of provisions
even though the country was well stocked [79]—the government
never mentioned the Battle of Vitoria. Official pieces were only
extracts designed to deceive the public. Clarke was ordered not to
mention broken and lost artillery in the *Moniteur*, and Napoleon
had Champagny extract from foreign archives only what might
justify the conduct of France.[80]

Another means of creating a false impression was the editing
of material before it was published. Cambacérès edited the discussions of the Council of State before they appeared in the *Moniteur*, and the text of the sentence of the Duke of Enghien was
altered before it appeared in the same paper. Because the government's changing the word "laws" to the more inclusive word
"measures" four days after the execution of the Duke of Enghien
seemed to imply approval of that event by the Legislative Body,
Fontanes secured the insertion of the only erratum ever printed
by the *Moniteur*, and that in the smallest possible type. Count
Louis Molé, Minister of Justice in 1813, complained that many of
Napoleon's phrases were inserted in place of his own. To a private
letter from Constantinople, Napoleon added that the Turks knew
English control of Egypt was worse for the Ottoman power than
French control. The *Moniteur* cleverly edited communications
so as to stir up popular emotion favorable to the Empire. Napoleon informed Maret that any changes he made in the notes answering Austria's manifesto issued in August of 1813 when it
joined the allies would be solely for publication purposes. Before

---

[79] Rose, *Napoleon*, II, 307.

[80] General Hector Fleischmann (ed.), *Memoirs of Count Miot de Melito*, tr.
by Mrs. Cashel Hoey and Mr. John Lillie (New York, 1881), 560; Department
of State, *Despatches* (Spain, George Erving to Madison, August 11, 1808);
Moniteur, 1808–13, *passim;* Napoleon, *Correspondance*, XII, 284; XVI, 446;
XIX, 183; XX, 317; Chaptal (E. A. Chaptal, ed.), *Souvenirs*, 301; Napoleon
(Brotonne, ed.), *Dernières lettres*, II, 166; Napoleon (Lecestre, comp.), *Lettres*,
II, 330; F. J. Maccunn, *The Contemporary English View of Napoleon* (London,
1914), 295–98; Robert Anchel, *Napoléon et les juifs* (Paris, 1928), 186; Murat
(Prince Murat, pub.), *Lettres*, VI, 304; Haussonville, *Église et empire*, IV, 31–35;
Périvier, *Napoléon journaliste*, 179.

permitting its appearance in the *Moniteur*, Napoleon altered a proclamation by Joseph in 1810 designed to unite the French and Spanish nations, and the *Gazette de Madrid*, copying the bulletins from the *Moniteur*, was to remove passages which might possibly shock Spain. Napoleon also ordered Bigot de Préameneu, successor to Portalis as Minister of Public Worship, to alter charges of the bishops before inserting them in the ecclesiastical press, and the *Moniteur* changed the Latin formula of the oath Cardinal Giovanni Battista Caprara took in 1802. Clarke was instructed to soften some passages before putting reports from the generals into the *Moniteur*, whose account of Spanish affairs on September 5, 1808, was changed before appearing in Spain in order to obtain the proper nuances for local effect. On January 4, 1811, Napoleon informed Berthier, "As I have cut out several things from the dispatch of Wellington which will be in tomorrow's *Moniteur*, I am sending it to you complete." From an article on British domination of the seas, he cut out a paragraph stating that Britain's maritime power was unparalleled in history.[81]

Two examples must suffice to show in detail the type of changes Napoleon made. The first is from the report of Marshal Brune on his entry into Stralsund on August 20, 1807: "earlier sovereign" was replaced by "ridiculous sovereign"; the "King had exposed himself" by "had been frightened by the dangers he had run." "To neutralize Stralsund" was replaced by the lengthy passage, "the most ridiculous proposition. One is to be pitied for having to deal with such a wild person. But the Swedes are even more to be pitied. Officers, soldiers, citizens, all groan at the caprices of their prince; all love France and admire Napoleon. In Sweden

[81] Thiers, *Histoire du consulat*, III, 302; Pasquier (Audiffret-Pasquier, ed., Roche, tr.), *Memoirs*, I, 199, 224; Napoleon (Chuquet, ed.), *Inédits napoléoniens*, I, 9; Sidney B. Fay, "Execution of the Duke d'Enghien," *American Historical Review*, IV (1898), 32; Joseph (Du Casse, ed.), *Mémoires*, VII, 183; IX, 85; Édouard Driault, *Austerlitz la fin du saint-empire (1804-1806) (Napoléon et l'Europe)* (Paris, 1912), 64; Napoleon, *Correspondance*, XIX, 547; XXVI, 72; Boulay de la Meurthe (ed.), *Documents sur la négociation du concordat*, V, 447; La Forest (Grandmaison, pub.), *Correspondance*, I, 288; Marquis Henri de Noailles, *Le comte Molé 1781-1855. Sa vie—ses mémoires* (3d ed.; Paris, 1922), I, 172; Napoleon (Picard and Tuetey, eds.), *Correspondance inédite*, II, 573; IV, 7; Ch. de Chênedollé, "Napoléon le grand et *l'Almanach de Gotha*," *Bulletin du bibliophile Belge*, VI (1850), 77.

the opinion of the King, except for twelve or fifteen wretches like Fersen and Armfeld, is held only by himself." [82]

The other lends support to the claim of Grenville that the *Moniteur* disfigured everything he said and to the statement in the Hamburg *Spectateur du Nord* that often French journalists distorted British parliamentary debates in unscrupulous fashion. The *Moniteur* left out of a speech with only seven paragraphs one which stated:

> The atrocious and unparalleled act of violence and treachery by which the Ruler of France tried to surprize and to enslave the Spanish nation, while it has excited in Spain a determined and unconquerable resistance against the usurpation and tyranny of the French Government, has . . . awakened in other nations . . . a determination to resist, by a new effort, the continued and increasing encroachments on their safety and independence.

Parts of other paragraphs were changed. For example, one portion of the speech read: "Although the uncertainty of all human events, and the vicissitudes attendant upon war, forbid too confident an expectation of a satisfactory issue to the present struggle against the common enemy of Europe, His Majesty commands us to congratulate you upon the splendid and important success which has recently crowned the arms of the Emperor of Austria, under the able and distinguished conduct of His Imperial Highness the Archduke Charles." But the *Moniteur* changed the sentence so that its meaning was altogether different: "The uncertainty of all human events, and the vicissitudes attendant upon war, forbid too confident an expectation of a satisfactory issue to the present struggle, for we have to struggle against an enemy of an active genius for whom everything thrives and whose plans, even the most incredible, are always accomplished." In the next paragraph "the efforts of Europe for its deliverance" was changed to "efforts of Austria." [83]

[82] Napoleon (Picard and Tuetey, eds.), *Correspondance inédite*, I, 608.

[83] *Moniteur*, 20 Floréal, Year X; July 10, 1809; *Spectateur du Nord*, March, 1800; "Falsification of the speech of the King of England at the time of the closing of Parliament June 21, 1809, by the *Moniteur*, July 10, 1809, page 754," in Harvard University collection of broadsides. The accuracy of the statements in this broadside was checked against the parliamentary debates and the *Moniteur*.

Such editing implies that leaving out items inconvenient to the French was common. Eugene, for example, was told to make sure that no paper mentioned his practice of using for charitable purposes the property of any ecclesiastic refusing to take the oath prescribed by the Concordat. When he re-established the Vienna papers in 1809, Napoleon ordered that the bulletins, proclamations, and orders of the day—all minus the phrases which might humiliate Austria—should be the first items inserted. He also kept quiet the fact that all the officers of the new companies formed in 1811 were going to be French.[84]

It must not be thought, however, that Napoleon always falsified materials of the types mentioned. The financial chaos of the Directory was as bad as he pictured it. Napoleon's claims that the enemy soldiers committed atrocities undoubtedly had some basis in fact, as did the charges that England was supporting revolt in western France. The report on French and allied losses at Quatre Bras was honest, and Wellington's report after Waterloo showed that the French accounts of their victories early in the campaign were accurate, at least to the extent of who won or lost. Other claims of the French were also supported by fact. France did have swarms of privateers preying on British commerce. The Continental System did damage British commerce sufficiently for the merchants to request an easier license system and for the special parliamentary committee on aid to commerce to recommend succor because the plight of commerce was so much worse than in 1793. One of the two sides in divided Switzerland did ask for French intervention. The allies likewise entered Switzerland, but they in turn claimed it was merely a French dependency. The *Argus* accounts of the revolutions in Constantinople and Algiers were reliable. It was true that the British lost heavily while embarking at Corunna and that the allies lost more heavily in capturing Paris than did the defenders. It was also true that Great

---

Another very interesting example of editing is the alteration of the *Almanach de Gotha* in 1808 in order to eliminate mention of Napoleon's enemies and enhance French prestige. Chênedollé, "Napoléon et *l'Almanach de Gotha*," *loc. cit.*, 69–80.

[84] *Moniteur*, June 27, 1815; Napoleon, *Correspondance*, XVII, 403; XIX, 11; Napoleon (Picard and Tuetey, eds.), *Correspondance inédite*, IV, 615.

Britain was as responsible as Napoleon for the resumption of war in 1803.[85]

Thus, Napoleon, in his use of propaganda devices, frequently relied on a slim, necessary base of truth. Consequently, it was the skill of his various distortions that gave the measure of his artistry and of his success.

[85] Department of State, *Despatches* (France, Armstrong to Madison, December 26, 1808; Armstrong to Smith, February 16, 1809; Joel Barlow to James Monroe, April 22, 1812; William Crawford to Monroe, January 16 and April 11, 1814); Abrantès, *Mémoires*, X, 212; Ernest Daudet, *La police et les chouans sous le consulat et l'empire, 1800–1815* (Paris, 1895), 40; *Moniteur*, Years X and XI, *passim*; Édouard Driault, *La politique extérieure du premier consul 1800–1803 (Napoléon et l'Europe)* (Paris, 1910), 284; Edmond Biré (ed.), *Mémoires du général d'Andigné*, 2 vols. (Paris, 1900–1901), II, 12; Frances Jackson (tr.), *Memoirs of the Count de Rochechouart* (London, 1920), 64; Napoleon, *Correspondance*, XXVIII, 294; Rose, *Napoleon*, II, 475; Schoell, *Recueil de pièces officielles*, II, 5; *Moniteur*, March 22, 1811; *Journal*, August 18, 1810; *Mémoires, souvenirs, opinions, et écrits du duc de Gaëte* (Vols. XXXVI and XXXVII, *Collection des mémoires relatifs à la révolution française*) (2 vols. Paris, 1926), I, 134. Charles d'Espinal, mayor of Fouchécourt, reported that the Cossacks "ate like the very devil" but did not pillage. However, Fouchécourt was not on the main line of travel. Charles Guyot, "Souvenirs de la première invasion," *Mémoires de l'académie de Stanislas*, 6th series, X(1913), 132–44.

Although an examination of the degree of accuracy in each of the items of Napoleon's message is outside the scope of this study, a few remarks regarding them may not be out of order. It is entirely possible that the English papers lied, but certainly no more than the French ones, and in Great Britain the government did not dictate what the papers should say. Far from growing worse, the British financial situation was better in 1815 than in 1789. France was perfectly correct in asserting that Great Britain did not live up to its constitution during the war, just as the United States has found it impossible to abide in wartime by all the provisions of its constitution. Great Britain did refuse to admit any interpretation other than her own of international law regarding freedom of the seas, even as France would have done had it been to her own selfish interest. Napoleon would have a hard time convincing the historian that he acted only for the welfare of France (unless he actually believed his own propaganda to the effect that he and France were synonymous), fought only in self-defense, and never violated a treaty. Undoubtedly the Bourbons had ruled only in the interest of a relatively small group in France. Despite Napoleon's claims, the coalitions against him were quite stable, falling apart only as a result of his victories. Ordinarily a victorious country is more accurate in its reports, but that did not seem to hold true for France under Napoleon. He pointed out the lack of cohesion among the allies but omitted mentioning the irritation in the states subordinate to France because of the development of French industry at their expense under the Continental System. Unquestionably the populace in foreign countries was at times war-weary; but France also had its draft troubles, and Napoleon's major purposes in fostering the arts and sciences were to make them serve him and to help keep public opinion quiet.

CHAPTER IX

THE EFFECT[1]

"The influence of words over men is astounding."—
NAPOLEON

A PROPAGANDIST CANNOT EXPECT TO REAP A SATISFACTORY HARVEST from each of his efforts, though he would like a fairly large percentage to be effective. When Napoleon's propaganda was ineffectual, one of the things which stands out is that incompetence on the part of his subordinates was often directly responsible.[2] The censors of the *Almanach de Gotha*, for example, permitted mention of the aunt of Gustavus IV (who was on the French black list) and overlooked references to an article which had been removed, thus permitting the reading public to suspect censorship. In other cases, eliminations of phrases rendered unintelligible what remained. The censorship also created a bad impression by suppressing unfavorable news which was generally known. As Napoleon wrote Clarke in 1809: "Make them realize, one and all, how much they discredit the Government by concealing information which can be picked up from every soldier who writes home from the front, and who is tempted because of such concealment to believe all the enemy's false reports." [3] An even more important adverse effect of the rigid censorship was a decline of interest in the press, with a resultant reduction in its potential propaganda

[1] For any period prior to the development of more or less scientific measurements of public opinion, a discussion of the effect of propaganda must be somewhat inadequate. The two main causes rendering any conclusions merely tentative are insufficiency of data and the biased nature of much of the evidence which does exist. Without an attempt to analyze its effectiveness, however, a study of Napoleon's propaganda would be incomplete. The material in Chapters II to VII should be considered in connection with the first part of this chapter.

[2] Napoleon, *Correspondance*, XIV, 551.

[3] Napoleon (Thompson, ed.), *Letters*, 247.

influence, because all the papers seemed to be the product of one news mill able to grind out only tendentious news. The number of subscribers in Paris, the departments, and the Confederation of the Rhine steadily dwindled, and by Napoleon's own confession the only paper read in France was the relatively independent *Journal de l'Empire*, which was able to increase the number of its subscribers.[4]

The Napoleonic efforts to establish an influential semiofficial press were no more successful. Fiévée even assured Napoleon that people read these papers merely to know what the government wanted them to think and then took exactly the opposite position.[5]

The *Moniteur* served Napoleon much better, even though its articles were not always effective. On St. Helena he claimed that "The terrible *Moniteur* that ruined so many reputations was constantly useful and favorable to me alone," and went on to defend it in the following terms: "The *Moniteur* has been reproached for the acrimony and virulence of its notes against the enemy. But before we condemn them, we are bound to take into consideration the benefits they may have produced, the anxiety they occasionally caused to a perplexed enemy, the terror they struck in a hesitating cabinet, the stimulus they gave to our allies, the confidence and audacity they inspired in our troops." [6] While not too much reliance can be placed on the statements of other papers [7] or of government officials speaking to the public—or even to Napoleon, whom they wished to flatter—there was probably some basis for the repeated reports that the *Moniteur* was effective.

Some of the French officials were relatively honest in their reports to Napoleon on the effectiveness of the *Moniteur*. Among

[4] Chênedollé, "Napoléon et *l'Almanach de Gotha*," *loc. cit.*, 74–78; Remacle (ed.), *Bonaparte et les Bourbons*, 362; Broc, *Vie en France*, 248; Napoleon, *Correspondance*, XV, 19; Salomon, *Geschichte des Zeitungswesens*, 142, 151; Périvier, *Napoléon journaliste*, 391; *Débats*, 24 Messidor, Year IX; Roederer (A. M. Roederer, pub.), *Œuvres*, VII, 241; Le Poittevin, *Liberté de la presse*, 239.

[5] Salmon, *Newspaper and Authority*, 322. Conard (*Napoléon et la Catalogne*, 366) reports the same use of the semiofficial *Diario de Barcelona*.

[6] Napoleon (Breed, ed.), *Opinions and Reflections*, 319; R. M. Johnston (comp.), *The Corsican: a Diary of Napoleon's Life in His Own Words* (Boston, 1910), 481.

[7] See, for example, *Mercure*, October 26, 1811; *Débats*, 1 Frimaire, Year X; *Curés*, July 23, 1809.

this group was Talleyrand, who announced that the treatment of the 1803 Irish revolt had created a good impression. Joseph said that the article on the peace negotiations in February, 1814, neutralized to some extent the effect of the evacuation of Châlons-sur-Marne. La Forest related that, even when they were not favorably received, articles in the official paper were carefully read. The police reports frequently mentioned that the *Moniteur* had wholesomely affected the attitude of the public. Fiévée admitted that articles in the *Moniteur* by Napoleon were effective because Napoleon knew public opinion, and he advocated unofficial articles in the official paper as an effective means of wielding influence.[8]

The evidence of those hostile to Napoleon is even more valuable. The Austrian ambassador, Prince Klemens von Metternich, reported home:

> Newspaper articles have thus so misled the public mind that everything which is said to put matters in their proper light is opposed by documents held to be official.
>
> . . . .
>
> I have a confused idea of having one day drawn your Excellency's attention to the editors of the Frankfurt and Augsburg Gazettes.
>
> There is a most urgent necessity to exercise some influence over newspapers in general, and particularly over these two, which never cease spreading lies, often of the most ridiculous nature, about us. It is from these that most of the articles are extracted which are found in the French journals. . . .
>
> A great fault which all the Governments, and particularly our own, have committed since the commencement of the French Revolution is that they have regarded as useless, as beneath their dignity and that of the good cause, and indeed even as dangerous, to speak truth to the public, and to speak it incessantly. This fact is never more incontestable than when the French are concerned. They have the game to themselves; they have only occupied an

---

[8] Talleyrand (Bertrand, ed.), *Lettres à Napoléon*, 41; La Forest (Grandmaison, pub.), *Correspondance*, IV, 531, 543; Aulard (ed.), *Paris sous le consulat* and *Paris sous le premier empire, passim;* E. d'Hauterive (ed.), *La police secrète, passim;* Joseph (Du Casse, ed.), *Mémoires*, X, 59; Fiévée, *Correspondance*, I, 81; II, 238–43. Fiévée's recommendation that an idea to be propagated be linked with an idea already dominant was psychologically sound.

empty place by seizing the desks of the journalists, and no one can reproach them with silence; they have taken up the weapon we have disdained to make use of, and they are now employing it against ourselves.

The use of a thing is confused everywhere with its abuse. . . .

There is not one of the above-mentioned papers which does not say under the heading of Vienna that we are in full negotiation on important points, or which does not publish lies about facts and individuals. The public cannot distinguish if news is true or false. False news has the air of being true if no one can be found to contradict it.

. . . I speak to you from a place where, more than anywhere else, I can appreciate the success of the efforts of the Government to influence the public. The newspapers are worth to Napoleon an army of three hundred thousand men, for such a force would not overlook the interior better, or frighten foreign Powers more, than half a dozen of his paid pamphleteers.[9]

Louis Gohier, President of the Directory, admitted that the *Moniteur* deceived all France. The agents of Louis XVIII reported that the *Moniteur* led many Bourbon partisans to accuse England alone for renewal of the war in 1803.[10]

Reports by scholars as well as by contemporaries also indicate the power of the *Moniteur*. One historian has stated that merely knowing that his name had appeared favorably in this paper made the average Frenchman ecstatic with joy. Another has affirmed that the *Moniteur* succeeded fully in embittering Anglo-Spanish relations in 1804, just as it was in large part responsible for the blind hatred against England experienced by the French.[11]

One reason for its effectiveness was the ability to reach all classes by being, directly or through reprints, the principal source of news. Mme de Rémusat was admittedly influenced by the

[9] Prince Richard Metternich (ed.), *Memoirs of Prince* [Klemens] *Metternich*, tr. by Mrs. Alexander Napier (London, 1880–81), II, 225–26.

[10] Louis-Jerome Gohier, *Mémoires de Louis-Jérôme Gohier, président du directoire au 18 brumaire* (*Mémoires des contemporains*), 2 vols. (Paris, 1824), I, 338; Périvier, *Napoléon journaliste*, 319; Remacle (ed.), *Bonaparte et les Bourbons*, 355. Another indication of the effect of the *Moniteur* is that Metternich advocated an official press edited by the allies in opposition to the official French paper.

[11] Fugier, *Napoléon et l'Espagne*, I, 294; Paul Holzhausen, *Bonaparte et la société parisienne* (Paris, 1914), 189.

Moniteur, despite the distrust resulting from constant deception. Rapp reported to Berthier in 1813 that the issues recounting the victories of Lützen and Bautzen had affected the garrisons most favorably. In 1815 Davout wrote General Étienne Gérard that the copies he was forwarding had caused a great sensation at Paris.[12]

Napoleon eagerly checked on the effects of the *Moniteur* [13] and was chagrined to learn that frequently they were not all that could be desired. For one thing, the paper did not reach as many people as Napoleon would have liked—partly because its large format frightened away prospective readers, even as the inconvenience of reading regular-sized papers on a subway train or a bus has contributed greatly to the popularity of today's tabloids. Perhaps La Forest's occasional reports that people did not believe the *Moniteur* was truthful tie in with Fiévée's notation that the *Moniteur* was actually affecting public opinion badly and that its articles did not produce all the results expected.[14]

The other papers were no more successful. During the Consulate a press campaign against the custom of reviving titles of nobility acted as a boomerang. At the time of the Cadoudal plot the government maintained that only a few individuals were involved, but its press articles left the impression that a huge number were implicated. La Forest stated that the effect of the poorly

---

[12] Rémusat (P. de Rémusat, pub.), *Lettres*, II, 162; Rémusat (P. de Rémusat, pub.), *Mémoires*, III, 614; A. Bulos (ed.), *Memoirs of General Count Rapp* (London, 1823), 295; Davout (Mazada, ed.), *Correspondance*, IV, 445; Fiévée, *Correspondance*, II, 110; Constant, *Journal*, 355.

[13] Napoleon (Lecestre, comp.), *Lettres*, I, 151, 211.

[14] *Moniteur*, 27 Nivôse, Year IX; Réal (Desclozeaux, ed.), *Indescrétions*, I, 125; Fiévée, *Correspondance*, II, 364. There are also indications by people hostile to Napoleon which may contain an element of truth, particularly the statement by Remacle that the accounts of Bonaparte's trip into Normandy aroused anger with the flatterers. Remacle (ed.), *Bonaparte et les Bourbons*, 184. Rémusat (*Mémoires* [P. de Rémusat, pub.] III, 334-35) says that Napoleon was irritated by the distrust with which the people read the papers. Abbé de Pradt (*Histoire de l'ambassade, Napoleon Pamphlets*) says the *Moniteur* was welcomed with derision. It might also be pointed out that foreign countries censored French papers before allowing their publication. *St. Petersburgische Zeitung*, September 23, 1804, in Ebeling, *Miscellaneous German Newspapers 1804–1805*. Such censorship could indicate two things: first, that these countries feared French propaganda; second, that the *Moniteur* did not have in foreign countries the effect desired by Napoleon.

edited *Gazette de Madrid* was only mediocre, and Tournon reported that the *Journal du Capitole* of Rome had almost no influence on public opinion. Napoleon himself said that although informed men already knew that he had not attacked the papacy, nothing could convince the falsely devout of that fact, and he complained that French papers did not sufficiently animate opinion even though they were read everywhere. Extracts from foreign papers had much more effect on French public opinion than articles written at Paris, because the French papers were believed to be dependent on the government, and the English, aware of Napoleon's control over the press, likewise concluded that its statements were generally false. The police reported that certain articles were so tendentious they were not believed; Fiévée substantiated this statement and said that the lack of confidence was so great the papers no longer directed opinion. He also commented on the stupidity of press articles dealing with colonial goods or the Bourse, or repeating for five weeks that a big battle would take place.[15]

In spite of their shortcomings, these other papers were not without value, for certain types of articles were more effective if they appeared in papers other than the *Moniteur*. An illustration of one such type was an item in the *Journal des Débats* on babblers which, according to the agents of the Bourbons, had helped silence these *gobe-mouches*. In 1811 La Forest reported that the political articles of the *Gazette de Madrid* were successful in influencing public opinion. In the following year Napoleon was able for a time to deceive the public on his military preparations. According to him, the French papers were significant in Europe, partly because they flattered the peoples reading them.

15 Lanzac de Laborie, *Paris sous Napoléon*, I, 150; Aulard (ed.), *Paris sous le consulat*, II, 791; III, 445; and *passim;* Aulard (ed.), *Paris sous le premier empire*, III, 593; and *passim;* E. d'Hauterive (ed.), *La police secrète*, II, 334; and *passim;* Henry Benjamin Constant de Rebecque, *Mémoires sur les cent jours* (Paris, 1822), 18; Napoleon, *Correspondance*, XI, 287; XIX, 183; Fiévée, *Correspondance*, II, 331–34, 381–86, 398–99; La Forest (Grandmaison, pub.), *Correspondance*, II, 94; V, 45, 117; Maccunn, *Contemporary English View of Napoleon*, 132. Madame de Rémusat (*Mémoires* [P. de Rémusat, pub.], III, 63, 614–15) says that the papers did not convince anyone because they were so untrustworthy. Another reason for the lack of effect in England of the *Moniteur* articles may have been that the papers of the opposition had frequently said virtually the same thing.

Adam Czartoryski's report to Alexander that a newspaper article was sufficient to reawaken Polish enthusiasm for months would seem to support Napoleon's contention.[16]

As with the press, the degree of success in using the different devices varied. It is probably true that the undiscriminating masses [17] believed news, even if false, while the few informed people protested. Thus, the story on the use of daggers against Bonaparte at Saint-Cloud conciliated public opinion, and Napoleon insisted that the exaggeration of his own forces had served his ends without diminishing his glory. Yet even the masses might doubt favorable news from other countries when news of their own region was palpably false, and the general belief that Bulletin 30 exaggerated the number of prisoners captured by the French in 1806 forced Napoleon to order the insertion of an article in the *Journal de l'Empire* to make the figures appear plausible. Fiévée thought it inadvisable to push the credulity of the French people too far.

> If the articles put into the *Moniteur* to reassure people on the war with Austria have not produced all the effect expected, one must not be astonished by it, but he can groan at it. It has too long been forgotten that if authority may sometimes silence the truth, it must never disguise it. Cleverness rarely succeeds with the French, who generally pride themselves on being clever; he who perceives that he has been deceived once by believing, prefers the risk of deceiving himself twenty times by refusing to believe to that of exposing himself to being a dupe.[18]

---

[16] La Forest (Grandmaison, pub.), *Correspondance*, 190; F.-A. Aulard, "Un rapport de Portalis sur la presse en l'an XI," *La révolution française*, XXXII (1897), 87; Thiers, *Histoire du consulat*, XIII, 180; Remacle (ed.), *Bonaparte et les Bourbons*, 246; Napoleon, *Correspondance*, XV, 277; Napoleon (Lecestre, comp.), *Lettres*, I, 330; Prince Ladislaus Czartoryski (pub.), *Alexandre Ier et le prince* [Adam] *Czartoryski. Correspondance particulière et conversations 1801-23* (Paris, 1865), 87.

[17] Fiévée (*Correspondance*, I, 169) advised against the use of caricatures because they were suitable only in countries where the masses counted for something. But Rose (Broadley, *Napoleon in Caricature*, xxxv) says they were as effective as the press laws and more so than the official plays.

[18] Fiévée, *Correspondance*, II, 364; Napoleon (Hinard, comp.), *Opinions et jugemens*, II, 251; Le Coz (Roussel, pub.), *Correspondance*, II, 391; Lanzac de Laborie, *Paris sous Napoléon*, I, 13; Napoleon, *Correspondance*, XIX, 571; Napoleon (Lumbroso, ed.), *Lettres inédites*, 119. A hostile witness who wrote up his observations later held that people did not believe the lies in the Paris papers during the Hundred Days. Un Vieux Marseillais [Laurent Lautard], *Esquisses*

Napoleon occasionally felt compelled to publish material he did not care to reveal, since, as Fiévée complained, official silence on unconcealable events revealed the fear of the government and was the surest means of forcing public opinion to become adverse.[19] Sudden changes in the objectives of the press propaganda usually produced a strange feeling, rather than the desired effect, among the people. Napoleon did succeed, however, in forcing the enemy to take the defensive in the charge-countercharge rivalry. One reason for the effectiveness of the bulletins was that they cited men who inspired confidence. According to the papers, Napoleon used letters effectively, and Davout reported that a letter to the corps under Lannes after the Battle of Jena, acknowledging what it had done and promising someday to detail its exploits in a bulletin, was very moving.[20]

Because of rigid government control of the stage, only seven plays produced by the big theaters under the Empire proved financially successful. Even Mme de Rémusat, whose husband was in direct charge of the theaters, confessed they merited the reproaches directed at them by the papers; a play entitled *Cyrus*, written by Chénier, was so palpably government-inspired that it was hissed and withdrawn from the repertoire. Yet the effect of reading the bulletins in the theaters was, on the whole, salutary, and the theaters did perform patriotic plays.[21]

The papers gave very favorable reviews to the music for the various fetes, claiming that it had a great emotional effect on the

---

historiques: Marseilles depuis 1789 jusqu'en 1815, 2 vols. (Marseille, 1844), 88, 256.

[19] Fiévée, *Correspondance*, II, 357-59.

[20] Joseph (Du Casse, ed.), *Mémoires*, III, 244; Evjen, "English Propaganda against Napoleon," 39; "La diplomatie de Napoléon Ier pendant les cent jours d'après des documents inédits," *Hundred Days;* Hatin, *Histoire de la presse*, VIII, 121; Davout (Mazada, ed.), *Correspondance*, I, xxvii; *Journal*, 26 Prairial, Year VIII; 14 Nivôse, Year XI; Metternich (R. Metternich, ed., Napier, tr.), *Memoirs*, II, 95. Méneval (*Memoirs* [Baron de Méneval, ed.], III, 187) says that the atrocity reports did not arouse the expected anger.

[21] Welschinger, *Censure sous l'empire*, 238, 254; Rémusat (P. de Rémusat, pub.), *Lettres*, I, 40; II, 45; Aulard (ed.), *Paris sous le premier empire*, II, 278; Broadley, *Napoleon in Caricature*, xxxv; Charpentier, *Napoléon et les hommes de lettres*, 85. At one time in 1806, Madame de Rémusat reported (*Mémoires* [P. de Rémusat, pub.], II, 45) that the whole effect was spoiled when a woman fainted during the reading of the mortality list by an actor who raised his voice for this portion of a bulletin.

people present. Yet this music was not the type of mechanical song having the greatest influence on the masses; it is impossible to ascertain the effect of such songs inspired by the government. The Minister of the Interior did state on one occasion, however, that music had a unifying effect upon France and had often enhanced the courage of the French soldiers.[22]

The fetes themselves were probably none too successful as propaganda moves, although the flag ceremonies may have been effective. At least there is no evidence to contradict or refute Joseph's announcement in 1806 that the public showed much joy at the ceremony of transporting flags, and it is true that the military fetes were the most impressive. Even of them Napoleon wrote, "You know what I think of these military pomps, but perhaps they are useful now [1813]." Too great a stress was placed upon the amusement angle for the celebrations to arouse thoughts of devotion to Napoleon or of patriotism; even the Champ de Mai of 1815 had little effect on the populace. In fact, one article in the *Journal de Paris* went so far as to advocate complete abolition as the only proper move concerning these festivities. In the Ile-de-France, Decaen multiplied the number of fetes without any effect. Indeed, one trouble was that there were so many fetes as to be monotonous.[23]

Some fetes, such as those at Amiens in the Year VIII, were nevertheless acclaimed as successful. The participants and spectators allegedly could never forget the ceremony for the first Legion of Honor awards, and Tournon reported that the presentation of money aroused the most lively gratitude in the Roman

[22] Aulard (ed.), *Paris sous le premier empire*, III, 174; *Moniteur*, 4 Messidor, Year VIII; 3 Vendémiaire, Year IX; Jullien, *Histoire de la poésie française*, I, 110; *Journal*, 20 Frimaire, Year IX. When Lucien made his statements, he was awarding prizes to the Conservatory of Music; his claims must therefore be to some extent disallowed. A pamphlet, *Notice particulière, The Empire: Undated Contemporary Pamphlets*, in Boulay de la Meurthe collection, says Napoleon used hawkers and singers effectively.

[23] *Church Affairs: Rennes.* Lanzac de Laborie, *Paris sous Napoléon*, I, 103; Napoleon, *Correspondance*, XXVI, 405; Aulard (ed.), *Paris sous le consulat*, II, 408; Wilhelm Adolf Schmidt (ed.), *Tableaux de la révolution française, publiés sur les papiers inédits du département et de la police secrète de Paris* (Leipzig, 1867–71), III, 482; *Journal*, 23 Frimaire, Year X; Prentout, *Ile de France sous Decaen*, 519; Alfred A. Cuvillier-Fleury (tr.), *Memoirs of Count Lavallette*, 2 vols. (London, 1831), II, 218; Lanzac de Laborie, *Paris sous Napoléon*, III, 14, 31; Joseph (Du Casse, ed.), *Mémoires*, I, 360.

populace. Jean Portalis may have been somewhat biased, but he announced to Napoleon that the civil ceremonies were nothing unless they were also religious; the religious ceremonies were generally depicted as going off well and arousing joy in the populace. Although the priests were opposed to celebrating the *décadi* during the early part of the Consulate, the police reported that they had absolutely no influence on this point, even where they were generally influential, as in towns like Marseille and Morbihan.[24]

In other respects than in ceremonies the clergy was useful. Satisfied by the Concordat, it had proven itself an excellent electoral agent in 1802 and had urged unity rather than any schism. It persuaded large numbers of the people to be vaccinated and had some effect on conscription, in each case affecting the interested but little-enlightened class.[25]

Efforts of the government to utilize the Church for propaganda purposes did not always prove successful. Napoleon tried futilely to win the Roman and Spanish clergy by having the French attend religious celebrations. In France, the influence of the refractory priests, described as frightful, was greater in many places than that of the juring clergy. In Lozère a curé had to leave the pulpit because a congregation composed of relatives of conscripts greeted his sermon on the anniversary of Austerlitz with such an uproar. Even in Paris in 1814 Joseph reported that no religious ceremony would have a good effect for Napoleon until the Pope was safely back in Rome, and Napoleon reprimanded his brother for holding long public prayers which adversely affected opinion.[26]

[24] Marie-Antoine, vicomte de Reiset, *Souvenirs du lieutenant général vicomte de Reiset, 1775–1836*, 3 vols. (Paris, 1899–1902), I, 140; Tournon (Moulard, pub.), *Lettres inédites*, 139; Lanzac de Laborie, *Paris sous Napoléon*, III, 57; Calonne, *Amiens*, 15; Holzhausen (Minart, tr.), *Société parisienne*, 93; Aulard (ed.), *Paris sous le consulat*, I, 431; Boulay de la Meurthe (ed.), *Documents sur la négociation du concordat*, V, 571.

[25] Calonne, *Amiens*, 40; *Débats*, 3 Vendémiaire, Year XI; "Pastoral Letter," *Church and Religious Affairs in Versailles during the Consulate and Empire;* E. d'Hauterive (ed.), *La police secrète, passim; Moniteur*, August 17, 1812; *Curés*, July 2, 1809.

[26] E. d'Hauterive (ed.), *La police secrète*, I, 100; III, 99; Wilhelm Hammer, *Napoleon als Feldherr, Regent, Staatsmann, und Politiker* (Stuttgart, 1833), 101; *Mercure*, September 10, 1808; F. Uzureau, "La séparation de l'église et de

As indicated in Chapter VI, the effect of the educational system might be hinted at by the literary efforts of the pupils. In 1801 there appeared a pamphlet, *Les élèves du prytanée de Paris au premier consul Bonaparte sur l'attentat du 3 nivôse*, consisting of one poem each by eleven pupils, and the pupils at the Juilly boarding school composed a poem entitled "Le Lion et le Léopard" on violation of the peace by England. Pupils of the Polytechnic School at Paris were one group expressing support of the war against England in 1803, and students were also ardent defenders of Paris in 1814. However, the unpopularity of the *lycées* resulting from their military discipline and from their stress upon mathematics and the physical sciences meant that Napoleon's education measures could not achieve the hoped-for results because the school system reached too small a proportion of the young people.[27]

Not expecting to affect the officers whom these schools helped develop, Napoleon did believe that proclamations and orders of the day usefully influence the unthinking rank and file of soldiers.[28] There is abundant evidence to testify that his conviction was well-founded.

Napoleon, Junot, General Jean Solignac, Joseph, the Spanish Junta, Augereau, Eugene, Jourdan, Jerome, General Henri Dombrowski and the General Confederation, Kléber, the Prefects of Var and Bouches-du-Rhône, the special commissioners in 1814, and Masséna were most prominent in receiving acclaim for their proclamations.[29] The statements of friendly commentators re-

---

l'état dans un grand diocèse (1800–1802)," *Revue des sciences ecclésiastiques et la science catholique* (July, 1907) (*Local Church and Religious Affairs during the Consulate and Empire: Secondary Material*); Conard, *Napoléon et la Catalogne*, 367; Joseph (Du Casse, ed.) *Mémoires*, X, 69; Napoleon, *Correspondance*, XXVII, 128. In light of these facts, the statement of the *Courrier de l'Europe*, March 2, 1809, that the French had won back the Spaniards by participating in the *Te Deum* cannot bear much weight.

[27] *Consulate: Contemporary Pamphlets Year 9; Moniteur*, 12 Prairial, Year XI; *Journal*, 23 Messidor, Year XI; Benaerts, *Régime consulaire en Bretagne*, xi; *Archives parlementaires*, IX, 402–403.

[28] Napoleon, *Correspondance*, XIX, 570.

[29] *Débats*, 10 Pluviôse, Year IX; 14 Brumaire, Year XI; *Empire*, December 16, 1807; January 29, 1813; Miot de Melito (Fleischmann, ed., Hoey and Lillie, trs.), *Memoirs*, 669; Bausset, *Mémoires*, I, 239; Aulard (ed.), *Paris sous le consulat*, III, 338; Pasquier (Audiffret-Pasquier, ed., Roche, tr.), *Memoirs*, III, 172; Stendhal, *Napoleon*, ed. by Henri Martineau, 2 vols. (Paris, 1930), I, 316; Con-

garding the effect of proclamations on the soldiers are buttressed by the reluctant admissions of hostile witnesses. As Mme de Rémusat grudgingly put it, "The Emperor made a few more proclamations to the army in his usual turgid style, but they are said to have produced a great effect." [30] In addition, proclamations produced the desired results among civilians—results naturally heightened when the proclamations were printed instead of circulated in manuscript. [31]

There were instances when the use of proclamations by the French was fruitless or harmful. A proclamation by General Miollis to the rebels of Fontana had no effect. Murat told Napoleon he would publish his proclamation even though he knew in advance that it would not have any result and that the best proclamation would be one naming the new King of Spain. Also, Murat's proclamations to the Italians in 1815 did not produce the desired effect. The pamphlet *Vie de Joachim Murat* said that nowhere did proclamations have less effect than in Tuscany, and Napoleon admitted proclamations were useless among the Poles. In 1809 Eugene's proclamation was successful among the Tyrolese, to whom it was addressed, but it aroused great dissatisfaction among the Bavarians. Although praising Bonaparte for pacifying the West, the Hamburg *Spectateur du Nord* bemoaned his proclamation insulting the rebel leaders. The proclamation from Potsdam, October 26, 1806, announcing new dangers and glory for the army, frightened Paris and helped turn the masses against the

---

stant, *Journal*, 349; Napoleon, *Correspondance*, XXXI, 82; Eugene (Du Casse, ed.), *Mémoires*, IV, 154; Jerome (Du Casse, ed.), *Mémoires*, III, 356; Murat (Prince Murat, pub.), *Lettres*, VI, 207; Joseph (Du Casse, ed.), *Mémoires*, I, 283; Handelsman, *Napoléon et la Pologne*, 226; Napoleon, *Commentaires*, III, 190; La Forest (Grandmaison, pub.), *Correspondance*, I, 54; *Moniteur*, 7 Prairial, Year VIII; August 17, 1810; *Mercure*, 7 Prairial, Year VIII.

[30] Rémusat (P. de Rémusat, pub.), *Mémoires*, II, 327.

[31] Napoleon, *Commentaires*, V, 431; Joseph Petit, *Maringo*, *Napoleon Pamphlets*, 8, in Boulay de la Meurthe collection; General Comte Philippe de Ségur, *La campagne de Russie* (Paris, n.d.), 26; *Moniteur*, 22 Fructidor, Year IX; Kielland, *Napoleon's Men and Methods*, 29; Aulard (ed.), *Paris sous le consulat*, III, 338; L. de Contenson (ed.), "Lettres du comte Louis de Périgord (1806-1807)," *Revue d'histoire diplomatique*, XLIII (1929), 114; Louis de Pontécoulant (ed.), *Souvenirs historiques et parlementaires du comte de Pontécoulant*, 3 vols. (Paris, 1863), III, 95, 315; Bourrienne (Phipps, ed.), *Memoirs*, IV, 72; Joseph (Du Casse, ed.), *Mémoires*, II, 69; Rapp (Bulos, ed.), *Memoirs*, 162, 203; Eugene (Du Casse, ed.), *Mémoires*, IV, 257; Leclerc (Roussier, pub.), *Lettres*, 250.

war; Leclerc complained of the type of proclamations reaching
Santo Domingo; and Marmont claimed that Eugene's publication
in 1814 of a proclamation to the Italians resulted in their revolting.[32]

There is very little direct evidence available as to the effect of
orders of the day, a medium first habitually exploited by Napoleon, who may even have devised their use.[33] It is therefore not
surprising that he wrote:

> I saw a *Letter to the army;* it was by Barère. I have not read it,
> but I think there is no need of speaking to the army; it does not
> read the vain prattling of pamphlets, and one word in the order of
> the day would do more than a hundred volumes of Cicero and
> Demosthenes. One can rouse the soldiers against England without
> speaking to them. . . . He [Barère] always thinks that the masses
> must be stirred; on the contrary, they should be directed without
> their noticing it. . . . There is no legal means of speaking to it
> [the army] other than through the order of the day. Everything
> else is intrigue and faction.[34]

The *Journal de l'Empire* of 23 Vendémiaire, Year XIV, announced that an order to the Bavarian troops aroused their patriotic indignation, and Murat reported that one of his orders of the
day had the most desirable effect.[35]

One of the most effective ways of arousing the enthusiasm of
the army was the Legion of Honor awards. In fact, although there
was discontent when the Legion of Honor was established, the

[32] Napoleon, *Correspondance,* XIV, 126; XXVIII, 113; *Moniteur,* 17 Pluviôse,
Year VIII; Eugene (Du Casse, ed.), *Mémoires,* VI, 166, 190; Rémusat (P. de Rémusat, pub.), *Lettres,* II, 88; Marmont, *Mémoires,* VI, 29; Murat (Prince Murat,
pub.), *Lettres,* VI, 30, 200. Alphonse Roserot (pub.), *Mémoires de Mme. de
Chastenay, 1771–1815,* 2 vols. (Paris, 1896), II, 258, says that Napoleon's incendiary
proclamations in 1813 and 1814 merely froze all hearts. Joseph (*Mémoires* [Du
Casse, ed.], III, 365) said that proclamations spread by the erstwhile King of
Naples had no effect, and Murat (*Lettres* [Prince Murat, pub.], VI, 166) reported
the same for Ferdinand's proclamation in Spain. But La Forest (*Correspondance*
[Grandmaison, pub.], I, 172) reported that proclamations by de La Cuesta increased confidence in the latter. General Jellachich's proclamation to the Tyrolese
aroused them, although proclamations by Archduke John were said to have had
no effect. Napoleon, *Correspondance,* XIX, 55.
[33] The only definite information available on them is that they came into
use between 1776 and 1813.
[34] Napoleon, *Correspondance,* IX, 511.
[35] Murat (Prince Murat, pub.), *Lettres,* V, 346.

soldiers developed a mania for earning the medal presented by the order. Therefore Napoleon could incite the soldiers against the Bourbons in 1814 with the claim that Louis XVIII's government had sold awards for thirty louis.[36]

Bulletins also had a very favorable effect during most of Napoleon's reign, because they contained only news advantageous to the French. Even the royalist Countess de Boigne admired Napoleon as a writer of bulletins, which were said to reach millions of people, and Metternich wrote:

> The daily bulletins which are published for the French army, and which inundate Germany and the whole of Europe, are a new invention which deserves the most serious attention. Designed less to report military facts than to mislead the public as to the spirit and principles of our government and our people, Bonaparte's cabinet thus brings itself into daily contact with all classes of society. It has given up the official style and adopted that of familiar conversation; each Bulletin brings on the scene personages whose respectability inspires confidence and men of the people who confirm what they wish to be taken for public feeling in the Austrian monarchy, and millions of readers end by accepting it as such.[37]

Appropriate phrases from the bulletins put on divisional flags served to inflame the soldiers. Eugene assured Berthier in 1806 that the bulletins made the Italian army sorry it was not in action.[38]

Naturally there was variation in the effectiveness of individual bulletins. Those expressing a desire for peace were even more effective than those containing accounts of dazzling victories. Both types helped quell rumors by providing concrete news and helped fill draft quotas by making people optimistic. There was,

[36] Rufus W. Griswold and H. B. Wallace, *Napoleon and the Marshals of the Empire* (Philadelphia, 1885), 208; *Empire*, April 6, 1815. The value of the Napoleonic medals was lessened by their lack of individuality and by excessive adulation. Edwards (ed.), *Napoleon Medals*, I, viii.

[37] Metternich (R. Metternich, ed., Napier, tr.), *Memoirs*, II, 95.

[38] Caulaincourt (Hanoteau, ed.), *Mémoires*, II, 354; *Empire*, July 6, 1807; Charles Nicoullaud (ed.), *Memoirs of the comtesse de Boigne* (New York, 1907), I, 188; Rémusat (P. de Rémusat, pub.), *Lettres*, II, 44; *Eugene* (Du Casse, ed.), *Mémoires*, I, 428; III, 206, 213; Aulard (ed.), *Paris sous le premier empire, passim*; E. d'Hauterive (ed.), *La police secrète, passim*; Joseph (Du Casse, ed.), *Mémoires*, I, 303–304, 343–44; III, 228; Butterfield, *Peace Tactics of Napoleon*, 135; Stenger, *Société française*, VI, 28; Rémusat (P. de Rémusat, pub.), *Mémoires*, II, 291.

however, a great deal of consternation caused by the bulletin on
Eylau and by Bulletin 29 of the Russian campaign. Fiévée reported
people's feelings would depend upon what the bulletins contained.
For the influencing of public opinion the human touches about
Napoleon himself were far from being the least important section
of the bulletins.[39]

Beginning with the 1812 campaign, however, these bulletins
were no longer able to form opinion in the way Napoleon desired.
For that reason, and because people knew the bulletins were untrustworthy and were written by him, he accepted Fiévée's advice
to discontinue them. Although Fiévée counseled semiofficial articles, the bulletins were replaced by official articles with the news
ostensibly relayed from the army to the press by the regent.[40]

The bulletins defeated their own purpose and, by not being
frank concerning French losses, caused people to become blasé
regarding their contents. Furthermore, the exaggerated news in
the bulletins lost much of its desired effect because of the prior
circulation of even more fantastic rumors.[41]

Napoleon's speeches to the troops were for the most part effective, arousing unanimous acclamations. His adieu to the Imperial Guard actually caused even hardened veterans to weep:

> Soldiers of my Old Guard, I bid you adieu. For twenty years I
> always found you on the road of glory and honor. In these last
> times, as in those of our prosperity, you have not ceased to be
> models of bravery and of fidelity. With men like you, our cause

[39] La Forest (Grandmaison, pub.), *Correspondance*, II, 345; Rémusat (P. de
Remusat, pub.), *Mémoires*, III, 473; Aulard (ed.), *Paris sous le premier empire*, II,
787, 799; Fiévée, *Correspondance*, III, 226–29; Rocquain, *Napoléon et Louis*, 78;
Joseph (Du Casse, ed.), *Mémoires*, I, 306.

[40] Fiévée, *Correspondance*, III, 239; Napoleon (Brotonne, ed.), *Lettres*, 499;
Lecomte, *Monde dramatique*, II, 789; Thiers, *Histoire du consulat*, XIX, 311. As
early as 1804 Napoleon had stated (*Correspondance*, IX, 451) that he was the
only reader of Mollien's bulletins.

[41] Joseph (Du Casse, ed.), *Mémoires*, I, 298; Aulard (ed.), *Paris sous le premier
empire*, III, 13; Rémusat (P. de Rémusat, pub.), *Lettres*, II, 105; E. d'Hauterive,
La police secrète, III, 156. Rémusat (*Mémoires* [P. de Rémusat, pub.], III, 466)
says the bulletins were freely criticized and only hired applause was heard
in the theaters. Countess d'Albany, who was very hostile to Napoleon, said
(*Lettres* [Pelissier, ed.], II, 178) the gossiping in the bulletins was worthy of an
old nun. The *Journal* of April 24, 1807, claimed the Russian bulletins fooled no
one; on January 7, 1813, however, Napoleon was sufficiently anxious about them
to write Francis I of Austria at great length to warn him not to believe the Russian
bulletins. Napoleon (Brotonne, ed.), *Lettres*, 414.

was not lost. But the war was interminable; there would have been civil war and France would have become only more unfortunate as a result of it. I have therefore sacrificed all our interests to those of the country; I am leaving. You, my friends, continue to serve France. Her welfare was my only thought; it will always be the object of my wishes. Do not pity my fate; if I have consented to survive, it is to continue to serve your glory; I want to write of the great things we have done together! Good-bye, my children. I should like to press you all to my heart; may I at least embrace your flag!

Good-bye once again, my old companions! May this last kiss pass into your hearts.[42]

Napoleon's praise or blame fired the troops to commit deeds of valor, just as his reproaches incited the Poles. As far as the soldiers were concerned, it was not even necessary for him to speak; his mere presence, which aroused great enthusiasm even among civilians, was enough to inspire them.[43]

Other speeches by Napoleon, especially those at the start of sessions of the legislature, were well received. Addresses delivered by Maret and some of those inserted in the press also proved useful.[44]

Although Napoleon was an effective speaker, he was completely successful only when addressing lower-class Frenchmen, when the effectiveness of his speeches depended on his thorough understanding of the mass mind. On the other hand, Napoleon's failure to understand the individual mind kept him from gaining favor with savants and foreign peoples, whose support he sought to win through speeches. By 1814, Napoleon's addresses no longer had any favorable effect. Even earlier the Parisians had greeted the public eulogies, all of the same tenor and obviously com-

[42] Napoleon, *Correspondance*, XXVII, 362.
[43] Jerome (Du Casse, ed.), *Mémoires*, II, 221; V, 394; Eugene (Du Casse, ed.), *Mémoires*, I, 77; Caulaincourt, *Mémoires*, II, 374; III, 178, 401; Louis Lejeune, *Souvenirs d'un officier de l'empire*, 2 vols. (Toulouse, 1851), II, 340; A. Pingaud, *Bonaparte président de la république italienne*, II, 465-77; Rovigo, *Memoirs*, Vol. II, Part II, 82; Jean Baptiste Barrès, *Souvenirs d'un officier de la grande armée*, pub. by Maurice Barrès (Paris, 1922), 55.
[44] *Empire*, January 3, 1814; Fiévée, *Correspondance*, III, 7, 59; *Moniteur*, 26 Brumaire, Year VIII; Rémusat (P. de Rémusat, pub.), *Lettres*, I, 281; Rémusat (P. de Rémusat, pub.), *Mémoires*, II, 288; Aulard (ed.), *Paris sous le consulat*, III, 310; IV, 690; Aulard (ed.), *Paris sous le premier empire*, III, 763.

manded, either with indifference or indignation. Fiévée reported that the speeches of the Senate and Legislative Body on Napoleon's personal safety at the time of the assassination plot had the effect of exculpating General Jean Moreau, whom Bonaparte wished to eliminate as a possible rival for public favor. Governmental attempts to have the pastors deliver long speeches in the provinces proved very unwise, as the people simply were not accustomed to them.[45]

The talk in the *salons* did not have much effect upon the mass of citizens, but certain rumors definitely did, although sometimes they were repeated so frequently that they no longer produced any effect. Napoleon refused to deny rumors that Brabant and Zeeland were to be united to France because those rumors furthered his policy. Rumors were most effective when other acts tended to support them.[46]

The French were unable to prevent hostile rumors, especially numerous in Spain, from grievously affecting public opinion, even though these rumors did not always upset public tranquillity. While Joseph, both in Naples and Spain, reported most frequently on the effect of the rumors circulated by the enemy, Marmont, Davout, and the police also sent in reports. One of the unfavorable results of these rumors was to increase the strength of the Spanish guerrillas, and a second was derision of the French government by its domestic enemies.[47]

[45] Émile Gabory, *Napoléon et la Vendée* (Paris, 1914), 383; Aulard, "Rapport de Portalis sur la presse," *loc. cit.*, 68; *Actes du second concile*, II, 248; *Débats*, 9 Frimaire, Year VIII; Miot de Melito (Fleischmann, ed., Hoey and Lillie, trs.), *Memoirs*, 284; Pasquier (Audiffret-Pasquier, ed., Roche, tr.), *Memoirs*, II, 65, 108; Fiévée, *Correspondance*, I, 211; Charpentier, *Napoléon et les hommes de lettres*, 17–18; Napoleon (Barral, pub.), *Messages*, 4. According to Thiébault, the speech of Napoleon at the Champ de Mai was not effective. Fernand Calmette (ed.), *Mémoires du général Thiébault*, 5 vols. (Paris, 1893–95), V, 331. Plancy (*Souvenirs* [Baron de Plancy, pub.], 429) makes the same report.

[46] Aulard (ed.), *Paris sous le premier empire*, I, 312; III, 461; Rocquain, *Napoléon et Louis*, xxxi; Marmont, *Mémoires*, III, 221. There is virtually no material additional to that in Chapter V on the effectiveness of rumors spread at the instigation of the French government. Marmont does say, though (*Mémoires*, IV, 206), that a rumor he spread of marching on Lisbon was too absurd to cause any uneasiness. Murat (*Lettres* [Prince Murat, pub.], V, 460) said a rumor he had spread was effective.

[47] Joseph (Du Casse, ed.), *Mémoires*, II, 27, 165, 188; IV, 265; VI, 54, 361; VIII, 170; Aulard (ed.), *Paris sous le consulat*, IV, 644; Aulard (ed.), *Paris sous le*

Officially inspired pamphlets, of which thousands of copies were printed and which circulated quite widely, had some effect, though the fraction of successful ones probably was not as large as was the case with some of the other mediums. The miscarriage of the pamphlet of Lucien and the displeasure aroused by that of Barère to the army have already been mentioned. *Du Jacobinisme des Anglais sur les mers* did not have the desired effect, and pamphlets were not successful in influencing Italy.[48]

Bessières reported that pamphlets had no effect in Spain, but Napoleon flatly contradicted his statement with the remark, "Spaniards are like other people." Later in the same month, on May 30, 1808, the *Journal de Paris* said that *Jugement sur les affaires d'Espagne*—which, in the light of the preceding sentence, might have been officially inspired—pleading for a new and strong dynasty, was most effective. There were several editions of Hauterive's pamphlet and Metternich credited French pamphleteers with helping form a public opinion favorable to France: "The dignity of silence observed by the right side does not impress the people; they blame us for maintaining silence, and it is necessary only to be in a foreign country, especially at a place where Bonaparte has chosen to spread all that odious pamphleteers emit daily against us, to be convinced of the truth of what I say." [49]

Since, in a more general way, the effect of Napoleon's propaganda was reflected in the state of public opinion, it is appropriate and necessary to examine that opinion in the territories under Napoleon's control.

---

premier empire, III, 444; Davout (Mazada, ed.), *Correspondance*, IV, 530; E. d'Hauterive (ed.), *La police secrète*, I, 6.

[48] Charpentier, *Napoléon et les hommes de lettres*, 84; A. Pingaud, *Bonaparte président de la république italienne*, II, 382; *Church and Religious Affairs during the Consulate and Empire: Contemporary Pamphlets*. Further evidence might be the statement of Napoleon at St. Helena (*Correspondance*, XXXII, 252) that pamphlets are powerless. Though he was speaking of pamphlets directed against himself, the ideas of Napoleon may have been partially formulated by his own experience.

[49] Napoleon, *Correspondance*, XVII, 71; *Metternich* (R. Metternich, ed., Napier, tr.), *Memoirs*, II, 95. Napoleon's repeated orders for official pamphlets demonstrate that he thought they were effective or could be so. Méneval (*Memoirs* [Baron de Méneval, ed.], II, 49) says that libelous pamphlets began circulating in 1806 and helped greatly to exasperate Europe against France.

Before 18 Brumaire the masses were opposed to the Directory but were sincerely attached to the republic. Weary from foreign war and domestic upheaval, they were interested primarily in peace and in the security of their own existence.[50]

Immediately after 18 Brumaire, Paris, having accepted Bonaparte, was calm and rather indifferent. When the government suppressed five of every six daily papers, Parisians did not protest much, partly because that same government was restoring law and order. Until the Battle of Marengo, Paris did not even display much interest in the victories in Italy, even though the civilians did aid the army.[51]

Although the government had to plead for troops in the spring of 1800, Bonaparte so thoroughly convinced the people that he was the man to right matters, and Marengo temporarily aroused such enthusiasm, that after this victory the army had more volunteers than it could handle. Indifference again appeared, however, and the police reported a tendency on the part of Parisians to purchase caricatures of Louis XVI and Marie Antoinette merely to occupy their minds with the memory of the Bourbon family. The plot of 3 Nivôse rekindled public opinion in favor of Bonaparte, and the blunt refusal of England to enter into peace negotiations likewise increased his popularity because the people thought England was blocking his sincere efforts to obtain for them that peace which was their most ardent desire.[52]

Although royalist and Jacobin propaganda was unable to change the opinion of the masses, certain regions, primarily in western France, remained royalist, and there was a tendency to-

[50] Marmont, *Mémoires*, II, 97; W. Schmidt (ed.), *Tableaux de la révolution*, III, 467; Iung, *Lucien Bonaparte*, I, 418.

[51] Welschinger, *Censure sous l'empire*, 13; Gershoy, *French Revolution and Napoleon*, 357; Aulard (ed.), *Paris sous le consulat*, I, 2, 184, 293, 300; *Moniteur*, 21 Ventôse, Year VIII; *Journal*, 27 Frimaire, Year VIII; *Moniteur*, 12 and 14 Frimaire, Year VIII.

[52] Gohier, *Mémoires*, I, 253; Lanzac de Laborie, *Paris sous Napoléon*, I, 87; Bourrienne (Phipps, ed.), *Memoirs*, II, 26; Barère (Carnot and David, eds., Payen-Payne, tr.), *Memoirs*, III, 108; *Débats*, 4 Messidor, Year VIII; Desmarest (Grasilier, ed.), *Quinze ans de haute police*, 58; A. Sayous (ed.), *Memoirs and Correspondence of Mallet du Pan, Illustrative of the History of the French Revolution*, 2 vols. (London, 1852), II, 449; Aulard (ed.), *Paris sous le consulat*, I, 639. Gohier claimed that a loan could be covered only by a lottery. There were thirty-one conspiracies against Napoleon on official record. Johnston (comp.), *The Corsican*, 473.

ward reaction. In these regions a large majority of the priests refused to make a declaration of submission to the constitution, and there was a religious and monarchical rising in the Vendée. Public opinion here was at best indifferent to political changes at Paris, but Bonaparte obtained a following by appointing magistrates who inspired confidence.[53]

The public was furious with Lucien in 1800, and there was a seditious movement in Toulouse because of the rise in grain prices. Yet the return of Bonaparte had caused great joy in the army, the colonies accepted the news of 18 Brumaire in the proper spirit, and in some regions every priest submitted to the constitution, which was announced as having been approved by the overwhelming vote of 3,011,007 to 1,562.[54]

France thought foreign powers had forced on her the war ended by the enthusiastically greeted Treaty of Lunéville. Although public opinion generally supported the government, Bonaparte lost popularity because the government securities fell, the government made too many arrests, and the people did not get the general peace they wanted. Despite the good morale of the army in Santo Domingo, there were draft troubles. Bayonne and Bordeaux were the scenes of Jacobin and Bourbonist troubles, and the return of the émigrés caused opposition even though they generally supported the government.[55]

In 1802 French interest in Swiss affairs became prominent. Although Switzerland was reported by the *Moniteur* to have been

[53] Calonne, *Amiens*, 2–3, 11, 16; Napoleon, *Commentaires*, IV, 77; Benaerts, *Régime consulaire en Bretagne*, 80, 182; Lanzac de Laborie, *Paris sous Napoléon*, I, 15, 118, 195; Aulard (ed.), *Paris sous le consulat*, I, 247; *Bulletin commercial, maritime, littéraire et politique du département de la Gironde*, 1 Nivôse, Year VIII; Vicomtesse Pauline Henriette Hyde de Neuville (ed.), *Mémoires et souvenirs du baron Hyde de Neuville*, 3 vols. (Paris, 1888–92), I, 294.

[54] Stenger, *Société française*, VI, 8; Roederer (A. M. Roederer, pub.), *Œuvres*, V, 349; *Débats*, 5 Pluviôse, 1 Germinal, and 19 and 28 Thermidor, Year VIII. The dismissal of Lucien had an effect on public opinion favorable to Bonaparte. Jahn (ed.), *Bonaparte, Talleyrand, et Stapfer*, 23.

[55] *Sbornik*, LXX, 151–54; Paul Marmottan, "Lucchesini ambassadeur de Prusse à Paris (1800–1810)," *Revue d'histoire diplomatique*, XLIII(1929), 458; *Journal*, 13 Frimaire, Year XI; Lanzac de Laborie, *Paris sous le consulat*, I, 239; Aulard (ed.), *Paris sous le consulat*, II, 179; Rovigo, *Memoirs*, Vol. I, Part I, 211; Leclerc (Roussier, pub.), *Lettres*, 54; Ernest Picard and Victor Paulier (eds.), *Mémoires et journaux du général Decaen*, 2 vols. (Paris, 1910–11), II, 250; *Spectateur du Nord*, February, 1801; Gabory, *Napoléon et la Vendée*, 124.

pleased with the change of 18 Brumaire, it was not wholly favorable to France; several cantonal diets, representing perhaps the majority of the population, rejected the idea of a bond with France. There were constant revolts in 1802, and the central government lost support. Although Vaud was the only canton where it was certain that France was loved more than feared, the cantons supported Napoleon in 1805. There was frequent desertion from the Swiss militia in 1807, and by 1813—partly because of Jesuit propaganda—most of the cantons were hostile to Napoleon. The captivity of the Pope at Fontainebleau was disastrous in its effects on Swiss public opinion, which welcomed the Bourbon restoration.[56]

In France itself, the Treaty of Amiens met with universal approval, although there was not much enthusiasm except at Amiens itself. The masses, particularly the peasants, expressed satisfaction with the Concordat, and the establishment of the Legion of Honor bound the army more closely to Bonaparte.[57]

Whether or not one believes with Fox that the hold of Bonaparte on the masses rested solely on their belief that he alone would have been able to obtain peace and that he was best able to maintain it, the general approval of the populace with the government was shown in 1802, when a vote approved Bonaparte's being Consul for life. Although the masses were interested primarily in bread and rest, one-half million more than in 1800 voted "yes" on the governmental change. Especially was the vote larger this time in the royalist regions. Yet this vote also gave evidence of discontent. The intellectual world was opposed to the life consulate; and the negative votes, cast largely in the army, were more than five times as numerous as those of 1800.[58]

[56] *Moniteur*, 3 Frimaire, Year VIII; *passim*; Jahn (ed.), *Bonaparte, Talleyrand, et Stapfer*, 99; *Débats*, 2 Floréal and 29 Thermidor, Year X; 4 Vendémiaire, Year XI; Germinal, Year III; Guillon, *Napoléon et la Suisse*, 260–61, 288; E. d'Hauterive (ed.), *La police secrète*, II, 113; III, 401. Thibaudeau says that the democratic party favored French mediation and the aristocrats tried to obtain help from Austria or England. A. C. Thibaudeau, *Bonaparte and the Consulate*, ed. by G. K. Fortescue (New York, 1908), 276.

[57] Calonne, *Amiens*, 27; Deutsch, "Lunéville to Pressburg," I, 52; Lanzac de Laborie, *Paris sous Napoléon*, I, 309; Stenger, *Sociéte française*, I, 214; Remacle (ed.), *Bonaparte et les Bourbons*, 21; Boulay de la Meurthe (ed.), *Documents sur la négociation du concordat*, V, 163–65.

[58] Remacle (ed.), *Bonaparte et les Bourbons*, 22–26, 60; Aulard (ed.), *Paris*

During 1802 there were other elements creating discontent. The Catholics were displeased with Bonaparte's issuance of the Organic Articles to supplement the Concordat of 1801. Although the Concordat itself re-established the Catholic Church in France, the Articles actually increased the power of the state in religious affairs. Besides, the reopening of the churches was by no means welcomed by everyone; the army, the republicans, and the *philosophes* were indifferent or hostile to the move. The establishment of the Legion of Honor created general dissatisfaction because it was feared that it was the first step toward creating a nobility. Even the troops were unresponsive; those who had embarked under protest for Santo Domingo became discouraged by fall. By that time, fear of a renewal of war, the depleted state of French commerce, and increased displeasure with draft levies were adding to the general unrest. Several members of the Legislative Body complained that in their departments public opinion was hostile.[59] In the Vendée, hatreds had been only partially extinguished. In Angers, opinion was sufficiently unsatisfactory for Napoleon to ask Lebrun what could be done to ameliorate it. On the whole, Bonaparte's popularity in 1802 was shown negatively, by the absence of unrest.[60]

sous le consulat, III, *passim;* Fox (Russell, ed.), *Memorials and Correspondence,* III, 382; Benaerts, *Régime consulaire en Bretagne*, ix–x, 247; Lanzac de Laborie, *Paris sous Napoléon*, I, 251; Department of State, *Despatches* (France, Livingston to Madison, March 26, 1802); F.-A. Aulard, "L'établissement du consulat à vie," *La révolution française*, XXVIII(1895), 336. The police reported that people preferred the life consulate to an extension of ten years. Aulard (ed.), *Paris sous le consulat*, III, 45; André Jacques, "L'esprit public à Metz au temps de Napoléon," *Revue des études napoléoniennes*, XXVII(1926), 102.

[59] A department (*département*) corresponds roughly to an American state, in that it is the largest subdivision in the nation. Smaller governmental units are the *arrondissement*, canton, and commune.

[60] Marmottan, "Lucchesini à Paris," *loc. cit.*, 458; Sir John Hall, *General Pichegru's Treason* (New York, 1915), 298; Lanzac de Laborie, *Paris sous Napoléon*, I, 251; Ernest Picard, *Bonaparte et Moreau* (Paris, 1905), 370; Remacle (ed.), *Bonaparte et les Bourbons*, 74–79, 198; Leclerc (Roussier, pub.), *Lettres,* 270; Department of State, *Despatches* (France, Livingston to Madison, June 24, 1802); Aulard (ed.), *Paris sous le consulat*, III, 7, 236, 284, 376; Maccunn, *Contemporary English View of Napoleon*, 54; Gabory, *Napoléon et la Vendée*, 356; Thiers, *Histoire du consulat*, IV, 18; Napoleon, *Correspondance*, VIII, 106. The agents of Louis XVIII reported that there was apathy, that the new bishops were in general dissatisfied, and that opinion had not made a step favorable to Bonaparte. Remacle (ed.), *Bonaparte et les Bourbons*, 66, 91, 107. The police reported that people liked the Legion. Aulard (ed.), *Paris sous le consulat*, IV, 63.

It was during this same year that Bonaparte established the Italian Republic. Its predecessor, the Cisalpine Republic, had at first been relieved at shaking off the French yoke, but by 1799 it was longing for French protection. The Italians reserved judgment in 1800 until the Battle of Marengo revealed the probable victor, and then they became enthusiastic. Although opinion in 1801 was very favorable, Napoleon did not care to risk free elections in the Cisalpine Republic or the removal of all the French troops. His attitude toward religion also helped win the masses, who were hoping for peace and the re-establishment of order. Reuniting to Lombardy people who had interests in common with it aroused grateful enthusiasm in this region, which did not regard the French as its friends; but the only really zealous partisans were those dependent on the Republic for a livelihood or those considering it a lesser evil than disorder.[61]

There was indifference evidenced at the convocation of the *consulta,* however, because too many of the promises in the proclamations to the Italians had not been fulfilled. The various regulations on censorship made little impression on the public. Although opinion in the various cities was generally favorable to the French, the draft produced only an infinitesimal part of its quota,[62] provoked discontent because the levies were too heavy, and in Tuscany even caused a little fear. In Piedmont there was hatred for the French, and Baron Friedrich von Humboldt wrote from Bologna that this hatred was general in all Italy.[63]

In fact, public opinion did become more hostile, partly because the people and the army were war-weary. Though the review of

[61] Driault, "Napoléon et Italie" *loc. cit.,* LXXXVIII, 37; *Débats,* 15 Messidor, Year VIII; A. Pingaud, *Bonaparte président de la république italienne,* I, 194–99, 203, 306; II, 361, 380; Driault, *Napoléon en Italie,* 49, 69, 424; Boulay de la Meurthe (ed.), *Documents sur la négociation du concordat,* II, 504.

[62] If the year 1806 is indicative of the others, the statement of Borel (*Gênes sous Napoléon Ier,* 155) that Genoese youth were so fond of wearing uniforms that the draft was accomplished readily is inaccurate; in that year Genoa yielded only one-half its quota and most of the draftees deserted on their way to the army. E. d'Hauterive (ed.), *La police secrète,* II, 402.

[63] A. Pingaud, *Bonaparte président de la république italienne,* II, 348; Murat (Prince Murat, pub.), *Lettres,* II, 316, 418; Benno Menzel, *Napoleons Politik in Oberitalien 1800–1805* (Magdeburg, 1912), 8, 30; Réal (Desclozeaux, ed.), *Indiscrétions,* I, 261; Paul Marmottan (ed.), "La grande-duchesse Élisa et Fouché," *Revue d'histoire diplomatique,* XL(1926), 399.

the Italian army by Napoleon in January, 1804, electrified the soldiers temporarily, weariness soon set in once again, and the generally poor morale of the army was evidenced by the number of desertions—4,000 in six months. Opinion was favorable in 1805 to the coronation of Napoleon as King of Italy. Although Joseph expressed satisfaction with the sentiments of the city of Naples on the celebration of Napoleon's birthday in 1806, at Genoa, only the French participated in the fete of August 15, and sentiment in Turin was also hostile. Furthermore, in 1808 feelings at Turin were bad because malevolent citizens were exploiting the news from Spain to incite the people to revolt. An attempt to curry favor, in the form of establishing the Order of the Iron Crown for civilians, did not produce the desired effect, but Eugene reported that public opinion, without being good, was not very bad and that the people could be led to love the French.[64]

In Rome the public showed great joy at the ratification of the Concordat. From then until 1809, when the French took control of the city, Roman public opinion was no concern of France. In this latter year, Rome was depicted as calm and well-disposed, but there, as in the rest of Italy, opinion grew steadily worse in spite of a beneficent rule. The clergy, with most of the monks refusing in 1810 to take the oath to the new government, undoubtedly influenced the public against Napoleon, and the people did not like conscription. Although news of the Concordat of Fontainebleau was welcomed, it could not counteract the unfavorable impression produced by the captivity of the Pope. News of Lützen and Bautzen and the deliverance of Saxony did give public opinion a shot in the arm, as did Murat's passage through Rome on his way to Naples.[65]

In 1814 the results of the battle of the Mincio River had a good

[64] Driault "Napoléon et Italie," *loc. cit.*, LXXXIX, 64; A. Pingaud, *Bonaparte président de la république italienne*, I, 400; II, 216, 279; Joseph (Du Casse, ed.), *Mémoires*, III, 124; Borel, *Gênes sous Napoléon Ier*, 155; Kielland, *Napoleon's Men and Methods*, 160; Driault, *Napoléon en Italie*, 326; Murat (Prince Murat, pub.), *Lettres*, VI, 280; E. d'Hauterive (ed.), *La police secrète*, II, 472; III, 85; Eugene (Du Casse, ed.), *Mémoires*, IV, 256.

[65] Boulay de la Meurthe (ed.), *Documents sur la négociation du concordat*, IV, 50; Tournon (Moulard, pub.), *Lettres inédites*, 85 and *passim*; Sir George Head (tr.), *Historical Memoirs of Cardinal Pacca, Prime Minister to Pius VII*, 2 vols. (London, 1850), I, 192; Haussonville, *Église et empire*, V, 329.

effect on the Italian morale, which was growing steadily worse. As soon as he had fallen, Napoleon was forgotten; and Italy, which did not show much emotion during the Hundred Days, was highly enthusiastic about the news of Waterloo.[66]

An invasion scare in England was the goal of a large-scale propaganda campaign launched in 1803. Although unable to convince enlightened people that an invasion of England would succeed, Napoleon did cause the superstitious masses to become so fearful that they kept invasion rumors afloat,[67] and almost the entire population thought Napoleon would make the attempt. Backed by intensive preparations, this propaganda forced the English government to undertake expensive defense measures, and it called forth huge amounts of popular counterpropaganda in the form of pamphlets, broadsides, and songs. At this time the supposed invincibility of Napoleon only added to the terror of the British public, which viewed him as the typical "enemy of mankind." [68]

Much to Napoleon's surprise, the report of Count Horace Sebastiani [69] caused a great sensation among the leaders of public opinion in England, and other acts of Napoleon sometimes had an effect contrary to that which he had desired: his statement that England by itself was unable to fight France increased the ranks of those hostile to him in England, and the death of the Duke of Enghien inflamed opinion against him. Yet the French statements that France would not allow exportation of any grain to England increased the bitterness shown against the cabinet by the peace-

[66] Eugene (Du Casse, ed.), *Mémoires*, X, 106; Joseph (Du Casse, ed.), *Mémoires*, X, 136; Borel, *Gênes sous Napoléon Ier*, 135; Davout (Mazada, ed.), *Correspondance*, IV, 426.

[67] H. V. Morton, *In Search of Scotland* (New York, 1930), 24, says that this propaganda was the start in the English language of the word "bogey," a corruption of "Boney" (Bonaparte).

[68] Wheeler and Broadley, *Napoleon and the Invasion of England*, II, 38, 43, 274, 285; Broadsides, De Paul University; Thomas Hague, *An Appeal to His Majesty, on the State of the Nation, the Talents and Dispositions of the Royal Dukes, and the Capacity of Ministers: with a Sketch of the Character and Power of Buonaparte* (Greenwich, 1810), 6; Maccunn, *Contemporary English View of Napoleon*, 137, 153, 295; Fox (Russell, ed.), *Memorials and Correspondence*, III, 232.

[69] Sebastiani, whose report indicated public opinion there was very favorable to France, was a special envoy of Napoleon to Turkey. The report said that France could reconquer Egypt with only a few thousand troops.

loving British populace, which welcomed the peace of Amiens even more heartily than did France.[70]

The most important event of 1803 influencing opinion within France was the renewal of war with England. As a result of official propaganda the nation rallied behind Bonaparte in his efforts against Britain, although the people of France had sincerely desired peace. Even royalist Vendée was anti-British; Napoleon later said he had won this region by the Concordat for the clergy and by public works for the poorer classes.[71]

Irrespective of the war, Fiévée reported that opinion had never been so excellent and so in accord since 1787—though a little later in the year he said it was considering European, rather than purely French, interests. He also cautioned Napoleon that although the French were weary of revolution, they were still sincerely in accord with the principles of 1789. Talleyrand declared that opinion was daily growing more favorable to the Legion of Honor, and the Bourbons admitted that Bonaparte's arrival at Lille and in Belgium aroused great joy and enthusiasm, but not as much as the papers claimed.[72]

These same Bourbon agents announced that the fete of August 15 was welcomed very coldly, partly because of the uneasiness caused by the many bankruptcies. Napoleon himself admitted that during the fall he was sitting on a volcano, and again there were troubles in connection with conscription. At the end of the year

[70] Wheeler and Broadley, *Napoleon and the Invasion of England*, 184; Coquelle, *Napoleon and England*, 38; Rose, *Napoleon*, I, 415; Ebbinghaus, *Napoleon, England und die Presse*, 25; Lanzac de Laborie, *Paris sous Napoléon*, I, 239. Irish opinion constantly manifested itself against England. Though Napoleon encouraged this opposition, it is impossible to state what the effect of his measures was on Irish sentiment.

[71] Department of State, *Despatches* (France, Livingston to Madison, March 24, 1803); Browning (ed.), *England and Napoleon*, 138, 227; Ney, *Memoirs*, II, 188, 206; Deutsch, "Lunéville to Pressburg," I, 280; Remacle (ed.), *Bonaparte et les Bourbons*, 346; Aulard (ed.), *Paris sous le consulat*, IV, *passim*; Napoleon (Kircheisen, comp., Collins, tr.), *Memoirs*, 106. The statement of Miot de Melito (*Memoirs* [Fleischmann, ed., Hoey and Lillie, trs.], 261) that opinion promptly declared itself against the war is biased.

[72] Fiévée, *Correspondance*, I, 80, 139, 152, 166; Talleyrand (Bertrand, ed.), *Lettres à Napoléon*, 101; Remacle (ed.), *Bonaparte et les Bourbons*, 355-58. Hence the Bourbon claims of hostility to Bonaparte, at least in Belgium, may be discounted. See Remacle (ed.), *Bonaparte et les Bourbons*, 266-315.

the police reported that Paris was seething with hidden discontent.[73]

Early in 1804 an uneasiness and even a hostile disposition began to make itself felt, and people began to long for the royal government. Their refusal to believe in the existence of a plot against Bonaparte until Georges Cadoudal and General Charles Pichegru were arrested reflected their attitude. When Moreau was accused of complicity in the plot, public opinion showed itself friendly to him, and the army at Boulogne was split between the partisans of Bonaparte and Moreau. There was general satisfaction at the lightness of his sentence. For Cadoudal and Pichegru there was, however, no public sympathy at Paris, even though people admired the courage shown by the former.[74] Although people generally believed that Bonaparte had ordered the death of Pichegru,[75] the net effect of the plot was to win support for Bonaparte.

Even before the sentences in this case had been pronounced, the execution of the Duke of Enghien had produced a sensation. Among the *bourgeoisie* not even the most ardent anti-Bourbonist approved the execution, and Napoleon was led to remark in the Council of State: "The population of Paris is a collection of blockheads who believe the most absurd reports. . . . I respect the decisions of public opinion when they are justly formed; but it has its caprices which we ought to learn to despise. It is the task of the government, and of those who support it, to enlighten the public, not to follow it in its wanderings." [76] The government succeeded, however, in convincing the average Frenchman that the duke had deserved his fate. Publicity given the activities of Drake and Smith more than counteracted whatever tendency there was to censure

---

[73] Remacle (ed.), *Bonaparte et les Bourbons,* 386; Napoleon (Kircheisen, comp., Collins, tr.), *Memoirs,* 108; Roederer (A. M. Roederer, pub.), *Œuvres,* III, 474; Aulard (ed.), *Paris sous le consulat,* IV, 577, 619; *Citoyen français,* 5 Ventôse, Year XI; *Débats,* 26 Prairial, Year XI.

[74] Aulard (ed.), *Paris sous le consulat,* IV, 650, 688, 720; Fiévée, *Correspondance,* I, 200–205, 228; Roederer (Vitrac, ed.), *Autour de Bonaparte,* 193; *Sbornik,* LXXVII, 641; G. W. de Lafayette (ed.), *Mémoires, correspondance et manuscrits du général Lafayette* (Paris, 1837–39), V, 215; *Moniteur,* 1 Germinal, Year XII.

[75] Rumor had it that Bonaparte's Mamelukes had strangled Pichegru in his cell. The rumor, as rumor so often is, was incorrect.

[76] Pelet (Hall, tr.), *Napoleon in Council,* 46–47.

the government, with the result that the Enghien affair likewise added to the strength of Bonaparte's government.[77]

These affairs ended factionalism and enabled Bonaparte to establish the Empire after a gradual improvement in public opinion throughout the summer and fall. The aristocrats, clergy, and even the army and republican areas approved the establishment of a new dynasty.

The people accepted hereditary rule, however, only because it seemed reassuring after what France had experienced. Bonaparte's personal popularity was at a low ebb, and the refusal of many royalists and republicans to participate in the plebiscite caused the total vote to be smaller than in 1802. Evidences of Parisian hostility to the government were the disputes and sarcastic comments on the first distribution of Legion of Honor crosses. Belgium had never been pleased with French rule, and in western France there were uprisings against conscription. Indeed, Fiévée was rather close to the mark when he said the government had lost control of public opinion.[78]

Upon restoration of the monarchy, public opinion was probably more concerned with the form of government than with France, for the police reported on 14 Vendémiaire, Year XIII, that "patriotism will be reborn when the astonishment at the revival of monarchy gives way to habit." During 1805 the public became progressively calmer, partly because the physical impossibility of evincing the constant enthusiasm desired by the government had already made it blasé. Yet it was moved by the spring maritime expeditions, admired Napoleon, and enthusiastically welcomed him on his trip to Milan for coronation as King of Italy. Even in Belgium, opinion became more friendly when the British govern-

[77] Department of State, *Despatches* (France, Livingston to Madison, March 29, 1804); Haussonville, *Église et empire*, I, 313; Deutsch, "Lunéville to Pressburg," I, 306; Thiers, *Histoire du consulat*, V, 17.

[78] Rémusat (P. de Rémusat, pub.), *Mémoires*, II, 19, 190; Department of State, *Despatches* (France, Livingston to Madison, July 25, 1804; August 8, 1804); *Sbornik*, LXXVII, 641; Roederer (Vitrac, ed.), *Autour de Bonaparte*, 192; Fiévée, *Correspondance*, I, 30; II, 6, 37, 73; Ney, *Memoirs*, 210; Aulard (ed.), *Paris sous le premier empire*, I, 3; E. d'Hauterive (ed.), *La police secrète*, I, 222 and *passim*; Charpentier, *Napoléon et les hommes de lettres*, 101; Benaerts, *Régime consulaire en Bretagne*, x, 344; Jacques, "Esprit public à Metz," *loc. cit.*, 103.

ment rejected the petition of the Catholics for civic rights.[79]

The decline of commerce caused some trouble, and opinion at Brest was becoming progressively worse. When orders for the embarkation of the infantry reached Brest and Toulon, there were a great many desertions. The news of Trafalgar affected Toulon more adversely than any other city, the effect in Paris, for example, being less sensational because at first the facts were so little known. There were also many complaints during the summer about the difficulty in filling the draft and about the priests' shielding refractory conscripts. Party spirit likewise manifested itself once more, and there were evidences of friendliness toward the Bourbons.[80]

The military successes of 1805 once more aroused enthusiasm, news of victories arousing ardor even in the conscripts and bringing in many who had refused to report or had deserted. Even before the fighting began, Fiévée reported that confidence in the armies was so great people would not believe any report, official or otherwise, that they had been defeated; and the transition from hopes of peace to actual warfare did not disturb public opinion. Opinion in Belgium, where the only grievance was the draft, was growing better. A prolonged interval between bulletins after the first few had been published caused enough uneasiness, however, for the people to welcome all rumors of peace. By October opinion was not so good as in September because of government decrees concerning the national guard and the stopping of bank notes.[81]

After the campaign of 1805, Naples fell under French control. There Joseph was welcomed by the only liberal class—the middle one, including all the proprietors—and appreciated for his mod-

[79] Fiévée, *Correspondance*, II, 64, 74; A. Pingaud, *Bonaparte président de la république italienne*, I, 337; Rémusat (P. de Rémusat, pub.), *Lettres*, I, 144; E. d'Hauterive (ed.), *La police secrète*, I, 448, 479, *passim;* Department of State, *Despatches* (France, Armstrong to Madison, August 20, 1805).

[80] E. d'Hauterive (ed.), *La police secrète*, I, 267, 380, *passim;* II, *passim;* Rémusat (P. de Rémusat, pub.), *Lettres*, I, 91; Miot de Melito (Fleischmann, ed., Hoey and Lillie, trs.), *Memoirs*, 390; Rémusat (P. de Rémusat, pub.), *Mémoires*, II, 299.

[81] Labédoyère, *Memoirs*, I, 392; Fiévée, *Correspondance*, II, 136, 150-52; Miot de Melito (Fleischmann, ed., Hoey and Lillie, trs.), *Memoirs*, 377; Constant, *Journal*, 349; Joseph (Du Casse, ed.), *Mémoires*, I, 295; E. d'Hauterive (ed.), *La police secrète, passim;* Rémusat (P. de Rémusat, pub.), *Lettres*, I, 384.

eration, but there was no national spirit supporting him and he had difficulty establishing tranquillity. Support of Joseph was so uncertain that Napoleon even disapproved the establishment of a home guard composed of picked men, and Roederer bluntly told his wife that the French were detested. Nevertheless, Masséna reported to Joseph that a huge majority of the people in Cosenza accepted the French as liberators. At Taranto and in most of Calabria opinion was hostile, but news of Napoleon's victories in 1806 gradually created submissiveness toward the government. During the latter part of 1807 opinion in Naples was calm, largely because English influence had been lessened by Napoleon's victories, the Treaty of Tilsit, and the return of the Ionian Islands and Cattaro to the French.[82]

Upon taking charge in 1808, Murat, always inclined to be optimistic in such matters, reported that opinion was favorable everywhere except at Rome proper and that even excommunications had not caused any desertions from the civic guard. While claiming at the end of the year that the opinion of the masses was excellent, he was obliged to admit there were not two thousand people in the whole kingdom favorably enough disposed to be willing to serve in his guard. In the spring of 1809 opinion was admittedly bad, but Murat reported that news of Napoleon's first victories against the Austrians in 1809 quieted the malevolent factions. In the summer Murat reported that opinion was so favorable as to surpass even his hopes, but the legionnaires of Calabria deserted in large numbers, as they did in 1810, when many sailors likewise deserted. The revolts which it was necessary to repress by force as late as 1813 show the continued hostility of the Neapolitans toward France.[83]

Meanwhile, enthusiasm in France reached a new high after Napoleon's return from the campaign of 1805, and, but for a few revolts, opinion remained good in 1806.[84] The recurring draft

[82] Joseph (Du Casse, ed.), *Mémoires*, II, 266, 299, 433; III, 150, 233, 236; IV, 1; *Empire*, 1806, *passim;* Driault, *Napoléon en Italie*, 412; Roederer (A. M. Roederer, pub.), *Œuvres*, IV, 73. In Naples and the other states ruled by the brothers of Napoleon the press always pictured the people's enthusiasm as being very great at sight of the rulers. Roederer was Joseph's Minister of Finance.

[83] Murat (Prince Murat, pub.), *Lettres*, VI, 282-83, 341; VII, *passim;* VIII, *passim; Empire*, April 18, 1813.

[84] This despite the assertion of Fiévée (*Correspondance*, II, 225) that there

troubles, some of them quite serious, were not nearly so wide-spread as previously, and the number declined throughout the summer. Despite a few pamphlets against the new catechism, the vast majority of the French accepted it. Party spirit seemed absolutely to have died out, and at Amiens there was popular enthusiasm because industry was on a better footing.[85]

The press exaggerated, however, in portraying the enthusiasm of the Jewish Assembly in 1806. Lack of enthusiasm was also shown in Drôme, where, because of the heavy taxes, not a single member of the congregation joined in the prayer for the government recited by the curé. During the campaign of 1806 enthusiasm for victories vanished within a few days after news of them reached Paris because the war-weary masses thought only of the misfortunes of war.[86]

The early part of 1807 saw some dissatisfaction resulting from the war, more especially from the battle of Eylau and the sparseness of military news. There were a great many desertions from the French army after Eylau, and lack of provisions dulled the keenness of the army's fighting edge. Yet, except near the end of the campaign and in the last quarter of the year, when increasing difficulty was experienced, the draft quotas were filled more easily than they had been in the past. Naturally the news of Tilsit caused great joy. The public was keenly aware of French prosperity, but it scarcely noticed the general amelioration in government finances. This year, the last of those marked by overwhelming victories, also marked the end of the three-year period during which Napoleon most nearly achieved universal popularity in France. The officially inspired rumor on the creation of titles was a real test of public opinion, and the police were able to report that it did not stir up a single objection.[87]

---

was no real public opinion on issues because too many people dabbled in politics and administration.

[85] Rapp (A. Bulos, ed.), *Memoirs*, 66; E. d'Hauterive (ed.), *La police secrète*, III, 38, and *passim*; Rémusat (P. de Rémusat, pub.), *Mémoires*, II, 345; Calonne, *Amiens*, 63.

[86] Anchel, *Napoléon et les juifs*, 156; E. d'Hauterive (ed.), *La police secrète*, II, 474; Rémusat (P. de Rémusat, pub.), *Lettres*, II, 88; Fiévée, *Correspondance*, II, 166.

[87] E. d'Hauterive (ed.), *La police secrète*, III, 159, *passim*; Macdonnell, *Napoleon and His Marshals*, 143; *Journal*, January 11, 1807; *Empire*, July 28, 1807;

A Polish state, the Duchy of Warsaw, reappeared in Europe with the Treaty of Tilsit. The Poles had looked to France for relief from the Prussian yoke, but, until the French had defeated the Russians, the city of Warsaw was the only place upon whose enthusiasm and active support Napoleon could rely. The news of the surrender of Danzig, and later of the cession of Galicia to Warsaw by Austria, made the finest impression on the people. Napoleon's influence remained all-powerful with the Poles as late as 1813, but he was disappointed with opinion in Lithuania.[88]

Spanish opinion should likewise have been a disappointment to Napoleon. Even before Napoleon established Joseph as King of Spain in 1808, Spain had grievances against France on the scores of commerce and the sale of Louisiana. While Murat was still in charge of French affairs in Spain, there were insurrections in the provinces, and a very serious one at Madrid on May 2, 1808— after Murat had reported that since about April 20 opinion was very favorable to France and the French press had devoted most of its space on Spain to recitals of popular support for French measures.[89]

Actually, however, there was strong backing for Ferdinand, whom the French were ousting, and strong dislike for de Godoy, the favorite of the Queen and of France. Seville revolted at news of the uprising in Madrid, and the attitude of the populace was demonstrated by the increase in the number of guerrillas. At the end of May, 1808, Murat admitted that malevolence had manifested itself, but La Forest was able to report that the dominant attitude in Spain was one of submission. In June the insurrection

---

Joseph de Maistre, *Œuvres complètes de J. de Maistre* (Vols. IX–XIII of *Bibliographie choisie des chefs-d'oeuvre français et étrangers*) (Lyon, 1884–86), X, 394; Mollien (Ch. Gomel, ed.), *Mémoires*, II, 102; Maccunn, *Contemporary English View of Napoleon*, 54; Aulard (ed.), *Paris sous le premier empire*, III, 336. Marseille, the greatest French port, suffered much from the maritime war. Therefore even dazzling land victories could never make opinion there wholly favorable to the Empire, as the city desired peace. Paul Gaffarel, "L'esprit public à Marseilles de 1800 à 1814," *Revue des études napoléoniennes*, IX(1916), 65, 77, 79; Morvan, *Soldat impérial*, II, 498.

[88] Murat (Prince Murat, pub.), *Lettres*, IV, 460, 474, 489; V, 28; Handelsman, *Napoléon et la Pologne*, 33, 226; Davout (Mazada, ed.), *Correspondance*, I, 331; A. Czartoryski (L. Czartoryski, pub.), *Alexandre Ier et le prince Czartoryski*, 86, 98, 237; Vandal, *Napoléon et Alexandre Ier*, III, 456, 514.

[89] Fugier, *Napoléon et l'Espagne*, I, 190, 194; Murat (Prince Murat, pub.), *Lettres*, VI, 38, *passim; Empire*, June 30, 1808, and *passim*.

began to spread widely, becoming so serious that Joseph was obliged to withdraw from Madrid. Only the advance of the French troops was able to restore tranquillity, but in Catalonia, perhaps the most exasperated of all Spanish provinces, the uneasiness resulting from the mere presence of the French caused a business stoppage leading to unemployment, for which the French were blamed.[90]

There was considerable desertion from the army, and even the attendants in Joseph's palace favored Ferdinand. Joseph himself complained, "Not one Spaniard has shown himself for me except those in the junta or traveling with me," and reported his inability to locate even a single spy. He also told Napoleon that Spain was unanimously opposed to the double abdication and abjuration of Charles IV and Ferdinand at Bayonne. The Spanish clergy was very influential, and it was universally hostile to the relatively liberal new government. When the Spanish constitution was published, it was treated with indifference in the provinces cowed by French troops, and elsewhere with contempt.[91]

Later in the summer the official news of the victory over General de La Cuesta and the capture of Saragossa created a favorable impression, and the popularity of Joseph increased sufficiently for even the draft to be successful at Madrid in September. However, Napoleon's refusal to delegate any authority to Joseph while he himself was in Spain lessened the consideration Joseph had acquired.[92]

The need for arresting large numbers in Madrid in 1809 showed that people were still none too friendly to Joseph's government. However, the French claimed that news of the British rout caused

[90] *Empire*, April 9, 1808; Murat (Prince Murat, pub.), *Lettres*, VI, 94, 166; La Forest (Grandmaison, pub.), *Correspondance*, I, 45, 53–66; Stanislaus Girardin, *Discours et opinions, journals et souvenirs de S. Girardin*, 4 vols. (Paris, 1828), IV, 126; Joseph (Du Casse, ed.), *Mémoires*, IV, 402; Conard, *Napoléon et la Catalogne*, 46–47, 65, 368.

[91] Joseph (Du Casse, ed.), *Mémoires*, IV, 343; Bausset, *Mémoires*, I, 272; Du Casse, "Napoléon et Joseph," *loc. cit.*, 350.

[92] La Forest (Grandmaison, pub.), *Correspondance*, I, 176, 232, 280; II, 9; Joseph (Du Casse, ed.), *Mémoires*, IV, 418; *Empire*, 1809, *passim*; Maria de las Mercedes, comtesse de Merlin, *Souvenirs et memoires de madame la comtesse Merlin*, 3 vols. (Paris, 1836), III, 101. La Forest reported on March 1, 1809 (*Correspondance* [Grandmaison, pub.] II, 104) that the government received no benefit from the fall of Saragossa.

great joy. Later in the year, though Joseph was able to conquer Andalusia, and though the French victory at Ocaña helped win over opinion, Joseph was dissatisfied with the spirit manifested by the people. Over one half of the employees in the ministries and government offices at Madrid took the oath of loyalty to the new government with mental reservations. If the *Journal de Paris* was correct in reporting that Aragon, where 22,000 rebels lived, was the most submissive of all Spanish provinces, the others must have been frightfully insurrectionary.[93]

At the start of 1810 Joseph seemed much more optimistic; at the end of the year he again confessed that opinion had not been conquered. Napoleon was still feared in Spain, but the French were definitely not loved. Although Joseph's popularity increased upon his return from France in 1811, he soon fell to an even lower level in the opinion of the people. As he himself put it: "Every day opinion becomes worse; it is formed by the nature of events and things." After this depression, opinion never climbed again in favor of Spain's Napoleonically appointed ruler.[94]

In the year during which Napoleon sought to obtain control of Spain, French public opinion, as viewed by the government, seemed only mediocre, largely because the people had become blasé and indifferent. To be sure, the public welcomed the establishment of the University and had stopped murmuring about high prices. The meeting of Alexander and Napoleon at Erfurt did propitiate opinion, and sentiment there was excellent. At Paris the police reported that public opinion was good as long as people had work, but warned that commerce was suffering. It also remarked on the uneasiness as to Spanish affairs, and Fiévée urged Napoleon to concentrate, not on attempting to increase the power of the government, but upon restoring confidence in it.[95]

---

[93] Girardin, *Discours,* IV, 302; Joseph (Du Casse, ed.), *Mémoires,* V, 328; VII, 105, 108; *Empire,* January 23, 1809; La Forest (Grandmaison, pub.), *Correspondance,* II, 372; Roederer (A. M. Roederer, pub.), *Œuvres,* IV, 35.

[94] Joseph (Du Casse, ed.), *Mémoires,* VII, 239, 356; VIII, 93, 256–57; Du Casse, "Napoléon et Joseph," *loc. cit.,* 377; La Forest (Grandmaison, pub.), *Correspondance,* III, 474; V, 304; VI, 132, 361.

[95] Grimaud, *Liberté d'enseignement,* 93; Aulard (ed.), *Paris sous le premier empire,* III, 652, 706; Fiévée, *Correspondance,* II, 324–27, 351, 372; Fouché (Beauchamp, ed.), *Mémoires,* 250; Paul Muller, *L'espionnage militaire sous Napoléon Ier* (Paris, 1896), 133; Rémusat (P. de Rémusat, pub.), *Mémoires,* III, 371.

The campaign of 1809 did not win popularity for the government: all classes were interested in peace and individual security, rather than in the conquest of the world. Because the people were uneasy and discontented, they tended to welcome adverse rumors. Political news was derided, and the public became actually bitter. Only a few officials showed any enthusiasm; patriotism lagged and only the British attack on Walcheren—not even the victories over Austria—was able to rearouse it. Although the Treaty of Vienna had not created too much enthusiasm, Fiévée asserted that after the campaign, public opinion would again favor the government if allowed to rest.[96]

Opinion was favorable to Napoleon's divorcing Josephine, but his marriage to Marie Louise failed to arouse enthusiasm—in fact, Paris was so hostile that the wedding party's itinerary avoided it completely. This marriage also increased religious opposition to Napoleon because his marriage with Josephine was still considered valid. Afraid actually to controvert the government, the public indicated its disapproval of Napoleon's second marriage by showing itself more favorable to the Pope than to Napoleon in their dispute about the appointment of bishops. The annexation of Holland created further opposition, and Maury, the Archbishop of Paris, related that public opinion did not proceed as the government desired.[97]

Holland never had wanted to be under French control, and early in the Consulate its attitude had led to French accusations that it was a British colony on the Continent. When France dictated its constitution in 1801, the vast majority of the Dutch— about five sixths—abstained from voting, and Bonaparte was obliged to count their votes as favorable in order to proclaim that the plebiscite had approved the new government.[98]

The year 1810 also marked the final acquisition by France of

[96] Fiévée, Correspondance, II, passim; III, 2–4; Lanzac de Laborie, Paris sous Napoléon, III, 56; VIII, 221; Thiers, Histoire du consulat, XI, 231; Calonne, Amiens, 65.

[97] Henri Welschinger, Le divorce de Napoléon (Paris, 1889), 10; Lanzac de Laborie, Paris sous Napoléon, III, 31–33; IV, 226; Vandal, Napoléon et Alexandre Ier, II, 293; Fabre de l'Aude, Mémoires et souvenirs d'un pair de France, 4 vols. (Paris, 1840), III, 259; Haussonville, Église et empire, IV, 31; Périvier, Napoléon journaliste, 387; Rovigo, Memoirs, Vol. II, Part II, 241.

[98] Mercure, 1 Fructidor, Year VIII; Spectateur du Nord, November, 1801; Rose, Napoleon, I, 318, 332.

territory in Germany. Bonaparte had, however, intervened immediately after the Treaty of Lunéville in order to reorganize Germany, which did not like the Imperial Recess. Upon renewal of war between France and England, Germany regarded the policy of each side as an evil but thought a French success would be more dangerous than a British one, though Count Charles de Labédoyère claimed everybody in Germany thought the British were the authors of the 1805 war. In 1805 public opinion in Berlin was temporarily turned against England by publication of several of Drake's letters.[99]

The start of patriotic German publications directed against France and designed to appeal to the masses came in 1806. The execution of Johann Palm, a Nuremberg publisher, for printing *Germany in Her Lowest Abasement*, had a terrible effect upon Germany. Even while the French troops were occupying Berlin, Napoleon had to warn Clarke not to allow any demonstrations, but the first bulletins of the Army of Spain were said to have overwhelmed the Berlin hotheads.[100]

In the Grand Duchy of Berg public opinion showed itself only with the defeats of France in Spain, beginning in 1809; there was a popular revolt in Westphalia at the same time, but the defeat of Austria once more quieted opinion there. In Austria the war of 1809 was decidedly popular, partly because it was thought necessary to restore the country's commerce, but Austrian attempts to arouse Bavaria against France failed.[101]

In 1811 there was a great deal of unrest and hatred against France in Westphalia, partly because all classes were financially ruined. This hostility to France not only became more intense but spread to the Hanseatic cities. After the retreat from Russia it was

---

[99] Deutsch, "Lunéville to Pressburg," I, 110, 331; Wilhelm Stroh, *Das Verhältnis zwischen Frankreich und England in den Jahren 1801–1803 im Urteil der politischen Literatur Deutschlands* (Berlin, 1914), 10, 52 ff.; Labédoyère, *Memoirs*, I, 364.

[100] Davout (Mazada, ed.), *Correspondance*, I, 254, 327; Méneval (Baron de Méneval, ed.), *Memoirs*, II, 49; Napoleon, *Correspondance*, XV, 429; Jerome (Du Casse, ed.), *Mémoires*, III, 295. The Army of Spain was very successful in 1808.

[101] Charles Schmidt, *Le grand-duché de Berg (1806–1813)* (Paris, 1905), 422–76; Eugene (Du Casse, ed.), *Mémoires*, IV, 275; Du Casse, "Napoléon et Jérôme," *loc. cit.*, 376; *Journal*, August 23, 1809; Mrs. Arthur Bell (ed.), *Memoirs of Baron Lejeune, Aide-de-camp to Marshals Berthier, Davout, and Oudinot*, 2 vols. (London, 1897), I, 339.

impossible to enforce any draft levies in Westphalia, and there was great discontent in Berg. In the parts of Prussia under French control there was a strong reaction against French rule, and in 1815 the inhabitants of the Rhineland joined in the bitter attacks on France.[102]

From Napoleon's viewpoint the most important event in 1811 was the birth of his son, but it is a moot point whether the joy expressed by the populace at this time was superficial or sincere.[103] Also, people were concerned because of the food shortage in 1811 and 1812.[104]

From the very start of 1812 French minds were occupied with the war which seemed imminent, and there were more volunteers early in 1812 than at any other time. Later on, as the war activities moved farther and farther from France, interest in them declined, perhaps partly because people were unable to divine the goal of the Russian expedition. Although there was no real discontent during the summer, hopes were not as outspoken as formerly, because it was impossible to grasp the grandeur of the undertaking. When people saw the defensive strategy of Russia, they were uneasy and began to hope for peace; but the faith of the masses in Napoleon was such as to weaken the effect of any bad news. In the fall, people were not vindictive against the members of the conspiracy organized by General Claude Malet, which caused only uneasiness and a resurgence of republican opinion, quiescent since the establishment of the Empire, and the whole Russian expedition brought about a general feeling of discouragement. A widespread weariness accompanied the consternation caused by the revelations of French losses in Bulletin 29.[105]

[102] Du Casse, "Napoléon et Jérôme," loc. cit., 376; Davout (Mazada, ed.), Correspondance, III, 523; V. Lombard de Langres, [no title], Napoleon Pamphlets, XXXV, 226; Empire, December 22, 1813; Marmont, Mémoires, IV, 125; Thiers, Histoire du consulat, XIX, 527-28.

[103] Secondary studies declare it was an ordered enthusiasm; contemporary accounts, by usually honest (and even hostile) reporters, state that it was real. Lanzac de Laborie, Paris sous Napoléon, III, 38; Calonne, Amiens, 68; Boigne (Nicoullaud, ed.), Memoirs I, 256; Fiévée, Correspondance, III, 106. There is the possibility that Fiévée was flattering Napoleon at this particular time.

[104] Lanzac de Laborie, Paris sous Napoléon, V, 251.

[105] Fiévée, Correspondance, III, 192, 196, 221, 227-28, 230, 243, 265-67, 272; Mollien (Ch. Gomel, ed.), Mémoires, III, 130-31, 174; Caulaincourt (Hanoteau, ed.), Mémoires, II, 196.

Even the masses were angered by the constant draft levies, and discontent became very evident. There was general blame for governmental activities and constant irony concerning its disasters; but it is significant that the spirit of the army was still good—in fact, even enthusiastic in the first battles, though this enthusiasm dwindled—and the confidence in Napoleon's military ability still predominated among the people.[106]

Napoleon was assured in 1813 and 1814 that if he brought about the peace for which there was a general cry, opinion would be excellent in two years. When the armistice failed to result in peace, general discouragement therefore followed. Although the workers demanded arms, people refused to defend their property and families except at their own homes. Paris remained quite calm, largely because the working classes were kept occupied on public works.[107]

When the armies and rulers of the allies entered Brussels in 1814, they were welcomed by the acclamations of the multitude. The French peasants fought against the invaders, but they were fighting for a much-needed and much-desired peace guaranteeing to France her natural limits; no longer were they fighting for Napoleon, whom they regarded as an obstacle to reaching their goal. Joseph warned Napoleon that the most he could expect from Paris was obedience, not any real defense, because war-weariness was so great, and he even reported that Paris would support whichever side promised the earlier peace. There were many desertions in Paris at this time, the soldiers no longer wanting to fight, but the army did serve as the nucleus of Bonapartism during the first restoration.[108]

[106] Department of State, *Despatches* (France, Thomas Barlow to Monroe, 1813 [?]); Fiévée, *Correspondance*, III, 319; Méneval (Baron de Méneval, ed.), *Memoirs*, III, 97; Gabory, *Napoléon et la Vendée*, 377; Pasquier (Audiffret-Pasquier, ed., Roche, tr.), *Memoirs*, II, 67; Marquise de La Tour du Pin, *Journal d'une femme de cinquante ans 1778–1815*, pub. by Count Aymar de Liedekerke-Beaufort, 2 vols. (Paris, 1913), II, 333; Gouvion St.-Cyr, *Mémoires*, III, 46; Calonne, *Amiens*, 71; Morvan, *Soldat impérial*, II, 504.

[107] Gouvion St.-Cyr, *Mémoires*, IV, 346; Chastenay (Roserot, pub.), *Mémoires*, II, 245; Charles A. Faré, *Lettres d'un jeune officier à sa mère, 1803–1814*, ed. by H. Faré (Paris, 1889), 310; Caulaincourt (Hanoteau, ed.), *Mémoires*, III, 13; Bausset, *Mémoires*, IV, 255; Gohier, *Mémoires*, II, 237; Joseph (Du Casse, ed.), *Mémoires*, X, 151.

[108] Frédéric Masson (ed.), *The Private Diaries of Marie Louise* (London,

On the other hand, the masses were glum at the time of the allied entry into Paris, and only a few donned white cockades. Large numbers did shout "*Vive les alliés*," but they were the same ones who would have hailed Napoleon with acclaim had he returned triumphant. The *bourgeoisie*, masses, and army did not like being forced to accept the dictation of foreigners; and, as the number of military men returning to Paris increased, the spirit of the populace became more hostile to the foreign troops. As for the Bourbons, the French had virtually forgotten them and did not request their restoration. It is probably true that Amiens, partly because it felt that the return of Louis meant the return of peace, was sincerely Bourbonian, and it is probably true that the Vendée gave Louis XVIII a spontaneous welcome, but the majority of France did not like the Bourbon dynasty. The government of Louis XVIII was unable to gain public confidence during the first eleven months of its rule. The lower classes and the workers' guilds still supported Napoleon, and the army, especially the class of young officers seeking promotion, was Imperialist. The press law and establishment of the senatorships for life created opposition. The claim that the royal government ruled by divine right accentuated discontent, and perhaps the most powerful of all causes of dissatisfaction was the apprehension that the clergy was regaining its old influence.[109]

1922), 217; Rose, Napoleon, II, 378; Léon-G. Pelissier (pub.), Lettres inédites du baron Guillaume Peyrusse écrites à son frère André pendant les campagnes de l'empire de 1809 à 1814 (Paris, 1894), 187; Guyot, "Souvenirs de la première invasion," loc. cit., 145; Castellane (Beaulaincourt-Marles, pub.), Journal, 253; Henri Marie Ghislain comte de Mérode, Souvenirs du comte de Mérode-Westerloo, 2 vols. (Brussels, 1864), I, 331; Joseph (Du Casse, ed.), Mémoires, X, 153, 195; Fain, Manuscrit de mil huit cent quatorze, 141; Méneval (Baron de Méneval, ed.), Memoirs, III, 187. L. Pingaud (Jean de Bry, 329) says that public opinion ceased to exist with the dislocation of the administrative machinery.

[109] Abrantès, Mémoires, IX, 295–96; Rochechouart (Jackson, tr.), Memoirs, 254; Pasquier (Audiffret-Pasquier, ed., Roche, tr.), Memoirs, II, 405; Department of State, Despatches (France, Crawford to Monroe, April 11, 1814; March 16 and 21, 1815); Joseph (Du Casse, ed.), Mémoires, X, 222; Raphael Ledos de Beaufort (ed.), Personal Recollections of the Late Duc de Broglie, 2 vols. (London, 1887), I, 241; Lafayette (G. Lafayette, ed.), Mémoires, V, 301; Gabory, Napoléon et la Vendée, 390; Calonne, Amiens, 79, 87; Miot de Melito (Fleischmann, ed., Hoey and Lillie, trs.), Memoirs, 686, 691; Lavalette, Memoirs, II, 157; A. Polovtsoff (ed.), Correspondance diplomatique des ambassadeurs et ministres de Russie en France avec leur gouvernment de 1814 à 1830, 3 vols. (St. Petersburg, 1902), I, 35, 144.

When it was learned that Napoleon had landed from Elba, treason became rife at Paris, and the shouts of *"Vive le roi"* were obviously farcical, the soldiers of the Paris garrison looking at each other and laughing as they said it. Napoleon did not win Marseille, however, and he left royalist Provence as quickly as possible; yet Louis was unable to arouse royalist Vendée to his defense before Napoleon had re-established himself. At Grenoble everybody turned out to see Napoleon, and peasants lined the roads merely to get a glimpse of him.[110]

In addition to peace, public opinion wanted Napoleon to restrict his own powers and to allow a truly national representation based on political guarantees. It also desired re-establishment of the jury system in its purity; security for the rights of individuals; an independent judiciary; freedom of the press; a responsible ministry; and abolition of property confiscation as a penalty.[111]

Napoleon's tolerance toward the press in 1815 helped win people, and many rallied to Napoleon to avoid a repetition of the invasion of 1814, during which they had been victims of the rage animating the enemies of France.[112]

There was, however, no universal fanaticism such as that characteristic of the Revolution, and opinion did not remain as favorable to Napoleon as it had been originally. The royalist revolt did break out in the Vendée, but it was not as spontaneous as in 1802. The Additional Act [113] did not satisfy the liberals, and the vote on it—1,288,357 in favor and 4,207 opposed—showed the indifference of the majority of the population, inasmuch as more than double that number had voted on the life consulate. Whatever

---

[110] Polovtsoff (ed.), *Correspondance diplomatique en France*, I, 164, 168–69; A.B.D.M. . . . , *Une année de la vie de l'empereur Napoléon, Napoleon Pamphlets*, XV; Paul Canestrier, "Comment fut annoncé aux gendarmes le retour de Napoléon en 1815," *Revue de la gendarmerie*, XII(1939), 427; Department of State, *Despatches* (France, Crawford to Monroe, March 16 and 21, 1815); Captain Léon Routier, *Récits d'un soldat de la république et de l'empire 1792–1830*, ed. by E. Routier (Paris, 1899), 169; Charles Jubé, "Les cent jours. Passage de l'empereur à Grenoble (mars 1815). Journal du colonel de gendarmerie Jubé," *Nouvelle revue rétrospective*, 3d semester(1896), 83; Rose, *Napoleon*, II, 444; Gabory, *Napoléon et la Vendée*, 431.

[111] *Correspondance inédite de Carnot avec Napoléon, pendant les cent jours* (Paris, 1819), 77.

[112] Thiers, *Histoire du consulat*, XIX, 482; Gautier, *Madame de Staël*, 378.

[113] Theoretically a supplement to Napoleon's earlier constitution, the Additional Act was in reality a new organic law for France.

enthusiasm the spectators at the Champ de Mai felt—and it was not too great—was not communicated to the departments, where opinion was dictated by local interests. There was a general failure on the part of the prefects to rally to the Emperor, and the clergy was still opposed to Napoleon. The new conscription, showing that the desire for rest and peace was not to be fulfilled, alienated some of the lower classes. Although secret discontent was said to be increasing even in the army, the garrison at Lille favored Napoleon, while the townspeople favored Louis XVIII. Of the towns in republican regions, sentiment at Paris was probably as unfavorable as at any place; Lyon was as enthusiastic as Grenoble, but its enthusiasm died out more rapidly. By June opinion was generally bad throughout the country.[114]

Napoleon's concern about public opinion was one of the striking characteristics of his approach to propaganda. Although at times professing not to care about public opinion and reprimanding his subordinates for heeding it, Napoleon was careful to check on it to the best of his ability. In fact, one of the major purposes of his trips throughout France was to ascertain the status of public opinion. In addition to using subordinate executives who sent in reports, Napoleon received confidential notices from individuals, of whom Fiévée was the only honest one; the senators reported on opinion; and diplomatic officials and military officers also collected data.[115]

[114] Macdonald (Rousset, ed., Siméon, tr.), *Recollections*, I, 100; II, 237; Marquis de Barral and Comte P. Durrieu, "Deux témoignages contemporains sur le retour de l'île d'Elbe," *Revue d'histoire diplomatique*, XXVI (1912), 158; Abrantès, *Mémoires*, IX, 592; Pasquier (Audiffret-Pasquier, ed., Roche, tr.), *Memoirs*, III, 202; Calonne, *Amiens*, 90; Baron Pierre Fleury de Chaboulon, *Mémoires pour servir à l'histoire de la vie privée, du retour, et du règne de Napoléon en 1815*, 2 vols. (London, 1819), II, 62; Grouchy (G. de Grouchy, ed.), *Mémoires*, III, 336; *Archives parlementaires*, XIV, 465–66; *Portefeuille de Napoléon*, in *Napoleon Pamphlets*, XXIII, in Boulay de la Meurthe collection; L'Aude, *Mémoires*, IV, 63; Miot de Melito (Fleischmann, ed., Hoey and Lillie, trs.), *Memoirs*, 695; Jacques Regnier, "Les préfets pendant les cent-jours," *Hundred Days: Secondary Material*, in Boulay de la Meurthe collection of pamphlets; *Correspondance inédite de Carnot*, 96; Bourrienne (Phipps, ed.), *Memoirs*, IV, 131; *Gazette de France*, June 3, 1815; Lavalette, *Memoirs*, II, 223.

[115] Napoleon (Thompson, ed.), *Letters*, 113, 277; Deutsch, "Lunéville to Pressburg," I, 76; Chaptal (E. A. Chaptal, ed.), *Souvenirs*, 367; Murat (Prince Murat, pub.), V and VI, *passim*; Napoleon, *Correspondance*, XVII, 49; La Forest (Grandmaison, pub.), *Correspondance*, I, 52; Rambaud, *L'Allemagne sous Napoléon Ier*, 134; Joseph (Du Casse, ed.), *Mémoires*, II, 114.

The attention which Napoleon devoted to formulating public opinion was an important and necessary phase of his policy, but he was sometimes too much occupied by his desire to convince people of his greatness. Fiévée complained about Napoleon's overzealousness along this line by saying, "Those ruling think they are loved only when people constantly shout at them that they are adored." No matter what period of Napoleon's reign one may examine, he will find directions for shaping opinion. During the Consulate he wrote his colleague Lebrun, "Tell me what could be done to ameliorate the state of public opinion, especially around Beaupreau (*arrondissement* of Angers)." Fouché was told in 1805, "Stir yourself a little more to prop up opinion." Davout in Warsaw was informed in 1807, "In our circumstances and in the country in which you are located, where war is desired, one must constantly pay great attention to rectifying opinions." During Napoleon's final fling in the Hundred Days he instructed Carnot: "Remind the prefect of Calvados that . . . he is not ordering the printing of anything to enlighten and move public opinion, that it is not thus that one serves his country.

"Write to the prefects of the North and make them feel the necessity of opposing writings to writings and of publicizing well that the cause in question today is that of the people against the nobles, of the peasants against the lords, and of the French against the foreigners. An appeal must be made everywhere to the honor and patriotism of the masses." [116]

Always, heavily, Napoleon relied on propaganda to facilitate and consolidate the victories which he won by the sword.

[116] Fiévée, *Correspondance*, II, 6; Napoleon, *Correspondance*, VIII, 106; X, 374; XVI, 115; XXVIII, 172.

CHAPTER X

CONCLUSION

THE EVIDENCE CONTAINED IN THE FOREGOING CHAPTERS CERTAINLY leaves no doubt that the French government under Napoleon devoted considerable attention to creating a favorable public opinion. Its propaganda, in which Napoleon was vitally interested, was occasionally ineffective because his subordinates were forced to rely excessively upon him; but they, if left completely to themselves, would probably have been no more successful. The fault lay, then, in Napoleon's inability or unwillingness wisely to delegate authority at appropriate times. In order to produce the greatest possible effect, it was at times essential that the public should not discern the role of the government; yet the people knew that the press was dominated by the government, could tell when articles were written by officials, and even perceived that the bulletins, a new medium, were written by Napoleon.

Official propaganda was almost never supplemented by that of private agencies. One of the outstanding defects in the use of the governmental machinery was the lack of a clear-cut program as to the role of each department. The existence of censorship bureaus in both the ministry of police and the ministry of the interior and the insertion of military news by the Major General, the Minister of War, and the Minister of Police illustrate this confusion of functions. No one man with ministerial influence co-ordinated the propaganda activities. Napoleon was "boss" in this field, as in others, but the trouble was precisely that he did have other fields requiring his care.

In view of the fact that Napoleon feared the influence of the clergy more than that of any other class, it is rather surprising that he utilized the minister of public worship so little. The ministers who played by far the most significant roles, both in controlling disadvantageous material and in inspiring favorable statements, were the ministers of police, the interior, and foreign affairs. The military organization was likewise important, especially for the distribution of propaganda materials.

Perhaps the greatest weakness of Napoleonic propaganda was its failure to adapt its messages and mediums to those whom it was designed to influence. There were times, to be sure, at which it satisfactorily appealed to distinct elements in the population: orders of the day appealed to the army; news of the Irish Catholics appealed to Catholics. But on the whole, confusion existed. The press was read largely by the *bourgeoisie*, yet many articles were so written as to appeal principally to the lower classes, even when there was no intention of reprinting the items in a form the masses might see. Fetes were for the masses, but the music and plays performed on such occasions did not appeal primarily to them, the plays being too replete with historical allusions and the music too complex. In spite of Napoleon's great reliance upon the *Moniteur* to influence foreign countries, it published many violent diatribes, designed for home consumption, which could only weaken its effect abroad.

Except for new laws and decrees granting the government stricter control of the various mediums, there were relatively few changes in method designed to increase the efficacy of the propaganda. The character of the fetes became less philosophical and more military. There was a definite trend toward a bilingual press in the non-French regions under Napoleon's control, and he attempted to exploit semiofficial papers. In 1810 the ministry of the interior began sending weekly circulars to the prefects to inform them of rumors, and it was enlarged by the addition of a censorship bureau for books. In 1811 the Minister Secretary of State was charged with editing and inserting all political articles appearing in the *Moniteur*. The minister of foreign affairs, who in 1806 had been ordered to write all the political articles in the official paper, now merely submitted to Maret articles relative to his own department. Several of the changes concerned the bulletins. The practice of reading them in the churches was discontinued as that of reading them in the theaters—in full or in extract—developed. Finally they were discontinued altogether in favor of a new form

of reporting military news. With the exception of these proce-
dural changes, the handling of propaganda remained the same
during the Consulate and Empire.

If Napoleon neglected any medium, it was that of handbills.
These were really unnecessary, however, because they would have
appealed mainly to the lower classes, who, with the army, were
the most favorably disposed toward Napoleon. He adapted his
message to their psychology, and any loss of popularity among
them was caused by events rather than by an insufficiency of
propaganda.

To these events Napoleon also adapted his propaganda activities
—occasionally changing objectives so rapidly that the public must
have been momentarily bewildered.[1] Attempts to divert public
opinion to less serious topics than those occupying it, to stifle
hostile rumors, to utilize various printing devices, and to develop
patriotism by means of the fetes were relatively unsuccessful. Devices which proved generally effective included letters, rhetorical
questions, ridicule, emotional vocabulary, space (much of it devoted to the question of neutrality in order to win allies), and
falsification. It is probably fair to conclude that on the whole
Napoleon's methods conform to the criteria established by the
best present-day students of propaganda.[2]

It is well known that propaganda has existed since ancient times
and that long before the time of Napoleon there had been government control of papers. Why, then, was Napoleon's propaganda
activity important? Because he made two real contributions to the
development of propaganda. He was the first sovereign to talk to
his subjects directly and frequently, partly through mediums such
as the bulletins and orders of the day, which he was the first to
exploit;[3] and in his utilization of the machinery of government,
he took a pioneering step toward systematic official propaganda
activity of the type we know today. In these two momentous
categories, Napoleon stands as the first modern propagandist.

[1] Under Mussolini the Italians were said to have suffered the same difficulty.
[2] As stated in the Introduction.
[3] Other countries soon copied the custom of reading bulletins in the theaters.

CRITICAL ESSAY ON AUTHORITIES

PERIODICALS AND SPECIAL ARTICLES

The following bibliography is selective only, designed to mention the most valuable works used. For that reason many articles in historical journals which would prove interesting and valuable have been omitted. More of these would be found in the *Revue des études napoléoniennes* than in any other. Those journals ranking behind it are *La révolution française, American Historical Review, Revue historique,* and *Revue d'histoire diplomatique.*

Among the noteworthy articles in these or other periodicals is Ch. de Chênedollé, "Napoléon le grand et *l'Almanach de Gotha*," *Bulletin du bibliophile belge,* VI (1850), 69–80, which is very good on the changes demanded by the censors. Victor Coffin, "Censorship and Literature under Napoleon I," *American Historical Review,* XXII (1916–17), 288–308, examines censorship in relation to the more noted writers. For information on the newspapers during the Napoleonic period, Karl Obser, "Zur Geschichte der badischen Presse in der Rheinbundzeit," *Zeitschrift für die Geschichte des Oberrheins,* XIV (1899), 111–36, is helpful. Page for page, August Fournier, "Napoleon I und das Theater," *Bühne und Welt,* 3d year (1900–1901), 541–47, 584–90, has more material on the theater than any other work. A detailed view of one secondary school is given by René Simon, "Un lycée sous l'empire: le lycée de Poitiers," *Revue des études napoléoniennes,* VII (1915), 324–40. Jean Babelon, "La médaille et les médailleurs sous le premier empire," *ibid.,* XXIX (1929), 199–202, supplements the full-length work on medals cited below. André Blum, "La caricature politique en France sous le consulat et l'empire," *ibid.,* XIII (1918), 296–312, gives specific titles of several cartoons. Sidney B. Fay, "Execution of the Duke d'Enghien," *American Historical Review,* III (1898), 629–40, and IV (1898), 21–37, contains some material on public opinion. The small amount of information on the same topic in Charles Guyot, "Souvenirs de la première invasion," *Mémoires de l'académie de Stanislas,* 6th Series, X (1913), 128–46, was found to be excellent. David Hannay, "Did Napoleon Mean to

Invade England?" *Macmillan's Magazine*, LXXXV (1902), 285–94, is an excellent discussion. Marquis de Barral and Comte P. Durrieu deal with public opinion during the Hundred Days in "Deux témoignages contemporains sur le retour de l'île d'Elbe," *Revue d'histoire diplomatique*, XXVI (1912), 153–60. Secondary discussions of public opinion are: Paul Gaffarel, "L'esprit public à Marseilles de 1800 à 1814," *Revue des études napoléoniennes*, IX (1916), 65–93; André Jacques, "L'esprit public à Metz au temps de Napoléon," *ibid.*, XXVII (1926), 101–10; and F. Uzureau, "La séparation de l'église et de l'état dans un grand diocèse (1800–1802)," *Revue des sciences ecclésiastiques et la science catholique* (July, 1907), in that part of the Boulay de la Meurthe pamphlet collection at Harvard entitled *Local Church and Religious Affairs during the Consulate and Empire: Secondary Material.*

SPECIAL STUDIES

Although Hans Thimme, *Weltkrieg ohne Waffen* (Stuttgart, 1932), has been called the best propaganda book in any language, more useful for the present study were Harold D. Lasswell, *Propaganda Technique in the World War* (New York, 1927), for the organizational aspect, and Leonard W. Doob, *Propaganda; its Psychology and Technique* (New York, 1935), for the psychological side. The other works cited in the footnote in the Introduction were not as helpful, but Edward Bonns and C. E. Carrier, *Putting It Over by Means and Methods of Exploitation* (New York, 1925), did have some material on method. All of them, plus F. C. Bartlett, *Political Propaganda* (Cambridge, 1940), were useful in the formulation of a general definition of propaganda.

In an exhaustive study, *Napoléon journaliste* (Paris, 1918), Antonin Périvier examines the personal role of Napoleon in the propaganda, and Therese Ebbinghaus, *Napoleon, England und die Presse, 1800–1803* (München, 1914), offers a thorough examination of the early anti-English phase of Bonaparte's press campaign. Several histories of the press in France tell how Napoleon utilized the papers to put across his ideas. Among them are Volumes VII and VIII of Louis Hatin, *Histoire politique et littéraire de la presse en France*, 8 vols. (Paris, 1859–61), and Henri Avenel, *Histoire de la presse française depuis 1789* (Paris, 1900). Lucy M. Salmon, *The Newspaper and Authority* (New York, 1923), naturally includes a study of Napoleonic France in its survey of how the press functions under a dictator. Henri Welschinger, *La censure sous le premier empire* (Paris, 1887), is the most complete study of the censorship phase, but the author is so desirous of showing censorship is unnecessary and disadvantageous that his anti-Napoleon bias sometimes causes a loss of objectivity. Likewise hostile to Napoleon is Gustave Le Poittevin, *La liberté de la presse depuis la révolution (1789–1815)* (Paris, 1901). A speech by M. van Schoor, *La presse sous le consulat et l'empire* (Brussels, 1899), is the best and most objective published work dealing exclusively with the press in Napoleonic France. Albert Vandal, *L'avènement de Bonaparte*, 2 vols. (Paris, 1910), is very good on the press and on public opinion. Robert Anchel, *Napoléon et les juifs* (Paris, 1928), contains a little on the Jews and on the newspapers. Also good on public opinion and on the inspired press is Paul Gautier, *Madame de Staël et Napoléon* (2d ed.; Paris, 1903). There are also some works dealing with subordinate regions which have a good deal of information on the press and public opinion in those areas. Volume II of Ludwig Salomon, *Geschichte des deutschen Zeitungswesens*, 3 vols. (Oldenburg, 1906), is excellent on newspapers in Germany. Jean Borel, *Gênes sous Napoléon Ier* (Paris, 1929), is fairly good. Pierre Conard, *Napoléon et la Catalogne, 1808–1814* (Paris, 1910), is excellent to early 1810.

Maurice Albert, *Les théâtres des boulevards, 1789–1848* (Paris, 1902), is excellent, and indispensable for a study of the theater under Napoleon. A list and analysis of each play presented, with an indication of its success, is found in Volumes I, VI, VII, and IX of L.-Henry Lecomte, *Histoire des théâtres de Paris, 1402–1904*, 10 vols. (Paris, 1905–10). The same author's *Napoléon et le monde dramatique* (Paris, 1912), is even more valuable. François H. Blaze, called Castil-Blaze, *Mémorial du Grand-Opéra* (Paris, 1847), a history of the Opéra from 1647 to 1847 is good, but short. The title of Hamil Grant, *Napoleon and the Artists* (London, 1917), is somewhat misleading, as it deals primarily with the theater and the press. Also good is Theodore Muret, *L'histoire par le théâtre, 1789–1851,* (1st series: *La révolution, le consulat, l'empire*) (Paris, 1865). Lew Rosen, *Napoleon's Opera-Glass* (London, 1897), deals with bulletins, proclamations, speeches, and music as well as with the theater; and Georg Storost considers all types of literature in *Napoleons I Stellung zur zeitgenössischen und klassischen französischen Literatur* (Schönebeck, 1914). John Charpentier, *Napoléon et les hommes de lettres de son temps* (4th ed.; Paris, 1935), is bitterly critical of Napoleon's treatment of writers. A work by Duchesse Laura d'Abrantès, *Histoire des salons de Paris*, 6 vols. (Paris, 1837–38), deals with Napoleon's efforts to control conversation.

The material available on music and poetry is rather disappointing because, except for Maurice Allem (ed.), *L'épopée napoléonienne dans la poésie française* (Paris, 1912), books specializing in these topics spend most of their time on the period from 1789 to 1799 or confine themselves too largely to criticism. Victor Jeanroy-Félix brings out some new points in *Nouvelle histoire de la littérature pendant la révolution et le premier empire* (Paris, 1886). Constant Pierre, *Musique des fêtes et cérémonies de la révolution française* (Paris, 1899), contains a little on the Consulate. Volume II of *Poésies révolutionnaires et contre-révolutionnaires*, 2 vols. (Paris, 1821), deals with some of the poems set to music. John Julian, *A Dictionary of Hymnology* (London, 1892), was useful only for a little material on the *Te Deums*.

François P.-G. Guizot, *De l'état des beaux-arts en France et du salon de 1810* (Paris, 1811), tells what was painted to glorify Napoleon and what effect these pictures had. No special work deals with the architectural and sculptural monuments, but Volume I of Edward Edwards (ed.), *The Napoleon Medals: a Complete Series of the Medals Struck in France, Italy, Great Britain, and Germany from the Commencement of the Empire in 1804 to the Restoration in 1815*, 2 vols. (London, 1837–40), shows what the government thought worthy of commemorating. A. M. Broadley, *Napoleon in Caricature, 1795–1821*, 2 vols. (London, 1911), is of value primarily for the introduction by John Holland Rose. The best collection of caricatures, unfortunately limited to only one topic, is found in Harold F. B. Wheeler and Alexander M. Broadley, *Napoleon and the Invasion of England, the Story of The Great Terror*, 2 vols. (London, 1907).

The two books which do most to explain the education setup under Napoleon are François V. A. Aulard, *Napoléon Ier et le monopole universitaire* (Paris, 1911), and Louis Grimaud, *Histoire de la liberté d'enseignement en France depuis la chute de l'ancien régime jusqu'à nos jours* (Paris, 1898), both of them hostile to Napoleon. Volumes I, II, and VI of Gilbert Stenger, *La société française pendant le consulat*, 6 vols. (Paris, 1903–1908), have some rather good material on proclamations, bulletins, and public opinion as well as on schools.

H. C. Deutsch, "Lunéville to Pressburg: a Study in Napoleonic Diplomacy, 1801–5," 2 vols. (unpublished Ph.D. thesis, Harvard, 1929), is quite good on the relationship between propaganda and diplomacy. Édouard Driault, *La politique extérieure du premier con-*

sul 1800–1803 (*Napoléon et l'Europe*) (Paris, 1910), also examines diplomacy from the angle of propaganda. *Napoléon en Italie* (*1800–1812*) (Paris, 1906), by the same author, is especially good on proclamations. Léon de la Sicotière, *Les conférences 1799–1800* (Angers, 1885), deals with both the proclamations and the press. Marcel Handelsman, *Napoléon et la Pologne 1806–1807* (Paris, 1909), shows very well how Napoleon handled Polish public opinion. H. Butterfield, *The Peace Tactics of Napoleon 1806–1808* (Cambridge, 1929), includes some material on the effect of French propaganda.

A. G. Macdonnell, *Napoleon and His Marshals* (New York, 1934), is quite good on the truthfulness of Napoleon's military propaganda. Verfasser des Napoleon, *Napoleon und Pitt, oder Wer wird siegen* (Hamburg, 1805), is quite impartial on the propaganda regarding the invasion of England. Baron A. de Calonne, *Histoire de la ville d'Amiens: Amiens au XIXe siècle* (Amiens, 1906), which contains valuable information on the effectiveness of French propaganda and on public opinion, also deals with the press. Volumes I, IV, V, VII, and VIII of Léon de Lanzac de Laborie, *Paris sous Napoléon*, 8 vols. (Paris, 1905–13), are very helpful and are the product of careful research. Despite the title, Comte Joseph d'Haussonville, *L'église romaine et le premier empire*, 5 vols. (3d ed.; Paris, 1870), is most valuable for material on public opinion. Perhaps F. J. Maccunn, *The Contemporary English View of Napoleon* (London, 1914), relies too much upon opinions of individuals in considering public opinion in England and the effect of Napoleon's propaganda measures on that country. Albert Pingaud, *Bonaparte président de la république italienne*, 2 vols. (Paris, 1914), is very good on public opinion in the Italian Republic, and Benno Menzel, *Napoleons Politik in Oberitalien 1800–1805* (Magdeburg, 1912), is quite good both on public opinion and on the truthfulness of French statements. Charles Schmidt, *Le grand-duché de Berg (1806–1813)* (Paris, 1905), has one chapter devoted solely to a study of public opinion, and Wilhelm Stroh, *Das Verhältnis zwischen Frankreich und England in den Jahren 1801–1803 im Urteil der politischen Literatur Deutschlands* (Berlin, 1914), gives an idea of the state of mind in Germany during the first three years of the nineteenth century.

MEMOIRS

The historian of the Napoleonic period finds a wealth of material in the memoirs of Napoleon's contemporaries. Among the most valuable memoirs on the propaganda phase of Napoleon's activities are those by his subordinates. Volumes I and III of Hippolyte Carnot and M. David (eds.) and V. Payen-Payne (tr.), *Memoirs of Bertrand Barère*, 4 vols. (London, 1896), must be used with caution but they contain much firsthand information on the press and its value to Napoleon. Comte Pierre François Réal, *Indiscrétions, 1798–1830. Souvenirs anecdotiques et politiques tirés du portefeuille d'un fonctionnaire de l'empire*, ed. by Musnier Desclozeaux, 2 vols. (Paris, 1835), describes how the prefect of police controlled the departmental press. Volumes III, IV, VI, VIII of A. M. Roederer (pub.), *Œuvres du comte P. L. Roederer*, 8 vols. (Paris, 1859), portray the press situation from the viewpoint of the editor of the *Journal de Paris* and also contain some information on the accuracy of Napoleon's claims and on public opinion.

Some fairly good material, buried among that which Napoleon wanted people to believe, is found in F. M. Kircheisen (comp.) and Frederick Collins (tr.), *Memoirs of Napoleon I Compiled from His Own Writings* (New York, 1929). Also valuable for studying the exploitation of government machinery were some of the memoirs of Napoleon's officials, especially those which contain letters to Napoleon. L. F. J. de Bausset, *Mémoires anecdotiques sur l'intérieur du palais et sur quelques événemens de l'empire depuis 1808 jusqu'au Ier mai 1814 pour servir à l'histoire de Napoléon*, 4 vols. (Paris, 1827–29), must be used carefully since there is no indication whether the author kept notes and since all the material is not firsthand. A. Du Casse (ed.), *Mémoires et correspondance politique et militaire du prince Eugène*, 10 vols. (Paris, 1858–60), was used primarily for the letters to Napoleon. Volumes II–IV of Marquis George de Grouchy (ed.), *Mémoires du maréchal de Grouchy*, 5 vols. (Paris, 1873–74), concern themselves primarily with justifying the marshal, but give helpful information on government machinery and on the accuracy of French propaganda. A. Du Casse (ed.), *Mémoires et correspondance du roi Jérôme et de la reine Catherine*, 7 vols. (Paris, 1861–66), and Joseph's *Mémoires et correspondance politique et militaire*, 10 vols. (Paris, 1853–54), also ed. by A. Du Casse, were used primarily for their correspondence with Napoleon. The fragments of correspondence found in the *Mémoires du maréchal Marmont, duc de Raguse de 1792 à 1841 imprimés sur le manuscrit original de l'auteur*, 9 vols. (2d ed.; Paris, 1857), were the justification for using the memoirs, just as the documents are the most valuable part of Baron de Plancy (pub.), *Souvenirs du comte de Plancy (1789–1816)* (Paris, 1904). Count Plancy was one of Napoleon's prefects. Another prefect was A. C. Thibaudeau, whose *Bonaparte and the Consulate,* tr. and ed. by G. K. Fortescue (New York, 1908), seems quite objective even though it is impossible to determine the extent of the author's reliance on notes. Baron Claude François de Méneval was Napoleon's private secretary, and his *Memoirs of Napoleon Bonaparte,* 3 vols. (New York, 1910), pub. by Baron Napoleon de Méneval, is based upon documents he retained. For material on the functioning of the military machine, Charles Jean Pelleport-Burête (ed.), *Souvenirs militaires et intimes du général v^{te} de Pelleport,* 2 vols. (Paris, 1857), is valuable. Comtesse Claire de Rémusat, *Mémoires, 1802–8,* 3 vols. (Paris, 1879–80), pub. by Paul de Rémusat, tells of theatrical affairs from the viewpoint of her husband, who was in charge of the big theaters. Volume I of Comtesse de Beaulaincourt-Marles (pub.), *Journal du maréchal de Castellane 1804–1862,* 5 vols. (2d ed.; Paris, 1895), is helpful for falsification in the propaganda. Duc d'Audiffret-Pasquier (ed.) and Charles E. Roche (tr.), *A History of my Time; Memoirs of Chancellor Pasquier,* 3 vols. (New York, 1893–94), is especially good on the authenticity of Napoleon's claims and quite enlightening on the effect of propaganda items and on public opinion. Frances Jackson (tr.), *Memoirs of the Count de Rochechouart* (London, 1920), deals with both falsification and public opinion. Volume I of Charles Nicoullaud (ed.), *Memoirs of the Comtesse de Boigne,* 3 vols. (New York, 1907), contains good material on public opinion and the effect of the propaganda, but it must be used with care as the memoirs were written solely from memory. Volume V of G. W. de Lafayette (ed.), *Mémoires, correspondance, et manuscrits du général Lafayette,* 12 vols. (Paris, 1837–39), is good on public opinion. Count Charles Labédoyère, *Memoirs of the Public and Private Life of Napoleon Bonaparte,* 2 vols. (London, 1837), likewise contains some information on public opinion. While ambassador to France, Metternich grudgingly had to concede the effectiveness of French propaganda, and his admissions are found in Volumes I and II of Prince Richard Metternich (ed.), and Mrs. Alexander Napier (tr.), *Memoirs of Prince Metternich,* 4 vols. (London, 1880–81). General Hector Fleischmann (ed.) and Mrs. Cashel Hoey and Mr. John Lillie (trs.), *Memoirs of Count Miot de Melito* (New York, 1881), is very good, and especially so on public opinion.

HISTORIES AND BIOGRAPHIES

These types of works are not especially valuable for the subject studied by the present book. The chief value of any survey history of the period, the most recent good one being Leo Gershoy, *The French Revolution and Napoleon* (New York, 1933), is its usefulness in checking the veracity of the propaganda. Hippolyte A. Taine, *The Modern Regime (The Origins of Contemporary France)*, tr. by John Durand, 2 vols. (New York, 1890–94), contains much material on education and some on censorship. Marie Joseph Adolphe Thiers, *Histoire du consulat et de l'empire faisant suite à l'histoire de la révolution française*, 20 vols. (Paris, 1845–62), includes some letters, the most useful of which deal with the effectiveness of proclamations and bulletins.

John Holland Rose, *The Life of Napoleon I*, 2 vols. (7th ed.; London, 1919), is sufficiently detailed to be of great help in detecting falsification, and it includes a little material on caricature. Theodore Iung, *Lucien Bonaparte et ses mémoires, 1775–1840*, 3 vols. (Paris, 1882–83), is rather unusual in that the author, who has remained objective, has tried to reconstruct Lucien's life from Lucien's manuscripts and other authentic documents. Léonce Pingaud, *Jean de Bry (1760–1835)* (Paris, 1909), is the life of a prefect which includes much valuable material on the administrative machinery, public opinion, and the press.

NEWSPAPERS

The French newspapers for the period 1799–1815 are by all odds the best source for the message Napoleon was trying to put across. Complete files of the two most important daily newspapers and of a leading weekly have therefore been examined for this period. They are: the official *Gazette nationale ou le Moniteur universel;* the leading paper from the standpoint of independence and circulation, the *Journal des Débats et Loix du Pouvoir législatif* (after 1805 entitled *Journal de l'Empire*); and the weekly, the *Mercure de France*. Most of the *Journal de Paris* was also used.

PAMPHLETS

The most valuable single source for religious affairs is the extensive Boulay de la Meurthe pamphlet collection at Harvard, which includes contemporary pamphlets on almost every aspect of religion, both from the broadly national and from the local viewpoint. Contemporary pamphlets not in this collection which received publicity include Citoyen Fonvielle, aîné, *Résultats possibles de la journée du 18 brumaire an VIII* (Paris, Year VIII); Alexandre Hauterive, *De l'état de la France à la fin de l'an VIII* (Paris, Year IX); and the anonymous *Aurons-nous la paix? ne l'aurons-nous pas? est-il possible de la faire avec l'Angleterre?* (Paris, 1800). P. F. Malingre, *Ode sur le premier consul* (Paris, Year X), is good for catchwords.

Only two later pamphlets merit citation at this point. Édouard Romberg, *Les journaux à Gand en 1815. Une page des cent-jours* (Brussels, 1896), has a somewhat misleading title, as most of its information is really prior to 1815. Hector Fleischmann, *Napoléon et la francmaçonnerie* (Paris, 1908), deals with Napoleon's effort to control one type of secret organization.

CORRESPONDENCE AND DIPLOMATIC DESPATCHES

By far the most valuable correspondence is that of Napoleon himself. In addition to dealing with what the propaganda mediums should say, it is the best source for Napoleon's exploitation of subordinates with regard to utilization of those propaganda mediums. Because the official edition of the *Correspondance de Napoléon Ier*, 32 vols. (Paris, 1858–70), is incomplete, various other editions have been published. Those which are indispensable are Ernest Picard and Louis Tuetey (eds.), *Correspondance inédite de Napoléon Ier conservée aux archives de la guerre*, 5 vols. (Paris, 1912–25); Léonce de Brotonne (ed.), *Dernières lettres inédites de Napoléon Ier*, 2 vols. (Paris, 1903), and *Lettres inédites de Napoléon Ier* (Paris, 1898); and L. Lecestre (comp.), *Lettres inédites de Napoléon Ier (an VIII–1815)* 2 vols. (2d ed.; Paris, 1897). Others less valuable but still useful include Alberto Lumbroso (ed.), *Cent quatre-vingt-trois lettres inédites de Napoléon* (Rome, 1899); J. M. Thompson (ed.), *Letters of Napoleon* (Oxford, 1934); Léon Cerf (comp.), *Lettres de Napoléon à Josephine* (Paris, 1928); Lady Mary Loyd (tr.), *New Letters of Napoleon I Omitted from the Edition Published under the Auspices of Napoleon III* (London, 1898); and Albert Du Casse (ed.), *Supplément à la correspondance de Napoléon Ier* (Paris, 1887). Other writings by Napoleon of some value, particularly for research in military propaganda, have been edited by Arthur Chuquet: *Inédits napoléoniens*, 2 vols. (Paris,

1913–19), and *Ordres et apostilles de Napoléon* (*1799–1815*), 4 vols. (Paris, 1911–12).

Likewise valuable was the correspondence of various officials. A. Roussel (pub.), *Correspondance de Le Coz, évêque constitutionnel d'Ille-et-Vilaine et archévêque de Besançon*, 2 vols. (Paris, 1900–1903), reveals how one cleric intervened in press affairs. Albert Jahn (ed.), *Bonaparte, Talleyrand, et Stapfer* (Zurich, 1869), has the correspondence of the Swiss minister to France from 1800 to 1803. Félix Rocquain, *Napoléon Ier et le roi Louis d'après les documents conservés aux archives nationales* (Paris, 1875), contains the letters of Louis to Napoleon while the former was King of Holland. Prince Murat (pub.), *Lettres et documents pour servir à l'histoire de Joachim Murat 1767–1815*, 8 vols. (Paris, 1908–14), is full of information regarding the role played by Napoleon's brother-in-law as propagandist. Religious matters were dealt with in the letters in A. Du Casse, *Histoire des négotiations diplomatiques relatives aux traités de Morfontaine, de Lunéville, et d'Amiens, pour faire suite aux Mémoires du roi Joseph, précédée de la correspondance inédite de l'empereur Napoléon Ier avec le cardinal Fesch*, 3 vols. (Paris, 1857). Information on papers and education is contained in Joseph Joubert, *Correspondance de J. Joubert* (9th ed.; Paris, 1895). The compilations of correspondence by officials most useful for the purpose of showing how the governmental organization was utilized were Geoffroy de Grandmaison (pub.), *Correspondance du comte de La Forest*, 7 vols. (Paris, 1904–13), La Forest being the ambassador of France to Spain from 1808 to 1813; Pierre Bertrand (ed.), *Lettres inédites de Talleyrand à Napoléon 1800–1809* (Paris, 1889); and Abbé Jacques Moulard (pub.), *Lettres inédites du comte Camille de Tournon, préfet de Rome, 1809–1814. Première partie: la Politique et l'Esprit public* (Paris, 1914). Useful as much for the accuracy of French propaganda as for use of government officials was Paul Roussier (pub.), *Lettres du général Leclerc* (Paris, 1937). Ch. de Mazada (ed.), *Correspondance du maréchal Davout prince d'Eckmühl, ses commandements, son ministère, 1801–15*, 4 vols. (Paris, 1885), is quite good on the press, on rumors which Davout was to combat, and on public opinion. M. Bail (ed.), *Correspondance de Bernadotte, prince-royal de Suède, avec Napoléon, depuis 1810 jusqu'en 1814* (Paris, 1819), is good for the accuracy of French propaganda even though the editor is most biased in favor of Napoleon. The despatches of Lord Whitworth and others which are found in Oscar Browning (ed.), *England and Napoleon in 1803* (London, 1887), deal both with the accuracy of Napoleon's claims and with public opinion. *Copies des lettres originales et dépêches des généraux, ministres, grands officiers d'état, etc.* (Paris, 1814), written to Napoleon at Dresden from Paris, contains some fairly good material on the false claims of French propaganda. *Correspondance et relations de J. Fiévée avec Bonaparte premier consul et empereur pendant onze an-nées (1802 à 1813)*, 3 vols. (Paris, 1836), containing personal reports to Napoleon on the reception accorded Napoleon's measures, is an excellent source on the effectiveness of French propaganda and on public opinion. Whenever statements favorable to Bonaparte are found in Comte L. Remacle (ed.), *Bonaparte et les Bourbons. Rela-tions secrètes des agents de Louis XVIII à Paris sous le consulat (1802–1803)* (Paris, 1899), they may probably be relied on. Another source of great value on French public opinion is *Die Berichte der russischen Gesandten aus Paris (1801–4)*, Vols. LXX and LXXVII of *Sbornik* (St. Petersburg, 1890–91). Prince Ladislaus Czartoryski (pub.), *Alex-andre Ier et le prince Czartoryski. Correspondance particulière et con-versations 1801–1823* (Paris, 1865), reveals much on Polish opinion. Volumes III and IV of Lord John Russell (ed.), *Memorials and Cor-respondence of C. J. Fox*, 4 vols. (London, 1853–57), were used as a check on the accuracy of French propaganda claims, but they actually proved most useful for the effectiveness of Napoleonic propaganda and for British public opinion. *The Substance of Some Letters, Written by an Englishman Resident at Paris during the Last Reign of the Emperor Napoleon* (Philadelphia, 1816), is quite good, the letters at first being dated considerably after the events but gradually catching up.

The only unprinted documents important enough to be cited here are all the despatches from 1799 to 1815 of the American ministers to France, located in the National Archives in Washington, D.C. These were found to be particularly valuable with regard to the accuracy of the French propaganda and to public opinion.

COMMENTARIES, SPEECHES, AND CON-TEMPORARY BOOKS OF SOURCES

The ideas expressed by Napoleon's favorite orator may be found in C. F. A. Fayot (pub.), *Collection complète des discours de M. de Fontanes* (Paris, 1821). Napoleon's speechs have been compiled and published by Georges Barral, *Messages et discours politiques* (Paris, 1896). His ideas on various topics may be found in Damas Hinard (comp.), *Napoléon. Ses opinions et jugemens sur les hommes et sur les choses,* 2 vols. (Paris, 1837–38); Lewis C. Breed (ed.), *The Opinions and Reflections of Napoleon* (Boston, 1926); and Adrien Dansette (comp.), *Vues politiques* (Paris, 1939), which is quite good on education. Written at St. Helena, *Commentaires de Napoléon premier,* 6 vols. (Paris, 1867), contain some fairly good information.

J. J. Lucet and Eckard (comps.), *Hommages poétiques à leurs majestés impériales et royales sur la naissance de S. M. le roi de Rome,* 2 vols. (Paris, 1811), indicates the popular tunes and shows how large a proportion of homages to Napoleon were written by government employees. A list of the works praising Napoleon may be compiled from *Journal typographique et bibliographique, 1799–1810,* of which one volume appeared annually and listed the books published in France during that year.

PRINTED COLLECTIONS OF DOCUMENTS

Archives parlementaires, 1787–1860: recueil complet des débats des chambres françaises, Series 2, 137 vols. (Paris, 1862–1913), being composed of supposedly stenographic reports of debates in the legislative chambers, contains many points the government wanted stressed. Comte Alfred Boulay de la Meurthe has edited a collection, *Documents sur la négociation du concordat et sur les autres rapports de la France avec le Saint-Siège en 1800 et 1801,* 6 vols. (Paris, 1891–1905), valuable for the press, public opinion, and religion. An indication as to how one of the legislative houses felt about press freedom may be gleaned from a book edited by the Secretary-General of the Council of State, Baron Jean Locré, *Discussions sur la liberté de la presse, la censure, la propriété littéraire, l'imprimerie et la librairie qui ont eu lieu dans le conseil d'état pendant les années 1808, 1809, 1810 et 1811* (Paris, 1819). There are a number of excellent sources on the effectiveness of French propaganda and on French public opinion. Heading the list are two collections of police reports and excerpts from the papers, edited by François V. A. Aulard: *Paris sous le consulat: recueil de documents pour l'histoire de l'esprit public à Paris,* 4 vols. (Paris, 1903–1909), and *Paris sous le premier empire: recueil de documents pour l'histoire de l'esprit public à Paris,* 3 vols. (Paris, 1912–23). Ernest d'Hauterive (ed.), *La police secrète du premier empire,* 3 vols. (Paris, 1908), is a collection of the daily police bulletins composed for Napoleon from 1804 to 1807. Volume III of Wilhelm Adolf Schmidt (ed.), *Tableaux de la révolution française, publiés sur les papiers inédits du département et de la police secrète de Paris,* 3 vols. (Leipzig, 1867–71), which cites approximately one seventh of the available documents for the period, contains some rather good material.

INDEX

catchwords, 178-79; attack on, is personalized, 186; blamed for items unpopular in France, 194; losses, 201
Enghien, Duke of, 10, 169, 197, 226, 228-29; commentaries on death of, forbidden, 53
England, 3, 31, 80, 180, 222-27; attacks concentrated on, 3; accused of inciting revolts, 3; accused of prolonging civil war in Switzerland, 3; attack on, 4, 154, 170; incites Austria and Prussia to war, 5; causes Russia to reject treaty, 5; wants perpetual war, 5; responsible for Spanish troubles, 6; ambitions, 6; disregards maritime rights of neutrals, 6; breaks agreements, 7; sends counterfeit money to Continent, 7; inhumanity of, 7-8; attempts poison warfare, 8; soldiers of, pillage Spain and Portugal, 8; refuses prisoner exchange, 8; privateers piratical, 9; treatment of Catholics, 9; inconsistency on religion, 9; financial problems, 11; commerce deteriorating, 12; unemployment, 12; crime and riots, 12; to be forced to discontinue subsidies, 12; morale, 12; unreliability of colonies, 12; selfishness of, 12; has no common interests with Continent, 12; exploits allies, 12-13; inimical to maritime nations, 13; not trusted by allies, 13; papers of, criticize allies, 13; futility of efforts, 14; navy of, does not capture ships, 15; loses allies, 15; defeats of, 15; results of acts, 15; royal family of, does not inspire confidence, 16; ministers poor, 16; violates constitution, 16; invasion of, 17, 160, 196, 226; position of, increasingly bad, 26; superiority of navy cannot prevent invasion of, 29-30; Napoleon attacks press of, 72; Napoleon obtains information from press of, 73; French attacks on, in pamphlets, 82-83; medals against, 162; charges against Napoleon, 169, 170 n.; rhetorical questions used to criticize, 173; attacks on, supported by history, 177; attacked in catchwords, 179; war guilt of, 200; lack of effect of Moniteur in, 207; public opinion in, 226; counterpropaganda of, 226
Engravings, 162
Esménard, Joseph, 39, 54, 150-51, 152, 154, 157; censor of Journal de l'Em-

pire, 49, 49 n.; editor of Mercure de France, 55
Étienne, Charles, 152, 155, 157; ode praising Napoleon, 33; censor of Journal de l'Empire, 49, 49 n.; editor of Journal de l'Empire, 55; heads police censorship, 78 n.
Eugene, 37, 58, 72, 76, 97, 98, 99, 100, 103, 104, 105, 111, 112, 114 n., 117, 118, 135, 164, 190, 195, 196, 200, 212, 214, 215, 225; suspends paper, 49; abolishes preliminary censorship in Kingdom of Italy, 50; receives orders on Italian press, 54; writes and inserts press articles, 65; and book censorship in Italy, 80-81; distributes pamphlets, 86; distributes bulletin, 92 n., 94-95; proclamation to Tyrolese, 101; effect of proclamation, 213

Falsification, 175 n.; of military strength, 188-90; of military losses, 190-92; of soldiers' behavior and supplies, 192-93; about situation in colonies, 193; on domestic affairs, 193-94; in international relations, 194; on governmental changes, 195; by lies, 195; by suppression of unfavorable information, 196-97; by prepublication editing of material, 197-200; effect of, 208-209, 246
Ferdinand, Prince of Asturias, 85, 176, 214 n., 233, 234; treatment of, by Napoleon, 27
Fesch, Card. Joseph, 94, 112, 117, 142
Festivals, 35, 134, 143, 180, 182, 227, 245-46; in Kingdom of Italy, 106; occasions for, 106-107, 129; type of celebration, 107-109; Napoleon and, 107-109; cost of, 110; publicity on, 110; difficulties, 110-11; free theater performances for, 155; music for, 159; success of, 210-11
Fetes, see Festivals
Fiévée, Joseph, 32, 57 n., 72, 203, 204, 206, 207, 209, 227, 229, 235, 236, 242-43; criticizes report on Dutch press, 41; editor of Journal de l'Empire, 55; minor press role of, 66; charges discrimination against Journal de l'Empire, 70; says government-inspired press articles are poor, 75; on rumors, 118; urges inspired texts, 129; urges limit on falsification, 208; advises discontinuance of bulletins, 216; on